Nature at War

This anthology is the first sustained examination of American involvement in World War II through an environmental lens. World War II was
a total and global war that involved the extraction, processing, and use
of vast quantities of natural resources. The wartime military-industrial
complex, the "Arsenal of Democracy," experienced tremendous economic growth and technological development, employing resources at
a higher intensity than ever before. The war years witnessed transformations in American agriculture; the proliferation of militarized landscapes; the popularization of chemical and pharmaceutical products; a
rapid increase in energy consumption and the development of nuclear
energy; a remaking of the nation's transportation networks; a shift in
population toward the Sunbelt and the West Coast; a vast expansion in
the federal government, in conjunction with industrial firms; and the
emergence of environmentalism. World War II represented a quantitative and qualitative leap in resource use, with lasting implications for
American government, science, society, health, and ecology.

THOMAS ROBERTSON is Executive Director of the United States Educational Foundation (USEF) Fulbright in Kathmandu, Nepal and the
author of *The Malthusian Moment: Global Population Growth and the
Birth of American Environmentalism* (2012).

RICHARD P. TUCKER is Adjunct Professor in the School for Environment and Sustainability at the University of Michigan. He is co-editor of
four multiauthor books on the environmental history of the two world
wars. His previous publications include *Insatiable Appetite: The United
States and the Ecological Degradation of the Tropical World* (2000).

NICHOLAS B. BREYFOGLE is Associate Professor of History at The Ohio
State University. He is the author/editor of seven volumes, including *Water
History: Readings and Sources* (2020) and *Eurasian Environments: Nature
and Ecology in Imperial Russian and Soviet History* (2018). Since 2007 he
has been coeditor of *Origins: Current Events in Historical Perspective.*

PETER MANSOOR is the General Raymond E. Mason Jr. Chair of
Military History at The Ohio State University. He is the author of three
books and co-editor of three volumes, including the award-winning *The
GI Offensive in Europe: The Triumph of American Infantry Divisions,
1941–1945* (1999).

Nature at War

American Environments and World War II

Edited by

THOMAS ROBERTSON
US Education Foundation, Nepal

RICHARD P. TUCKER
University of Michigan

NICHOLAS B. BREYFOGLE
The Ohio State University

PETER MANSOOR
The Ohio State University

CAMBRIDGE
UNIVERSITY PRESS

University Printing House, Cambridge CB2 8BS, United Kingdom

One Liberty Plaza, 20th Floor, New York, NY 10006, USA

477 Williamstown Road, Port Melbourne, VIC 3207, Australia

314–321, 3rd Floor, Plot 3, Splendor Forum, Jasola District Centre,
New Delhi – 110025, India

79 Anson Road, #06–04/06, Singapore 079906

Cambridge University Press is part of the University of Cambridge.

It furthers the University's mission by disseminating knowledge in the pursuit of
education, learning, and research at the highest international levels of excellence.

www.cambridge.org
Information on this title: www.cambridge.org/9781108419765
DOI: 10.1017/9781108304146

First published 2020

Printed in the United Kingdom by TJ International Ltd, Padstow Cornwall

A catalogue record for this publication is available from the British Library.

ISBN 978-1-108-41976-5 Hardback
ISBN 978-1-108-41207-0 Paperback

Contents

Figures

Tables and Charts

Tables

Charts

Maps

Contributors

Kellen Backer is Faculty Fellow in the Humanities at Syracuse University. He is the author of *"Food Will Win the War and Write the Peace"*: *World War II and the Making of an American Industrial Food System*.

Joel R. Bius is Assistant Professor of National Security Studies and Associate Dean of Education at the Air Command and Staff College. He is the author of *Smoke 'Em If You Got 'Em: The Rise and Fall of the Military Cigarette Ration*.

Brian Black is Professor of Environmental Studies and History and Head of the Division of Arts and Humanities at Pennsylvania State University, Altoona. His publications include *Petrolia: The Landscape of America's First Oil Boom, Crude Reality: Petroleum in World History*, and *Gettysburg Contested: 150 Years of Preserving America's Most Cherished Landscape*.

Kent Curtis is Associate Professor of Environmental History at Ohio State University, Mansfield, and author of *Gambling on Ore: The Nature of Metal Mining in the United States, 1860–1910*.

Ryan H. Edgington is author of *Range Wars: The Environmental Contest for the White Sands Missile Range*.

Sarah S. Elkind is Professor of History at San Diego State University. Her publications include *Bay Cities and Water Politics: The Battle for Resources in Boston and Oakland, 1880–1930*, and *How Local Politics Shape Federal Policy: Business, Power and the Environment in Twentieth Century Los Angeles*.

Martha N. Gardner is Associate Professor of History and Social Sciences at Massachusetts College of Pharmacy and Health Science.

Jean Mansavage is a historian and Research Branch Chief at the US Air Force Historical Studies Office. She is author of *Natural Defense: U.S. Air Force Origins of the Department of Defense Natural Resources Conservation Program.*

Peter Mansoor is Professor of Military History at Ohio State University. His publications include *The GI Offensive in Europe: The Triumph of American Infantry Divisions, 1941–1945, Baghdad at Sunrise: A Brigade Commander's War in Iraq*, and *Surge: My Journey with General David Petraeus and the Remaking of the Iraq* War. He is also the coeditor of *Hybrid Warfare: Fighting Complex Opponents from the Ancient World to the Present, Grand Strategy and Military Alliances*, and *The Culture of Military Organizations.*

Christopher M. Rein is the Managing Editor of Air University Press at Maxwell Air Force Base, Alabama. He is the author of *Alabamians in Blue: Freedmen, Unionists, and the Civil War in the Cotton State, Multi-Domain Battle in the Southwest Pacific Theater of World War II*, and *The North African Air Campaign: US Army Air Forces from El Alamein to Salerno.*

Thomas Robertson is the author of *The Malthusian Moment: Global Population Growth and the Birth of American Environmentalism*, and coeditor with Jenny Leigh Smith, *Transplanting Modernity? New Histories of Technology, Development, and Environment.*

Kendra Smith-Howard is Associate Professor of History at the State University of New York, Albany, and author of *Pure and Modern Milk: An Environmental History since 1900.*

Richard P. Tucker is Adjunct Professor in the School for Environment and Sustainability, University of Michigan. His publications include *Insatiable Appetite: The United States and the Ecological Degradation of the Tropical World.*

Christopher W. Wells is Professor of Environmental Studies at Macalester College, author of *Car Country: An Environmental History*, and editor of *Environmental Justice in Postwar America: A Documentary Reader.*

Preface

American Environments and World War II

Peter Mansoor

World War II was the largest and most destructive conflict in human history. It was an existential struggle that pitted irreconcilable political systems and ideologies against one another across the globe in a decade of violence unlike any other. There is little doubt today that the United States had to engage in the fighting, especially after the Japanese attack on Pearl Harbor on December 7, 1941. The conflict was, in the words of historians Allan Millett and Williamson Murray, "a war to be won."[1] As the world's largest industrial power, the United States put forth a supreme effort to produce the weapons, munitions, and military formations essential to achieving victory.[2] When the war finally ended, the finale signaled by atomic mushroom clouds over Hiroshima and Nagasaki, upward of 60 million people had perished in the inferno.[3] Of course, the human toll represented only part of the devastation; global environments also suffered greatly. The growth and devastation of World War II significantly changed American landscapes as well. The war created or significantly expanded a number of industries, put land to new uses, spurred urbanization, and left a legacy of pollution that would in time create a new term: superfund site.

[1] Allan R. Millett and Williamson Murray, *A War to Be Won: Fighting the Second World War* (Cambridge, MA: Belknap Press, 2000).

[2] The most comprehensive study of the American political economy during World War II is Paul A. C. Koistinen, *Arsenal of World War II: The Political Economy of American Warfare, 1941–1945* (Lawrence: University Press of Kansas, 2004).

[3] This is perhaps a low estimate, in as much as 50 million civilians may have perished in China alone. Statistics from the US National World War II museum website, www.nationalww2museum.org/learn/education/for-students/ww2-history/ww2-by-the-numbers/world-wide-deaths.html (accessed July 29, 2019).

Before considering how World War II changed America, it is useful to consider the magnitude of the war effort. World War II was the last great industrial total war, engulfing in its fiery embrace entire peoples, economies, and armed forces. Emerging from the throes of the Great Depression, the US gross domestic product increased from $97.1 billion in 1939 to $185.1 billion in 1944.[4] Expenditures on national defense during this period increased from $1.7 billion to $86.3 billion; by 1945, nearly half the economy was engaged in war production.[5] Manufacturers tripled their output; Ford Motor Company alone produced more durable goods than Italy.[6] Nothing was impossible with victory at stake. When the War Department asked the president of Chrysler Corporation, K. T. Keller, if his company could make tanks, he immediately responded "Yes," before adding, "What's a tank look like?"[7]

The American people made good on President Franklin D. Roosevelt's desire to make the United States the arsenal of democracy. Between 1939 and 1945, the United States produced 303,695 planes, 10 battleships, 27 fleet carriers, 110 escort carriers, 211 submarines, 907 cruisers/destroyers/destroyer escorts, 82,000 landing craft, 41,000 artillery pieces, 60,973 tanks, 2,400,000 vehicles of all types, 12,500,000 rifles, 41,000,000,000 rounds of ammunition, and 3 atomic bombs.[8] In the peak war years of 1942–1944, the United States alone produced more combat munitions than all its allies put together and nearly twice as much as the combined Axis powers.[9] In just one year (1943), the United States produced more tanks than Germany did during the entire war.[10] "I know how you defeated us," remarked a German prisoner as he marched past

---

[4] "Real Gross Domestic Product, Chained (1937) Dollars," US Department of Commerce Bureau of Economic Analysis, https://bea.gov/iTable/iTable.cfm?ReqID=9&step=1#reqid= 9&step=3&isuri=1&904=1939&903=7&906=q&905=1945&910=x&911=0 (accessed July 29, 2019).

[5] Ibid.   [6] Richard Overy, *Why the Allies Won* (New York: W. W. Norton, 1995), 195.

[7] Scott Burgess, "Detroit's Production Battle to Win World War II," *Motor Trend*, October 9, 2015, www.motortrend.com/news/detroits-production-battle-to-win-world-war-ii/ (accessed July 29, 2019).

[8] These numbers vary somewhat with each source, but the general idea is the same – US production during World War II was massive. The numbers quoted are from the National WWII Museum, "By the Numbers: Wartime Production," www.nationalww2museum.org/ learn/education/for-students/ww2-history/ww2-by-the-numbers/wartime-production.html (accessed July 29, 2019).

[9] Koistinen, *Arsenal of World War II*, 499, table 2.

[10] Alan Gropman, "Industrial Mobilization," in *The Big "L": American Logistics in World War II*, ed. Alan Gropman (Washington, DC: NDU Press, 1997), 55.

one of the many supply dumps in Normandy. "You piled up the supplies and let them fall on us."[11]

The United States was the arsenal for its allies as well – democratic or otherwise. "This is a war of engines and octanes," Soviet Premier Josef Stalin declared as he rose to toast his allied comrades at a banquet at the Tehran conference in November 1943. "I drink to the American auto industry and the American oil industry."[12] Stalin was correct on all counts. Through the Lend-Lease program the United States transferred $46 billion in raw materials, munitions, and weapons to its allies, primarily the British Empire and the Soviet Union.[13] "Long before American troops had engaged the Germans in large-scale fighting," President Harry S. Truman reported to Congress in early 1946, "lend-lease tanks and jeeps, communication equipment, rolling stock, planes, guns, and heavy artillery were aiding the defenders of Stalingrad and helping General Montgomery's Eighth Army hold and repulse the Afrika Korps in Egypt."[14] Lend-Lease recipients received 45,000 planes, helping the allies to gain and maintain air superiority.[15] The Soviet Union alone received 14,700 planes, 7,000 tanks, 52,000 jeeps, and 375,000 trucks, without which the Red Army would have been sorely pressed to sustain the enormous land offensives that crushed the Wehrmacht in the last two years of the war.[16]

The massive increase in wartime production was made possible by the conversion of civilian industry to defense usage and the creation of new plants.[17] US manufacturers built 40 engine and propeller plants between 1940 and 1943, many of them with government funding. Floor space increased from 13 million square feet to more than 167 million square feet in the same period.[18] The most impressive facility was Ford's Willow

---

[11] Quoted in Barry J. Dysart, "Materialschlact: The 'Materiel Battle' in the European Theater," in *The Big "L": American Logistics in World War II*, ed. Alan Gropman (Washington, DC: NDU Press, 1997), 339. Material superiority was only one of the reasons behind Allied victory, however. For a discussion of other factors, see Overy, *Why the Allies Won*.

[12] John A. Thompson, *A Sense of Power: The Roots of America's Global Role* (New York: Cornell University Press, 2015), 197.

[13] President of the United States, *Twenty-First Report to Congress on Lend-Lease Operations* (Washington, DC: Government Printing Office, 1946), table 2, 14. The figure of $46 billion is in 1945 dollars, equivalent to $621 billion in 2017 dollars.

[14] Ibid., 12.   [15] Ibid., 15.   [16] Ibid., 25.

[17] Amazingly, civilian consumption in the United States increased slightly during the war, the only nation of the major combatants in which this occurred.

[18] Gropman, "Industrial Mobilization," 55.

Run, a massive, newly built factory 25 miles west of Detroit that by spring 1944 was churning out a B-24 heavy bomber every hour. With these new facilities came workers, housing, and transportation infrastructure that changed the landscape of suburban America.[19] According to historians Hugh Conway and James Toth, the vast array of newly constructed infrastructure "revised the correlation of American labor, raw material, transport, and electrical power across the land. The result was a far more extensive, cohesive, flexible, and dynamic pattern of production than anything the world had previously known. It revolutionized the capital underpinnings of the American economy not only for the war but also for the peace in the aftermath."[20] But it was not just the economy that would be forever altered; American landscapes would never be the same again.

The Manhattan Project, which by 1945 made the United States the world's first atomic power, involved laboratories in Chicago and Berkeley, uranium production facilities in Tennessee, plutonium production facilities in Washington, and a laboratory and integration facility in the newly constructed town of Los Alamos, New Mexico. At the height of the effort in June 1944, the Manhattan Engineer District employed nearly 129,000 people, of whom 84,500 were construction workers, 40,500 operated facilities, 1,800 were civil service employees, and 1,800 were military personnel.[21] The world's first atomic detonation occurred on US soil on July 16, 1945, at Trinity Site in the Jornada del Muerto Desert near Alamogordo, New Mexico. The explosion of the man-made Plutonium-239 fission device measured 22 kilotons of TNT and broke windows 120 miles distant, while the heat of the blast melted the desert sand and turned it into a green glassy substance christened trinitite. Watching the blast, the scientific leader of the Manhattan Project, Dr. J. Robert Oppenheimer, recalled a verse from Hindu scripture, "Now I am become Death, the destroyer of worlds."[22] He was correct in more ways than one. Nuclear material can quickly destroy mankind with the

[19] For an examination of how Willow Run changed the greater Detroit area, see Sarah Jo Peterson, *Planning the Home Front: Building Bombers and Communities at Willow Run* (Chicago: University of Chicago Press, 2013).

[20] Hugh Conway and James E. Toth, "Building Victory's Foundation: Infrastructure," in *The Big "L": American Logistics in World War II*, ed. Alan Gropman (Washington, DC: NDU Press, 1997), 194.

[21] Vincent C. Jones, *Manhattan: The Army and the Atomic Bomb* (Washington, DC: Center of Military History, 1985), 344.

[22] J. Robert Oppenheimer Oral History, Atomic Archive, www.atomicarchive.com/Movies/Movie8.shtml (accessed July 29, 2019).

explosion of a thousand suns, or it can more quietly destroy life with highly toxic radioactive fallout and pollution of soil and water. The toxic effects of atomic devices were not well understood in 1945; what the military personnel and scientists working on the Manhattan Project did know is the war had to be won, and the atomic bomb was essential to that purpose.

All this production was for one purpose: to win the war. Doing so required more than just weapons, however. The United States would organize and train 89 ground divisions, 243 air combat groups, and a two-ocean navy that at its peak numbered 6,768 vessels. These forces needed vast areas for posts, camps, bases, and training areas, soldiers often building their facilities as they organized and trained for combat.[23] Armies maneuvered in Louisiana, Tennessee, the Carolinas, and at the Desert Training Center in California. The legacy structure of military forts across the West was soon overwhelmed by the expansion and creation of huge bases such as Fort Bragg, North Carolina; Fort Knox, Kentucky; and Camp Hood, Texas. Military activity changed the landscape in many ways, and although some of this base structure was downsized or closed after 1945, much of it remained to house US armed forces during and after the Cold War.[24]

The United States was not just the arsenal of democracy; it was also the granary of democracy. American farmers ramped up production for the war effort, assisted by generous government policy that allowed prices for foodstuffs and livestock to rise by as much as 100 percent, while subsidies encouraged production of essential war products, such as cotton and tobacco.[25] Americans supported the war effort by rationing, recycling, and building "Victory Gardens" to ease the burden on the agricultural industry to feed both the nation and its armed forces. The success of American agriculture was so complete that by the end of the war in 1945 American farmers were feeding the people of every major ally *and*

[23] For an examination of the mobilization and training of US infantry divisions in the US Army during World War II, see Peter R. Mansoor, *The GI Offensive in Europe: The Triumph of American Infantry Divisions, 1941–1945* (Lawrence: University Press of Kansas, 1999), chs. 2 and 3.

[24] Ironically, the devotion of land to military purposes, which has staved off the march of suburbia and agribusiness, has been a boon to some endangered species, such as the desert tortoise in Fort Irwin, California, and the red cockaded woodpecker in Fort Bragg, North Carolina.

[25] Millett and Murray, *A War to Be Won*, 529. Given the fact that most GIs smoked, the designation of tobacco as a critical agricultural product is not as strange as it appears on its face.

conquered enemy except China.[26] The war accelerated the industrialization of American agriculture, in the process turning a land of family farms into one of vast conglomerates run by an increasingly narrow percentage of the population.

World War II, then, was a milestone in the economic and environmental history of the United States. The former story has been well researched; the latter history largely remains to be written. The intent of this collection of essays, the result of a conference sponsored by the Mershon Center for International Security Studies in February 2016 on the campus of The Ohio State University, is to fill some of the gaps in the environmental history of the United States during World War II. The editors and authors present this work in the hope that it will shed light on the vast changes to American landscapes during World War II – a war that had to be won, but that continues to shape modern America in profound ways.

---

[26] For a comprehensive perspective on the role of agriculture and food in World War II, see Lizzie Collingham, *Taste of War: World War II and the Battle for Food* (New York: Penguin, 2012).

Acknowledgments

This volume began as a series of papers presented at the conference "The Nature of War: American Environments and World War II," at the Mershon Center for International Security Studies at The Ohio State University, February 25–27, 2016. During the conference, we realized there was a fascinating new story to tell, and so we set about revising the papers and fashioning them into a volume that would explain how World War II shaped the American environment as we experience it today. The editors would like to thank the following organizations for their generous funding of the conference and book: the Mershon Center for International Security Studies, the Society for Military History, The Ohio State University Department of History, and the Sustainable and Resilient Economy Discovery Theme at Ohio State. In addition to those scholars whose chapters appear in this volume, we would also like to recognize the other participants who made the conference so very productive and exciting: Charles Closmann, Anastasia Day, Roger Lotchin, Derek Lee Nelson, Chris Otter, and Sam White. We would also like to acknowledge: Steven Blalock and Kyle McCray from the Mershon Center, whose tireless organization and budget support made the conference possible; Mark Sokolsky for his excellent editorial assistance; the anonymous reviewers of the manuscript for their insightful comments and helpful suggestions; and last but certainly not least Debbie Gershenowitz and her excellent team at Cambridge University Press.

Introduction

Total War and American Nature

Thomas Robertson and Richard P. Tucker

SICILY, 1943: THE "MIGHT OF MATERIAL"

When we send an expedition to Sicily, where does it begin? Well it begins at
two places practically. It begins on the farms of *this* country, and in the
mines of *this* country.

     – Franklin Roosevelt, July 1943[1]

In late summer 1943, famed war correspondent Ernie Pyle sat above a
newly constructed port in Sicily – the island near Italy's toe that Anglo-
American forces had invaded in early July – taking in the scene below.
Pyle had sailed with Allied troops across the Mediterranean from North
Africa. Before D-day in Normandy 11 months later, the Sicily campaign –
Operation Husky – was the largest seaborne invasion in history, involving
an astonishing armada of nearly 3,000 ships. "There is no way of
conveying the enormous size of that fleet," wrote Pyle. "On the horizon
it resembled a distant city. It covered half the skyline.... Even to be part of
it was frightening."[2]

    Those ships delivered 180,000 soldiers onshore but also 14,000
vehicles, 600 tanks, and 1,800 large guns – half of this huge quantity
during the attack's first 48 hours. Many landing craft carried not people
but supplies; 20 carried water alone.[3] In subsequent days, other supplies

---

[1] A. J. Baime, *The Arsenal of Democracy: FDR, Detroit, and an Epic Quest to Arm an America at War* (Boston: Houghton Mifflin Harcourt, 2014), 210.

[2] Ernie Pyle, *Brave Men* (New York: H. Holt and Co., 1944), 8.

[3] James Dunn, "Engineers in Sicily," in *Builders and Fighters: US Army Engineers in World War II*, ed. Barry W. Fowle (Fort Belvoir, VA: Office of History, US Army Corp of Engineers, 1992), 408.

FIGURE I.1 LST carrying innumerable supplies for the US military, Invasion of Cape Gloucester, New Britain, December 24, 1943. Records of the US Coast Guard; Activities, Facilities, Personalities, 1785–1967, Record Group 26, National Archives and Records Administration (NARA), Image 513188.
Source: Image in the public domain

would follow: food, fuel, ammunition, spare parts, medicine, maps, cigarettes, tents, radios and telephones, and much, much more – everything that a modern army needed, and modern armies needed a great deal. "We kept pouring men and machines into Sicily," Ernie Pyle observed, "as though it were a giant hopper" (see Figure I.1).[4]

American abundance of natural resources, and the ability to mobilize and focus them, gave the Allied soldiers, sailors, and airmen a tremendous advantage everywhere they fought. Each US soldier in the field was backed by roughly 67 pounds of equipment and supplies.[5] "When an American soldier goes over from here," President Roosevelt emphasized to the press corps a few weeks after the Sicily invasion begun, "he is fully equipped, not only his clothing, but also all of the munitions that are assigned to him, which include almost everything – guns, rifles, machine

[4] Pyle, *Brave Men*, 24.
[5] Daniel Yergin, *The Prize: The Epic Quest for Oil, Money, and Power* (New York: Free Press, 2003), 382. In the Pacific each American soldier was supported by four tons of supplies but each Japanese soldier by only two pounds. Richard Overy, *Why the Allies Won* (New York: W. W. Norton, 1995), 210.

guns and ammunition, artillery small and large, tanks, planes, trucks, and everything else."[6]

"Everything else" included powerful tools that also gave the Allies a great advantage: vast amounts of oil and gas, far more than in any previous war; huge quantities of food, packaged for easy storage and delivery and designed to last for months; detailed maps of Sicily's rugged terrain, drawn from the aerial photographs that had become essential before any battle; boxes and boxes of cigarettes, provided by the military in generous quantities for tired and nervous troops; medicines like antibiotics, newly developed and available in large quantities; and chemicals such as DDT, a newly synthesized substance that helped prevent a typhus outbreak among troops and civilians in mainland Italy the next year. Watching the varied supplies pile higher and higher on Sicily's shores, Pyle had an epiphany: "Suddenly I realized what all this was. It was America's long-awaited power of production finally rolling into the far places where it had to go."[7]

That power of production proved decisive. In 1943, US productive capacity began to tip the tide in favor of the Allies. "To a large degree, the improvement in the military situation [in 1943]," historians Robert Coakley and Richard Leighton have written, "was a result of the huge outpouring of munitions from American factories and of ships from American yards."[8]

World War II was a war of hundreds of thousands of guns, tanks, and planes, and thousands of other products. One prominent historian has called it a "gross national product war."[9] As such, it was also a war of mines, farms, and factories – largely industrial or industrializing sites where slices of nature were extracted and processed into military machines and materiel.

---

[6] Franklin D. Roosevelt: "Excerpts from the Press Conference," July 27, 1943. Online by Gerhard Peters and John T. Woolley, *The American Presidency Project*, www.presidency .ucsb.edu/documents/excerpts-from-the-press-conference-14 (accessed October 23, 2018).

[7] Pyle, *Brave Men*, 25.

[8] Robert W. Coakley and Richard M. Leighton, *Global Logistics and Strategy: 1943–1945* (Washington, DC: US Government Printing Office, 1955), 601, quoted in Doris Kearns Goodwin, *No Ordinary Time: Franklin and Eleanor Roosevelt and the Home Front in World War II* (New York: Simon & Schuster, 2013), 450.

[9] Russell Weigley, *The American Way of War: A History of United States Military Strategy and Policy* (New York: MacMillan, 1973), 146. Indeed, the concept of the gross national product (GNP) was developed in 1942 by economists to determine whether the United States had the productive capacity to meet the needs of the nation's World War II Victory Program. Jim Lacey, *Keep from All Thoughtful Men: How US Economists Won World War II* (Annapolis, MD: Naval Institute Press, 2011), 45.

Nothing showed the Allies' dependence on American productive landscapes better than the "fireside" chat that Franklin Delano Roosevelt gave on July 28, 1943, two and a half weeks after the first soldiers splashed ashore on Sicily's beaches. As they sat in living rooms by their radios, Americans listened as President Roosevelt explained the import of Sicily. "I think the first crack in the Axis has come," Roosevelt announced with signature mix of gravity and optimism. "The criminal, corrupt Fascist regime in Italy is going to pieces."

But the job was far from done and still uncertain, the president stressed. Ultimate success, he emphasized, depended on what happened not in Europe but thousands of miles away: on the American home front that produced the weapons and other supplies that Allied soldiers carried with them. American power, Roosevelt said, came from America's farms and mines, its natural resources and productive capacity:

Behind the invasion forces ... were thousands of ships and planes guarding the long, perilous sea lanes, carrying the men, carrying the equipment and the supplies to the point of attack. And behind all these were the railroad lines and the highways here back home that carried the men and the munitions to the ports of embarkation – there were the factories and the mines and the farms here back home that turned out the materials – there were the training camps here back home where the men learned how to perform the strange and difficult and dangerous tasks which were to meet them on the beaches and in the deserts and in the mountains.[10]

FDR's words help us see what distinguished World War II from earlier conflicts. The Allied invasion force included not just an army of soldiers and sailors but an army of supplies and equipment of unprecedented scale and scope. Watching these supplies move ashore in Sicily, Pyle spoke of "the might of material."[11] All these materials – each soldier, ship, and plane – relied upon transportation networks, fuel, factories, mines, and farms. The war, Roosevelt was saying, demanded not just amassing a large military force but drawing together critical materials from all possible sources, near and far, and concentrating them into one enormous, mobile, lethal force. It was indeed a GNP war, a war of total mobilization.[12]

---

[10] Franklin D. Roosevelt, "Fireside Chat 25: On the Fall of Mussolini" (speech, Washington, DC, July 28, 1943) UVA Miller Centre, https://millercenter.org/the-presidency/presidential-speeches/july-28-1943-fireside-chat-25-fall-mussolini (accessed October 6, 2018).

[11] Pyle, *Brave Men*, 25.

[12] Paul Kennedy expands on this theme. "Gigantic productive power means little in wartime unless it is harnessed and its resources are directed to the right places. Total steel output means nothing at all until it is directed toward well-designed Essex class carriers.

Wars can be understood many ways – politically, strategically, economically, socially, personally. They also can be understood environmentally. Geography and supplies shape strategy and outcomes, and battles remake coastlines, fields, and forests. Less well known is how, even far from the battle zones, the need for supplies militarize landscapes and remake ecosystems.

No war transformed natural environments more than World War II – a total, global conflict that saw massive fighting across four continents and four oceans and drew resources from around the planet. The discussion of "total war" – the state's capacity to mobilize nearly all human and natural resources for the military effort – has rarely engaged its underlying environmental preconditions, even though total war entails massive and even transformative interventions into natural systems. More than any previous war, World War II achieved this total mobilization of resources across the world. The United States played a decisive role in the war and the story of its astoundingly rapid accumulation of military capacity is well known. Yet, surprisingly, historians have hardly explored the environmental dimensions of the American home-front transformation.

This volume examines the environmental aspects of the war, not in far off battlefields but on and near US soil, often with long-term consequences that linger even today. We investigate these matters by pursuing the clues provided by FDR's Fireside Chat on the home front. We look at the transportation networks that made World War II into a "war of transportation," the mines that yielded "strategic" minerals, the farms that transformed soil and seed into fiber and nutrition, the factories that forged the guns and munitions, and the training camps that molded skilled fighters and new methods. The location, abundance, and quality of these resources – shaped by new technologies and new logistical strategies – created the "might of material" that transformed the United States into the Arsenal of Democracy. American geology, hydrology, geography, and biology all mattered. Minerals, coastlines, rivers and wetlands, forests, and atmospheres, as well as farmlands, cities, and other human-built environments, shaped the war and were deeply transformed by it.

Aluminum and rubber and copper mean nothing until they are given to the B-29 construction program. Skilled workers mean nothing until Ben Moreell [of the Seabees] organizes them." Paul M. Kennedy, *Engineers of Victory: The Problem Solvers Who Turned the Tide in the Second World War* (Toronto: HarperCollins Publishers, 2013), 351. "Sheer numbers were not enough." Ibid., 363.

What made large and lethal American fighting forces in Europe and the Far East possible was a marshaling of material resources – physical objects and energy – drawn from forests, waterways, and soils around the United States and, indeed, around the world. Organizing these resources required new organizational tools and methods, and left behind a legacy of transformed landscapes, powerful new technological tools, and ideas about nature that would shape American relations with nature for decades to come.

In 1938, before massive wartime spending began, most Americans lived in small towns, farms, or small urban areas; traveled by rail; and had never heard of penicillin, DDT, or atomic bombs. By 1945, the scales had tipped decidedly toward military-industrial urban areas, the Sunbelt, machine and chemical agriculture, air travel, oil-based materials, such as nylon, and a Keynesian "growth" economy stressing government-sponsored consumption. The war spurred in the United States a vastly expanded production capacity and powerful new economic tools: a new military-industrial geography and transformed sense of time and space; new "miracle" technologies and a new material culture; new forms and quantities of waste and pollution; and new ideas about nature's fragility. In sum, the war forged the world we live in – not just the political and economic order but also the built environment, material culture, and intellectual topography, not to mention American landscapes near and far.

Understanding the environmental dimensions of the war provides a novel, penetrating way to understand not just World War II – the most crucial of all events in recent American history – but its lasting impact on American society.

ENVIRONMENTAL TRANSFORMATIONS IN THE UNITED STATES DURING WORLD WAR II

If the Second World War touched every portion of the outside world, its domestic impact reached into every corner of the United States as well.
Historian Roger Lotchin[13]

Before the mid-nineteenth century, preindustrial warfare had created only limited, local impact on natural environments. The environmental

[13] Roger Lotchin, "Turning the Good War Bad?," *Journal of Urban History* 33, no. 2 (2007): 175.

impacts of warfare in medieval Europe, for instance, were small-scale and limited, resulting from sieges of fortified castles and towns, the cutting of selected species of trees (such as Yew trees for longbows), disruption of watercourses, and scorched earth campaigns, or *chevauchées*, designed to deprive populations of essential food and supplies.[14] Armaments were limited in destructive power, military transport systems were still largely limited to human marching and horseback, and environments usually recovered quickly from the effects of war.

Industrial wars in the nineteenth century, especially the American Civil War, changed all that permanently. The Civil War was a transitional war, exhibiting both traditional dimensions and the new power of industrial systems, foreshadowing what was to come.[15] Bringing together huge armies for several years of warfare and introducing factory production and rail transport, the Civil War both shaped and was shaped by nature. The North-South conflict shows many of the main concerns of environmental historians of war: the impact of battlefields on war and war on battlefields; changing forms of resource consumption and energy use; the overlap of health, disease, and warfare; new forms of governmental planning; and changing ideas of nature.

Fifty years later, World War I showed how interlinked war and nature had become in the industrial age and highlights the tremendous transformative power of national security imperatives not just on human systems but also on ecologies, hydrologies, and geologies. Nature factored into World War I in many of the same ways it did with the Civil War – through strategy, battlefield destruction, resource mobilization, disease landscapes, and state planning. Of these, the United States was, at first, initially mostly involved with resource mobilization, supplying England,

---

[14] Richard C. Hoffmann, *An Environmental History of Medieval Europe* (Cambridge: Cambridge University Press, 2014); Bruce M. S. Campbell, *The Great Transition: Climate, Disease and Society in the Late Medieval World* (Cambridge: Cambridge University Press, 2016).

[15] Lisa M. Brady, *War upon the Land: Military Strategy and the Transformation of Southern Landscapes during the American Civil War* (Athens: University of Georgia Press, 2012); Mark Fiege, "Gettysburg and the Organic Nature of the American Civil War," in Richard P. Tucker and Edmund Russell, *Natural Enemy, Natural Ally: Toward an Environmental History of Warfare* (Corvallis: Oregon State University Press, 2004), 93–109; Megan Kate Nelson, *Ruin Nation: Destruction and the American Civil War* (Athens: University of Georgia Press, 2012); Kathryn Shively Meier, *Nature's Civil War: Common Soldiers and the Environment in 1862 Virginia* (Chapel Hill: University of North Carolina Press, 2013); Brian Allen Drake, ed., *The Blue, the Gray, and the Green: Toward an Environmental History of the Civil War* (Athens: University of Georgia Press, 2015).

France, and others with food, industrial equipment, horses, and more.[16] Factories and fields rapidly increased the production of steel and copper, timber, grain, rubber, and petroleum.[17] New productive technologies yielded new forms of pollution.

During the Great War, to coordinate government-industry relations and allocate resources, the US federal government created a series of regulatory agencies, centered on the War Industries Board, which brought together federal officials and heads of the major industrial corporations. The military-industrial complex began to take shape. But traditional opposition to a powerful federal government was still widespread, so most of those agencies were dismantled quickly after November 1918, and the US military downsized once again.[18] The aftermath of World War II would be very different.

Expanding and institutionalizing many of the developments of the Civil War and World War I, World War II played a transformative role in creating the world we live in today – its built environment, material culture, and intellectual geography, as well as American landscapes around the country.

This book's chapters explore the rise of the two most important factors shaping environmental change during the second half of the century: national security concerns and a related technology-driven growth economy. We see the emergence of the military-industrial political economy, the birth of "big science" and the modern university; techno-optimism; the consolidation of corporate agriculture and the industrial food system; the coming of age of West Coast cities, such as Seattle and Los Angeles; the profound remaking of Detroit, Birmingham, New Orleans, and indeed, of much of urban America; and, finally, the demographic shifts that define America today – the rural to urban

---

[16] Tait Keller, "Mobilizing Nature for the First World War: An Introduction," in *Environmental Histories of the First World War*, ed. Richard P. Tucker, Tait Keller, J. R. McNeill, and Martin Schmid (Cambridge: Cambridge University Press, 2018), 1–16; Paul A. C. Koistinen, *Mobilizing for Modern War: The Political Economy of American Warfare, 1865–1919* (Lawrence: University Press of Kansas, 1997).

[17] Richard P. Tucker, "War and the Environment," in *At War: The Military and American Culture in the Twentieth Century and Beyond*, ed. David Kieran and Edwin A. Martini (New Brunswick, NJ: Rutgers University Press, 2018), 240–257.

[18] Roger Chickering and Stig Förster, eds., *The Shadows of Total War: Europe, East Asia, and the United States, 1919–1939* (Cambridge: Cambridge University Press, 2003); Williamson Murray and Allan R. Millett, eds., *Military Innovation in the Interwar Period* (Cambridge: Cambridge University Press, 1996); Joseph Maiolo, *Cry Havoc: How the Arms Race Drove the World to War, 1931–1941* (New York: Basic Books, 2010).

shift, the Great Migration of African Americans to urban and western cities, and the general shift to the Sunbelt. Nature played a role in, and was shaped by, all these changes.

Most noticeably, the war years produced, in the words of economic historian Robert Gordon, an "economic miracle."[19] Factory floor space and productivity shot upward. From 1942 to 1945, ship building times dropped by 67 percent. Steel production grew from 67 million tons per year in 1940 to 89 million tons in 1944, even as the number of workers remained constant – the change owing entirely to productivity gains. Overall, between 1940 and 1945, productivity per worker-hour climbed by 21 percent. Plant capacity grew as well. By 1945, the United States had 50 percent more productive capacity than in 1940.[20] These gains – along with the devastation of much of the rest of the industrial world – jumpstarted America's postwar economy. "Every part of the postwar manufacturing sector had been deeply involved in making military equipment or its components," Gordon notes, "and the lessons learned from the war translated into permanent efficiency gains after the war."[21] The early 1940s saw America's Keynes-inspired growth-based "guns and butter" economy – the modern economic approach that would drive postwar prosperity and environmental transformation – take shape.

The American military juggernaut mobilized resources on an unprecedented scale and with new planning and technological power from all over the United States and, indeed, all over the world. In 1945, a government report evocatively described the material needs of modern warfare. Echoing FDR's 1943 home-front speech, it described the transformations to forests, fields, rivers, and streams that made it possible:

War is indeed a story of arms and men; of supplies as well as soldiers. An army cannot fight a modern war with naked fists; front lines are unavoidably inhered to supply lines. And these supply lines reach all the way back along "red ball" truck lines [in Europe's western front], rails, and the bridge of ships to the ordnance plants, shipyards and plane assembly plants; to factories making bearings, gears, radio tubes, and thousands of other components; to petroleum wells and refineries producing the power for bombers and fighters, trucks and jeeps; to copper, iron, lead, zinc, and coal mines; to farms and forests. The story of the battle of supply is

---

[19] Robert J. Gordon, *The Rise and Fall of American Growth: The US Standard of Living since the Civil War* (Princeton, NJ: Princeton University Press, 2016), 537.

[20] D'ann Campbell and Richard Jensen, "Domestic Life, War Effort, and Economy," in *The Oxford Companion to World War II* (Oxford: Oxford University Press, 2001), 1180–1182.

[21] Gordon, *The Rise and Fall of American Growth*, 550.

the story of the production of all the raw materials and components, of all the assembly processes, and of all the management skill and labor that go into the making of a modern war machine.[22]

Because of the modern military machine – and the new production, new assembly processes, and new management skills that comprised it – "the demands on resources," as the Interior Department noted a few years later, "had become permanently higher."[23] Nothing shows this new productive efficiency's impact on resources better than wartime forestry. The nation's forests felt the pressure of war, as the federal Forest Service worked closely with the military to maximize war production, often by clearcutting entire stands of trees. Efficient collaboration expanded the timber products industry's technological, organizational, and financial capacity to penetrate further and more efficiently into both previously managed and previously untouched forest zones. New equipment was designed and new logging roads were bulldozed.[24] In this and other industries, the war expanded productive capacity exponentially; this new capacity would alter landscapes for decades to come.

The change was not just quantitative but also qualitative. Many of the technologies that drove America's productivity jump manipulated nature in unprecedented ways and with new intensity, ushering in unintended and previously unknown environmental consequences. David Lilienthal, writing in 1944, noted the wartime "machines of wizardry" that were spinning out "the stuff of a way of life new to this world."[25] Because of the length of the war, the tremendous innovations of previous decades, and the new determination with which governments mobilized these innovations and pursued others, scores of new technologies emerged during and immediately after the war – some decades in the making and applied with new wartime urgency, and others newly developed by scientists commissioned by the military. These technologies were unlike anything the world had ever seen. Taken together they entailed vast new human powers to alter the earth.

[22] US War Production Board, *War Production in 1944* (Washington, DC: Government Printing Office, 1945), 25.
[23] Department of Interior, *Years of Progress, 1945–1952* (Washington, DC: Government Printing Office, 1953), 3.
[24] Richard P. Tucker, "The World Wars and the Globalization of Timber Cutting," in *Natural Enemy, Natural Ally: Toward an Environmental History of* War, ed. Richard P. Tucker and Edmund Russell (Corvallis: Oregon State University Press, 2004), 110–141.
[25] David Lilienthal, *TVA: Democracy on the March* (New York: Harper & Brothers, 1944), 3.

The list of new tools invented or vastly transformed and popularized by the war is astonishing: atomic weapons; synthetics, such as plastic and nylon; new metal alloys; drugs like penicillin; sonar; airplane technology, including jet engines; DDT, insecticides, and herbicides; bulldozers and earth-moving equipment; assembly line housing that led to cookie-cutter suburban houses; and the first computers. All deployed unprecedented forms of power to manipulate environments, and many were applied with a reckless disregard for environmental consequences that modern readers would find shocking, but that was believed necessary to achieve victory. At the time, for instance, few Americans gave much thought to the ecological damage that DDT could spread.

Vastly scaled up production deploying powerful new technologies dirtied the nation's air and water in new ways and on a new scale. Few places were hit harder than the big cities that saw rapid defense-industry growth. "The war," historian Roger Lotchin has noted, "poured tons of pollutants into the atmosphere and into the waterways. By 1945, places like Pittsburgh and the other Ohio and Mississippi River cities had so much smoke in the air that they had to turn the street lights on at noon, dust bowl style." In Los Angeles, Lotchin adds, the war "actually created the smog problem."[26] Military-industrial sites also bore the brunt, including the massive Willow Run airplane factory outside Detroit, as described in this volume, and places such as Niagara, New York. The consequences could be long term. In Niagara, New York in 1941, the Hooker Chemical Company began dumping toxic wastes in nearby Love Canal, which it sealed over in 1953 and sold to the local school board to construct an elementary school and a residential neighborhood. In the late 1970s, local residents began noticing a surprising number of miscarriages and other health problems debilitating their loved ones and neighbors. Scientists soon connected these illnesses to the chemicals stored under the ground on which they lived. Love Canal became a symbol of modern society's environmental recklessness, spurring the federal Superfund program aimed at cleaning up the nation's worst polluted areas, many of which, like this one, dated to World War II military production. Scores of such military-industrial wastelands dot the nation's map, often near to where thousands of Americans – often working class or minority – live.[27] Most

---

[26] Roger Lotchin, "Turning the Good War Bad?," *Journal of Urban History* 33, no. 2 (2007): 176.

[27] Richard S. Newman, *Love Canal: A Toxic History from Colonial Times to the Present* (New York: Oxford University Press, 2016), 74–77.

of the nation's Superfund sites, the nation's most toxic landscapes, have military origins, and most have World War II stories. At the end of the Cold War, there were more than 19,000 contaminated sites in over 1,700 active military facilities across the country.[28]

The war also profoundly reordered American geography. Wartime national security imperatives recast the spatial arrangement of the United States, creating a military-industrial geography layered upon the nineteenth-century capitalist geography that had organized American landscapes by what could be profitably marketed and sold. The war ushered in a more integrated, urban, militarized, high-tech industrial country, with big shifts away from rural areas in favor of northern and coastal cities and the Sunbelt, and with many more links outside the United States than ever before. At its core, this military-industrial geography consisted of a network of militarized spaces, such as bases, and militarized industries, such as chemical and aviation factories, linked together and to a global network of suppliers and military bases by a road, rail, shipping, and air system remade by wartime needs and technologies. It was a more interconnected, mobile landscape, with people and material moving around more frequently, faster, and farther than ever before. Speed took on new urgency. Rail use reached new peaks, yet the war made air travel, trucks, highways, and mass shipping the way of the future.

This new geography demanded huge quantities of energy. Undergirding this new system, in addition to a vast transportation network, was an energy network of oil and electricity layered upon the earlier system of coal. Much of new wartime geography took shape in places where cheap electricity was available in prodigious amounts, particularly New Deal landscapes such as the Pacific Northwest and Tennessee Valley. Cheap oil also became critical, creating a huge infrastructure, such as around New Orleans, as well as a thousand and one spin-off products. The placement of industries in the Sunbelt would have been impossible without large amounts of electricity that powered air conditioners to make factories habitable for workers in the intense summer heat. New energy-intensive patterns of work and leisure also emerged.

This environmental transformation also included new environmental sciences "discovered," studied, and engineered, particularly in nuclear

---

[28] John McNeill and David Painter, "America's Military Footprint: Environmental Implications of the US Army since 1789," in *War and the Environment: Military Destruction in the Modern Age*, ed. Charles E. Closmann (College Station: Texas A&M University Press, 2009), 23.

physics, chemistry, and biology. Not only did the war open up the new and powerfully unpredictable frontier of subatomic particles, but it also marshaled modern chemistry to create scores of substances that no human had ever encountered before, such as alloys, plastics, and DDT, as well as new biological tools, such as penicillin, that altered the very architecture of life. All this – new technologies; new more powerful forms of energy; new uses of physics, chemistry, and biology – enabled unprecedentedly powerful manipulations of nature and left behind an archipelago of toxic dead zones.

Along with creating a new geography, the war created a military material culture that shaped daily life for decades. Of course, no one could miss the military nature of the thousands of troops and scores of military bases, which became common and permanent features of the landscape. But World War II's national security imperatives, technologies, and patterns of organization also seeped into and shaped ordinary civilian life in ways that many people recognized at the time but, decades later, are largely forgotten, even though their impact still lives on. This was the "way of life new to this world" that David Lilienthal wrote of in 1944.[29] To the extent that we live in northern cities or the Sunbelt, work at defense industries or companies that support them, eat processed food from fertilizer-fed fields (and cover leftovers in Saran Wrap), smoke cigarettes, travel by airplane, wear and use petroleum-based clothes and products, use aluminum and a host of alloys, and rely upon antibiotics when we get sick, we are drawing from the material culture developed for military purposes and spread during World War II. Of course, the Cold War reinforced and added to this military material culture, but it was World War II that started things, putting the basic patterns in place. After the war, Americans lived in landscapes and navigated a daily material world that World War II and the demands of national security had transformed profoundly from earlier decades. As historian Roger Lotchin noted, the war reached into every corner of the United States.

The federal government organized, administered, and regulated the creation of thousands of militarized landscapes.[30] In sharp contrast to previous wars, the federal government, in the name of national security,

[29] Lilienthal, *TVA: Democracy on the March*, 3.
[30] For the concept of militarized landscapes, see Chris Pearson, Peter Coates, and Tim Cole, eds., *Militarized Landscapes from Gettysburg to Salisbury Plain* (London: Continuum, 2010); David G. Havlick, *Bombs Away: Militarization, Conservation, and Ecological Restoration* (Chicago: University of Chicago Press, 2018).

took on a wide variety of environmental management activities. This transformation involved new planning tools and new forms of knowledge. The federal government had been expanding its authority, particularly in the realm of resource and environmental planning during the New Deal, but World War II marked a decided shift, a maturation of the "environmental-management state." The federal government's expanded role included direct ownership of vast amounts of acreage for military bases, as well as federal survey and infrastructure development programs in the far-flung corners of the republic, including Alaska, Hawaii, and the Panama Canal zone. Federal initiatives included national conservation drives and natural resource planning through organizations such as the War Production Board; planning in every sector of the economy; economic tools to monitor and spur consumption; and research and programming in physics, chemistry, earth sciences, engineering, and public health.

In sum, the war was global and total in fighting, but also in natural resource mobilization. It not only drew materials from all over the United States and the globe, but also, in the process, it intensified relations with nature, deploying new technologies and extractive systems to pull and channel as much productive power (or destructive power) as possible out of each mine, each farm field, each river, and each human – indeed, out of each molecule and atom of matter. This is what total war was about. This all-encompassing, more intensified war mobilization remade American landscapes. In some sectors, such as rural land use, the changes were smaller; the war accelerated trends that had first emerged well before. In other areas, however, the war brought more fundamental and far-reaching changes, such as with industrial capacity, energy, patterns of mineral use, pollution, and urban environments. In some cases, the changes were immediately visible; in others, the seeds of changes were sown – often in the form of new military strategies, new technologies, or new social patterns – that would take full form only with the passage of time.

ENVIRONMENTAL CHANGES EXPLORED IN THIS VOLUME

The contributors to this book examine 12 dimensions of the wartime environmental experience of the United States in depth. After Peter Mansoor's powerful preface, the book is divided into six parts. Part I examines World War II's new military strategies and how these strategies drew from and changed American landscapes, often in unprecedented ways. Unlike the trench-based combat of World War I, mobile combat dominated World War II, requiring thousands of vehicles and planes. It was a war of transport, mobility, and speed – of tanks, ships, and airplanes. What technologies and environmental conditions made this new warfare possible and with what short-term and long-term impact? In Chapter 1, Christopher W. Wells and Thomas Robertson examine airplanes and transportation, focusing on factories that built airplanes, such as the gargantuan Willow Run factory outside Detroit; the materials, such as aluminum and rubber, marshaled from around the United States and the world to make them; the transport system that linked these landscapes of extraction and production; the new scale and power of the productive technologies involved; their waste products; and the related new ideas that emerged during the war.

In Chapter 2, Jean Mansavage examines the tremendous land requirements of the US military because of the new strategies of tank and air warfare. During World War II, great swathes of the American countryside came under the control of the military – 20 times the area it controlled before the war – and stayed in government hands for decades. The development of bases brought short- and long-term changes to nearby forests, mountains, rivers, and coastal zones. Sometimes the bases closed off lands to development, but often they developed the land, including into military industrial sites that left behind a legacy of toxic contamination.

Part II examines two of the key resources – metals and petroleum – that made World War II possible. Without these materials, a global war that traversed oceans and vast continents was unthinkable. It was a war of metals – of iron and steel for sure, but also of aluminum, copper, and scores of others (see Figure I.2). As *National Geographic* put it in 1942, it was the "age of alloys," without which no modern war machine could function. "More than any other struggle in history, this is a war of many metals, and the lack of a single one may be a blow far worse than the loss of a battle."[31] In Chapter 3, Kent Curtis examines this story, arguing that this massive demand required mining of both old and new sites at breakneck speed; as a result, mining sites and their surrounding areas were badly scarred. He further shows that even during the prewar strategic buildup, anxiety that domestic sites would prove inadequate to supply a massive war led to a search for sources of strategic minerals far beyond American borders. Of the 136 raw materials that the US government

---

[31] Frederick Vosburgh, "Metal Sinews of Strength," *National Geographic* 81 (April 1, 1942): 457.

FIGURE 1.2 Deal Cornell, "Back Them Up with Metal" (poster) (Washington, DC: Government Printing Office, 1943). A government-issued poster that shows the importance of metal in modern warfare.
Source: Image in the public domain

listed as strategic and critical at the beginning of the war, 48 came from outside the United States. The notes of one planner from 1945 give a sense of the situation:

We had to import tantalite for vacuum tubes; balsa wood for Mosquito bombers; kapok for life preservers; loofa sponges for filters in marine engines; mahogany for aircraft and PT boats; tin ore; chrome, manganese, and nickel to toughen our steel; natural rubber; burlap and rope fibers; and many other vital war needs. ... our productive machine would have been seriously hampered without them.[32]

American strategic hegemony over global resources was emerging. These strategic materials, although only a small percentage of total war materials, carried outsized importance. Perhaps nothing was more important than oil, a form of energy essential to mobile warfare. During the war, the US Army became the single largest consumer of oil and other petroleum products in the world, a pattern that would continue for

---

[32] US War Production Board, *War Production in 1944* (Washington, DC: Government Printing Office, 1944), 22.

decades. By one estimate, an American armored division in World War II required approximately 60,000 gallons of gasoline daily.[33] Creating a guaranteed system of supply for a vast military and industrial apparatus transformed economies, political systems, and environments around the United States and the world. Chapter 4, by Brian Black, documents many of these important changes.

Part III examines the organic supplies needed to feed the war machine. Chapter 5 examines agriculture. During the war, Kendra Smith-Howard argues, farming became "an act of national security" with both short-lived and longer-lasting changes. In the short term, the war did not bring out deep immediate changes in agricultural practices, but it set the stage for dramatic changes immediately after the war, fueled by mechanization and the use of chemical fertilizers, herbicides, and antibiotics. Smith-Howard tells these stories with close attention to the on-the-ground reality during the war years.

Food, Kellen Backer argues in Chapter 6, also became a weapon in World War II. American farmers kept US and allied troops fed and content while enemy armies struggled to find sufficient supplies. Backer documents the war's cross-cutting trends. Through "victory gardens" and food conservation efforts, thousands of Americans learned more about locally grown agriculture. At the same time, and with greater long-term consequences, wartime research and development yielded a more industrialized food system, removed from soil and fields and seasonal patterns and full of processed products such as canned, frozen, and dehydrated foods. Americans have never eaten the same since, with lasting environmental and health consequences.

In Chapter 7, Joel R. Bius examines cigarettes and their consequences, from soil to human bodies. Cigarettes – and the nicotine they contained – gave a boost to weary workers on the home front and soldiers on distant shores. They too became a weapon of war, prompting calls for greater tobacco production and a relaxation of New Deal conservation measures. But farmers and policy makers, remembering the washed away fields that tobacco had created over the decades, mostly resisted a rollback of conservation measures. Indeed, no better case exists, as Bius notes, that the wartime "drive for greater production had limits." At the same time, though, generous government tobacco distribution to troops devastated the human environment. World War II subsidies for cigarettes created,

[33] McNeill and Painter, "America's Military Footprint: Environmental Implications of the US Army since 1789," 23.

Bius argues, "a deadly habit that seared the lungs of America's fighting men and their families for generations."

Part IV examines two of the most heavily reconfigured landscapes of the war, coastal zones and urban centers, particularly in the Southeast and in Southern California. In 1940, Christopher M. Rein writes in Chapter 8, the Southeast and the Gulf Coast had been a malarial backwater, with little development and small populations. By the end of the war, though, permanent military bases, federal dollars, and a massive expansion in the region's petrochemical infrastructure had remade the region, most noticeably in the growth of industrial infrastructure and the mushrooming of urban areas such as Houston, New Orleans, Baton Rouge, Mobile, and Tampa. Much of this development came in environmentally vulnerable coastal areas.

In Chapter 9, Sarah S. Elkind analyzes the wartime politics of industrial pollution in Los Angeles. As in many other US cities, especially along the entire West Coast, Los Angeles's political leaders saw a major opportunity for federal contracts – for naval and aeronautics industries in particular – to build the city's industrial and political power. The politicization of wartime industrial growth operated on every level, from local to federal. In Los Angeles this process was contested: political and community leaders were conflicted about the environmental stress of oil production, which produced a notorious level of smog.

Part V examines two types of "landscapes" newly explored and manipulated by scientists during the war: the molecular and subatomic realms. In the molecular landscape, as Martha N. Gardner explores in Chapter 10, the massive acceleration and diversification of the chemical and pharmaceutical industries had profound though largely unforeseen consequences for public health and the environment. She examines the histories of DDT, the germicide Hexachlorophene, and penicillin, the grandparent of the antibiotics industry. Each of them transformed an industry and shaped long-term environmental dynamics. Chemicals and antibiotics created industries that, together with the new herbicides, created chemically saturated ecosystems and societies. The stakes for both public health and environmental health would be high.

In Chapter 11, Ryan H. Edgington takes a novel and revealing approach to one of the best known environmental stories of World War II: the development of nuclear weapons. While documenting the rise of "big science" and what it meant for human-nature relations, he focuses on how three landscapes were experienced by the people who lived there – Los Alamos, New Mexico, the community that had seen wave after wave of migrants and that now saw a new wave of wealthy scientific, federal arrivals; the Navajo lands that produced uranium for the nuclear bombs, as well as cancer for many local residents; and the Trinity Test Site, former ranch land that became a scientific laboratory and, eventually, a national and global landmark. "Nuclear technologies did not merely explode in far off places," Edgington writes. "They reshaped scores of local landscapes across the United States where people had long lived and worked."

Finally, Chapter 12 focuses on how total war shaped the thinking of conservationists. Examining the wartime writings of David Brower, Aldo Leopold, Rachel Carson, and other mid-century thinkers, it argues that national security imperatives created problems and knowledges that spurred the shift from early-twentieth-century "conservation" thinking to the 1960s "environmental movement." Even as it reinforced the conservationist call for efficient natural resource development, the extensive resource mobilization and new technologies of total war during the 1940s, which set patterns followed during the Cold War, sowed the seeds for new environmentalist perspectives emphasizing ecological science, deep skepticism of technology, and natural limits.

In sum, global war ushered in the Age of Acceleration across the United States and around the world. The central dimensions of accelerating ecological deterioration became increasingly evident in the 20 years that followed the war. The expansions of these years were unprecedented, as the population boom, widespread consumerism, accelerating technological capacity of industry, and concentration of capital devoured natural resources (especially fossil fuels) and created a global scourge of toxic pollution.[34] World War II shaped all these trends, and the United States became the dominant engine of those transformations for the postwar world.

---

[34] Major sources on the "great acceleration" include J. R. McNeill and Peter Engelke, *The Great Acceleration: An Environmental History of the Anthropocene since 1945* (Cambridge, MA: Belknap Press of Harvard University Press, 2014).

PART I

NEW WEAPONS, NEW SPACES

A War of Mobility

Transportation, American Productive Power,
and the Environment during World War II

Thomas Robertson and Christopher W. Wells

We knew that we would have to fight a highly motorized mechanized
war – or a *losing war*.
  – Donald Nelson, Chairman of the War Production Board[1]

World War II was a global war. It was a war of transport, mobility, and
speed, fought in the far corners of the planet, across four continents and
four oceans. It was also a gross national product war, fought with huge
armies equipped with the fruits of modern industry – guns, artillery,
tanks, trucks, airplanes, and thousands of other tools and supplies. To
fight a war of men and material simultaneously on opposite sides of the
earth, the United States needed weapons of speed and distance, such as
the airplane, but also tools of mobile transport, such as heavy trucks –
and they needed them in record numbers. The United States also required
a transportation infrastructure at home (and abroad) that could deliver
people and resources where needed for production and warfare.

Building hundreds of thousands of airplanes and millions of new
trucks, combined with creating the substantial, far-flung transportation
infrastructures to support them, spurred significant and lasting environmental changes: a new pattern of extracting resources, some of which
came from the United States and some from overseas; a host of new
industrial sites and expanded production capacity, which brought environmentally destructive practices; a new geography, together with an
accelerated culture of mobility; and new ideas about modern life,

[1] A. J. Baime, *The Arsenal of Democracy: FDR, Detroit, and an Epic Quest to Arm an
America at War* (Boston: Houghton Mifflin Harcourt, 2014), 135.

technology, and nature – and, especially, a sense of fragility in the face of humanity's growing technological prowess. Remaking extractive and productive landscapes and the transportation systems that connected them during the war created patterns, technologies, and ideas that shaped American relationships with nature well into the future.

BUILDING AN AVIATION INDUSTRY

Many of the more distinctive environmental changes that World War II prompted in the United States – new materials, technologies, productive power, and ideas – flowed from the stunning growth, in just a few short years, of the American aviation industry. Between 1940 and 1943, the American military's air force grew from tiny to gargantuan. In September 1939, the United States possessed 2,470 aircraft; in July 1944, it had nearly 80,000. In late 1939, the United States had 17 airbases; by 1943, it possessed 345 main bases, 116 subbases, and 322 auxiliary fields – most of which had also been expanded and improved during the war. In June 1938, the General Headquarters Air Force, a predecessor to the Army Air Force (AAF), enlisted more than 20,000; in March 1945, it had almost 1.9 million men and women, roughly one in six of all military personnel.[2] Of the planes the United States had in 1939, only 23 were truly modern aircraft – B-17 bombers – which by the end of the war had been surpassed in size, speed, power, and capacity for devastation.[3]

Massive air power was not possible without industrial facilities that gobbled up massive amounts of materials and left behind a significant environmental mark. During the war, the United States possessed great productive advantages over other countries in steel, automobiles, oil, and – eventually – in aviation. But the war did not start that way. In 1938, US production of planes, including both military and civilian, totaled more than 3,600 aircraft. In May 1940, President Franklin Roosevelt shocked the nation by calling for a yearly output of 50,000 planes, an almost unimaginable number. The United States had produced only about 50,000 aircraft in its entire history until then. But one-third of those were made in World War I, so planners knew that wartime emergency

---

[2] David T. Courtwright, *Sky as Frontier: Adventure, Aviation, and Empire* (College Station: Texas A & M University Press, 2005), 118.

[3] D'ann Campbell and Richard Jensen, "Domestic Life, War Effort, and Economy," in *The Oxford Companion to World War II* (Oxford: Oxford University Press, 2001), 1180–1182. See also John Bell Rae, *Climb to Greatness: The American Aircraft Industry, 1920–1960* (Cambridge, MA: MIT Press, 1968).

measures could yield big results. By early 1944, the United States could produce 110,000 planes a year. In total, the United States produced 300,000 planes during the war (see Figure 1.1).[4]

The buildup began long before the United States entered the war in December 1941. In 1939, the federal government allocated $68 million for military aircraft production. At the time, only 15 plants made airframes, engines, and propellers. By 1940, 41 factories did so, and, by 1943, more than 80. More than 2.1 million American men and women worked in the aircraft industry.[5] In the run-up to American involvement in the war, the country began spending lavishly on airports, disbursing $40 million in 1939 and another $95 million in 1941.[6]

None of this would have been possible without the automobile industry. "Automotive conversion," the War Production Board's Donald Nelson wrote, "was the first and biggest item on our agenda. The story of production for war ... centers around the story of conversion of our automotive industry – the most colossal aggregation of industrial might in history."[7] It was not just the size of the auto industry that mattered; more important was that no industry could match the auto industry's mastery of assembly-line mass production. Ultimately, the United States won the war, as A. J. Baime notes, with thousands of "Oldsmobile cannon shells, Packard marine and aviation engines, Buick aviation engines, Dodge gyrocompasses and ambulances, Studebaker troop transporters, Cadillac tanks and Howitzer cannons, Dodge shortwave radio sets, Chrysler field kitchens, A. C. spark plug 50 caliber Browning machine guns."[8] This was just one of many ways in which the aircraft and automobile were interlinked during the war.

Much of this prodigious production occurred in and around Detroit, as the city's automakers redirected their prowess in mass production toward establishing the United States as the "arsenal of democracy." Almost as soon as the United States entered the war, Detroit's automakers stopped building cars for civilians, shifting to a round-the-clock, seven-day-a-week schedule of war production. By war's end, only the chemical industry giant DuPont outstripped General Motors as a producer for the American military. The nation's largest automaker churned out a vast range of

---

[4] Roger E. Bilstein, *Flight in America: From the Wrights to the Astronauts* (Baltimore: Johns Hopkins University Press, 2001), 159–160. Also see Donald M. Pattillo, *Pushing the Envelope: The American Aircraft Industry* (Ann Arbor: University of Michigan Press, 2000).
[5] Courtwright, *Sky as Frontier*, 96–97.   [6] Ibid.
[7] Baime, *The Arsenal of Democracy*, 135.   [8] Ibid., 136.

FIGURE 1.1 Garrett Price, "Pour It On" (poster) (Washington, DC: War
Production Board, 1942). Library of Congress Prints and Photographs Division
Washington, DC, Reproduction Number: LC-USZC4-6032.
Source: Image in the public domain

military goods, including tank and airplane engines; complete bombers and fighter planes; tanks, trucks, and armored vehicles; and an array of cannons, machine guns, carbines, and mortar and artillery shells, among other war products. Ford and Chrysler ranked eighth and ninth, respectively, in military production, making a similarly wide range of war materiel. Smaller automakers like Willys and Packard also did their part.[9] By war's end, no less than 30 percent of the nation's total military equipment was pounded, welded, and bolted together in southeastern Michigan.[10]

No better example of the auto industry's involvement in wartime airplane production – and of the new scale and intensity of interactions with nature during the war – exists than the Ford Motor Company's massive Willow Run plant, built early in the war to make B-24 Liberators. Backed with the promise of a federal contract, Edsel Ford carved out the huge industrial facility from soybean fields 25 miles west of Detroit, near Ypsilanti. The airfield emerged first, in 1941, with workers bulldozing 650,000 cubic yards of dirt, and laying down 16 miles of sewers and 58 miles of drain tile.[11] The plant was monstrous: 67 acres under one roof. The *Washington Post* called it "the greatest single manufacturing plant the world had ever seen." Inside, the *Post* reported, "All 16 major league baseball teams could play simultaneous games before crowds of 30,000 each.... And there would still be room enough left over for a full-sized football game before an additional 30,000 spectators."[12] Before the end of the war, Willow Run would be rolling out a new B-24 bomber every hour.[13]

Building the B-24 – which stretched 110 feet from wingtip to wingtip and weighed 35,000 pounds – required tremendous quantities of materials from the near and far corners of the earth: aluminum, rubber, plastic, steel, and several other metals. The bomber's skin consisted of thin sheets of aluminum. Nearly 5 miles of wire and 4,000 feet of rubber and metal tubing snaked within each plane, circulating fuel, oil, oxygen, de-icing fluid, and hydraulic fluid. Eighteen self-sealing rubber fuel tanks inside the wings held 16,320 pounds (2,320 gallons) of 100-octane gasoline. Three rubber tires, each of them three feet high and capable of supporting nearly

[9] On World War II auto industry production, see Automobile Manufacturers Association, *Freedom's Arsenal: The Story of the Automotive Council for War Production* (Detroit: Automobile Manufacturers Association, 1950).
[10] Baime, *The Arsenal of Democracy*, 259. [11] Ibid., 108. [12] Ibid., 143.
[13] On Willow Run, also see David T. Courtwright, *Sky as Frontier: Adventure, Aviation, and Empire* (College Station: Texas A&M University Press, 2005), 118.

27,000 pounds, rolled beneath the plane. Four radial engines generated
the equivalent of 56 Ford V8 engines, or of a total of 4,800 horses. Four
generators, each enough to power an average household, churned out
electricity. Overall, aluminum made up 85 percent of the plane; steel 13
percent; brass, copper, and bronze 0.66 percent; magnesium 0.33 percent;
and rubber, glass, and plastic 1.01 percent.[14] A railroad spur delivered
these materials to Willow Run; four 30,000-pound cranes unloaded and
distributed them.

The plant was divided into manufacturing and assembly sections.
To stamp out bomber parts, metalworkers used hydraulic presses, some
weighing 700,000 pounds. Welders and blacksmiths shaped sheet metal
and 3,000 separate parts. Twenty-nine miles of ceiling conveyors ferried
parts and materials around the plant. Machines – drills, lathes, x-ray
machines, jigs, and presses – spread throughout the work areas. Pipes
circulated oxygen, paraffin, machine oil, compressed air, steam, acetyl-
ene, hydrogen, oxygen, and two kinds of gasoline – 73 octane for trucks
and cars, 100 octane for airplanes.[15]

From an environmental perspective, perhaps the most significant area
of the factory was the metals lab, the physical location where the "age of
alloys" was created. Here, to make high-performance alloys – new metal-
lic mixtures that would remake American material culture – foundry
workers mixed molten aluminum and steel with copper, chromium,
molybdenum, tungsten, vanadium, and, especially, carbon.[16] They often
used acid and cyanide.

Windowless because of wartime blackouts, the factory relied on
156,000 40-watt Sylvania fluorescent bulbs. Hundreds of machines generated an ear-splitting clatter and scream. One worker described the
factory floor's otherworldly environment: "The roar of the machinery;
the special din of the rivet guns, absolutely deafening nearby; the
throbbing crash of giant metal presses; busy little service trucks rushing
down endless aisles under the blue white fluorescent lights; the strange
far-reaching line of half-born skyships growing wings under swarms of
workers meeting deadlines."[17] (At another wartime aviation factory,
one writer described the "banshee din of air-riveting hammers and the
high-pitched swearing of tortured souls." It was, he said, a "nerve-
shattering existence."[18])

---

[14] Baime, *The Arsenal of Democracy*, 90, 96, 164.   [15] Ibid., 97.   [16] Ibid., 146.
[17] Ibid., 18, 140.
[18] Hurd Barrett, "Bombers by the Pound," *Saturday Evening Post*, February 24, 1940.

A small army of workers, including African Americans recruited from the South and women, took turns keeping Willow Run churning around the clock. Employment peaked in the spring of 1943 at 42,331. Housing employees in the nearest hamlet, which had only 331 residents before the war, posed a particular problem. By 1942, shantytowns without clean drinking water and sewage systems sprang up.[19] Eventually the government constructed "Bomber City" for workers, a sprawling complex of one- and two-bedroom apartments. Some officials hoped to apply the latest urban planning principles to these wartime settlements to prevent problems. Their hopes were rejected. "The military's concern for delivery speed and reliability," writes Sarah Jo Peterson, "overwhelmed all other criteria."[20]

It is hard to know exactly how much factories like Willow Run contaminated the water, air, and soil. At the time, very few people gave much thought to industrial pollution, and factories kept few records. But one indication is the toxic sludge pond containing PCBs that collected some plant waste beginning in 1942 and for decades afterward.[21] Yet the pollution from a plant of this size extended beyond this. Guided by ignorance and constrained by few regulations, most American factories spewed substantial amounts of dirty air, contaminated water, and toxic solid waste. On top of this, great urgency drove all military production: "speed and more speed" according to one top planner.[22] "Facilities for production," Roosevelt announced in his 1942 State of the Union, "must be ready to turn out munitions and equipment at top speed."[23] This sense of urgency, coupled with an inexperienced workforce, pushed factories to implement many new techniques without proper testing, resulting in widespread corner-cutting, such as the dumping of chemicals.

Willow Run was only one of scores of aviation industrial sites. Similar aircraft factories remade local economies and environments in aviation production pockets scattered around the country. Aircraft factories making aircraft frames, propellers, parts and engines sprung up around

[19] Baime, *The Arsenal of Democracy*, 146–149.

[20] Sarah Jo Peterson, *Planning the Home Front: Building Bombers and Communities at Willow Run* (Chicago: University of Chicago Press, 2013), 32. Also see Douglas Karsner, "Aviation and Airports: The Impact on the Economic and Geographic Structure of American Cities, 1940s–1980s," *Journal of Urban History* 23, no. 4 (1997): 406–436.

[21] "Public Health Assessment: Willow Run Sludge Lagoon," Public Health Assessments and Health Consultations, Agency for Toxic Substances & Disease Registry, www.atsdr.cdc .gov/hac/pha/pha.asp?docid=479&pg=1 (accessed July 18, 2016).

[22] Baime, *The Arsenal of Democracy*, 85.   [23] Ibid., 69.

Detroit, New York City, Chicago, Wichita (the "air capital" of America),
Seattle, and a few Sunbelt locations, such as Los Angeles and Georgia,
in a process of geographic reconfiguration one scholar has called the
"Military Remapping of America."[24] The Bell Aircraft Plant in Marietta,
GA, which drew resources from Tennessee Valley aluminum plants,
occupied a 3,000-acre plot. The biggest single factory, the Dodge plant
in Chicago, which produced Wright-cyclone engines for the B-29 "Superfortress" and sat on land that in 1942 was just a grassy prairie, occupied
6.5 million square feet of work area (covering 30 city blocks), as much
floor space as occupied by the entire aircraft engine industry early in
1941.[25] These factories all contaminated local ecosystems with new
chemicals and byproducts. Boeing Plant 2, located along the Duwamish
River in Seattle, later became a Superfund site because of PCBs and a
range of other hazardous materials in its soil and groundwater, including
chromium, copper, and cadmium, cyanide, petroleum products, and
chlorinated solvents such as trychlorethylene.[26] Similarly, new air bases
were also industrial sites that polluted local soil and water and consumed
great stretches of American territory, particularly in the Sunbelt, a term
coined by the AAF. By the war's end, AAF bases covered 19.7 million
acres.[27] Besides the pollution, airplane factories and bases required new
local infrastructure and housing. They also pulled materials from around
the country and the world.

MINING NATURE TO MAKE PLANES

Procuring the vast range and quantity of materials for airplane
production – the total mobilization of materials required by new military
strategy – also dramatically rearranged nature, often with significant
environmental consequences. The many minerals and other materials
demanded by an aviation-driving military strategy all came from the earth
somewhere – often outside of the United States. As Brian Black also shows
in Chapter 4, digging up and transporting these materials transformed not
just the earth but also the lives of many people along the way.

[24] Ann R. Markusen, *The Rise of the Gunbelt: The Military Remapping of Industrial America* (New York: Oxford University Press, 1991).
[25] Rae, *Climb to Greatness*, 143.
[26] Environmental Protection Agency, "Hazardous Waste Cleanup: Boeing Plant 2, Tukwila, Washington," www.epa.gov/hwcorrectiveactionsites/hazardous-waste-cleanup-boeing-plant-2-tukwila-washington (accessed July 25, 2019).
[27] Rae, *Climb to Greatness*, 16.

At the war's outset, the United States lacked domestic sources for many materials essential for a massive military. In 1940, the United States possessed just 15 percent of the raw materials needed for even a two-year military emergency.[28] Supplies for airplanes – including rubber, copper, ferroalloys, and, especially, aluminum – particularly worried planners.[29]

Aluminum was to the mid-twentieth century what iron and steel were to the late nineteenth century: the era's defining material. Its widespread availability gave birth to spectacular innovations and yielded shiny new aesthetics. Above all, aluminum created modern airplanes, and, with them, modern warfare. "The aluminum industry helped to modernize warfare," Mimi Sheller has noted, "and warfare helped to modernize the aluminum industry."[30] As strong as iron or steel but much lighter, aluminum enabled planes to carry more, fly faster, and travel farther than ever before. Aluminum made up 60 percent of a modern heavy bomber's engines, 90 percent of its wings and fuselage, all its propellers, as well as rivets, wires, cables, rods, and electrical equipment.[31] "Aluminum," one observer noted in 1951, "has become the most important single bulk material of modern warfare. No fighting is possible, and no war can be carried to a successful conclusion today, without using and destroying vast quantities of aluminum."[32]

Between 1939 and 1943, American aluminum production multiplied sixfold, eclipsing the growth of all other essential metals.[33] At first, the United States obtained most of its bauxite – the ore in which aluminum is found – from mines in Suriname. But in 1942, despite new air bases and other heavy fortifications, German U-boats disrupted this supply. During a single three-week period in early fall, German submarines ignited a crisis by torpedoing 15 bauxite carriers and cutting deliveries by more than 75,000 tons. Launching an "all-out" program to develop domestic sources, the War Production Board turned to bauxite from Arkansas, newly useable because of a technological breakthrough called the

[28] Alfred E. Eckes, *The United States and the Global Struggle for Minerals* (Austin: University of Texas Press, 1979), 94.

[29] For Canadian aluminum production, see Matthew Evenden's pioneering work, "Aluminum, Commodity Chains, and the Environmental History of the Second World War," *Environmental History* 16, no. 1 (January 1, 2011): 69–93. Also see Matthew Evenden, *Allied Power: Mobilizing Hydro-Electricity during Canada's Second World War* (Toronto: University of Toronto Press, 2015).

[30] Mimi Sheller, *Aluminum Dreams: The Making of Light Modernity* (Cambridge, MA: MIT Press, 2014), 62.

[31] Ibid., 70.   [32] Ibid., 61.   [33] Ibid., 70.

lime-soda sintering process.[34] In 1941, foreign suppliers provided 54 percent of America's bauxite; in 1943, even as aluminum production increased dramatically, they supplied less than 20 percent.[35] "Had the United States not possessed a deposit of bauxite in Arkansas," a 1952 government commission explained, "it might have been forced to cut back on airplane production."[36]

Like most mining, bauxite mining came at an environmental cost. Aluminum comes from reddish bauxite ore pulled from the earth in strip mines. In these mines, workers rip away the earth's trees and other vegetation to uncover the ore mixed with soil and rock below. Bauxite mines leave behind vast pools of red mud, and often disrupt local streams and contaminate groundwater.

The ore was then transported to processing plants, which were located near massive hydroelectric dams because of the tremendous quantities of electricity needed to remove impurities. Indeed, so much electricity was needed that aluminum has been called "packaged electricity" or "solidified electricity."[37] During the war, reduction plants near Niagara Falls in New York, the Tennessee Valley in Tennessee and North Carolina, and the Bonneville Dam in Washington processed most American aluminum.[38] Without the huge amounts of power produced by New Deal dams in the Tennessee and Columbia River valleys, started during the New Deal and expanded during the war, it is unlikely that the United States could have reached the astonishing production heights it did. In the Pacific Northwest, half of the 8.5 billion kilowatt-hours of electricity produced during the war's last year went into producing more than half a billion pounds of aluminum – one-third of the nation's total. That was enough, a proud Bureau of Reclamation official pointed out, to produce 10,000 B-29s or 150,000 fighter planes.[39]

Securing the many little-known materials essential to the bauxite refining process became a top national security priority. No better example

[34] Eckes, *The United States and the Global Struggle for Minerals*, 107.   [35] Ibid., 115.
[36] President's Materials Policy Commission, *Resources for Freedom, Vol. 1* (Washington, DC: US Government Printing Office, 1952), 157.
[37] Brad Barham, Stephen G. Bunker, and Denis O'Hearn, *States, Firms, and Raw Materials: The World Economy and Ecology of Aluminum* (Madison: University of Wisconsin Press, 1994), cited in Sheller, *Aluminum Dreams*, 148.
[38] National Resources Planning Board, *Industrial Location and National Resources, December, 1942* (Washington, DC: Government Printing Office, 1943), 178.
[39] Department of Interior, *Annual Report, 1945* (Washington, DC: Government Printing Office, 1945), 45.

exists than cryolite, a scarce material used as a bath in the alumina smelter pots and critical to the electrolytic process. No cryolite, no aluminum – and no American air force. In 1939, the only known accessible location of cryolite in the world lay within the Ivigtut mine on the west coast of Greenland, a Danish colony. In April 1941, after Germany took over Denmark, yet still six months before Pearl Harbor, the US Army moved in to secure the site.[40]

American airplanes also required large quantities of high-octane fuel. "Aviation," Secretary of the Interior Harold Ickes noted, "is a creature of petroleum." Planes, he said, were "oil in the air." You could imagine electric or coal automobiles, he said, but not electric or coal airplanes.[41] In particular, modern aircraft demanded special gasoline: 100-octane fuel. This new "super" fuel, which contained lots of lead, ramped up the power of engines, fueling greater speed and steeper climbs. "Without high-octane gasoline," the War Production Board noted in 1944, "the huge bombers – the B-29's, the Liberators, and the Flying Fortresses – and the fast fighter planes – the Mustangs, the Hellcats, and the Black Widows – might have been built, but they could not have been flown. It is the high-octane gasoline that makes possible the quick take-off speed, the long range, the high altitude, and the heavy loads of modern planes."[42] Fueled by oil, heavy bombers delivered destruction with greater intensity and on a broader scale than ever before.

In addition to aluminum and fuel, numerous other raw materials linked airplane production to environmental change and destruction. Take rubber, for instance. As Japan swept through the world's major rubber-producing region in Southeast Asia, including the British Malay States and the Dutch East Indies, the United States lost its chief source of rubber. In 1942, the US government created the Emergency Rubber Project, a "Manhattan Project of plant sciences" that was, according to historian Mark Finlay, comparable to some degree to the nuclear bomb project "in terms of scale, urgency, and interdisciplinary scope."[43] Rubber was needed, President Roosevelt told the nation in June 1942,

[40] Evenden, "Aluminum, Commodity Chains, and the Environmental History of the Second World War," 81–82.
[41] Harold L. Ickes, *Fightin' Oil* (New York: A. A. Knopf, 1943), 153.
[42] US War Production Board, *War Production in 1944* (Washington, DC: Government Printing Office, 1945), 46. Also see Wright W. Gary, "Super Fuel: 100 Octane Gasoline," *Flying* 31 (July 1942): 43–44.
[43] Mark R. Finlay, *Growing American Rubber: Strategic Plants and the Politics of National Security* (New Brunswick, NJ: Rutgers University Press, 2009), 141.

to "build the planes to bomb Tokyo and Berlin" and to "build the tanks to crush the enemy wherever we may find him."[44] Copper – also crucial for planes – provides another example. "Not a ship sails, not a plane flies, and not a shot is fired but copper has somewhere entered its production," a 1944 War Production Board report noted.[45] Copper came mostly from mines in the US West and Latin America.

Ferroalloys posed particular concerns. Used in the production of high-performance steel and central to the emerging new material culture, ferroalloys typically originated overseas. The United States produced sufficient molybdenum and had a reliable source of nickel in Canada, but all other materials for alloys came from far-off lands more difficult to access during wartime. In 1942, for example, 89 percent of America's chromite came from overseas, along with 87 percent of the manganese, 78 percent of the cobalt, 64 percent of the tungsten, and 38 percent of the vanadium.[46]

Of these, chromite held particular importance for aviation and reveals the worldwide supply network on which aviation depended. Between 1940 and 1945, chromite – which produced chrome for gun barrels, naval armor, and aircraft engines – jumped in consumption by 70 percent. Chromium-bearing ore came from all over the world. As prewar Filipino sources were cut off, and numerous domestic sources in California, Montana, and Oregon proved to be too low in quality, the United States turned to Cuba, Russia, Turkey, New Caledonia, and especially Southern Rhodesia (Zimbabwe) and South Africa. Between 1940 and mid-1945, South Africa provided the United States with 680,000 tons of ore and Rhodesia more than 1 million tons. In the end, low chromite supplies created anxiety but ultimately proved sufficient; the government's reserve stockpile grew, even while meeting all military requirements.[47] Chromite became a bigger problem for Germany. In summer 1943, German supplies of chromium fell to under six months of production. If it ran out, Nazi materials expert Albert Speer warned Adolf Hitler, "the manufacture of planes, tanks, motor vehicles, tank shells, U-boats, and almost the

[44] Seth Garfield, *In Search of the Amazon: Brazil, the United States, and the Nature of a Region* (Chapel Hill, NC: Duke University Press, 2013), 83.
[45] US War Production Board, *War Production in 1944*, 33.
[46] Elliot M. Helfgott, "The Ferro-Alloys Production and Control 1940–45," in *Industrial Mobilization for War History of the War Production Board and Predecessor Agencies, 1940–1945; Vol. II. Materials and Products* (Washington, DC: Civilian Production Administration, 1947), 2–3.
[47] Ibid.

entire gamut of artillery would have to cease."[48] Had the war continued much longer, chromite might have become the factor that tipped the fate of the war in the Allies' favor.

In the same way that rapid wartime expansion illuminated the environmental underpinnings of the aviation industry, war also exposed how deeply the car-and-highway–based transportation system of the United States, itself so crucial to the aircraft and war production system, depended on natural systems and resources. The high priority that wartime leaders placed on getting people and resources to sites of military production helps highlight both the variety and depth of this dependence.

Almost as soon as the war began, for example, war planners launched rationing systems designed to divert the most strategically important raw materials harvested from nature from civilian to military purposes. Even the automobile, despite its prominent role in everyday American life, had to bow before military demands in the face of materials shortages. Soon after the United States entered the war, the nation's leaders determined that steel, the major component of automobiles, was too precious a military resource to use to build private vehicles. As a result, official limits on automobile construction went into effect on January 1, 1942, and on February 10 – following a short ceremony by workers at the Ford Motor Company – the last private automobile rolled off a Detroit assembly line for the remainder of the war.[49] In addition to restrictions on buying new cars, natural resource shortages made it difficult for car owners to maintain their accustomed driving habits. Fuel derived from oil, for example, became scarce on the East Coast almost as soon as the United States officially entered the war, in December 1941, when German U-boats declared open season on American oil tankers. Officials immediately instituted a program of gasoline rationing on the East Coast and expanded the practice into a national rationing system in

---

[48] Albert Speer, *Inside the Third Reich* (New York: Simon & Schuster, 1970), 316, as quoted in Eckes, *The United States and the Global Struggle for Minerals*, 117.

[49] David M. Kennedy, *Freedom from Fear: The American People in Depression and War, 1929–1945* (New York: Oxford University Press, 2001), 645; Allan Nevins and Frank Ernest Hill, *Ford: Decline and Rebirth, 1933–1962* (New York: Scribner, 1963), 198–199.

November.[50] Rubber tires, too, made from the sap of rubber trees, were in desperately short supply. After Japan occupied Southeast Asia, where vast rubber tree plantations produced a majority of the world's rubber, the federal government imposed a national 35 mph speed limit to preserve tires as long as possible.[51] Limited access to key materials also constrained highway builders: tar, asphalt, and steel shortages translated into strict limits on all nonessential highway construction, bringing the interwar highway construction boom to an end.[52]

Unable to replace aging vehicles with new ones and facing constraints on their use of gasoline and rubber, many car owners heeded the active pleas of business and government leaders to help conserve scarce resources by finding alternative means of getting around for the duration of the war. Reflecting this trend, urban public transportation systems surged to levels of popularity that they had not seen in more than a decade. After holding steady at around 10 billion rides per year between 1935 and 1941, ridership jumped after Pearl Harbor, nearly doubling to 19 billion by 1945.[53]

But growing ridership indicated more than just a practical response to wartime limits on driving. It also reflected the successful efforts of government and industry leaders to conserve a crucial natural resource: oil. Officials made a concerted attempt, for example, to cast a patriotic light on alternative forms of transportation like walking to work. In addition, to reduce congestion, conserve oil, and encourage commuting using public transportation, transportation officials coordinated with businesses to stagger their starting times with the dual aims of reducing peak demand and increasing the carrying capacity of buses and streetcars. In Atlanta, for example, officials announced that a new system of staggered work hours had increased the number of passengers that the city's

---

[50] "Gasoline Rationing," *New York Times*, April 27, 1942, 14. See also Daniel Yergin, *The Prize: The Epic Quest for Oil, Money, and Power* (New York: Simon & Schuster, 1991), 375; Federal Highway Administration, *America's Highways, 1776–1976: A History of the Federal-Aid Program* (Washington, DC: Government Printing Office, 1976), 145–147.

[51] "Tire Rationing," *New York Times*, December 28, 1945, 12. See also Finlay, *Growing American Rubber*.

[52] Bruce E. Seely, *Building the American Highway System: Engineers as Policy Makers* (Philadelphia: Temple University Press, 1987); Federal Highway Administration, *America's Highways*, 147.

[53] Bureau of the Census, *Historical Statistics of the United States, Colonial Times to 1957* (Washington, DC: Government Printing Office, 1960), 464.

existing fleet of 455 buses could handle by an amount equivalent to introducing 90 new buses to the system.[54]

Despite the resurgence of urban public transportation systems and the limits on driving that came with rationing oil and rubber, the steady spread of car-dependent landscapes in the United States during the inter-war decades – marked especially by the movement of industrial factories toward the urban periphery, and amplified by a shift in the demographics of factory workers – meant that most American defense workers commuted by automobile.[55] In Kansas, for example, one study revealed that 93 percent of an airplane manufacturing facility's workers arrived at work in a car. Yet inadequate public transportation was not to blame. More important was the fact that factory workers, who before World War I had tended to concentrate in dense working-class neighborhoods that were easy to serve with streetcar lines, had begun during the interwar years to disperse into neighborhoods scattered across broad metropolitan regions much too extensive for public transportation to get them to work efficiently. According to the Kansas study, 81 percent of workers lived at least five miles away from work, and 17 percent lived more than 10 miles away. This reality prompted Thomas MacDonald, the longtime chief of the Public Roads Administration, to conclude early in the war that it was unrealistic to think that public transportation alone could meet the needs of anything more than a small proportion of the nation's 10 million defense plant workers.[56]

Concluding that only private automobiles could do the job, government efforts focused on reducing overall oil consumption by encouraging workers to carpool. With lone drivers stigmatized as unpatriotic, the number of riders per car swelled from a prewar average of less than two to a wartime average closer to four.[57] Yet even carpooling's most ardent advocates never presented it as anything other than a temporary, short-term "sacrifice" borne of wartime necessity to conserve oil. War may have

---

[54] J. T. Thompson, "Wartime Highway Transportation Problems," *Convention Group Meetings 1942* (Washington, DC: American Association of State Highway Officials, 1943), 114–124, as cited in Federal Highway Administration, *America's Highways*, 148.

[55] For an extended argument about the spread of car-dependent landscapes, see Christopher W. Wells, *Car Country: An Environmental History* (Seattle: University of Washington Press, 2012).

[56] Thompson, "Wartime Highway Transportation Problems," 114–124, as cited in Federal Highway Administration, *America's Highways*, 148.

[57] Ibid.

shrunk the rates at which American motorists consumed natural resources like oil and rubber, but motorists changed their behavior with the clear understanding that they would revert back to "normal" patterns of resource consumption after the war.

At the same time that natural resource shortages forced automakers, highway builders, and motorists to reorient their accustomed behaviors, the strategic demands of war introduced a new set of priorities for highway maintenance and construction. Rather than spreading available money around over a huge national system, as had happened during the interwar years, highway builders concentrated their investments in strategic priorities.

Before World War II, American highway policy had focused on reshaping the country's landscapes by bringing the extensive national road system up to basic minimum standards. Early in the century, the vast majority of highways were rural routes that served predominantly local traffic, and most states devoted the few resources they had to bringing the more heavily traveled routes up to basic minimum standards of passability. Even after the watershed Federal Highway Act of 1921, federal highway policy focused on creating a coordinated national system of highways built with an eye on meeting only the needs of existing traffic, which over much of the system was quite light by today's standards. Because highway builders only built the biggest, sturdiest, most advanced highways in areas with heavy traffic – often settling for thin pavements, steeper grades, and narrow widths in less-trafficked portions – the system's highways formed more of an erratic patchwork than a consistent, coordinated system. The highway system "is narrow where it should be wide, and sometimes wide where it could be narrow," declared *Fortune* in June 1941. "The system suggests exactly what it has been: the result of years and years of improvisations ... subject to local and state and federal authority, which do not necessarily work together."[58]

As the war in Europe grew ever more ominous, the nation took faltering but important steps to address the highway system's strategic deficiencies. In June 1940, President Roosevelt ordered the Federal Works Administrator to assess the national highway system from the perspective of national defense. The Public Roads Administration's resulting report in February 1941, *Highways for the National Defense*, identified a range of

---

[58] "The US Highway System," *Fortune* 23 (June 1941): 91–95, 91 (quotation).

pressing needs. Defense operations would require efforts in three areas: first, constructing a range of new roads on military reservations; second, making significant improvements to roads providing access to military facilities and defense industries; and third, building "tactical roads" that would give the military easier "access to more or less isolated points of strategic importance." In addition to these direct defense needs, the report also found significant deficiencies in the trunk highway system, especially in the form of bridges and long stretches of highway incapable of carrying heavy trucks loaded with war materiel.[59] The Defense Highway Act of 1941 allocated the relatively small amount of $150 million "for the correction of critical deficiencies in highways and bridges essential to the national defense."[60]

Reshaping the environments around defense facilities by improving their "access roads" became critical to an all-out war effort. For example, the construction of the world's largest office building – the Pentagon – also required reshaping the surrounding environment with a completely new network of highways to serve its 54,000 defense workers. The system of roads serving the three bridges over the Potomac also got a makeover to relieve their regular traffic jams.[61] Factories, too, needed new facilities to make it easier for the daily crush of defense workers arriving at factory gates in automobiles. In addition to building "Bomber City" to accommodate the crush of workers at Ford's giant Willow Run facility, for example, the state built a $9.5 million high-speed, limited-access highway – still a design novelty at the time – complete with double- and triple-level crossings in and out of the facility's gargantuan parking areas, to accommodate workers during shift changes.[62] In addition to the obvious local environmental consequences of building this new infrastructure, the new highway, interchange, and parking lots reified the site's dependence on automobile-based transportation, which had its own environmental implications. As was typical of so many other defense industry workers, most Willow Run workers commuted by car, despite scarcities of gasoline and rubber; also,

---

[59] US Bureau of Public Roads, *Highways for the National Defense* (Washington, DC: Government Printing Office, 1941), esp. 8–14.

[60] "Defense Highway Bill Enacted," *American City* 56 (December 1941): 105. On the process for identifying "essential" projects, see "Programming Federal Aid Projects Essential to the National Defense," *Roads and Streets* 85 (February 1942): 42–43.

[61] Joseph Barnett, "The New War Department Building Road Network," *Civil Engineering* 13 (March 1943): 127–130.

[62] Curtis Fuller, "Moving Workers to Willow Run," *Flying* 33 (August 1943): 79.

typically, most drivers carpooled, with each automobile carrying on average 3.1 workers.[63]

But rebuilding the environment around factories was important for reasons beyond just giving workers better access; the wartime focus on building better access roads also presaged the growing, environmentally significant role of big trucks in the American transportation system generally and within defense industries specifically. In Michigan, for example, studies of defense plants revealed that the vast majority of factories trucked in at least half of their materials over highways and trucked out over half of their products. Of these, 13 percent depended entirely on trucks to supply their operations.[64] The growing reliance on trucks rather than railroads reflected both improvements in truck design, which allowed them to carry heavier loads more reliably, and the flexibility of operation that they offered compared to railroads for industrial operations that were increasingly spread widely over metropolitan regions.[65]

Although useful, heavy trucks were also destructive, pounding highways – and especially the lightly traveled rural portions of the nation's highway system that were not designed to carry heavy loads – which made maintaining key supply routes a strategically vital investment. In the American countryside, beyond the high-quality highways that provided direct access to specific defense plants, the expanded use of heavy trucks exposed the inadequacies of the interwar period's inconsistent highway design standards. Setting aside other deficiencies of the highway system, like limited sight distances, hazardously sharp curves, and dangerously narrow widths, *Highways for the National Defense* identified roughly 14,000 miles of paved primary route highways that could not handle 9,000-pound wheel loads, as well as 2,436 bridges that it deemed "substandard in their capacity to carry the heaviest equipment and ordnance."[66] Given wartime rationing and limited access to funds, it was nearly impossible even to maintain the nation's highways in the face of wartime demands, much less to improve them to the consistently high standards that extensive use of heavy trucks for long-distance

[63] Peterson, *Planning the Home Front*, 200.

[64] Thompson, "Wartime Highway Transportation Problems," 114–124, as cited in Federal Highway Administration, *America's Highways*, 148.

[65] Robert J. Gordon, *The Rise and Fall of American Growth: The US Standard of Living since the Civil War* (Princeton, NJ: Princeton University Press, 2016), 561. William E. Rudolph, "Strategic Roads of the World: Notes on Recent Developments," *Geographical Review* 33, no. 1 (January 1, 1943): 110.

[66] *Highways for the National Defense*, 42, 26 (quotation).

transportation required. Some states attempted to preserve their roads by enforcing weight limits, but political pressure to sacrifice the long-term integrity of highways on behalf of wartime exigencies won the day.[67] Remaking the American landscape with a new national system of highways that could cater to heavy trucks would have to wait until after the war – but wartime experiences would eventually factor heavily into the final form of the postwar Interstate system.

STRATEGIC HIGHWAYS IN LATIN AMERICA AND ALASKA

As a window onto the ways that wartime imperatives for transportation infrastructure shaped landscapes and American relationships with nature, no highway projects were more important than the two major "tactical" roads that the United States prioritized during the war – the Alaskan-Canadian Military Highway (known as the "Alcan" highway), and the Pan-American Highway. First, both highways demonstrate the nation's commitment to using transportation infrastructure to assert control over valuable natural resources and strategically important areas, even when they were remote, difficult to access, and located outside the boundaries of the United States. Using transportation infrastructure to exert such control opened sizable territories to new efforts to extract natural resources. Second, both highway-building efforts embodied important ideas about the interrelationships among nature, construction technologies such as bulldozers and aerial surveys, and progress as they evolved against the backdrop of an ongoing war, setting the stage for postwar relationships.

Though plans for the Alcan and Pan-American highway projects originated in the interwar decades, both took on new strategic significance during the war, which prompted the US government to prioritize immediate construction. This required the United States to assume the lion's share of construction costs and to send American construction crews into the field. The Pan-American Highway, the planned route for which ran from the US border town of Laredo, Texas, through Central America and on to Buenos Aires and Rio de Janeiro, represented a potential supply line more secure from U-boat attack than traditional shipping lanes. "Ships still are the principal means of moving commodities in inter-American trade," explained an American official in *Scientific American* about the new importance of highways. "It is the long sea distance which makes this

[67] Federal Highway Administration, *America's Highways*, 145–147.

menace to our shipping so crucial. If transportation between the Americas over the long sea routes can be sharply reduced and if, at the same time, a continuous flow of essential supplies can be maintained, we are on the way to a solution of the problem."[68] Providing overland routes for the flow of strategic materials, including copper, bauxite, and rubber for airplanes, would directly serve military priorities.

The Alcan Highway gave the United States a safe overland alternative to shipping to and from Alaska, and beyond that to Asia. Even more importantly, it supported a reliable air route to what one geographer described as "the most strategic area on the continent."[69] "[T]he road now being shoved through the British Columbia and Yukon fastness is more than a highway," a *Saturday Evening Post* article explained. "It is the land counterpart of an air route which ranks in importance with those our fighting planes travel to the Near East and South Pacific." Before the highway went through, the "route" was little more than an unconnected string of landing strips newly carved out of the otherwise continuous forests of the region, which gave Alaska-bound planes places to stop and refuel. These were much easier to supply by truck than by plane, and the highway helped transform the isolated landing strips into what the *Post* described as a full-fledged "wilderness airway."[70] In addition, as Col. J. K. Tully explained, the highway made navigating the route much safer, giving pilots access to emergency landing strips and providing "a trace for our airmen to fly along."[71] Airplanes, at the same time, used new aerial surveying methods that made it easier to map out where the highway should go in rough, remote, and poorly mapped regions.

In addition to creating more secure transportation links to distant but strategically important areas, both highway projects improved the ability of the United States to assert control over valuable natural resources like oil and rubber in South America and timber and minerals in Canada. "The universal shortage of ship transportation has increased the importance of the Pan-American Highway as a potentially vital factor, not only

---

[68] Edwin W. James, "Highways to Strategic Materials," *Scientific American* 168 (March 1943): 110. On the failure to fully achieve an entirely overland connection, see Shawn W. Miller, "Minding the Gap: Pan-Americanisms's Highway, American Environmentalism, and Remembering the Failure to Close the Darién Gap," *Environmental History* 19 (April 2014): 189–216.

[69] S. C. Ells, "Alaska Highway," *Canadian Geographical Journal* 28 (March 1944): 105.

[70] V. H. Jorgensen Jr., "Our New Land and Air Route to Alaska," *Saturday Evening Post,* November 7, 1942, 16.

[71] Ibid., 105.

in the 'Battle of Supply Lines,' but also in the 'Battle for Raw Materials,'" an American official explained in *Scientific American*. "South America is veritably a storehouse of strategic materials for the great munition industries of the Arsenal of Democracy, and is now more important than ever before as a source of strategic materials formerly obtained from the Far East."[72] In the case of the Alcan Highway, the transportation functions clearly outweighed immediate access to natural resources, but its builders nonetheless extolled the ways that the road would open the area to "mining, lumbering, agricultural production ... and the development of such hydro-power as may be required."[73]

Both highway projects also illustrate evolving wartime ideas about nature, technology, and progress, as well as the ways that the patterns of the natural world affected the contours of the war effort. The formidable natural obstacles confronting road builders permeated press accounts of both highways. Writers characterized portions of the Pan-American route as impenetrable "uncharted jungle" that "had not even been surveyed," noting that the pass over the Andes outside Santiago was "closed by snow from seven to nine months of the year."[74] Other sections traversed "a great diversity of terrain and climate, arid desert country, tropical rain forest, and alpine scenery."[75] For the Alcan Highway, descriptions reached almost poetic heights:

Mud so deep that even tractors were swallowed up, dust ankle high which rose in clouds like a dense fog so that a convoy of trucks could be spotted from many miles away, jellylike muskeg which had to be bridged with corduroy, cold, drizzling rain, frigid nights, vicious black flies, and ravenous gnats – all these now are part of the epic of the road.... There were only three points of access in Alaska, Yukon Territory, and British Columbia and only one settlement which could be called a town on the entire route. The country was a wilderness and some of it was barely explored. There were no adequate maps and, of course, no detailed survey for the route.[76]

The *Rotarian* ran a photo essay on the highway's construction featuring packhorses, mules, and dogsleds hauling supplies, rugged campsites, and

---

[72] James, "Highways to Strategic Materials," 110.   [73] Ells, "Alaska Highway," 118.

[74] Richard Tewkesbury, "Jungle Journey for a Hemisphere Highway," *Scholastic* 40 (May 18, 1942): 28 (first quotation); Walter Holbrook, "The Pan-American Highway Nears Completion," *Popular Science* 139 (August 1941): 33 (second quotation), 35 (third quotation).

[75] Herbert Charles Lanks, "The Pan-American Highway," *Canadian Geographical Journal* 26 (April 1943): 162.

[76] Froelich Rainey, "Alaskan Highway an Engineering Epic," *National Geographic* 83 (February 1943): 143.

a variety of wild animals, including wolves, grizzly bears, and mountain sheep.[77] *Reader's Digest* dubbed the highway "one of the great wilderness undertakings of American history."[78]

Yet the descriptions of quaking muskeg bogs and impenetrable jungles, extreme heat and numbing cold, dangerous wild animals and swarming insects always provided a backdrop for the more important story: the victories over nature achieved by American ingenuity, hard work, and technological prowess.[79] Heavy earth-moving machinery conjured descriptions nearly as poetic as those of the wilderness. According to *National Geographic:*

Giant lumbering 20-ton caterpillar tractors led the attack on the forest. Equipped with broad cutting blades or bulldozers, they advanced into standing timber and simply pushed it aside, trunks, stumps, and all. Working back and forth across a blazed right-of-way, they mowed down the thick timber as if it were no more than a field of cornstalks. The machines were like wild boars rooting and snorting in the jungle.[80]

Not to be outdone, *Life* also conjured images of a technological sublime overcoming an equally sublime nature, describing the highway as "a raw streak of sodden earth punched through the wilderness with roaring bulldozers and power shovels. The highway is the greatest achievement of the Engineers' history, surpassing even the construction of the Panama Canal in sheer efficiency of subduing Nature."[81] As in the struggle against the Axis, American technological might would triumph, even against the powerful forces of nature.

In these projects as well as building projects in the main theaters of war, the United States developed technologies and ideas about nature that profoundly shaped postwar highway building and other construction. As Francesca Ammon has pointed out, the massive earthmoving equipment that became widespread during the war and that was portrayed in heroic terms fueled a revolution in large scale, no-holds-barred construction

---

[77] Alfred Milotte and Elma Milotte, "That Highway to Alaska," *Rotarian* 59 (November 1941): 21–26.

[78] Richard Lewis Neuberger, "Our Battlefront in the Wilderness," *Reader's Digest* 41 (August 1942): 48.

[79] For broader discussions about using big technological systems and infrastructure networks to dominate and control the unruly forces of nature, see David E. Nye, *American Technological Sublime* (Cambridge, MA: MIT Press, 1994) and Maria Kaika, *City of Flows: Modernity, Nature, and the City* (New York: Routledge, 2005).

[80] Rainey, "Alaskan Highway an Engineering Epic," 154.

[81] "Alaska Highway: Army Engineers Punch It through the Wilderness," *Life*, September 14, 1942, 45.

thinking best described by a 1954 *Time* article: "Today, there is almost no project too big to tackle, no reasonable limit to reshaping the earth to make it more productive."[82]

The postwar Interstate system was planned during the war years, in part because domestic construction was so limited. The system appeared in its broad outlines in the 1939 *Toll Roads and Free Roads* report, and in its more specific form in the 1944 report, *Interregional Highways*, which Congress approved by legislation in 1944 without any dedicated funding, setting up over a decade of political wrangling that ended with the creation of a dedicated funding system in 1956.

Despite their wartime plans, though, highway planners failed to anticipate the major environmental consequences that the Interstate system would have: restructuring cities and creating car dependence by further decentralizing the urban economy; making long-distance travel more comfortable and economically efficient; and the rise of heavy trucking, including long-distance trucking, which required much higher highway construction standards than wartime planners anticipated. Wartime planners combined the planning mindset of the interwar period with the reality of new wartime needs, new technologies, and new ideas about conquering nature to advance the idea and the routes of the Interstates.

WORLD WAR II AND PERCEPTIONS OF NATURE

As with the strategic highways and changes in the highway system, the wartime revolution in air power and air transport created new links between humans, technology, and nature. Beyond expanding productive capacity and rearranging landscapes through new patterns of resource use, pollution, and transportation, aviation also began to alter how Americans perceived geography and nature. "More than anything except the telephone," Harold Ickes wrote in 1943, "aviation is cutting down time and space."[83] A 1941 Mid-Continent Airlines advertisement summed up the war's effect: "The times call for speed."[84]

Within the United States, faster, more frequent, and more reliable air service linked countryside with city, state with state, and region with region, forging the modern system of air transportation. Direct intercity

---

[82] Francesca Ammon, *Bulldozer: Demolition and Clearance of the Postwar Landscape* (New Haven, CT: Yale University Press, 2016), 60.

[83] Ickes, *Fightin' Oil*, 154.

[84] Mid-Continent Airlines Ad, 1941, Zawasky Scrapbook, Minnesota Historical Society.

flights became more common. Minneapolis, for instance, gained fast direct service to New York, Washington, Detroit, and Cleveland.[85] City officials began to see air service as not just useful but essential. "Good airline service is necessary to the commercial life of a city," a Detroit city official argued in 1944. "Wartime has emphasized that fact in a most convincing manner."[86]

Because of aviation and the war, Americans learned more about other countries and their connections to those countries and gained a new understanding of the earth. "The modern airplane," the Republican leader Wendell Wilkie wrote in 1943, "creates a new geographical dimension.... A navigable ocean of air blankets the whole surface of the globe. There are no distant places any longer."[87] The war, Ickes added, is "a world war in every sense of the word, and nothing but petroleum, plus aviation, has made it so."[88]

Aerial interconnection made many Americans feel increasingly vulnerable. The Pearl Harbor attacks shattered a sense of safety; the bombing of cities heightened anxieties. Alexander de Seversky's *Victory through Air Power*, a 1943 Book of the Month Club selection, stressed an America prone to aerial attack.[89] "Everybody," another observer wrote, "is being put in the front lines."[90]

For some, greater interconnection meant that the United States had no choice but to engage more internationally. "The world is small and the world is one," Willkie wrote, rejecting the isolationist leanings of many within his party. "The American people must grasp these new realities if they are to play their essential part in winning the war and building a world of peace and freedom."[91]

Five aerial supply routes linked the United States to the war's main arenas: across the North Atlantic to Great Britain, across the mid-Atlantic to North Africa via the Azores, across the south Atlantic from Brazil to central Africa and the Middle East, northwest from Minneapolis and

---

[85] *Minneapolis Daily Times*, September 30, 1943, Curry Scrapbook, Northwest Airlines Collection, Box 54, Minnesota Historical Society.

[86] Karsner, "Aviation and Airports," 412.

[87] Sam Howe Verhovek, *Jet Age: The Comet, the 707, and the Race to Shrink the World* (London: Portfolio, 2011), 98.

[88] Ickes, *Fightin' Oil*, 153.

[89] Susan Schulten, *The Geographical Imagination in America, 1880–1950* (Chicago: University of Chicago Press, 2001).

[90] John Hamilton Jouett, "Aviation after the War," *Flying* 31 (July 1942): 24.

[91] Verhovek, *Jet Age*, 98.

Seattle through Alaska to northeast Asia, and across the south Pacific from Hawaii to Australia.[92] US-built airfields around the world, from the Caribbean to the North Atlantic, from the South Pacific to China and Northeast India increased capacity and encouraged new routes after the war. New wartime airports at Gander in Newfoundland and Shannon in Ireland, built to enable four-engine bombers and transports to fly from the United States to Britain, eventually reduced peacetime flying time for commercial flights from New York to London to 15 hours.[93] All these new routes added to Americans' knowledge of different places and shrank their conceptions of space.

A shrinking planet also encouraged "one-world" thinking, an emphasis on universality and open borders. "In the air," wrote Adolf Berle, a Roosevelt advisor and State Department official in charge of aviation, "there is no excuse for an attempt to revive the 16th-and 17th-century conceptions for a modern British East India Company or Portuguese trading monopoly or Spanish Main conception."[94]

The war also gave rise to new cartographic visions that shifted the focus from the "seaman's view" focused on oceans to the "airman's view."[95] In *Human Geography for the Air Age* (1942) and *Global Geography* (1944), George Renner called for new maps and a new geography. The oversized oceans of the traditional Mercator projection had given Americans an exaggerated sense of protective distance from Europe and Asia. Renner's "World Map for the Air Age," which centered on the North Pole and showed US proximity to Russia and northern Europe, sold more in its first year than any other map in Rand McNally's history.[96]

Many maps began to provide an airplane pilot's view of the earth, elevated and integrative. Calling himself an artist and publishing in *Fortune*, Richard Edes Harrison made maps that, according to Susan Schulten, "resemble a photograph of the earth from a distance." They showed relationships "left hidden on more traditional maps" and through this perspective "silently – yet insistently – forced the reader to conclude that

[92] Wesley Frank Craven and James Lea Cate, *The Army Air Forces in World War II, Volume I* (Chicago: University of Chicago Press, 1958), 312.

[93] Peter J. Hugill, *World Trade since 1431: Geography, Technology, and Capitalism* (Baltimore: Johns Hopkins University Press, 1993), 282.

[94] Verhovek, *Jet Age*, 98.

[95] Alan K. Henrikson, "The Map as an 'Idea': The Role of Cartographic Imagery during the Second World War," *Cartography and Geographic Information Science* 2, no. 1 (1975): 19–53.

[96] Schulten, *The Geographical Imagination in America, 1880–1950*, 138.

the world had been reshaped through the advent of aviation."[97] Making maps for the *Los Angeles Times*, Charles Owens also presented scenes of the earth from an elevated oblique angle.[98]

One interesting wartime map from Rand McNally – a 12-inch translucent "air globe" – gave the names of a few crucial places but left out all factors made seemingly irrelevant by air travel, including oceans, mountains, and national borders. Rand McNally and American Airlines marketed it to teach, in their words, "the concept of freedom of the air and the universality of air transportation."[99]

Airplanes brought about another important change in perspective. Airplanes and aerial bombardment of cities became a prime example of modern technology gone awry, fueling an antimodernism that brought with it a reevaluation and celebration of nature. As technological civilization seemed more and more violent and depraved, nature emerged as more and more pure, peaceful, and restorative.

No one shows this shift better than Charles Lindbergh, the famous pilot who symbolized technological optimism during the 1920s and who became a vocal and influential environmentalist during the 1960s and 1970s. World War II dramatically transformed Lindbergh's thinking. As part of the "America First" movement, Lindbergh had at first opposed US involvement in the war but after Pearl Harbor found several ways to contribute, including as a test pilot at the Willow Run plant, a War Department advisor, and even as a combat pilot in the Pacific War. One day at Willow Run changed his life forever. On a test run at 43,000 feet in the skies above the massive factory, a faulty oxygen gauge caused Lindbergh to black out. By the narrowest of margins, he made it back to earth safely, but walked away from his plane with an altered view of technology, the war, and the earth. Approaching the huge Willow Run factory that day, he felt different. Whereas once he had seen the factory's bomber production line as "a marvelous feat of engineering," he now saw it, as he recounted in a 1948 book, as "a terrible giant's womb, growling, clanging, giving birth to robots which were killing people by the thousands each day as they destroyed the culture of Europe.... Only two years before on this same spot, I would've been surrounded by hickories, maples, and oaks. Scientific man could now touch a forest in Michigan with his wand, and by so doing wipe out

[97] Ibid., 214–218, quotations from 215, 214, 215.
[98] Denis E. Cosgrove and William L. Fox, *Photography and Flight* (London: Reaktion, 2010), 57.
[99] Schulten, *The Geographical Imagination in America, 1880–1950*, 139.

European cities.... Here I watched a steel door lift and an airplane roll outside; while, in reality, the walls of the cathedral fell and children died."[100]

Flying into Munich in 1945, Lindbergh saw the devastation that aerial bombing had wrought:

As human death pierces through a room, that city pierced the sky. I forgot farms and villages, trenches and tank tracks. I could no longer see the beauty of the earth or experience the joy of flight. As we drew closer, the features of death emerged – troubled streets, gutted buildings, ragged walls. *This* had been a city inhabited by men! Street after street lined with blasted factories, offices, and homes – open roofs and fallen floors, smudged by fire, deserted by life. And this was only one of the bombed cities of Europe; there were scores of them.... How fragile civilization had become, viewed through the lens of modern science; how vulnerable to the eye of the bombardier.[101]

Lindbergh filled his 1948 book "Of Flight and Life" with similar observations. A profound shift to a more "environmental" approach to modern life was underway.

CONCLUSION

Lindbergh's ruminations on the growing capacity of technology to wreak havoc on the environment and on human communities, developed in part from the cockpit of an airplane, focused on the awesome devastation of modern war and particularly on ruin rained down from the sky. Yet Lindbergh's reflections also contained the seed of a more ecological world-view, prompted by the destructive violence of war, which stressed both the fragility and the interconnectedness of nature. If the shambles of European cities pointed backward toward military bases launching massive bombing runs, they also pointed backward toward industrial landscapes of production like Willow Run, where workers hammered and riveted together the modern instruments of war, and then even further backward toward landscapes of extraction, where workers drilled, dug, grew, and collected the dizzying array of raw materials that made up the modern airplane.

Paying attention to these landscapes of production and extraction thus helps bring the environmental footprint of World War II – and the new relationships with nature that it created – into sharper focus. The mass production of "flying resources" like airplanes meant solidifying control over rare raw materials, wherever they were found around the globe, and

---

[100] Charles A. Lindbergh, *Of Flight and Life* (New York: Scribner's Sons, 1948), 9.
[101] Ibid., 16–17.

then shepherding them securely during wartime conditions toward American assembly lines. It meant turning former potato fields into vast new aviation facilities while repurposing the productive capacity of the already massive automotive industry, replacing the mass production of private automobiles with that of airplanes (while also churning out a stunning range of armaments and heavy trucks) under conditions that favored speed and quantity at all costs. And it meant thinking strategically about where to allocate limited home front resources, even when that meant redirecting valuable resources from dominant peacetime industries, encouraging people to abandon aging automobiles for busses and streetcars, and redirecting highway investments toward industrial access roads and strategic highways outside the United States. In the process, the nation remade both extractive and productive landscapes – at home and abroad – along with the transportation systems that connected them.

The crucible of war fostered a range of environmentally significant ideas as well. To exert control over strategically vital resources, the United States created a range of more secure transportation routes – both on the ground and in the air – that highlighted its growing capacity to direct its technological prowess toward subduing even the wildest, most distant environments. Airplanes gave surveyors a tool that helped them reduce even the most remote landscapes to detailed technical drawings, while bulldozers made it possible to transform even the most rugged landscapes with unprecedented ease and speed. In addition to making wild nature seem less forbidding, and somewhat more vulnerable, in the face of advanced technology, airplanes and trucks also changed the ways that people perceived geography and geographical relationships, shrinking space, strengthening knowledge of (and connections to) a greater number of places, and encouraging more ambitious planning for new transportation infrastructure, such as the Interstate highway system and a truly national system of commercial airports.

Thus, the United States left the war on a kind of environmental collision course. On the one hand, there was tremendous expanded productive capacity, technological development, and faith in heroic technologies to transform nature for the benefit of humanity. Mobile technologies accelerated, and with them the pace of life. But on the other hand, the war also brought greater pollution, violence, death, and the seeds of antimodernist ideologies that grew stronger over time. Together these new forces shaped American relationships with nature well into the future.

2

For Land's Sake

World War II Military Land Acquisition and Alteration

Jean Mansavage

On March 2, 1942, just four months after the attack on Pearl Harbor, Lt. Col. James H. "Jimmy" Doolittle assembled 80 US Army Air Forces (USAAF) airmen at Eglin Airfield on the Florida Panhandle to prepare for Special Aviation Project #1 – the Doolittle Tokyo Raid – that would strike the heart of the Japanese empire. Eglin, a secluded base on the Gulf of Mexico, provided an ideal location to train. There, to prepare for the secret April 1942 mission, 16 B–25 Mitchell bomber crews rehearsed short-field takeoffs that replicated an aircraft carrier's truncated 450-foot runway, practiced navigation over open water, simulated evasive actions, and perfected low-level bombing techniques.[1]

Eglin Airfield proved a tremendous asset for the daring Doolittle Raid and, throughout the war, provided an excellent testing area for the B-17 Flying Fortress, the B-29 Superfortress, and the US version of the German V-1 missile, the JB-2 Loon (see Figure 2.1). Today, Eglin is the largest US Air Force installation in the world, comprised of 725 square miles of land – more than half the size of Rhode Island – as well as 125,000 square miles of water.[2]

---

[1] Carroll V. Glines, *The Doolittle Raid: America's Daring First Strike against Japan* (Atglen, PA: Schiffer Publishing, 1991), 28–37; B-25 History Project, "Training for the Doolittle Raid on Tokyo," https://b-25history.org/doolittle/training.htm (accessed August 24, 2016); Wesley F. Craven and James L. Cate, *The Army Air Forces in World War II, Vol. 6: Men and Planes* (Chicago: University of Chicago Press, 1955), 129, 160.

[2] National Park Service, "Eglin Field Historic District," www.nps.gov/articles/eglin-field-historic-district.htm (accessed August 24, 2016); Historical Branch, Army Air Forces Proving Ground Command, "History of the Army Air Forces Proving Ground Command: Background of Eglin Field, 1933–1940" (reprint, Eglin AFB, Florida: Office of History,

FIGURE 2.1 Doolittle Raider training aircraft preparing for short takeoff at Eglin Airfield, March 1942. Note the sandy soil and longleaf pine trees.
Source: US Army Air Forces courtesy Doolittleraider.org. Image in the public domain

Like the majority of modern Department of Defense (DOD) installations that had their origins in World War II, Eglin grew from a marginal military facility to an established base during the war. It had possessed a mere 1,500-acre landing strip in 1937, but in October 1940 the US Forest Service (USFS) ceded nearly 400,000 acres – 625 square miles – of the Choctawhatchee National Forest to the US Department of War, which radically enlarged Eglin (see Map 2.1). President Theodore Roosevelt had originally designated the Choctawhatchee National Forest in November 1908, and the USFS began restoring cutover longleaf pine stands and protecting naval stores (see Figure 2.2). In May 1933, Camp F-3, Company 1402 of the Civilian Conservation Corps (CCC) established a camp in the forest near Niceville, employing 225 enrollees to construct fire lookout towers, improve timber stands, and build roads and recreational facilities (see Figure 2.3). After the War Department assumed control of the forest in 1940, a new CCC unit helped build runways and other

Armament Division, 1989), 4, 9; Eglin Joint Land Use Study Policy Committee and Technical Advisory Group, "Eglin Air Force Base Joint Land Use Study," June 2009, http://gis.okaloosafl.com/jlus/docs/final/INDIVIDUAL%20SECTIONS/1_Title%20Cover %20Page%20&%20TOC.pdf (accessed August 24, 2016).

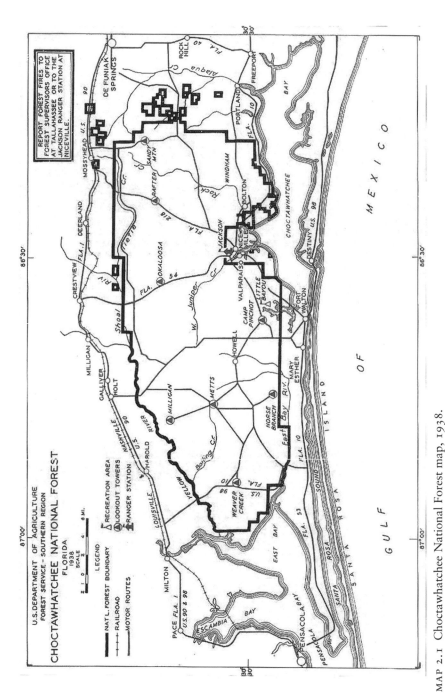

MAP 2.1 Choctawhatchee National Forest map, 1938.
Source: *Florida National Forests*, Department of Agriculture, US Forest Service, (Washington, DC: US Government Printing Office, 1939). Image in the public domain

53

FIGURE 2.2 Naval stores operation in West Florida during the 1920s. The turpentine is being extracted from an old growth longleaf pine stand in what used to be Choctawhatchee National Forest, now Eglin AFB, in Walton or Okaloosa County, 1922.
Source: US Department of Agriculture, Bureau of Forestry, National Archives and Records Administration (NARA). NARA Local Identifier: 95-GP-4273-16532. Image in the public domain

FIGURE 2.3 Metts lookout tower area of Civilian Conservation Corps Camp located in the Choctawhatchee National Forest, 1934.
Source: US Air Force, Eglin Air Force Base Natural Resources Division. Image in the public domain

structures at Eglin. In July 1942, the CCC transferred the camp to the USAAF. While the Forest Service had cursed the Choctawhatchee because of its low timber yields, military officers recognized the forest's assets. The tract was big, unpopulated, isolated, and cheap; moreover, it boasted splendid weather, flat contours, and provided unimpeded access to infinite water ranges over which to train – attributes of an ideal proving ground.[3]

OVERVIEW

Eglin was only one of thousands of military facilities that sprang up across the country as the United States mobilized for World War II. This chapter explains several fundamental reasons why the US Departments of War (Army and Army Air Forces) and Navy (Navy and Marine Corps) expanded exponentially to fight this war. The chapter also enumerates and describes the types of property required for different military training and production purposes; describes where and how the military obtained the acreage; and discusses the long-term environmental consequences of the military's stewardship of this land.

Historically, Americans have held an ingrained aversion to maintaining a large standing army. As a result, the size of the US military has fluctuated according to the nature and magnitude of the threat to the nation's security. Until technology reduced the distance that insulated the United States from international conflicts, American military forces were organized around a small professional nucleus that expanded – in numbers of personnel and in the extent of property holdings – during times of war. After World War I, the national desire for peace, and later the Great Depression, hindered military development politically and financially, but imminent threat of war in 1939 demanded that the United States begin preparing to fight.[4]

---

[3] Eglin Field Forestry Section, "Forest Section History," August 21, 1951, 1–2; M. L. Grant, "Camp Report [Fla F-3]," Emergency Conservation work, Office of the Director, September 25, 1939; Robert G. Pasquill Jr., "Civilian Corps Company 1402: Company History, Camp F-3, Niceville, Florida," n.d., all Box 1, Jackson Guard Environmental Records, Eglin AFB Natural Resources Division Archives; Historical Branch, Army Air Forces Proving Ground Command, "History of the Army Air Forces Proving Ground Command," 1, 8–9, 61, 80, 93–98; Douglas G. Brinkley, *The Wilderness Warrior: Theodore Roosevelt and the Crusade for America* (New York: HarperCollins, 2009), 737.

[4] John Elsberg, ed., *American Military History* (Washington, DC: US Army Center of Military History, 1989), 14–15; John Whiteclay Chambers, *To Raise an Army* (New York: The Free Press, 1987), 2.

In the years preceding and during World War II, as technological advances expanded the reach of military forces and implements of war, the US military required sizeable areas of land to prepare for battle. New weapons delivered increased speed, agility, and range, and to train effectively with them, defense agencies required tremendous amounts of acreage. In addition, these arms altered strategies and tactics, with larger, combined-arms military formations requiring unparalleled numbers of recruits who needed vast expanses on which to maneuver.

One of the first steps toward US military readiness included acquiring a substantial amount of land on which to billet and train its troops. Opportunely, an abundance of inexpensive public domain property in the Depression-era United States enabled the military to mobilize without delay and with minimum investment. In the 150 years leading up to World War II, the US military had accumulated approximately 2.6 million acres. Between 1939 and 1945, it procured 20 times that total, more than 52 million acres of land, a collective area larger than the state of Kansas. Much, although not all, of it stayed in the military's hands for most of the Cold War period. More than half of the land that the defense establishment leased or purchased during the conflict was located in the southern third of the country, the region known today as the Sunbelt. Indeed, just as the availability of land shaped the early growth and development of the nation, it proved a critical component of America's arsenal during World War II.[5]

Initially, the military's acquisition of property abruptly altered prevailing land uses: it converted grazing districts into bombing ranges, cornfields to ordnance works, apple orchards to plutonium reactors, marshlands to docking facilities, and coastal national parks to aircraft warning stations. This wartime activity spurred sustained, intensive use and often generated significant environmental contamination ranging from fuels and cleaning solvents to heavy metals, unexploded ordnance, and low-level radioactive waste. Ensuing Cold War–era training

[5] Alvin T. M. Lee, "Getting and Using Land in Time of War," in *Land: USDA Yearbook of Agriculture* (Washington, DC: Government Printing Office, 1958), 87; Alvin T. M. Lee, *Acquisition and Use of Land for Military and War Production Purposes, World War II* (Washington, DC: US Department of Agriculture, 1947), 4–5, 106–109; Craven and Cate, *Army Air Forces in World War II*, 6: 120–168; US Department of Defense, Deputy Under Secretary of Defense, Installations and Environment, "Base Structure Report: Fiscal Year 2015 Baseline, A Summary of the Department of Defense's Real Property Inventory," 14–15, www.acq.osd.mil/eie/Downloads/BSI/Base%20Structure%20Report%20FY15.pdf (accessed September 30, 2016).

exercises, weapons testing, and military hardware maintenance – and the great influx of people working on the bases – further fouled and otherwise damaged nearby ecosystems. The advent of enhanced environmental standards in the 1960s and 1970s forced DOD to begin remediation of past contamination and to alter its ecosystem management practices. Because a large proportion of installations still in the military inventory in the 2010s originated during World War II, the continued military land stewardship activities over the intervening 70 years have generated long-lasting, though not always permanent, environmental legacies.[6] In some instances, as discussed at the end of this chapter, the result is a paradoxically positive long-term effect of the military's World War II land procurement the creation of large, sanctuary-like habitats that are protected from human encroachment.

MODERN WARFARE AND THE DEMAND FOR LAND

In March 1938, after Germany annexed Austria, the United States awakened to the likelihood of a second world war. A year later, Germany seized Czechoslovakia, and in September 1939 it invaded Poland. Despite widespread isolationist sentiment in the United States, President Franklin D. Roosevelt heeded his advisors' dire warnings and launched preparedness efforts. Spurred by continued German aggression in Europe and the fall of France in June 1940, Congress approved large military mobilization appropriations and granted preparedness powers, 18 months before the Japanese attack on Pearl Harbor.

The astonishingly rapid German victories demonstrated how developments in weapons technology, doctrine, and organizational structure during the interwar period had fundamentally transformed all levels of modern warfare. Combined with significant increases in troop numbers, these innovations required a massive quantity of arms and more extensive

---

[6] This contamination is well documented in many works, including Seth Shulman, *The Threat at Home: Confronting the Toxic Legacy of the US Military* (Boston: Beacon Press, 1992); Richard A. Wegman Jr. and Harold G. Bailey, "The Challenge of Cleaning Up Military Wastes When US Bases Are Closed," *Ecological Law Quarterly* 21, no. 4 (September 1994), 866–949; David M. Bearden, "Cleanup of US Military Munitions: Authorities, Status, Costs," Congressional Research Service Report 22862, April 2008; Peter Eisler, "Pollution Cleanups Pit Pentagon against Regulators," *USA Today*, October 10, 2004; Robert F. Durant, *The Greening of the US Military: Environmental Policy, National Security, and Organizational Change* (Washington, DC: Georgetown University Press, 2007).

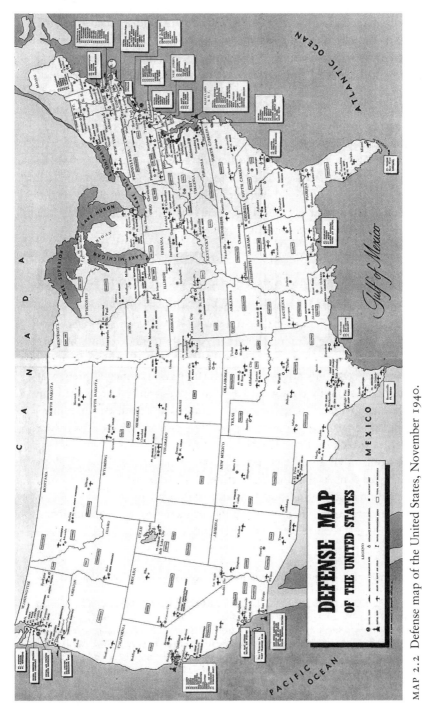

MAP 2.2 Defense map of the United States, November 1940.

Source: Rand McNally and Company, found in NARA, Record Group 114, Records of the Natural Resources Conservation Service (1875–2002) includes History of the Soil Conservation Service (1935–1971), Entry A1–1039, Box 1, War Department (General). Image in the public domain

training facilities. This unprecedented expansion of training and production in the United States compelled the acquisition of sizeable areas of land, with inevitable environmental consequences. During World War I, the Allied and Central Powers had deadlocked on the Western Front for four years. Until late in the war neither side could break the stalemate created by trenches, barbed wire, massive amounts of artillery, and machine guns. This war of attrition ended only when the Allies, fortified by the arrival of US forces and tanks, outlasted German manpower reserves in the autumn of 1918. Two decades later, in 1939 and 1940, the German military dismantled that relatively static model of warfare by deploying mechanized formations to quickly penetrate opposing armies and to exploit their rear areas, throwing them into confusion. Further, the Japanese attack on Pearl Harbor, made possible by a modern carrier fleet, meant the United States would have to fight a two-ocean, truly global war – at sea, in the air, and on the ground.

In response to the Axis onslaught, the US military armed and trained its forces for a new form of mechanized warfare that involved large interservice formations of specialized troops using weapons notable for increased speed, mobility, and firepower. These weapons platforms included faster, more agile tanks, artillery, antitank guns, and antiaircraft armament; larger, heavier, metalized aircraft with sophisticated navigational technology; larger radar-equipped ships and aircraft carriers; and innovative amphibious vehicles. Troops training on each of these systems needed significantly more space than those using earlier generations of weapons. Advances in vehicle mechanization and motorization required substantially greater maneuver area to conduct exercises; long-range artillery and modern antiaircraft guns demanded extended target ranges; and innovative amphibious vehicles necessitated development of new coastal training grounds. Furthermore, the United States had to develop its armories and war industries, which obliged US manufacturers to retool and expand. New technologies, tactics, and strategies compelled the war and navy departments to enlarge existing encampments and construct new training facilities, airfields, and bombing and artillery ranges, in addition to ordnance plants and depots, aircraft, tank, landing craft factories, and shipyards, all of which claimed substantial amounts of land (see Map 2.2).[7]

---

[7] Works that explore the impact of the evolution of military technology and its influence on tactics and strategy in the twentieth century include Williamson Murray and Allan R. Millett, eds., *Military Innovation in the Interwar Period* (New York: Cambridge

During World War I, the US Army did not need extensive training areas for its troop formations. Division-sized units in that conflict occupied a much smaller frontage than their World War II counterparts. Furthermore, in the earlier conflict US forces prepared for combat behind the protection of a stabilized front in France, with American service members receiving limited training stateside before they embarked for Europe. This arrangement permitted the army to use temporary cantonments for housing troops because men quickly shipped out to France. In contrast, German conquest of much of Europe in the early stages of World War II dictated that before they arrived in Europe for battle, US Army formations had to be fully prepared to fight as coherent, large, combined-arms forces.[8] In response, the military expanded its bases and built thousands of new housing, recreational, medical, and educational structures that would last the war's duration and in many cases well beyond.[9]

These facilities also had to accommodate dramatic increases in the number of troops that began entering the armed forces soon after Congress mobilized the National Guard and created the first peacetime draft in September 1940. Approximately 4.7 million American soldiers, sailors, airmen, and Marines served during World War I; nearly four times as many (16.1 million) served in World War II, with greatly increasing numbers entering the military as the war continued (see Table 2.1). Because of the global nature of the conflict, the American military also

University Press, 1996); Trevor N. Dupuy, *The Evolution of Weapons and Warfare* (Fairfax, VA: Hero Books, 1989), 202–277; Martin van Creveld, *Technology and War: From 2000 B.C. to the Present* (New York: Free Press, 1989), 153–232; Allan R. Millett and Peter Maslowski, *For the Common Defense: A Military History of the United States of America* (New York: Free Press, 1984), 363–392, which also provides a thorough bibliography of relevant sources.

[8] Large US Army units during World War II included the following ranges of personnel numbers: Division – 10,000 to 15,500; Corps (Army Corps) – 65,000 to 90,000; Army – 200,000 to 400,000. *The Officers' Guide: A Ready Reference to Customs, Correct Procedures Which Pertain to the Commissioned Officers of the Army of the United States,* 8th ed. (Harrisburg, PA: Military Service Publishing Company, 1942), 29–32; Kent R. Greenfield, Robert R. Palmer, and Bell I. Wiley, *The Organization of Ground Combat Troops* (Washington, DC: US Army Center of Military History, 1947), 200–306, 320, 363–373.

[9] William A. Hamilton Jr., "Statistics: Construction and Real Estate" (Washington, DC: US Army Chief of Military History, 1953), 1; Henry L. Stimson, Secretary of War, testimony, US Senate, Hearings, "Investigation of the National Defense Program," 77th Cong., 1st Sess. Part 1, April 1941, 2–6.

TABLE 2.1 *Military personnel strength during World Wars I and II*

Year	Army (includes Army Air Corps)	Navy (includes Marines)	Total
1917	(Apr. 1) 190,000	(Apr. 6) 99,000	289,000
1918	(Nov. 1) 3,665,000	(Nov. 11) 605,000	4,270,000
1940	653,000	245,000	898,000
1941	1,522,000	376,000	1,898,000
1942	3,074,000	784,000	3,858,000
1943	6,993,000	2,053,000	9,046,000
1944	7,993,000	3,454,000	11,447,000
1945	8,266,000	3,860,000	12,126,000

Sources: US Department of Commerce, *Statistical Abstract of the United States, 1944–45*, 174–176; *Statistical Abstract of the United States, 1946*, 221–222; *Statistical Abstract of the United States, 1919* (Washington, DC: GPO, 1945, 1946, 1920), 728–729. Numbers can vary among sources by exact date of the year that numbers were tabulated and for the navy, by inclusion of the number of Coast Guard personnel.

needed training grounds to prepare to fight in all types of terrain – jungles, deserts, mountains, oceans, shores – and climates – tropical, arid, polar, and temperate.[10]

Military mobilization for World War II demanded rapid new construction. Before the United States could produce guns, planes, and tanks, it had to assemble defense plants; before it could send troops into battle, it had to provide proper living areas and training grounds for new inductees. None of this development, however, could begin without land on which to build.[11] Thus, the availability in 1940 of contiguous stretches of sparsely populated public domain land in western states and submarginal agricultural and forest land in southern states was a windfall for the military. If defense agencies had been compelled to buy all the lands

[10] Hamilton, "Statistics: Construction and Real Estate," 1.
[11] US Senate, S. Rep. 347, "Acquisition of Additional Land for Military Purposes," 76th Cong, 1st Sess., May 1939, 1–2; US Senate, Hearings, "Investigation of the National Defense Program," 77th Cong., 1st Sess., April 1941, Part 1, 5–7, 193–194; US Senate, Special Committee Investigating the National Defense Program, "Investigation of the National Defense Program," 77th Cong, 1st Sess., October 1941, Part 8, 2493; Lenore Fine and Jesse A. Remington, *The Corps of Engineers: Construction in the United States* (Washington, DC: US Army Center of Military History, 1972), 174–175; US Navy Department, *Building the Navy's Bases in World War II, Part I* (Washington, DC: Government Printing Office, 1947), 111–112.

TABLE 2.2 *Ownership status of land used by US Military during World War II*

	War Department	Navy Department	Total acres	Percent of total
Owned as of June 30, 1940	2,116,862	499,961	2,616,823	5.0
Purchased during World War II	5,728,876	1,017,080	6,745,956	12.8
Other federally owned under temporary use agreements	28,340,132	4,739,753	33,079,885	62.7
Leased from citizens, state, and local governments	9,685,031	600,000	10,285,031	19.5
Totals	45,870,901	6,856,794	52,727,695	100.0

Source: Alvin T. M. Lee, *Acquisition and Use of Land for Military and War Production Purposes, World War II* (Washington, DC: US Department of Agriculture, 1947), 4–5.

temporarily needed for prosecution of the war, the expenditure would have been prohibitive and time would have been lost.[12]

The land acquisition task that fell to the Army Quartermaster Corps' Real Estate Branch was unprecedented. On June 30, 1940, the War Department occupied 2.1 million acres of land, while the Navy Department possessed an additional 500,000 acres. In 1940 alone, the military required eight million more acres, 14 times the roughly 571,000 acres the military acquired during World War I.[13] Over the course of World War II, the two military departments purchased roughly 6.7 million acres from private owners, leased 10.3 million acres from individuals and state and local governments, and used 33.1 million acres of public domain and other federal lands (see Table 2.2).[14]

THE GEOGRAPHY OF SITE SELECTION

Military considerations drove where to build, as did the need for rapid and cost-effective construction. The armed forces preferred expanding existing military camps before establishing new ones on federal, state-owned, or private property, although need quickly outpaced available

[12] L. A. Reuss and O. O. McCracken, *Federal Rural Lands* (Washington, DC: US Department of Agriculture, 1947), 14.

[13] Fine and Remington, *Corps of Engineers*, 94, 174–175; US House Committee Hearings, "Survey of Real Estate Owned or Controlled by War Department," 66th Cong., 3rd Sess., and 67th Sess. 1st Sess., January 1921, 16.

[14] Lee, *Acquisition and Use of Land*, 5.

space.[15] Each military function – ordnance, airfields, training grounds, and maneuver areas – required a specific type of land.

Airfields necessitated high-quality acreage. The best parcels had well-drained, level land with adjacent open space to avoid expensive tree-clearing costs. The USAAF needed a minimum of 160 acres for an auxiliary landing field, 2,500 acres for a primary field, and additional land for main airfields with barracks, hangars, and aircraft maintenance facilities.[16] Flight innovations during the war also increased the amount of land required. For example, the B-29 Superfortress, the aircraft designed for the long over-water flights necessary to attack the Japanese homeland, called for "super airports" to sustain their exceptionally heavy loads, rapid landing speeds, and powerful propeller blasts. Runways had to be longer and wider, pavement more durable, and grades less steep than for other aircraft.[17] The expanded Eglin Airfield in Florida met these requirements.

The army positioned its ground force training camps and maneuver areas on lands not well suited for agriculture, but commonly near sizeable cities with railroad and social facilities for large numbers of men. It sought to locate these facilities where the climate would allow year-round instruction, except where it conducted cold-weather and desert training exercises. Military camps and artillery ranges varied in size from 25,000 to 100,000 acres (39 and 156 square miles, respectively), depending on the type of training. The army required sites large enough to train division-sized forces, with ample space for housing, drill fields, and ranges for artillery, machine guns, pistols, mortars, antitank guns, and grenade courses. Additionally, the chosen locations required level areas for housing, woods and fields for tactical exercises, streams for practice constructing pontoon bridges and water crossings, and ground suitable for mechanized forces. The encampments also needed adequate utilities, water supplies, sewage disposal facilities, electrical power supplies, and telephone connections. Sites chosen for these posts had to have a sufficient local labor supply for construction and a nearby population center for civilian contact and commercial facilities.[18]

[15] Fine and Remington, *Corps of Engineers*, 138; US Senate, Hearings, "Investigation of the National Defense Program," 77th Cong., 1st Sess., Part 1, 182–183.

[16] Lee, "Getting and Using Land," 87–88.

[17] Jerold E. Brown, *Where Eagles Land: Planning and Development of US Army Airfields, 1910–1941* (London: Greenwood Press, 1990), 2–5; Fine and Remington, *Corps of Engineers*, 614–649.

[18] Lee, *Acquisition and Use of Land*, 4; US Senate, Hearings, "Investigation of the National Defense Program," 77th Cong., 1st Sess., April 1941, Part 1, 200–204.

FIGURE 2.4 Main Street in Taylors Creek, a village that was evacuated to create Camp Stewart area, near Hinesville, Georgia, 1941.
Source: US Farm Security Administration/Office of War Information, Library of Congress digital identification: fsa 8c05214 //hdl.loc.gov/loc.pnp/fsa.8c05214. Image in the public domain

Camp Stewart (later Fort Stewart) is illustrative of a typical large army facility developed during World War II (see Figure 2.4). In August 1940, the War Department leased 5,000 acres near Hinesville, Georgia, 40 miles southwest of Savannah, to serve as an antiaircraft artillery training and firing area. Subsequent land purchases stretched the reservation to more than 280,000 acres (about 437 square miles), displacing an estimated 1,500 farm families and tenants, almost evenly divided between blacks and whites. In 1940, the government paid landowners on average $15 per acre for land that had been covered in corn and intercropped with peanuts and soybeans.[19]

---

[19] US Senate Hearings, "National Defense Migration," 77th Cong., 1st Sess., March 1941, Part 11, 4743; Fort Stewart Museum, "Fort Stewart Fact Sheet," www.stewart.army.mil/info/?id=417 (accessed April 7, 2016); Craig S. Pascoe and John Rieken, "Fort Stewart," in *New Georgia Encyclopedia*, www.georgiaencyclopedia.org/articles/government-politics/fort-stewart (accessed April 7, 2016); City of Hinesville, GA, "Short History of Liberty

The South Georgia land proved ideal for the army's needs. The acreage could accommodate four regiments, 2,500 men at a time, and the terrain supported antiaircraft exercises. The climate permitted year-round training, three nearby Civilian Conservation Corps camps supplied ample construction workers, and existing defense installations, particularly Fort Screven and USAAF Hunter Field, were nearby. Further, the land was cheap, few people lived on it, and it had a first-class road and a railroad that provided links to Hinesville, the county seat of 500 people.[20]

In the western United States during early 1942, the navy purchased 4,000 acres (roughly six square miles) of a 107,000-acre ranch located near present-day Irvine, California, to establish Marine Air Corps Station El Toro. Named for the nearby community of 130 inhabitants, the air station, which the Marines commissioned in 1943, provided facilities for two air groups to train combat pilots. A few miles from the Pacific Ocean, the location was without fog most of the year, the Santa Fe Railroad ran along the site's western border, and the Marine Corps' primary West Coast infantry training base, Camp Pendleton, was nearby. The El Toro land had belonged to James Irvine Jr., who cultivated black and lima beans on the property. In addition to fourteen 250-man wooden dormitories, the Marines built an airfield with three asphalt runways and underground gasoline storage tanks. El Toro remained active after the war and in 1950 became the permanent center of Marine Corps aviation on the West Coast.[21]

Between the two coasts, the military acquired thousands of contiguous acres of land in isolated regions to permit high-speed fighter planes to

County," www.cityofhinesville.org/DocumentView.aspx?DID=313 (accessed November 8, 2016); Liberty County Historical Society, "Agricultural and Cattle Raising (1934)," https://libertyhistory.org/history/timelines/timelines-1930-1940/agriculture-and-cattle-raising-1934 (accessed November 8, 2016).

[20] US Senate, Hearings, "Investigation of the National Defense Program," 77th Cong., 1st Sess., April 1941, Part 1, 201–202; US Senate Hearings, "National Defense Migration," 77th Cong., 1st Sess., March 1941, Part 11, 4742–4749; Fort Stewart Museum, "Fort Stewart Fact Sheet," Craig S. Pascoe and John Rieken, "Fort Stewart," in *New Georgia Encyclopedia*, second reference from fn. 21, www.georgiaencyclopedia.org/articles/government-politics/fort-stewart (accessed April 7, 2016).

[21] Navy Department, *Building the Navy's Bases*, 258, 260; Naval Facilities Engineering Command, Base Realignment and Closure (BRAC) Program Management Office, "Former Marine Air Station El Toro," www.bracpmo.navy.mil/brac_bases/california/former_mcas_el_toro.html (accessed July 5, 2016); M. L. Shettle Jr., "Historic California Posts, Camps Stations and Airfields: Marine Corps Air Station, El Toro, California," www.militarymuseum.org/MCASElToro.html (accessed July 5, 2016).

perfect air-to-air gunnery tactics; heavy bombers to practice dropping live ammunition; and testing of nascent rocket and atomic weapons systems. The war and navy departments placed most bombing and artillery ranges on the poorest land available, primarily inferior public domain grazing acreage in western states and in limited areas of eastern woodlands, where costly land prices otherwise hindered development of large ranges.[22]

For the highly secretive Manhattan Project, the war department purchased and leased approximately 550,000 acres (about 860 square miles) for the program's main installations in Tennessee, New Mexico, and Washington. At Los Alamos, New Mexico, the US Forest Service provided 46,000 acres of the Santa Fe National Forest. The War Department bought another 8,900 acres of largely semiarid forest and grazing lands on the eastern slopes of the Jemez Mountains from a small number of private owners. In Tennessee, the Manhattan District acquired roughly 59,000 acres for the Clinton Engineer Works (later Oak Ridge National Laboratory), of which it purchased 56,000 acres for about $47 an acre from landowners of Roane and Anderson Counties on the western slope of the Cumberland Plateau. During the Great Depression, the region had been ravaged by floods, and a peach blight had further devastated the local economy. The Tennessee Valley Authority (TVA) had completed a dam nearby in 1942 that created navigable waterways and generated additional electricity – necessary infrastructure for the army's nuclear research facility. However, the TVA's use of eminent domain in the 1930s to acquire the land also uprooted hundreds of farmers from productive river-bottom farms. The Hanford Engineer Works site at Richland, Washington, included nearly 71,000 federally-held acres; 86,000 state- and county-controlled acres; 46,000 acres owned by railroad companies; and more than 225,000 acres belonging to private citizens and corporations. Private landowners had mostly planted fruits, asparagus, mint, and alfalfa. The flat, arid environment perfectly suited the plutonium production facility. Government officials considered it a remote, isolated wasteland, with abundant water from the Columbia River for electricity, and far enough inland to diminish concerns of an enemy attack. New Deal dams constructed nearby in the name of land reclamation, navigation improvement, and electricity

[22] Alvin T. M. Lee, "Land Acquisition Program of the War and Navy Departments," *Journal of Farm Economics* 29 (November 1947), 892; Lee, *Acquisition and Use of Land*, 10–12, 31.

production were the logical lure for the army's plutonium producing nuclear reactors.[23]

Geography also shaped ordnance plant site selection. Foremost, to thwart possible enemy attack, plants had to be placed inland from US borders and geographically dispersed. The War Department wanted plants manufacturing war chemicals and equipment located between the Appalachian and Rocky Mountains no closer than 200 miles from the nation's borders and near to related factories positioned in five areas of the eastern half of this zone.[24] The army required high-quality agricultural land for the 29 completely new ordnance plants because engineers needed level land for excavating heavy building foundations and deep soil to diminish shocks in the event of an explosion. Production processes demanded sufficient local water supplies for sparkless steam power. Also, the land had to lie in open country, with 5,000- to 10,000-acre buffer zones to keep a single explosion from triggering a chain reaction, and for the general safety of residents. The plant location had to sit near enough to population centers for an adequate labor supply and close to rail and highway transportation to bring in raw materials and ship the finished armaments.[25]

Badger Ordnance Works, 30 miles northwest of Madison, Wisconsin, was a typical ordnance facility. Built in 1942 on 10,565 acres (16.5 square miles) of fertile cultivated and pastured land, Badger produced smokeless gunpowder, solid rocket propellant fuel, and nitroglycerin for incorporation into small arms, cannons, grenades, and small rockets.[26] The War Department selected the Badger site largely because it consisted of gently rolling, less vulnerable interior lands with adequate drainage and excellent load-bearing capabilities far from large population centers. The facility was accessible by rail from significant shipping centers in

[23] Vincent C. Jones, *Manhattan: The Army and the Atomic Bomb* (Washington, DC: US Army Center of Military History, 1985), 319–343; Roane County Office of Emergency Services, "Roane County Natural Hazard Mitigation Plan," September 2010, 6–9; David Harvey, *History of the Hanford Site, 1943–1990* (Richland, WA: Pacific Northwest National Laboratory, n.d.), 3–6; Richard White, *The Organic Machine: The Remaking of the Columbia River* (New York: Hill and Wang, 1995), 53–58, 81–88.

[24] Fine and Remington, *Corps of Engineers*, 134–136, map on 136.

[25] Lee, "Getting and Using Land," 88; Fine and Remington, *Corps of Engineers*, 134–137. Of 35 manufacturing plants, the War Department had to find 29 new tracts for its munitions projects.

[26] US Army Joint Munitions Command (AMSJM), "Badger Army Ammunition Plant Historical Review, 1941–2006" (Rock Island, IL: AMSJM History Office, 2006), 4, 8.

Milwaukee, Chicago, St. Louis, St. Paul, and Kansas City, and the Wisconsin River flowed on the eastern boundary of the property.[27]

Political factors also influenced the selection of one community over another for defense projects, and local interests frequently clashed. Businessmen campaigned to have war-related industries located in their towns to increase payrolls and trade. But local landowners typically protested site development, as it meant the loss of their farms and homes.[28] In the case of Badger Ordnance, many citizens questioned the sacrifice of rich farmland for the powder plant, as there was a sandy agricultural wasteland less than an hour north in Adams County. Almost 30 years after the war, Leo T. Crowley, a Wisconsin banker who was chairman of the Federal Deposit Insurance Corporation from 1934 to 1945, revealed that he had lobbied Gen. George C. Marshall to establish the plant near Baraboo. Crowley's friend, Rowland L. "Bud" Williams, then president of the Chicago and Northwestern Railroad that ran through the area, wanted the additional business. Crowley's relationship as an economic advisor to President Roosevelt likely influenced the army's final site decision.[29]

Presidential advisors also argued for placement of military installations and production plants in nonindustrial areas in the South and West to help boost those regions out of the Depression.[30] The defense economy that emerged during the war contributed directly to development of what an Army Air Corps official in 1944 termed the "sunshine belt." This region south of the 37th parallel provided ideal training environs with little rainfall, mild winters, and friendly terrain from Georgia to California.[31]

Between 1941 and 1945, wartime mobilization injected more than $4 billion of military investment into the South, transforming the region. In addition to training facilities and airfields, the war and navy departments brought new shipyards to the coasts of Virginia, Florida, Texas,

[27] Louis F. Reuter Jr., *Historical Report: Badger Ordnance Works, Book 1, Period Ending December 31, 1942,* "Exhibits for Introduction, #2," NARA, RG 156, Records of the Office of the Chief of Ordnance, Entry 646.

[28] Fine and Remington, *Corps of Engineers,* 177–184.

[29] Michael J. Goc, *Powder, People and Place: Badger Ordnance Works and the Sauk Prairie* (Friendship, WI: New Past Press, 2002), 75–77; "Leo T. Crowley to Retire from Milwaukee Road," *Chicago Tribune,* October 18, 1963, section 3, 7.

[30] US Senate Hearings, "National Defense Migration," 77th Cong., 1st Sess., Part 16, 6545–6547.

[31] US Army Air Corps, "History of the West Coast Air Corps Training Center: Moffett Field, California, 8 July 1940–7 December 1941," 145–148, quotation on 148, Air Force Historical Studies Office Microfilm Collection, reel A2313.

North Carolina, and Mississippi; munitions and chemical warfare plants to Alabama; a bomber aircraft factory to Georgia; bauxite mining to Arkansas; and atomic weapons development to Tennessee. Scores of new military installations and supply depots stimulated new service industries from Virginia to Texas. The populations of 39 out of 48 southern urban areas grew dramatically: for example, Mobile, Alabama, grew by 61 percent and Norfolk, Virginia, by 57 percent.[32]

In western states, war requirements also created new shipyards, aircraft plants, aluminum and steel factories, and weapons research facilities. Because the West served as the staging area for the war in the Pacific, the military established training camps, supply and munitions depots, and testing grounds throughout the region. Prior to the war, few large urban areas existed in the West, and mobilization hastened the growth of existing cities. San Diego doubled in size, and San Francisco and Los Angeles each grew by 30 percent in four years. Internal migration also increased racial and ethnic diversity in the West, particularly in the cities.[33]

After the war, many military installations in this "sunshine belt" remained active and were enlarged, while others were placed on standby status and used by National Guard or Reserve units. Thus, World War II military expansion in the American South and West brought lasting change to the American landscape, such as infrastructure development, resource use, habitat destruction, and pollution, though it also prevented human development on some lands and preserved native habitat. Postwar, military service members and civilian employees permanently relocated to this region, laying the foundation for the Sunbelt's massive urban and suburban development.[34]

METHODS OF MILITARY LAND ACQUISITION AND ALTERATION IN WARTIME

Military land procurement during wartime fundamentally differed from peacetime practices. During World War II, land acquisition happened

---

[32] Gerald D. Nash, *The Crucial Era: The Great Depression and World War II, 1929–1945* (New York: St. Martin's Press, 1992), 157–161; Pete Daniel, "Going Among Strangers: Southern Reactions to World War II," *Journal of American History* 77, no. 3 (December 1990), 886–911.

[33] Nash, *The Crucial Era*, 162–166.

[34] Gilbert S. Guinn, "A Different Frontier: Aviation, the Army Air Forces, and the Evolution of the Sunshine Belt," *Aerospace Historian* 29, no. 4 (Spring/March 1982), 44.

hurriedly, with little time to consider alternatives. The armed forces secured acreage largely by leasing it from individuals and federal, state, and local agencies and by purchasing it from private citizens. Over the course of the war, the military leased approximately 43.3 million acres of primarily federal-, state-, and municipal-owned land, significantly more than the 6.7 million acres it purchased from private owners (see Table 2.2).[35] The US military preferred to lease federal land through executive orders, public land orders, and use permits instead of buying real estate because the process was fast, cost practically nothing, disrupted local populations only minimally, and reduced postwar property disposal problems. In general, defense agencies borrowed unimproved public land – raw acreage devoid of any development, construction, or site preparation – because laws required the government to restore property to its original condition or pay damages, which would often cost more than purchasing the property.[36]

The land the military leased from state governments in the West for bombing ranges tended to be interspersed with federally owned land and Native American reservations. In some states, the armed services arranged exchanges of the intermingled land for acreage outside of military reservations because the states were reluctant to sell the property outright. Municipal entities often leased civil airfields and the adjacent lands to the military. Cites frequently offered leases for one dollar per year, extended water and power lines, and sponsored housing projects for officers and their families in an effort to woo investment to the area. The selection of municipal airports saved the army considerable time and effort because the infrastructure already existed for the facilities.[37]

Land management bureaus and agencies of the US Departments of the Interior and Agriculture furnished the most federal land leased to the military, primarily in Oregon, Nevada, Arizona, California, New Mexico, and Utah. In the West, the federal government still owned large, contiguous swaths of public domain property in national forests, wildlife areas, Native American reservations, reclamation territories held for irrigation development, public water reserves, and otherwise vacant land. In the eastern and southeastern states, where less public domain land remained, the military leased forested tracts that were primarily cutover lands or privately owned, namely by paper and lumber companies and turpentine

[35] Lee, *Acquisition and Use of Land*, 3–22.   [36] Ibid., 9–23.
[37] Ibid., 10–11; Fine and Remington, *Corps of Engineers*, 133–134.

operators. The military converted many of these forest and grazing lands into bombing and artillery ranges.[38]

Throughout the conflict, the war and navy departments collaborated with the Department of the Interior's Fish and Wildlife Service (FWS) to repurpose more than 4.6 million acres of land on 33 national wildlife refuges in 18 states and the territory of Alaska as bombing and gunnery ranges, air bases, emergency landing fields, maneuver areas, docking facilities, and as recreational areas for men in training camps. Much of this acreage lay on property withdrawn during Depression-era submarginal land retirement programs in the South and Midwest. Several refuges acted as extensions of adjacent military artillery and gunnery ranges, including Patuxent National Wildlife Refuge (NWR) near Fort Meade, Maryland, and Wichita Mountains NWR, which adjoined Fort Sill, Oklahoma. The FWS also opened large sections of refuge lands to grazing, hay cutting, grain production, and nominal timber harvesting.[39]

Because the armed forces did not use FWS refuge areas with high concentrations of wildlife, little harm came to the fauna from these activities. Generally, the army was sympathetic to wildlife concerns. For example, upon President Roosevelt's request, the army spared nesting and resting grounds for the last remaining flock of Trumpeter Swans near Yellowstone National Park. It also withdrew plans to use moose-calving grounds on Kenai Peninsula in Alaska when wildlife managers raised objections. However, severe wartime damage did occur on the Aleutian Islands Refuge in Alaska, where 83,000 US troops established a presence on 18 islands to eradicate a 10,000-man Japanese force on two islands, Attu and Kiska, at the tip of the Aleutian Island chain.[40]

During the war, the National Park Service (NPS) issued nearly 2,000 permits for use of its facilities for short-term maneuvers. The military operated in nearly all the national parks along the Pacific, Atlantic, and Gulf Coasts, such as Acadia, Olympic, and Glacier Bay National Parks

---

[38] Lee, *Acquisition and Use of Land*, 12–13, 106–110.

[39] Information Service, US Department of the Interior [US Fish and Wildlife Service], "Wildlife in Wartime," August 7, 1943, 2; Michael W. Giese, "A Federal Foundation for Wildlife Conservation: The Evolution of the National Wildlife Refuge System, 1920–1968" (PhD diss., American University, 2008), 180–183.

[40] Correspondence between Harold L. Ickes, Secretary of Interior, and President Franklin D. Roosevelt in Edgar B. Nixon, *Franklin D. Roosevelt & Conservation, 1911–1945* (Hyde Park, NY: General Services Administration, 1957), 540–541; Information Service, "Wildlife in Wartime," August 7, 1943, 2; Giese, "A Federal Foundation for Wildlife Conservation," 180–183.

and Fort Pulaski and Cabrillo Monuments, using those sites for defense installations and aircraft warning service posts. NPS specialists assisted with alpine warfare training at Mount Rainier and Mount McKinley (now Denali) National Parks and supported desert warfare training at parks in Arizona and southern California. The services also established recreation camps at the Grand Canyon, Sequoia, Mount McKinley, and Carlsbad Caverns parks and a rehabilitation facility for 7,000 patients in Yosemite's Ahwahnee Hotel.[41]

Secretary of the Interior Harold L. Ickes and NPS director Newton B. Drury were staunch conservationists who sought to protect national parks from unnecessary military use. Drury, with Ickes's support, refused requests for the harvest of Sitka spruce trees in Olympic National Park for airplane construction, as had been done during World War I, and limited cattle and sheep grazing throughout the national parks. By 1946, the NPS terminated most of the military's permits and returned the parks to their former condition as quickly as possible, but it also permanently transferred six land parcels totaling about 10,000 acres to the armed forces. The military left some parks in poor condition and changed the character of others. For example, at Cabrillo, the navy constructed batteries and observation posts near the Old Spanish Lighthouse, while the army's use of Hawaii National Park for motorized maneuvers and firing practice caused extensive damage to the forests and other terrain and littered the area with unexploded ordnance.[42]

The US Forest Service provided military use permits for 2.8 million acres of land under its stewardship, including the area ceded to the military for Eglin Airfield. By May 1946, the military had returned almost 1.4 million acres to the USFS. Overall, the greatest effect the war had on national forest land related to the use of its resources. The volume of timber harvested from those stands increased 89 percent between 1940 and 1944, although loggers kept mostly within the accepted standards of sustained-yield management on federal timber lands. These forests fed a wartime economy hungry for raw timber. According to historian Richard P. Tucker, "Construction lumber, which had consumed 27 billion board feet in 1941, rose sharply to 35 billion annually during the war,

---

[41] Janet A. McDonnell, "'Far-Reaching Effects:' The United States Military and the National Parks during World War II," *George Wright Forum* 32, no. 1 (2015): 89–110; McDonnell, "World War II: Defending Park Values and Resources," *Public Historian* 29, no. 4 (Fall 2007): 15–33.

[42] McDonnell, "Far-Reaching Effects," 90, 102, 105–106; McDonnell, "Defending Park Values and Resources," 18, 30–31.

TABLE 2.3 *Major use of land before purchase by the war and navy departments during World War II*

	War Department	Navy Department	Total acres	Percent of total
Cropland	1,434,229	272,510	1,706,739	25.8
Pasture and Range	2,061,705	413,079	2,474,784	37.4
Woodland and Forest	1,888,028	269,085	2,157,113	32.6
Swamps, Waste, Urban, and Misc.	218,496	62,406	280,902	4.2
Totals*	5,602,458	1,017,080	6,619,538	100.0

Source: Alvin T. M. Lee, *Acquisition and Use of Land for Military and War Production Purposes, World War II* (Washington, DC: US Department of Agriculture, 1947), 30.

partly because of a huge program of military camp construction in the early months of the war." Concurrently, tree plantings in national forests decreased 96 percent due to manpower and funding shortages. Grazing in the forests declined marginally, and the estimated population of big game increased 16 percent.[43]

Laws that prohibited defense agencies from constructing permanent improvements on leased land led the military to purchase outright from private owners about 13 percent of the total land it acquired.[44] This type of acreage tended to have the highest use capabilities: of the total 6.7 million acres, about one-quarter had been cropland, one-third pasture and rangeland, and one-third woodland and forest, with the remainder in miscellaneous uses (see Table 2.3). In order of size, purchased parcels occurred primarily in California, Texas, Georgia, and Florida.[45]

When voluntary sale of land could not be arranged, the federal government took possession primarily though the General Condemnation Statute (1888) and the Declaration of Taking Act (1931), with additional legislative authorities granted during the war. The military's purchase of private property displaced an estimated 60,000 families from roughly 30,000 farms (see Map 2.3). The hurried acquisition of sizeable amounts of contiguous farmland during the war devastated the economic and

[43] Reuss and McCracken, *Federal Rural Lands*, 14, 21–25; quotation in Richard P. Tucker, "The World Wars and the Globalization of Timber Cutting," in *Natural Enemy, Natural Ally: Toward an Environmental History of Warfare*, ed. Edmund Russell and Richard P. Tucker (Corvallis: Oregon State University Press, 2004), 127.
[44] Lee, *Acquisition and Use of Land*, 5, 9–11; Fine and Remington, *Corps of Engineers*, 175–177.
[45] Lee, *Acquisition and Use of Land*, 29–32, 106–108, 110.

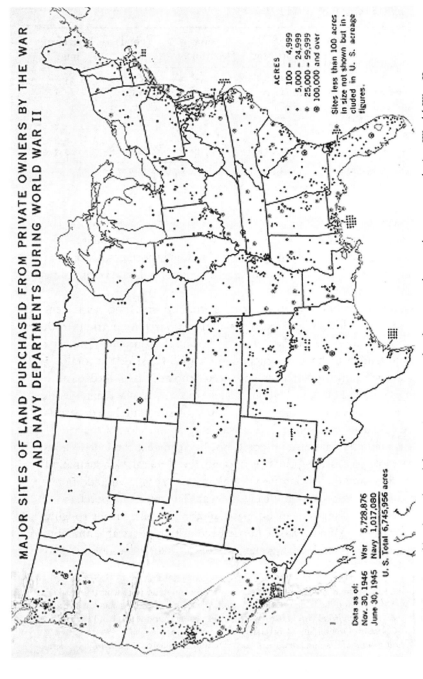

MAP 2.3 Major sites of land purchased from private owners by the war and navy departments during World War II.
Source: Alvin T. M. Lee, *Acquisition and Use of Land for Military and War Production Purposes, World War II* (Washington, DC: US Department of Agriculture, 1947), 7. Image in the public domain

social patterns of community life in certain areas. Lifelong residents scattered to new locales, school and road districts dissolved or combined with others, and tax bases withered.[46]

Toward the war's end, the Surplus Property Act of 1944 directed defense agencies to divest themselves of unneeded real estate. Almost all of the 10.3 million acres that the military leased from individuals and state and local governments reverted to the original proprietors after the conflict because most leases were stipulated to last only for the war's duration. About one-third of the 33.1 million acres (9.3 million acres) of public domain and federal lands that other agencies had transferred to the military during the war reverted to their former tenants by June 1947. The military determined after the war that about a quarter of the land it had purchased or obtained through condemnation from private owners (1.6 million acres of the 6.7 million acres) was surplus, of which former owners reclaimed almost 1 million acres. However, federal officials declared that roughly one-third of this purchased land, about 2.5 million acres, was submarginal for agricultural use and as a result retained it in public ownership for forestry and grazing purposes.[47]

While the government restored some wartime land to its original owners and managers, the military's overall acreage increased from its prewar level largely because of evolving weapons systems such as tanks, bombers, amphibious vehicles, and long-range artillery, as well as nuclear testing, which required more space for safety and secrecy purposes. Overall, between June 1943 and June 1944, military-controlled landholdings of all types peaked at 52.7 million acres. By June 1945, after the Allies achieved victory in Europe, that amount fell to a roughly 25.1 million acres. As of October 1949, inventories showed the military retained a total of 23.1 million acres. However, Cold War exigencies led to a renewed defense buildup, and by June 1956, the military's landholdings rose to 27.6 million acres, of which 16.9 million acres were lands removed from the public domain.[48]

---

[46] 25 Stat. 357, Aug. 1, 1888, 40 U. S. C. 257, 258; 46 Stat. 1421, 1422, Feb. 26, 1931, 40 U. S. C., Sec. 258a–258e; US Department of Justice, Lands Division, *Acquisition of Property for War Purposes* (Washington, DC: Government Printing Office, 1944), 50–51; Lee, *Acquisition and Use of Land*, 23–26, 33–34; Lee, "Land Acquisition Program of the War and Navy Departments," 898, 904–905.

[47] 58 Stat. 765, Oct. 3, 1944, 50 U. S. C. 1611–1646; Lee, *Acquisition and Use of Land*, 97–104.

[48] No single, comprehensive defense agency inventory of its World War II and early Cold War landholdings exists. The author has cited the most authoritative sources available on the subject. Lee, *Acquisition and Use of Land*, 5; Reuss and McCracken, *Federal Rural*

ENVIRONMENTAL LEGACIES

The US military's ready access to abundant, inexpensive land allowed its massive combined-arms forces to arrive on the World War II battlefields fully capable of unleashing faster, heavier, and more lethal weapons against its foes. During the war, military leaders – whose only substantive environmental concerns involved erosion, dust, and pest control – were largely ignorant of the long-term environmental effects of their activities. Their mission to fight and win wars did not account for the skills needed to properly manage the ballooning military land inventory. During the war, munitions production on formerly fertile farmlands, live-fire exercises on national forests turned into testing ranges, and improper disposal of munitions on newly restricted grazing lands contaminated millions of acres of land with hazardous and toxic compounds.

Throughout the early Cold War, military land managers focused on multiple-use hunting and fishing programs and sustained-yield timber production and did not prioritize other environmental concerns. During this time, DOD became the country's biggest polluter, tainting soil and water with volatile organic chemicals, industrial solvents, and nuclear waste. In the 1970s and 1980s, the exponential increase of environmental legislation gradually shifted the Defense Department's land management emphasis from consumptive uses of natural resources to strategies that complied with new environmental protection and remediation laws. In particular, through the National Environmental Protection Act (NEPA, 1969), Congress required DOD to conduct environmental remediation programs to address contamination from hazardous materials at active installations, formerly used defense sites, and other locations across the United States. By 1980, the Comprehensive Environmental Response, Compensation, and Liability Act (CERCLA, 1980) created the "Superfund" for remediation and established strict financial liability for the Defense Department to clean up environmental contamination on its installations. As of 1992, DOD possessed nearly 20,000 individual toxic waste sites and 81 percent of the

---

Lands, 54; US House of Representatives, Hearings, "Withdrawal and Utilization of the Public Lands of the United States," 84th Cong., 2d Sess., January–May 1956, 50; US House of Representatives, H. Rep. 1074, "Area, In Acres, of Lands in Federal Ownership," 81st Cong., 2nd Sess., September 1950, 12–14; US House of Representatives, H. Rep. 215, "Withdrawal and Utilization of the Public Lands of the United States," 85th Cong., 1st Sess., March 1957, 13.

properties on the federal facility National Priority List, commonly known as Superfund sites.[49]

Cold War exigencies permitted the defense establishment to flout environmental regulations through to the end of the 1980s. Not until the first decade of the post–Cold War era (1991–2001) did US politicians and policy makers compel the military to more effectively reconcile its defense mission with environmental laws. By the mid-to-late 1990s, the US military, reflecting the evolving national sentiment that favored increased environmental protection and the new sciences of restoration ecology and conservation biology, began implementing a more proactive, integrated ecosystem management approach. Certainly, the Pentagon has not always prioritized ecological stewardship, and the military's motives for landscape conservation is focused on sustaining its mission, not altruism. But slowly, the Defense Department has recognized that proper natural resource management maintains the ecological integrity of its property and ultimately preserves and provides the realistic training conditions that are essential to military readiness.[50]

As of 2018, most existing active military installations, and dozens that have closed over the last 30 years, trace their origins to the World War II era.[51] The following examples demonstrate how many of the land use and

[49] Jean A. Mansavage, *Natural Defense: US Air Force Origins of the Department of Defense Natural Resources Conservation Program* (Washington, DC: Air Force History and Museums Program, 2014), 39–40, 103–111; Durant, *The Greening of the US Military*, xi, 6–9, 77–82; 42 U.S.C. §4321 et seq. (1969); 42 U.S.C. §9601 et seq. (1980).

[50] Durant, *The Greening of the US Military*, 2, 6–9; Thomas H. Lillie and John J. Fittipaldi, "Evolution of Ecosystem Management for Stewardship of US Military Lands," in *Achieving Environmental Security: Ecosystem Services and Human Welfare*, ed. P. H. Liotta et al. (Amsterdam: IOS Press, 2010), 87–94; Office of the Deputy under Secretary of Defense (Installations and Environment), *Defense Environmental Quality Program Annual Report to Congress for Fiscal Year 2001*, "Sustainable Range Management" (June 2002), 85–86; The Nature Conservancy, "The Military and Nature: Our Partnership with the Department of Defense," March 7, 2013, www.nature.org/newsfeatures/specialfeatures/partnership-with-the-department-of-defense.xml (accessed May 6, 2013); Robert B. Shaw et al., "Training a Global Force: Sustaining Army Land for 21st Century Readiness," in *Military Geography from Peace to War*, ed. Eugene J. Palka and Francis A. Galgano (New York: McGraw Hill, 2005), 379–94; J. Douglas Ripley, "Legal and Policy Background," in *Conserving Biodiversity on Military Lands: A Guide for Natural Resources Managers*, ed. Nancy Benton, J. Douglas Ripley, and Fred Powledge (Arlington, VA: NatureServe, 2008), 54–73.

[51] Frederick J. Shaw, *Locating Air Force Base Sites: History's Legacy* (Washington, DC: Air Force History and Museums Program, 2004), 25–47, 203. As of 2003, 94 percent of the active major Air Force installations in the continental United States had been active during World War II; Department of Defense, "Base Structure Report: Fiscal Year 2015 Baseline," 29–67.

pollution patterns set during World War II continued and expanded during the Cold War decades and eventually became subject – often willingly, sometimes grudgingly – to evolving environmental remediation regulations.

Fort Stewart, Georgia

In 1940, the army removed a significant land area from active agricultural use and suppressed future human encroachment. Sustained military activity dating from World War II generated extensive environmental contamination, including unexploded ordnance on firing ranges and toxic chemicals from fuel operations and fire training facilities that leached into the soil and ground water. Since World War II, Fort Stewart has remained a principal army training complex, with only short idle periods between 1945 and 1950 and mid-1972 to 1974. As required by 1970s environmental laws, the army initiated contaminant prevention, remediation, and mitigation efforts that have helped the land recover from extreme use.[52]

Since 2005, army personnel at Fort Stewart have reduced by 75 percent the use of toxic and hazardous chemicals through Resource Conservation and Recovery Act (1976) training and proactive measures by the garrison's Environmental Division; however, the effects of the remaining hazardous material on fauna are not known. According to a 1993 statement from the US Army Environmental Center, the military rarely conducts field studies about the effects of toxic contaminants on wildlife unless there has been "noticeable and unusual wildlife mortality, failed breeding, or physical disfigurement." Where contamination risks to wildlife are extreme, the military constructs fences and emits simulated distress calls to warn wildlife away from the poisonous areas while it attempts to remove toxic materials and filter ground water to diminish the hazards. What is known is that implementation of a prescribed controlled burning program on Fort Stewart has created the largest remaining acreage of a longleaf pine-wiregrass ecosystem, which in turn sustains several threatened and endangered animal species.[53]

[52] Fort Stewart Museum, "Fort Stewart Fact Sheet"; US Army, "FY 2011 Secretary of Defense Environmental Awards: Army Nomination for Environmental Restoration – Fort Stewart/Hunter Army Airfield," www.denix.osd.mil/awards/previous-years/fy11secdef/eri/fort-stewart-hunter-army-airfield/ (accessed June 21, 2016).

[53] US Army, 3rd Infantry, Fort Stewart/Hunter AFB: "Hazardous Materials," www.stewart.army.mil/info/?id=511 (accessed August 31, 2016); Fort Stewart Museum, "Fort

Marine Corps Air Station, El Toro, California

Aviation activities at the base for more than 50 years starting in World War II, combined with nonexistent or lax fledgling environmental laws and inadequate disposal methods, contaminated the soil and groundwater at El Toro with volatile and semivolatile organic compounds, petroleum hydrocarbons, arsenic, and metals. In the mid-1980s, the Department of the Navy identified the sources of contamination and began environmental remediation (see Figure 2.5). In 1990, while the base was still active, the Environmental Protection Agency assigned it to its Superfund list.[54] In 1999, the navy decommissioned El Toro but continued its restoration program. By 2014, through soil sampling, excavation activities, and groundwater treatment, the navy and local agencies had cleaned up the contamination to the point that it no longer posed a risk to human health or the environment. In 2015 private builders began developing 9,500 homes and parkland in the middle of the former air station, with some of the other restored property used for agriculture.[55]

Stewart Fact Sheet"; US Army, "FY 2011 Secretary of Defense Environmental Awards"; Michael J. Lawrence et al., "The Effects of Modern War and Military Activities on Biodiversity and the Environment," *Environmental Review* 23, no. 4 (2015): 443–460; quotation from Michael Tennesen, National Wildlife Federation, "Can the Military Clean Up Its Act?," www.nwf.org/en/Magazines/National-Wildlife/1993/Can-the-Military-Clean-Up-Its-Act (accessed June 26, 2018) (the Army Environmental Center in 1993 is the Army Environmental Command located at Fort Sam Houston, San Antonio, Texas in 2018); Albert G. Way, *Conserving Southern Longleaf: Herbert Stoddard and the Rise of Ecological Land Management* (Athens: University of Georgia Press, 2011), 172–199.

[54] Center for Disease Control and Prevention (CDCP), "Public Health Assessments and Health Consultations, El Toro Marine Corps Air Station, Santa Ana, Orange County California," www.atsdr.cdc.gov/hac/pha/PHA.asp?docid=19&pg=1 (accessed July 6, 2016); Environmental Protection Agency, "Superfund Site: El Toro Marine Corps Air Station, El Toro, CA," https://cumulis.epa.gov/supercpad/SiteProfiles/index.cfm?fuseaction=second.schedule&id=0902770#Milestone (accessed July 30, 2019); Naval Facilities Engineering Command, "Second Five-Year Review Fact Sheet: Installation Restoration Program Sites 3, 5, 16, 17, 18, 24, and Anomaly Area 3 Former Marine Air Corps Station El Toro Irvine, California," February 2015, (found under February 2015, Fact Sheet Second Five-Year Review), www.bracpmo.navy.mil/brac_bases/california/former_mcas_el_toro/documents.html (accessed July 6, 2016).

[55] CDCP, "Public Health Assessments"; Tony Barboza, "Much of Old Irvine Air Base Is Removed from List of Hazardous Sites," *Los Angeles Times*, January 27, 2014, articles.latimes.com/2014/jan/27/local/la-me-0128-el-toro-20140128 (accessed July 5, 2016).

FIGURE 2.5 Aerial view of Marine Corps Air Station, El Toro, California, 1962 (left) and 1993 (right).
Source: Department of Defense. Department of the Navy Naval Imaging Command, NARA. NARA Local Identifier for 1962 figure: 330-CFD-DN-SN-85-06097. NARA Local Identifier for 1993 figure: 330-CFD-DN-ST-94-00718. Images in the public domain

Badger Ordnance Works, Baraboo, Wisconsin

After World War II, the army maintained Badger on standby status, reactivating it for the Korean and Vietnam wars. In 1975, the plant ceased production of explosives, and in 1997, the Defense Department decommissioned the facility (see Figure 2.6). In its final closing, Badger left behind an environmental legacy of toxic solvents, metals, and explosive waste onsite that had contaminated the nearby air, water, and soil. For the past three decades, the army has been conducting cleanup efforts: soil and water have been remediated, nearly 1,400 buildings demolished, and utility lines and railroad tracks removed.[56] Badger's final closing in 1997 initiated another shift in land use, with an inadvertent positive outcome: it has become a refuge for numerous rare bird and plant species. In 2016, the army transferred portions of the property to public and private conservation groups, creating the Sauk Prairie Recreation Area.[57]

Eglin Air Force Base, Florida

Eglin of the late 2010s exhibits an enigmatic environmental paradox: although military lands are often highly contaminated with unexploded

---

[56] AMSJM, "Badger Army Ammunition Plant," 13–14.
[57] Ibid.; US Army Toxic and Hazardous Materials Agency, *Remedial Investigation Badger Army Ammunition Plant Baraboo, Wisconsin* (Aberdeen Proving Ground, MD: US Army Environmental Center, 1993), ES1–11; Wisconsin Department of Natural Resources, "Property Master Plans: Sauk Prairie Recreation Area," https://dnr.wi.gov/topic/lands/propertyplanning/saukPrairie/ (accessed November 4, 2015).

FIGURE 2.6 View looking east of the main entrance gate of Badger Ordnance Works toward the Wisconsin River, May 1942.
Source: US Army, NARA, RG 156, Records of the Office of the Chief of Ordnance (1797–1988), Box A45. Image in the public domain

ordnance and other hazardous materials, because of their remoteness and lack of human development, they are highly biologically diverse. While this base has experienced the same contamination problems as the installations mentioned in the preceding text, it employs a robust environmental quality team to reduce risks and maintain compliance with environmental regulations. As of 2018, Eglin is the largest forested military reservation in the United States, providing 227,000 acres open for public recreational use, with only 60,000 acres permanently closed to the public. Roughly 400,000 acres are unimproved forests and beaches with diverse habitats that sustain eleven federally listed threatened and endangered species, including loggerhead sea turtles, red-cockaded woodpeckers, and Okaloosa darters. Eglin's military mission is relatively compatible with biodiversity goals: because it is an air force base, damage from tanks and tracked vehicles is minimal, and wildfires caused by training exercises have unintentionally improved the longleaf pine habitat nearby.[58] These conservation activities are not limited

[58] Eglin Joint Land Use Study Policy Group, "Eglin Air Force Base Joint Land Use Study"; Department of Defense, "Fiscal Year 2013 Secretary of Defense Environmental Awards: Eglin Air Force Base, Natural Resources Team"; Carlton Ward Jr., "Bombing Range Is National Example for Wildlife Conservation," *National Geographic Blog*, April 1, 2015, https://blog.nationalgeographic.org/2015/04/01/bombing-range-is-national-example-for-wildlife-conservation/ (accessed July 8, 2016); Richard J. Blaustein, "Biodiversity Hotspot: The Florida Panhandle," *BioScience* 58, no. 9 (October 2008): 784–790; Way, *Conserving Southern Longleaf*, 172–199; Mansavage, *Natural Defense*, 36–46, 94–98.

to Eglin but have become the new norm at installations across the United States, where fostering environmental sustainability has become conscious decision rather than a happenstance.

CONCLUSIONS

Innovations in military technology revolutionized the strategy and tactics unleashed to wage World War II. These new ways of war, and the mammoth US fighting force that executed them, required large expanses of land to train and perfect military maneuvers. During the conflict, the military's ready access to the quantity and quality of land it needed for defense plants, weapons testing, and troop training proved a substantial, and often forgotten, asset to the American war effort.[59] Immediately after the war, the armed forces returned some of the surplus leased property to its former owners or tenants. However, defense agencies retained most of the permanent installations they had established on purchased properties and on large expanses of land transferred or leased from the federal public domain. The majority of land the military kept, both leased and purchased, was located in southern and western Sunbelt states where weather, topography, and isolation offered favorable conditions for military activities. While mobilization for World War II rejuvenated the entire US economy, it also radically transformed the South and West and facilitated the creation of today's Sunbelt.

The environmental vestiges of World War II defense land acquisition manifested immediately and persisted over decades. When the military first procured new land, it altered the prevailing land uses and as a result, changed landscapes. Intense military use during World War II and the Cold War, coupled with limited environmental and waste disposal knowledge and laws, created significant soil, air, and water contamination. The development of environmental science and the statutes that followed, and later waves of base closures, revealed a toxic legacy of poor ecological practices on military installations. Numerous congressional investigations, news media exposés, and scholarly works have detailed the enduring impact of the military's improper waste disposal methods, use of uncontrolled toxic materials, inadequate fuel storage facilities, and unexploded ordnance hazards.[60]

Beginning in the early 1970s, Congress has required that all the military services comply with modern environmental regulations on currently active military installations. Although much work remains, decommissioned

---

[59] Lee, *Acquisition and Use of Land*, 4–5.   [60] See note 6.

installations have undergone extensive remediation efforts and are being repurposed as economic development districts, wildlife refuges, and recreational areas. A lesser-known sequel to the military's procurement of vast amounts of land for World War II is the current-day, vigorous maintenance of ecologically diverse habitats for more than 550 threatened and endangered plants and animals on more than 25 million acres of active military land in the United States. After decades of adversely impacting the land, the Department of Defense is slowly and unevenly emerging as an unexpected agent of environmental restoration and conservation while still sustaining its training areas and ranges for military use.[61]

---

[61] US Department of Defense, "Base Structure Report: Fiscal Year 2015 Baseline," 14–15; NatureServe, "Species at Risk on Department of Defense Lands: 2014 Updated Analysis, Report, and Maps," February 2015-Legacy Project 14–772, iii–iv, 10; Department of Defense Natural Resources Program, factsheet "Species at Risk on DoD Lands," August 2016.

PART II

MILITARY MATERIALS I (METALS AND ENERGY)

3

"Tanks Are Born Underground"

Mining and World War II

Kent Curtis

A WAR OF METALS

One of the essential material realities of the World War II military conflict was the overwhelming flow of metals.

We can see the central reality of metals at all scales of the war. Young American men jumping into the frigid ocean off Omaha Beach on the morning of June 6, 1944, to give one of the more well-known battlefield examples, faced waves of machine-gun fire and pulses of artillery. They were keenly aware of the deadly, hurling metal all around them. "When I landed on Omaha Beach and hit that sand, I got behind any obstacle I could," remembered Felix Branham. "Guys would try to get behind stones as big as coconuts, anything you could get behind, maybe even as small as a baseball. You'd try to keep the bullets away. They were firing at us with everything. I dare say we were on the beach an hour and a half with bullets flying. Bullets nicked off of my helmet. One went through my ammo belt."[1] Almost 1,500 Americans were killed at Omaha Beach that morning, and twice as many were wounded, bodies pierced by high speed metal and explosive minerals. At Omaha, the most storied of the five beachheads, almost everything went wrong that morning, leaving most of the first two waves of soldiers sitting ducks for the well-armed German defenses. "Men burdened with equipment and explosives were excellent targets for enemy fire as they unloaded in water often several feet deep," reported the army on the tragedy six months later. The surviving

[1] Felix Branham, "The True Story from Felix Branham," https://imgur.com/gallery/oDVv PIV (accessed September 30, 2018).

American soldiers experienced the terror described by Branham, the primal fear of machine guns pinning them down in open territory – metal spraying like rain across vast stretches of space. Once these soldiers secured the beach, they began to reverse the flow of metals, in the form of the tanks, machines, and armaments unloaded onto the beach ready for service.[2]

While the flow of metals initially felt one-sided against Americans at Omaha Beach on D-Day, the four other beaches targeted for invasion along 45 miles of the Normandy coast that day saw metals moving quickly in the other direction, right into the guts of German defenses. British and Canadian battalions landed men, tanks, machines, field weapons, and piles upon piles of ammunition, rockets, artillery shells, and grenades at Gold, Juno, and Sword Beaches, 25 miles east of Omaha. The American Fourth Infantry experienced similar luck at Utah Beach, 20 miles to the west of Omaha. Operation Overlord, as the invasion had been code named, was designed to land the war materials quickly enough to prevent a German resupply and counterattack. At the direction of the Allied Commanders, the Cotentin peninsula had become a modern war zone, a highly planned and highly constructed space in which large groups of armed men would kill each other with the best weapons and strategies they can muster. In the case of World War II, this meant mustering a great deal of metal.[3]

The assaults along the beaches of Normandy represented the most disposable end of an intensive metals-based assault strategy. Out in the near-shore waters, steel barrels of all sizes mounted on gunships directed metal projectiles, often containing dangerous explosives and shrapnel, at high speeds toward enemy soldiers and positions as steadily and accurately as possible. Overhead aluminum airplanes delivered steel-encapsulated explosives and mineralized firestorms to defensive positions and dropped well-armed soldiers behind enemy lines. On the seas, enormous steel vessels reinforced to withstand assault ferried soldiers and machine guns and weapons and ammunition to the conflict theater. All this fixed war capital created nimble ocean, land, and air mobility and was made possible by internal combustion engines – steel blocks containing a complex tangles of components made of steel and copper alloys.

[2] *Omaha Beachhead: (6 June–13 June 1944)*, American Forces in Action Series, No. 7 (Historical Division: War Department, 1945), 43.
[3] Ibid., 28–38.

This strategy put more metal everywhere. "One striking difference between this war and the previous one," editors of the *Engineering and Mining Journal* noted, "is the greater amount of metal now needed per man in the armed forces."[4] Indeed, each soldier had been assigned about 20 pounds of metal-dependent war materials. They strapped a pound and a half of bullet and shrapnel repellent steel to their heads. They also carried a nine-pound semiautomatic rifle containing metal parts made of about five pounds of various alloys of steel and copper. Capable of emptying an eight-cartridge magazine as quickly as the trigger could be pulled, the semiautomatic rifle gave American soldiers the advantage of moving metal more quickly into the battlefield conflict. Each soldier also carried another eight pounds of iron, copper, and lead alloyed cartridges in belts slung across their shoulders or wrapped around their waists. They carried a pound and half of steel in the spade attached to a backpack in which food rations were sealed in about a half-pound of tin. Another pound or two of iron and lead alloys were fabricated into the hand grenades attached to most of their belts, riveted with ounces of brass and steel. Those soldiers assigned communication roles often carried another 30 to 40 pounds of copper and iron alloys in radio equipment.[5]

The overall volume of metal-fabricated war materials generated is staggering. Between 1939 and 1945, the United States produced 42 trillion rounds of small arms ammunition,[6] 22 million Hadfield steel helmets, 6.5 million rifles, 6 million carbines, 2.7 million machine guns, and half a million bazooka rocket launchers to fire the 15 million bazooka rockets they made. In addition to the 20 pounds of metal carried by each individual soldier, each of the battalions also brought seemingly unlimited supplies of additional ammunition, rockets, bombs, and mortars that they moved with motorized trucks (2.5 million in all), tanks (200,000), and aircraft (500,000).[7] They also hauled along cannons, large howitzers, and

---

4 "Metal Mining – No. 1 Industry," *E&MJ* 143, no. 1 (January 1942): 31.
5 Bureau of Mines and the US Geological Survey, *Mineral Resources of the United States* (Washington, DC: Bureau of Mines, 1948), 52–56, 77–81, 93–99, 116–126, 130–133, 198–202.
6 To put some perspective on how many bullets this represents, a single person firing a World War II Garand semiautomatic rifle (if they did not have to change cartridges every eight bullets) would require more than 500 years of steady firing to run out of bullets.
7 By contrast, the entire commercial airline fleet in the United States in 2016 was more than 7,000, with about 5,000 flying each day. Aeroweb, "US Commercial Aircraft Fleet 2017: Number of Aircraft by Model, Type, Manufacturer, and Airline," www.fi-aeroweb.com/US-Commercial-Aircraft-Fleet.html (accessed January 27, 2017).

antitank weapons, to say nothing of the massive flotilla of ships (100,000), which were carrying more guns, cannons, and artillery, including those mounted on the ships, along with stores of ammunition.[8]

Alloys helped to create the special qualities – hardness, durability, heat resistance, strength – that would be fabricated into ships, airplanes, tanks, engines, guns, rockets, bombs, munitions.[9] Iron forms the bulk of material, but the industrial age had demanded new material qualities not found in pure iron.[10] Very small quantities of ferro-alloys like manganese, chromite, and tungsten were added to iron to create material much more suitable for the needs of capital-intensive production and, as it turned out, capital-intensive warfare. A small addition of manganese, for example, decreased iron's brittleness and increased its hardness without additional processing. With 13 percent manganese, steel became bulletproof. Known as "Hadfield steel," this material was pressed into the M-1 helmets whose bullet-repelling abilities saved the lives of countless soldiers, including Felix Branham. A small addition of chromite gave iron the ability to withstand sudden steep increases in heat and stress without changing shape or losing tensile strength. It was a key component in the internal engine valves and pistons powering the vehicles entering France on D-Day, as well as the 1.5 million M-1 Garand rifle barrels with which American soldiers would eventually overwhelm the German defenses. Tungsten added to iron hardened and increased its durability, making it a critical material for the machine tools that helped men fabricate all the war supplies as well as for armor-piercing shells. The alloys combined

[8] John Davis Morgan, "The Domestic Mining Industry of the United States in World War II: A Critical Study of the Economic Mobilization of the Mineral Base of National Power" (PhD diss., Pennsylvania State College, 1948), 36–40. The output of the US War Production Program from July 1940 to July 1945 is summarized in R. Elberton Smith, *The Army and Economic Mobilization* (Washington, DC: Office of the Chief of Military History, Department of the Army, 1959), 203.

[9] Shadia Jamil Ikhmayies et al., *Characterization of Minerals, Metals, and Materials 2016: Proceedings of a Symposium Sponsored by the Materials Characterization Committee of the Extraction and Processing Division of the Minerals, Metals & Materials Society (TMS) Held during TMS 2016, 145th Annual Meeting & Exhibition, February 14–18, 2016* (Hoboken, NJ: Wiley, 2016); Erik Lassner and Wolf-Dieter Schubert, *Tungsten: Properties, Chemistry, Technology of the Element, Alloys, and Chemical Compounds* (New York: Kluwer Academic/Plenum Publishers, 1999).

[10] Pure iron is not naturally suited for the stresses, intensity, and high-energy wear of modern warfare. Iron, and even oxidized steel, is generally brittle, easily worn, and can be fractured by heat. Until the nineteenth century, the traditional method to strengthen steel was heat stress, a hammer on an anvil pounding red-hot iron, which was far too slow and energy inefficient for mass production purposes.

TABLE 3.1 *Total percentage of metals used by the United States in World War II*

Metal	Percentage used
Iron	94.5
Copper	2.54
Lead	1.03
Chromite	0.85
Manganese	1.02
Antimony	0.04
Tungsten	8.06×10^{-6}

Source: Morgan, *The Domestic Mining Industry of the United States in World War II*, 47, 61, 67, 81, 83, 88, 115, and 118.

represented just more than 2 percent of the metal content of weaponry, but, without them, all of the iron in the world wouldn't have been sufficient for the fight (see Table 3.1).

The other major industrial metal – contributing as much volume as lead (bullets and batteries) and the alloys combined – was copper. Combined with tin, it became tough, springy brass, which provided the perfect combination of bounce and durability needed for the bullet casings that would help propel lead-antimony bullets out of rifles. But pure copper was also essential for its conductivity. The Interior Department referred to copper in 1942 as "literally the nervous system of a warring nation." Pure copper was "the *sine qua non* of communications."[11] The author might have added that, without copper wiring, the tens of millions of internal combustion engines mobilizing tanks, trucks, airplanes, and ships could not deliver an electric spark to the vaporized gasoline whose explosion generated the energy of mobility. The role of lead in bullets and batteries cannot be overstated either.[12]

Cumulatively during the war, the US military consumed 827 million tons of iron, 22 million tons of copper, 9 million tons of lead, 9 million tons of manganese, 8 million tons of chromite, 300 thousand tons of antimony, and 70 tons of tungsten. In total more than 110 million cubic yards of metal, enough material to fill ten football-field-sized rectangles

---

[11] US Department of the Interior, *The War Program of the Department of the Interior* (Washington, DC: Department of Interior, 1942), 33.

[12] Dave "Leather" Draper, "Electronic Ignition," June 2005, www.jetav8r.com/Vision/Igni tion/CDI.html (accessed August 5, 2019).

almost one mile high. This impressive volume of war metals, comprised of 94 percent iron, 3 percent copper, 1 percent each lead, manganese, and chromite, and less than 1 percent antimony and tungsten combined, represented the relative percentage of mineral consumption for an advanced industrialized economy generally, leaving only aluminum (a newcomer during World War II), whose production volume began well below that of antimony at the outset but exceeded that of lead during the peak production years of 1943–1945, off the list.[13]

This incredible volume of ore set the United States apart from other combatants and represented a critical part of their strategy in the war. All parties to the conflict brought abundant metals to the battlefield, but in the end the Allied forces, led by US war production, produced more weapons, vehicles, bombs, and rockets and sent more waves of men with more motorized vehicles and weapons, assisted by fleets of fighting ships and air armadas, sufficient to wear down and eventually annihilate the very well-armed German and Japanese military forces.[14] "[T]he sheer quantity of American resources," declared historian Alfred Eckes, "would overwhelm the Axis."[15] According to military historian Robert Patterson, the Allies brought a "scale far surpassing that of the Axis powers." Whether the scale of material *by itself* explains the ultimate victory of Allied forces in World War II remains a contentious issue among military historians, but no one denies that an abundance of metals in particular defined this conflict unlike any that had come before.[16]

---

[13] The estimate are summaries of production data in Morgan, *The Domestic Mining Industry of the United States in World War II*, 47, 61, 67, 81, 83, 87, 88, and 115. According to the planning department, most of the steel was used in high-explosive shells. I will not address the sudden rise of the bauxite/aluminum industry. Its story tacks closely to the development of inexpensive electrical power along the Columbia River.

[14] As Maj. General Orlando Wood put it, "the battle of quantity was won." Orlando Wood, "Foreword" to Constance McLaughlin Green, Harry C. Thomson and Peter C. Roots, *The Ordnance Department: Planning Munitions for War, The United States Army in World War II: The Technical Services*, ed. Kent Roberts Greenfield (Washington DC: Center of Military History, US Army, 1990), vii.

[15] Alfred E. Eckes, *The United States and the Global Struggle for Minerals* (Austin: University of Texas Press, 1979), 90.

[16] This notion that Allied abundance explains Allied victory has been challenged by some military historians, including Peter Mansoor. See Richard Overy, *Why the Allies Won* (New York: W. W. Norton, 1995), John Sloan Brown, *Draftee Division: The 88th Infantry Division in World War II* (Lexington: University of Kentucky Press, 2014), Kitt Bond, *When the Odds Were Even* (Novato, CA: Presidio Press, 2006) and Peter Mansoor, *The GI Offensive in Europe* (Lawrence: University of Kansas Press, 1999).

A METALS ECONOMY

World War II was a war of abundant metals because, for all of the nations engaged in the conflict, modern nation-state economic growth had been built atop a growing set of metal production and fabrication practices.

Access to mineral resources had been critical to the post-1870 production acceleration, accompanying the widespread application of fossil fuel energy. Together they correlated large increases in metal output in the primary industrializing regions of Europe, North America, and Asia, launching what has been called the "second" industrial revolution. In all cases, this flurry of activity had grown atop an abundance of raw materials whose production, movement – and, within a few major industries like steel, copper, and oil – allocation was increasingly centralized through large management hierarchies, allowing unprecedented efficiencies through coordination and communication along the length of the supply chain. The institutional reorganizations and expansion of control by large capital-investing corporate institutions remade the industrialized regions of the world into powerhouses of economic production. Their key strategy in this effort was to centralize coordination of the supply chain of the nation's key natural resources including metals. The efficiencies achieved through coordination facilitated historic increases in material growth through a steady increase in material output at lower per unit costs. No nation's mineral production accelerated as quickly and broadly as that of the United States, but Great Britain and several European nations maintained access to enough raw material at a sufficient rate to keep pace per capita.[17]

Rapid industrial growth translated directly into unprecedented increases in material demand – more wood, more fiber, more food, and more minerals over and above the natural demand increase accompanying population growth. Some of these resources were products of the organic natural world and were (at least in theory) renewable. A conservation and preservation movement had emerged in the United States at the end of the nineteenth century to manage forest and water resources; agriculture would receive its own attention in the 1930s. But *mineral* resources were nonrenewable and, as a result, presented an altogether different set of conservation problems. Unlike trees, wheat, corn, cotton, or wool, which grow back, mineral deposits are permanently depleted in

[17] Alfred Chandler, *The Visible Hand: The Managerial Revolution in American Business* (Cambridge, MA: Belknap Press of Harvard University Press, 1977).

their exploitation. In an expanding industrialized economy, the finite quantities of metal meant a growing appetite for what would necessarily become an ever-scarcer resource. Mineral deposits also presented a more complicated difficulty than just being nonrenewable: they were naturally invisible. Ore was buried in the earth, so it could only be evaluated through excavation and removal. Because the natural processes depositing ore were stochastic, representing the random reordering of the chaotic material substrata comprising the planet, the actual extent of any ore discovered was only as dependable as what could be seen. Both layers of uncertainty could be mitigated through careful prospecting and systematic mine development, but these were extremely costly endeavors and had led to a general concentration of mining activities into very large, highly capitalized oligopolies by the early years of the twentieth century.[18]

Another absolute fact of mineral exploitation was the unequal distribution of mineral materials globally. A set of determined realities had taken place long before humans emerged on earth. The geological origin of ores puts them into an entirely distinct scale of time from human history. They are the results of geomorphology unfolding over millions of years within events taking tens and hundreds of millions of years to occur. From our foreshortened perspective, they are a permanent trace buried in specific places. For this reason, unlike crops and livestock, which are mobile, ores are only available where they were left millions of years ago. The United States uncovered significant deposits of mineral resources during the nineteenth century in its eastern and western mountains. Great Britain possessed an abundance of coal and copper. Germany possessed iron and coal but squabbled with France and Poland over ownership. Russia possessed an enormous eastern frontier mirroring the United States' West. Each of the leading industrialized nations began with some favorable level of domestic resources on which to begin metals-based developments.[19]

While most of the industrialized nations launched their new economies based on large domestic deposits, or on deposits within geographies under their control, the acceleration of growth and the growing diversity of demand after the 1880s soon outstripped their abilities to find everything they needed within their existing domestic economy. Such conditions

[18] See Kent A. Curtis, *Gambling on Ore: The Nature of Metal Mining in the United States, 1865–1910* (Boulder: University Press of Colorado, 2013).
[19] Colin J. Dixon, *Atlas of Economic Mineral Deposits* (Ithaca, NY: Cornell University Press, 1979).

increased pressure on industrialized nations to develop favorable trade relationships, or enforce heavy-handed colonial relationships, with places that contained needed minerals. Through the end of the nineteenth century and into the twentieth, this established a new and much more perilous set of international arrangements, what Eric Hobsbawm has called a "global empire." For Hobsbawm, this empire was comprised of a few large core nations that exercised colonial control over weaker peripheral states and regions. But, from the perspective of supply-chain dependability, these new relationships meant that core industries in the leading nations were becoming more materially dependent upon increasingly uncertain and difficult to access mineral resources from afar. But because of the growing demand for a greater diversity of scarcer domestic resources, the question of access to minerals would become one of the most critical for industrialized and industrializing national economies in the 30 years between 1880 and the strategic alliances that led to World War I.[20]

Between the 1880s and the 1910s, men of finance and capital worked out these challenges in a generally open market economy within which they sought to access and trade minerals and metals on a global scale. *Laissez faire* liberal capitalism allowed the engine of industrial demand to determine the direction of raw material development, and nation-states followed the lead of industry in developing foreign relationships that created access to materials not produced domestically. But with the onset of World War I, nation-states suddenly found themselves concerned with metal production. In the United States in particular, World War I served to highlight and expose the critical web of interdependencies and potential scarcities lying at the heart of modern mass production system. "[T]he world faced a scramble for raw materials," historian Alfred Eckes reported about the breakdown of the global system of trade in those years. Deeply committed to free-market economics, US war planners allowed prices to rise according to demand throughout the war. This policy created a disastrous level of overcapacity, particularly in large fixed capital investments like mining industries, when the war ended. The high prices encouraged many mining operations to exhaust all of their known ore reserves during the war boom, depleting domestic supplies.[21]

---

[20] Eric J. Hobsbawm, *The Age of Empire, 1875–1914* (New York: Pantheon, 1987). Eckes, *Global Struggle*.

[21] Eckes, *Global Struggle*, see especially chapters 1 and 2. K. Leith and D. M. Liddel, *The Mineral Resources of the United States and Its Capacity for Production* (Washington, DC: National Resources Committee, 1936), 25. Eckes, *Global Struggle*, 25–55.

US war industries successfully engaged mass production to produce armaments and ammunition for World War I. However, government and business planners depended too much on flawed assumptions that would hamper the long-term prospects of the US mining industry: that there was a natural abundance of ore to be recovered, that increased demand would lead to new prospecting discoveries, and that free markets were the best way to balance supply and demand during war emergencies. Wartime demand drove up prices sufficiently to encourage the exploitation of low-grade ores not otherwise economical to mine, but this merely further reduced already-scarce strategic US resources. More importantly, war-time demand exposed planners to the web of global mineral dependencies lurking behind mass production. No single nation could go it alone materially. "No one of us lives through a single day without in some way getting help from all the other continents," William Redfield wrote in his popular 1926 book, *Dependent America*.[22] Planners saw this, but after 1918 national economies nevertheless returned to the prewar path of nationalist economic competition amid international material interdependency. The failure to address these mineral uncertainties in the wake of the Great War left in place volatile international interdependencies and the potential for a reignited international conflict.[23]

JOHN KENNETH LEITH AND A GLOBAL ECONOMIC GEOLOGY

Modern mass-production economies had gained access to the combination of mineral resources through domestic developments and foreign relations. The need to sustain a steady flow of raw materials as modern mass production consumed ever-greater volumes of goods necessitated a growing set of sometimes fragile international relationships that exposed supply chains to geographic and political risks beyond their domestic control.

Few people understood the breadth and depth of the global mineral interdependencies better than John Kenneth Leith. Leith had been a student of Charles Van Hise, the founder and first director of the University of Wisconsin's Geology Department and a leading conservation figure in the early twentieth century. Together the men had pioneered

---

[22] William C. Redfield, *Dependent America: A Study of the Economic Bases of Our International Relations* (Boston and New York: Houghton Mifflin Company, 1926), 13.
[23] Richard Overy, "Raw and Synthetic Materials," in *Oxford Companion to World War II* (New York: Oxford University Press, 2001), 727–730.

the study of economic geology, which was part science and part commerce. The goal was to learn strategies for overcoming the layers of uncertainty about ore deposits, and to increase the geographical scope of economically valuable geological knowledge. Van Hise and Leith had focused specifically on iron ore deposits in most of their private consulting work, but they had also come to know a great deal about the global patterns of mineral deposition generally. This knowledge had made Leith valuable during World War I, when he had been a mineral advisor to President Woodrow Wilson. He had also joined the administration at the Paris peace talks in 1919, only to be marginalized and sidelined first by Wilson's more abstract agenda and then by the failure of the League of Nations in Congress back home. He returned to the university and the lucrative private consulting work his status, knowledge, and connections provided.[24]

Like many careful observers, Leith walked away from the horrors of World War I believing that the combination of industrial might and nation-state self-preservation had been both a cause and a critical factor in the carnage of the European conflict. When industrialized states sought to secure access to scarce or finite resources, the resulting conflicts were also industrialized. Men like Leith and Woodrow Wilson sought new international institutions and new policy strategies to address the unique new resource challenges embedded in the modern economy. From these experiences, Leith began to assemble an understanding of global mineral resources that would inform his vision until the rumblings of World War II forced him to rethink and improvise a new strategy for the United States under the duress of expediency.[25]

In 1925, Leith summed up the best professional knowledge about the tensions and dangers inherent in the existing structure of nation-states' interdependencies in an article published in *Foreign Affairs*, "The Political Control of Mineral Resources." In his article, Leith called for new global policies around mineral resources that better reflected the growing dependencies of industrial and industrializing economies on mineral resources in underdeveloped regions. Two realities informed Leith's overall argument. The first was that global mineral consumption had increased at an unprecedented rate since the early twentieth century. "The world has used more of its mineral resources in the last twenty

---

[24] Sylvia Wallace McGrath, *Charles Kenneth Leith: Scientific Advisor* (Madison: University of Wisconsin Press, 1971), especially 95–110.
[25] Ibid.

years," Leith pointed out in 1925, "than *in all preceding time*, and there is nothing to indicate any slackening of the acceleration." Alongside this historic growth in consumption had emerged the geographic fact that all of the minerals needed for modern industrial life were not abundant in the core nations. Iron and coal were concentrated in the United States, England, and parts of Germany and France, he wrote. More pressing and more complicated were the deposits of the ferroalloys, the key minerals needed in the production of industrial quality iron and steel and the same trace alloys needed for warfare. These were spread across the world, concentrated in more than a dozen different states and regions, each with varying levels of economic development.[26]

A rapid breakdown of this web of material movement and exchange had quickly escalated conditions prior to World War I. Leith pointed out that the critical and diverse interdependencies created high risks in times of international conflict. He estimated that three-quarters of the entire global mineral production took place in a mere 30 major locations. A large share was moving internationally, with "nearly a third of the world's mineral tonnage mov[ing] across international boundaries."[27] Moreover, Leith noted that it was extremely unlikely that any new major ore discoveries would appear. In other words, by 1925, the geography of global mineral deposits, if not their exact extent, was fairly well known. Based on these circumstances, Leith called on the United States and Great Britain to found an international body designed to manage the world's mineral resources to avoid future conflicts. He believed an approach that acknowledged "the basic connection between mineral resources and national prosperity" was needed to ensure and protect existing global mineral resources for all nations, to facilitate the equitable international movement of these resources, and to protect less-developed regions from unfair exploitation practices by stronger powers in need of their resources.[28]

Leith's long experience in economic geology and his global understanding of mineral resources put him in the unique position of seeing the tensions inherent in metal-dependent industrialized nation-states, as well as the perilous conditions already in place. Two unwelcome outcomes appeared to Leith to be impending if an internationalization of mineral resources did not take place. The first was that the leading industrialized

[26] C. K. Leith, "The Political Control of Mineral Resources," *Foreign Affairs* 3, no. 4 (July 1925): 541. My emphasis.
[27] Ibid., 545.   [28] Ibid., 551.

powers would exploit smaller economically and militarily weak nations possessing needed minerals. The second was that leading industrialized nations were bound to engage in conflict in the future over scarce mineral resources. Leith pointed out these new and potentially dangerous interdependencies rooted in the metals-dependent economy, and he created a path forward designed to minimize, if not eliminate, conflict over these resources – cooperation instead of competition, collaboration instead of conflict. But such collaboration would not come to pass; Leith's insights, accurate as they would turn out to be, went unheeded.[29]

Affirming Leith, historian Alfred Eckes suggests nationalistic aggression and the expansionary moves of each of the Axis powers in the 1930s derived from "underlying structural problem" of "the uneven global distribution of raw materials among industrial states."[30] Nation-states with access to minerals, like the United States, England, and France, held a distinct advantage in industrial development over the eventual Axis powers, each of which, for different reasons, was much more alienated from the same. When the global economic depression descended in the 1930s, nations sought to insulate their domestic economies from the global fluctuations. For the future Allies, this meant curtailing exports and quickly securing needed imports based on existing international relationships (including their extensive and exploitative colonial holdings). For the future Axis powers, this meant attaining new territories that provided needed minerals to address resource deficits. Italy's need for coal and oil, for example, helps explain its invasion of Ethiopia. Japan invaded Manchuria to access iron ore. Hitler's *lebensraum* was not just living space for German people, but access to "the raw materials and food basis of our nation."[31] Germany also purchased large amounts of abundant mineral products from the United States, including petroleum, coal, steel, and copper. The soon-to-be aggressor nations built up war machines to support expansionist activities that would allow them a larger degree of mineral autonomy from the then dangerously volatile global economy.[32] Their actions did not emerge out of a vacuum but had roots in genuine material needs.[33]

---

[29] McGrath, *Charles Kenneth Leith*, 160–176.   [30] Eckes, *Global Struggle, 58.*

[31] Berenice A. Carroll, *Design for Total War: Arms and Economics in the Third Reich* (The Hague: Mouton, 1968), 103.

[32] Eckes, *Global Struggle*. See especially chapter 3, "Minerals and the Origins of World War II," 57–88. Overy, "Raw and Synthetic Materials," 727.

[33] Tyler Priest, *Global Gambits: Big Steel and the US Quest for Manganese*, International History Series (Westport, CT: Greenwood/Praeger Press, 2003), 147.

Everything leading industrialized nations needed to know about the perils that precipitated conflict in the middle of the twentieth century had been anticipated by Leith in 1925, and probably understood by him during, if not before, World War I. But nation-states that have successfully consolidated power through the development of a metals supply chain were not going to willingly give up any advantage. For all the frequent claims of Anglo supremacy in leadership that echoed down the nineteenth and into the twentieth centuries, at this critical moment, with global economic power and leadership and a very public vision describing the necessary path, neither the United States nor Great Britain displayed the political leadership to engage in the difficult global policy making needed to avert future international conflict.

CREATING THE STOCKPILE

By the time Leith was called back into public service in 1939, the opportunity for the internationalization of minerals was long gone. Countries had consolidated control over the resources they still held and leading economies were enmeshed in the Great Depression. "Leith's presence," wrote Alfred Eckes, "gave continuity to the mineral procurement work" from the previous war effort. Leith had also helped undertake a national survey of mineral resources in 1936 as a consultant to Franklin Roosevelt's New Deal Interior Department. The study had revealed that the United States was seriously deficient in key alloys – nickel, tin, antimony, manganese, tungsten, chromite – and its mineral reserves were on a downward trend in the production of iron, copper, lead, and zinc ores. If the United States hoped to engage in production levels similar to those experienced in the 1920s, it was going to have to lean heavily on other nations for much of its critical strategic material. "These minerals are all necessities and our dependence upon foreign suppliers either now or in the very near future must be recognized," Leith had implored at the time.[34]

When the war began in Europe in 1939, Leith was asked to be a member of a mineral procurement planning team. In the face of the impending need for a wide variety of alloys for war production, Leith suggested that the United States begin buying ahead of need, purchasing as much strategic raw ore as was available anywhere at a reasonable price up to an amount equaling the production demand of a two-front war for

---

[34] Leith and Liddell, *The Mineral Resources of the United States*, 2.

one year. Large mineral processing facilities like Anaconda's Washoe Works in Montana or the Kennecott Garfield Smelter in Salt Lake City each had practiced stockpiling of ores for years, always seeking to mine or purchase raw ore well ahead of its reduction to metal. The stockpile, in effect, created a buffer against the uncertainties of raw ore production, insuring that processing technologies always had adequate ore on hand to maintain steady production. Because transportation of ore during wartime, especially on the seas, was fraught with danger, the most logical strategy was to purchase as much of this foreign material as could be had at any given time at a certain pace ahead of need and store it domestically in case of emergency.

This time Congress listened to Leith's recommendations. In the summer of 1939 Congress codified Leith's core mineral policy recommendation in the Strategic Minerals Act. The act called for the purchase and storage of $100 million in strategic minerals with the goal of building and maintaining a store of strategic material large enough to sustain a multifront war for an entire year. The stockpile meant that in the possible but unlikely event that the United States got cut off from trade routes for any reason, it would have an ability to keep fighting for a length of time. The concept was accepted, but in 1939 the price was still considered too high. Congress only appropriated $10 million of the $100 million budget. Appropriations would grow in 1940 and take over the domestic minerals economy by the second half of 1941.[35]

More importantly, the 1939 Act also created brand new roles for the US Geological Survey (USGS) and the Bureau of Mines (BoM). Previously operating as data centers and aggregators of privately produced knowledge, the act placed them on the front lines of both knowledge production and resource development. It also expanded their work internationally. To help ensure the production of critical strategic minerals bound for the strategic reserves, as well as into the military production flow, the agencies were empowered to prospect, finance, and develop opportunities for strategic mineral production. The new duties included a new geographical scope: the agencies were empowered (and encouraged) to expand this work overseas – particularly into Central and South America, as well as in southern Africa and Asia. They also acquired a budget to build and

---

[35] "Latest List of Strategic and Critical Materials," *E&MJ* 143, no. 1 (January 1942): 71. The top seven strategic metals listed (since January 30, 1940) were, in alphabetical order, antimony, chromium, manganese, mercury, nickel, tin, and tungsten.

operate testing facilities and to pilot sampling plants and test new processing technologies.[36]

The combined efforts of the empowered USGS and BoM identified,
catalogued, verified, and offered support to more than 200 producing
mines for iron, copper, lead, antimony, zinc, manganese, and tungsten
across 30 states during the war. Domestically, the mineral prospecting
and development industry received more sustained public dollars in
government-funded investigations than at any time in its history. The
BoM had encouraged increased motorization of iron extracting in the
Minnesota Iron Range, for example, to increase the volume of raw output
for efficiencies of scale. When trucks replaced railroads in open pit mines,
companies could also be nimble and fine-tune their responses to the
vagaries of ore deposits.[37] The BoM took core samples in each of the
mining regions in every mining state in the nation. It also financed
processing plants, like ASARCO's huge zinc plant in Amarillo, Texas or
the exclusive manganese ore–processing facility in Anaconda, Montana.
The former was to work newly imported zinc ores for the war effort; the
latter worked ores ordinarily discarded by the Anaconda Copper Company. Elsewhere, the BoM developed an unsuccessful chrome smelting
experiment using Oregon and Montana ores to demonstrate the potential
for domestic chrome production. Throughout the war, similar efforts
were undertaken across the West. The *Engineering and Mining Journal*
celebrated the passage of the Strategic Minerals Act in early 1940, noting
the $500,000 appropriation to be provided to the BoM and USGS for
"investigation" by which "a broad program of reconnaissance and
exploration was inaugurated by the two government bureaus." The
United States spent hundreds of thousands of dollars seeking sources of
domestic and foreign ores for the metal-hungry war production effort. It
was "the greatest search for metals ever undertaken by the [Geological]
Survey," the *Journal* reported.[38]

---

[36] Historian Gerald Nash, in his widely read study, *World War II and the American West:
   Reshaping the Economy* (Lincoln: University of Nebraska Press, 1990), claimed that
   federal and military planners had ignored the domestic mining industry in favor of
   imported ores and that the only reason World War II did not boost mining the same
   way World War I had was a lack of will on the part of Congress to protect domestic
   mining industry. In fact, nothing could be further from the truth.

[37] According to the editors, "During the 1940 season several of the independent operators
   will use trucks in all mining operations." In "The Use of Trucks in Iron Mines," *E&MJ*
   141, no. 1 (January 1940): 79.

[38] "Editorial," *E&MJ* 141, no. 7 (July 1940): 49; "Editorial," *E&MJ* 144, no. 11
   (1943) : 127.

Every month during the early years of preparation the *Engineering and Mining Journal* brought reports from the field of federal prospecting and discovery. By December 1939, the BoM and USGS had surveyed seven sites in six western states – Oregon, Nevada (two times), Montana, Idaho, Wyoming – in all cases seeking metal alloys deposits, mostly chromium and tungsten, but also antimony. The processes involved building roads into mountains with bulldozers, clearing large strips of forest where ore lodes were expected, bulldozing deep trenches to the bed rock, drilling deep into the rock with diamond drills, and extracting the core material to send off to a government lab for sampling. The 1940 report was typical, including a range of activities from opening new lodes and testing old lodes to encouraging the development of private holdings.

The Geological Survey and Bureau of Mines data led to the exploration of the important San Manuel copper deposits north of Tucson, Arizona, where the Magma Company blocked out more than 425 million tons of 0.8 percent copper ore, containing some gold, silver, and molybdenum. And near Salem, Oregon, the Bureau of Mines found a substantial body of cobalt-copper ore. In central Idaho private operators developed the nation's principal supply of tungsten and largest source of antimony based on initial studies done in the Department of Interior.[39]

Across the mining regions of the United States, old claims came back to life upon solid knowledge of ore deposits made by new drilling techniques and the careful consideration of topographical and geological clues by the teams of federal experts. Others were abandoned forever by the same processes of scientific evaluation.[40]

Probably the most important work accomplished by the federal agencies working in tandem with private interests and producers during the war was the development of new mass-processing techniques for low-grade ores found in nineteenth-century tailings and twentieth-century ore lodes. None of the major industrial metals escaped these concerns. Iron producers, who continued to hold substantial deposits of rich ore, began to work lower grade deposits ahead of the complete exhaustion of higher grade, in an effort to extend the life of their holdings. By 1943, dump

---

[39] Eckes, *Global Struggle*, 114.

[40] Ibid. Also see Donald H. McLaughlin, "Government's Role in a National Mineral Policy," *Mining Engineering* 1, no. 4 (April 1949): 43–47. Charles F. Jackson, "In Quest of Strategic Mineral Supplies: Bureau and Survey Cooperate in Investigating Potential Mineral Resources," *E&MJ* 140, no. 12 (December 1939): 43–46.

trucks and conveyor belts replaced trains in the open cut iron pits across the Lake Superior region.[41] Major iron producers also found the need to add an additional sorting technique to their large plants. In these operations, pulverized iron and mill tailings would be worked through grinders and screens, first using gravity, and then using floatation to increase the ore content sufficient to allow preliminary smelting.[42] The industry press had been suggesting such improvements to operators in the iron, copper, and lead industries since the 1930s, but the impetus of the war encouraged widespread and concerted attention to the low-grade material left in the mines and left as waste by older, less efficient mining techniques.[43] Experimental plants in Texas, Montana, Idaho, and California each tested different strategies for beneficiation or floatation techniques. The floatation technique is somewhat misnamed. It is, in reality, a froth-enhanced chemical separation technique in which pulverized rock material containing trace amounts of ore is put into a chemical solution and agitated to a froth with giant metal blades. The frothy oily admixture, which chemically attracts the ore, leaves the waste rock to drop to the bottom of the tanks. The ore-saturated foam is swept from the top and sent through dryers, where it is formed into firing bricks for smelting. Each ore compound required different chemical signatures for the technique to work, and the core work of these experimental plants was to determine effective techniques for specific ores.[44] This work helped to identify appropriate chemical admixtures for different ore types and to perfect floatation strategies for the different materials and chemical reactions, increasing the economic potential of a whole new class of low-grade ore. As early as 1942, the industry reported that floatation methods "studied in laboratory pilot plants by private companies and the Bureau

[41] "Iron Ore Goes to War," *E&MJ* 144, no. 8 (1943): 76–77.
[42] Joseph Rudolph, "Iron-Ore Beneficiation," *E&MJ* 141, no. 2 (February 1940): 83–84. E. W. Davis, "The Iron Country," *E&MJ* 142, no. 8 (August 1941): 148.
[43] T. B. Counselman, "Dollars in Current Tailings of Mesabi Washing Plants: An Estimate of Profits Now Lost in Cases Where the Use of Floatation Might Increase Recovery," *E&MJ* 140, no. 4 (April 1939): 34–36. See also "Watson Trucks Advertisement," *E&MJ* 145, no. 3 (March 1944): 4.
[44] "Mineral Field Studies," *E&MJ* 140, no. 9 (September 1939): 70–72. Charles F. Jackson, "In Quest of Strategic Mineral Supplies: Bureau and Survey Cooperate in Investigating Potential Mineral Resources," *E&MJ* 140, no. 12 (December 1939): 43–46. Edmund S. Leaver, "The Laboratory Part in Strategic Mineral Projects: Reno Experiment Station of the United States Bureau of Mines Completed 4,580 Analyses and Tests on Samples Received in the Fourth Quarter of 1939 from the Investigation under Way." *E&MJ* 141, no. 2 (February 1940): 33–35.

of Mines are now being successfully employed in commercial production on an increasing scale."[45]

While these efforts combined to squeeze more ore out of existing low-grade domestic deposits, despite every effort, they were not able to meet wartime needs completely in any metal but iron. Some metals, like copper and lead, were simply on a decline in output. Other metals, including critical alloys like manganese, chromium, tungsten, and antimony, would have to be significantly or entirely sourced from overseas. Thus, based on the inability of domestic sources to completely satisfy the estimated production needs for a wartime economy, "[f]or the first time in its history, the United States Geological Survey [would] go outside the United States in search of deposits of strategic minerals as part of the defense program."[46] During 1939 and 1940, USGS and BoM explorations in Bolivia, Brazil, and Mexico determined that sufficient iron, tin, copper, and some manganese ore could be provisioned from these regions for war demand, and Congress was asked to appropriate additional funds to support such developments. With these emerging economic ties, Congress also decided to secure all the Western Hemisphere and, in late 1940, declared it off-limits to German and Japanese trade – a declaration that could only be enforced by bluster and espionage. Nevertheless, within months Japan expanded its control over Indochina and the Philippines and Germany moved onto the Scandinavian peninsula, both efforts to secure strategic reserves of war minerals.[47]

As might be expected, the quest for strategic metals transformed US relationships with countries in South and Central America, as the United States sent its federal geologists and mining engineers into the nations in those regions to find replacement minerals for the Asian Pacific suppliers of critical alloys. By 1939, Chilean copper ore represented almost one-third of all copper ore smelted annually in the United States; additional copper production was cultivated in northern Mexico, adding to this import total. Before the United States entered the war, Brazil had also become a source of iron ore, offsetting losses from China. The Department

[45] "Mine Equipment," *E&MJ* 143, no. 2 (February 1942): 97. V. H. Gottschalk, "The Uncommon Metals: Most of Them Required for Emergency Program," *E&MJ* 143, no. 2 (February 1942): 89–90. Gottschalk mentions new BoM-operated pilot and sample plants for manganese, tungsten, and chromium in Nevada, South Dakota, and Colorado.

[46] "Strategic Surveys," *E&MJ* 141, no. 7 (July 1940): 70.

[47] S. E. Lavrov, "Indo-China and Its Mineral Wealth," *E&MJ* 142, no. 1 (January 1941): 53–57. There is an excellent map of Indochina's mineral resources on p. 55.

of Interior began institutionalizing their international mission in these years. "A small group of Interior's Geological Survey and Bureau of Mines personnel ventured to Latin America, Africa, and Asia to help develop mineral reserves as part of the State Department's Interdepartmental Committee on Scientific and Cultural Cooperation that funded the nascent form of technical assistance to Latin American countries in the Institute of Inter-American affairs."[48] The agencies made contacts, assessed production, and transferred dollars while frequently worrying about Nazi competition. They worked throughout the war, assuming access to production output throughout the Caribbean, Central America, and South America. In Mexico, these activities led to mutual distrust, with the Mexican state asserting its sovereignty whenever it felt US officials were too forceful. In Bolivia, the state was much more amenable and sought an ore contract in early 1942. Contracts and developments were also established to import Brazilian manganese and iron, Cuban manganese, Bolivian tungsten and tin, Mexican antimony and copper, and Chilean copper and other trace metals.[49]

The infusion of cash and security from the United States and an interest in rapid development served wartime metal ore needs but also facilitated excessive violence. Between 1939 and 1942 United States annual investments in Bolivian tin – a critical component in brass – grew from $804,000 to $41 million. Bolivian laborers, who had been recruited at poverty wages, were asked to meet nearly impossible output targets and went on strike, asking for better wages and improved working conditions. The Bolivian government suggested to US foreign officials that these strikers were being paid and influenced by Nazi propagandists. US officials looked the other way when Bolivian government forces violently put down the strike, killing as many as 400 workers in the process.

Despite these foreign interventions and all the reasonable domestic encouragement they could muster, ore managers could never achieve even a one-year stockpile of the needed strategic materials.[50]

While the experienced Leith had become a guiding hand, most government planners (and the entire mining industry) were initially unwilling to believe that American natural resources would not be sufficient and all sides had to engage in a "feasibility dispute" out of which military

[48] Megan Black, "Interior's Exterior: The State, Mining Companies, and Resource Ideologies in the Four Point Program," *Diplomatic History* 40, no. 1 (January 2016): 83.
[49] Eckes, *Global Struggle*, 99–102.
[50] Ibid., 103–111. McGrath, *Charles Kenneth Leith*, 195.

ambitions were reconciled to American production realities. The outcome was a mine-to-producer, materials tracking system by which planners would reward domestic producers for overproduction to ensure adequate domestic allocations to meet the war demands. In other words, by the time the United States entered the war, it had developed a demand system that controlled prices and exceeded immediate production needs by a significant enough margin to assure access to sufficient ores and metals under the conditions of uncertainty inherent in mineral production. Alongside the system, USGS and BoM, under the quiet guidance of Charles Leith, had mapped and identified sources for many of the needed mineral ores both domestically and internationally, and were carefully tracking their production. Knowing more about supply and demand and supply chain networks in this way, however – even with the successful provisioning of a two-front war kicked into high gear in 1944 – left planners more uncertain than ever.

SCARCITY AMIDST ABUNDANCE

Given the sudden acceleration and scale of the economy that helped to produce an Allied victory in World War II, it comes as a surprise to learn that war material planners, and especially those concerned with metals for war production, experienced anxious feelings of scarcity prior to, during, and even after the war. From their perspective, ample material to assure victory in World War II was never a forgone conclusion. They found that they could not always identify sufficient minerals and metals in the quantities that they wanted, and not once were any of the strategic stockpiles sufficiently stocked. The buildup to mid-1944 and the successful invasion of Europe left mining industry experts giddy at their success and already planning for postwar surpluses by the fall of that year. But when Germany and Japan had continued to resist well into winter 1945, the most clear-headed among them recognized that such a level of production could not sustain itself indefinitely, or even, perhaps, past the end of the new year.

Because of a careful and meticulous accounting and large built-in demand buffers (stockpiles), war producers could confidently churn out war goods at a predetermined rate without experiencing any significant material shortages. During 1943 and 1944, after the four-year windup in preparation, producers coasted on this planning bubble. But for planners and far-sighted industry experts who could view the entire supply chain as a dynamic metabolic process designed to produce this planning bubble over time out of a nonrenewable, stochastic natural resource, the experience was fraught with peril. In addition to witnessing a shrinking domestic copper ore production, iron, lead, and zinc were also increasing output on the back of ever-lower grades of ore. As a result, the volume of foreign ore imports grew steadily in these years. Particularly troubling was the expanding list of strategic metals for which US domestic production was either too small or nonexistent, and so sources had to be found elsewhere, necessitating shipment over dangerous and uncertain transportation routes. Thus, deep in the heart of the United States' World War II saturation strategy, planners watched as mineral supply uncertainties grew like a cancer.[51]

Leith's recommendation to stockpile ores followed the older mining tradition of miners excavating more than enough ore to pay for processing before building a smelter. The simple fact of mine production was that one never knew how much ore a mine held without accessing and extracting that ore to the surface, which then depleted the mine. It creates a kind of material irony, where one's perception of their mine was based on something it no longer contained. To overcome the certain depletion of all veins at an uncertain point in the future, as well as to defend against potential strikes in the mines, sustained inclement weather, or other random chaos, large processing facilities maintained a significant surplus of workable ore to use if necessary to keep production on schedule. The practice of stockpiling gave ore processors and metal producers normative control over the flow of raw metals and alloys by always mining more than was needed. Leith had seen and approved of these levels of control in the private economy, and under the duress of expediency he adopted the same strategy on behalf of war production for the United States.

These practices created two sets of production goals for the Interior agencies, one that met the immediate needs of the military, including the production of forces of overwhelming abundance in munitions and technology, and another that sought to store a two-year stockpile of raw ore. Together these goals represented an ore and metal acquisition target three times larger than the war effort alone.

At the heart of the war of metal abundance, mineral policy had embedded the profound and unavoidable *experience* of scarcity. Stockpiling created in effect a permanent nation-state demand for a surplus of low-cost high-grade material and engaged the federal bureaucracies, at

---

[51] Eckes, *Global Struggle*, 102–103. McGrath, *Charles Kenneth Leith*, 167–197.

the behest of military readiness, to confront the ongoing uncertainties that accompany mineral exploitation. The stockpiles of ore provided a cushion against which production could lean if raw materials were otherwise scarce in the market. It allowed bullets and bombs to made without cease. But the legislative requirements to have material on hand for an extended conflict were never achieved for any of the growing list of strategic metals – not during the war, not after the war. For those charged with fulfilling this requirement, there emerged a nagging sense that the United States did not have access to and might never store enough mineral resources. The policy cultivated a sense of scarcity about ore reserves at the same time it maintained a generally abundant output of metals.

In 1948, the USGS and the Department of the Interior copublished the results of its five-year study of US mineral resources during the war. Their assessment was that because of lack of planning after experiences of scarcity in World War I, and because of the rise of a consumptive middle class in the 1920s, the United States went into World War II materially ill-prepared. "The United States learned in the First World War that it was deficient in several essential metals and minerals, and the tremendous growth in annual rates of consumption since then has aggravated these deficiencies," the authors wrote. As "the foundation that supports [the United States'] great industrial economy, making possible a high standard of living and its present leading position in world affairs," metals acquisition was no small matter. But mineral resources were "exhaustible" and "mineral wealth has been depleting at an ever-increasing rate." The report estimated that there had been a 22-fold increase in metal consumption in the United States since 1880 and warned that "the difficulties of obtaining adequate mineral supplies during the recent war emphasize the exhaustible nature of mineral resources."[52]

Indeed, their own data emphasized the growing scarcity of mineral resources. In 1939, mineral resource planners initially identified seven "strategic minerals" for which insufficient domestic resources already existed. Based on residual knowledge from World War I, this list included antimony, chromium, manganese, mercury, nickel, tin, and tungsten. These were all critical war materials. Antimony, alloyed with lead, hardens the soft metal for bullets. It also enhances conductivity in batteries. Mercury, a material highly sensitive to changes in temperature and air pressure, improved the accuracy of measuring devices. The rest were iron

---

[52] Bureau of Mines and the US Geological Survey, *Mineral Resources of the United States* (Washington, DC: Bureau of Mines, 1948), 1, 3, 7.

alloys that added either hardness or durability to steel products. By the end of the war the study had "amassed more data on mineral deposits than had ever before been assembled." By 1948, mineral planners had expanded this list to include a total of *thirty-nine commodity metals* in which the United States was facing serious domestic shortages if not outright absences. World War II, they concluded, "demonstrated weaknesses in the nation's mineral position and emphasized the need for doing something about it."[53]

World War II marked a new stage in the American state's management and control of natural resources, which had begun a half-century earlier around forests and wildlife, extending nation-state interests to the identification and acquisition of mineral ores in the service of war production. But the American state did not seek to understand and control resources in a vacuum. They stepped into trying to manage a natural resource unevenly distributed around the world, at a time when their domestic production was experiencing declining reserves, and in the midst of a geopolitical conflict rooted in both the geography and ultimate scarcity of a natural resource. The results both defined the battlefields of World War II and created the outlines of a new geopolitical order where understanding and control of a vast set of mineral resources became crucial to nation-state maintenance for the standoff of superpowers that descended into the Cold War.

INTO THE COLD WAR

By the late 1930s, when the prospect of war became a growing reality, neither endlessly abundant domestic mineral resources nor sufficient access to adequate foreign supplies of alloys had existed as operable realities. The exhaustion of most of the United States' richest ore deposits and the economic exhaustion created by the Great Depression had left American mining in shambles. The volumes of material ultimately brought to bear by Allied forces against the Germans and Japanese was in no way a given when hostilities broke out in Europe in 1939. It had resulted from a new approach to nation-state control of mineral resources, which was a careful understanding of the nature of mineral ores by the state apparatus for the first time. Indeed, only after Germany had made its expansionist, militaristic intentions clear did the United States expand its environmental management capacity to include the

[53] Ibid.

careful attention to and even management of mineral resources. But without the sudden promise of an infusion of cash and the technical support by mining experts, the domestic industry would not have recovered from its Depression low.[54]

US stockpiling goals, which made good geopolitical sense in an uncertain world under assault by larger militarized nation-states, left the USGS and BoM with a deep fear about mineral scarcity. They had never met and were not on track to meet the stockpiling goals. Moreover, as the postwar euphoria ground into a new Cold War fear, the importance of trying to maintain those stockpiles and being prepared for another war continued to press on material planners in the USGS and the BoM. World War II failed to fully resolve the nagging mineral uncertainties that had shaped geopolitical relationships among industrialized nations through half a century of growth and military conflict. Instead, the relationships between two of the largest Allies – the Soviet Union, which had contributed more human life to the war than any other single nation, and the United States, which had done the same with military goods – deteriorated into a series of territorial standoffs, more often than not related to strategic mineral resources.

Following the war, Truman embedded the stockpiling mission into the emergent National Security State. Mining and mineral production of key strategic materials was thus elevated to a level of national security. "The strategic minerals stockpiling program, expanded in 1946 and again after 1947 by the National Security Resources Board (NSRD) in the interdepartmental munitions board – both set up under the 1947 National Security Act – with advice from the state department and mining experts, was designed to make up for the US deficiency in minerals." In other words, the mission first blazed by USGS and BoM engineers and bureaucrats during World War II, lived on into the Cold War, with the security state directing the environmental management state to identify, access, and exploit mineral deposits around the world. Institutions like Eximbank, which dominated mineral investments in South America, came into existence precisely to ease the way. "Eximbank lending to Latin America facilitated US access to strategic minerals."[55]

[54] Wright, "American Economic Success"; Bureau of Mines and the US Geological Survey, *Mineral Resources of the United States*, 1947.

[55] Tyler Priest, "Banking on Development: Brazil in the United States' Search for Strategic Minerals, 1945–1953," *The International History Review* 21, no. 2 (June 1999): 297–330. Quotations from 305–306 and 330.

Tension and conflict over the intention of Interior agents, who neither achieved their stockpile quotas nor stimulated new domestic mining in the United States, began to blend with more general doubts about the loyalty of many New Deal–era State Department employees by the emergent anticommunist mission of the security agencies. These uncertainties bubbled to the surface in hearings in 1953, out of which would also come a report about material scarcity. "[T]he testimony received by the committee has revealed a shocking shortage of certain strategic and critical materials in the national stockpile."[56] The implication by the congressional inquisitors was that Interior's inability to create the required volume of ore on hand was part of a larger conspiracy to enrich foreign nations and deny American producers the opportunity to gain from the ongoing military demand for strategic metals. "We have become dependent upon foreign nations across one or both oceans for many of the materials without which we cannot fight a war or support our economic structure," one congressman complained. Meanwhile, American mills sat idle and once-productive mines went unworked, he continued. Without the perspective of men like Charles Kenneth Leith, who retired to Wisconsin after the war, congressional representatives could only see these circumstances through the eyes of their constituents, who felt neglected. Their choice to understand the situation as a conspiracy was perhaps more calculated. But the shortages were indisputable. Stockpiles were supposed to have reached capacity by 1951, but the deadline was pushed back to 1953 and then to 1958. As Leith could have told them, they would be pushed back indefinitely; that was the nature of ore production. But they never asked him.[57]

This failure to meet quotas over time raised suspicions of more conservative congressmembers, making them more willing to believe conspiracies about potential plots against the United States from within. During a congressional hearing in 1953, some members went so far as to suggest that it was State Department policy "which culminated in the dependencies on foreign sources of essential material."[58] Without a clear understanding of the complexities and scarcities related to mineral production in the United States, nor any interest in knowing how international markets in minerals worked, these members of Congress assumed a

---

[56] US Senate, Committee on Interior and Insular Affairs, *Stockpile and Accessibility of Strategic and Critical Materials to the United States in Time of War* (Washington, DC: Government Printing Office, 1953), part 10, 2.
[57] Ibid., 2   [58] Ibid., 3.

perfect and available supply of domestic ores whose access was hindered by political means alone.

This was coupled with the troubling fact that most known high-grade ore deposits had been significantly depleted, forcing mineral processers to use an increasingly lower grade of ore, more output, and creating therefore a larger mining and material processing footprint.[59]

The production innovations developed to address the low-grade American ores in the face of high wartime demand turned out to be extremely utilitarian in American and global mining well into the twenty-first century. Planners and economic geologists were absolutely correct that global high-grade ore deposits were exhausted, and the likelihood of a new find was very low. But the ore quality was only part of the mining equation. The cost of the metal output could be kept low with low grade ores by initiating technologies of mass production. For minerals, this included a new scale of production and new processing techniques. Not just iron mines, but copper, and lead, and other non-ferrous metals were now harvested through open-cutting techniques. "Mass destruction," in Tim LeCain's provocative description, where explosives blow off overburden and pulverize ore seams, which are loaded by enormous mobile bucket loaders onto huge dump trucks, which ferry the material to extensive conveyor belts to deliver the rocky material to sorters and into floatation mills, after which it will be rendered into an orelike material of sufficient metal content to afford smelting. Despite its apparent absolute limits as a natural material (mineral ore is deposited and unchanging), it turned out that automation and economies of scale could increase the value of deposits by lowering mining costs. A wave of automation and new bulk reduction methods began to return US output of iron, copper, zinc, and lead to a growth phase in the 1950s and 1960s, one that ultimately exceeded prewar outputs several times over. This meant that mineral processing industries were grinding through exponentially larger volumes of lower and lower grade metal-bearing material, leaving behind millions of acres of open pits and growing mountains of increasingly toxic tailings, which would become the lion's share of EPA Superfund "megasites" in the twenty-first century.[60]

---

[59] See Timothy J. LeCain, *Mass Destruction: The Men and Giant Mines the Wired America and Scarred the Planet* (New Brunswick, NJ: Rutgers University Press, 2009).

[60] Committee on Superfund Site Assessment and Remediation in the Coeur d'Alene River Basin, *Superfund and Mining Megasites* (Washington, DC: National Research Council, 2005).

The experience of scarcity and the ongoing efforts to prevent it were not just embedded in the planning motives in the Interior Department and Department of Defense, or used as fodder in a brewing ideological war, they also appear to have trickled up into a new set of broader cultural anxieties. BoM experts began to help American producers exploit lower and lower grade minerals, thereby increasing domestic output throughout the 1950s and 1960s. Yet a rhetoric of declining resources emerged at the same time, along with rising science-skepticism in the wake of the use of nuclear weapons. Potential scarcity became a recurrent trope within the neo-Malthusian thread of the late-twentieth-century environmental movement. Where war planners and economic geologists could calculate market demand, estimate global reserves, and anticipate both acute and eventual long-term scarcities of raw materials, the neo-Mathusians saw the ever-growing demand from population growth chewing ever more rapidly through finite resources. The sense of scarcity emerging from the close tracking of ore production by World War II planners had morphed into apocalyptic claims of impending scarcity for the planet and the potential end of civilization as we know it.[61]

Meanwhile, real scarcity of strategic resources continued to shape the hot parts of the Cold War. Based on known mining methods and known global deposits in the middle 1920s, Leith had warned of impending mineral scarcity and heightened competition between industrial nation-states whose mineral appetites would only grow at the same time rate that resources would diminish. His warning went unheeded, and the resulting resource frictions helped to precipitate World War II. Throughout the war, the United States, perhaps more than any other of the warring nations, committed its environmental management state apparatus (in the guise of the USGS and the BoM) to the work of finding and encouraging the exploitation of strategic minerals. As the war gave way to the Cold War, the same activities became part of the security state mission and mapped the geography of Cold War–era conflicts – Korea, Vietnam, Afghanistan, Chile, Bolivia, Cuba, and parts of Africa – all revolved in part around access to key strategic minerals.

"To procure ore men have wandered far and wide, and thus while the introduction of metal induced a more rapid concentration at the heart of the civilized mass, it caused a proportionate expansion at the

---

[61] See, for example, Paul Ehrlich, *The Population Bomb: Population Control or Race to Oblivion* (New York: Ballantine Books, 1970).

circumference," Brooks Adams wrote in 1903.[62] It would be no less true as the United States emerged into empire status after World War II. The geography, rhythm, and rhetoric of mining came to dominate the foreign policy, land-use policy, and cultural vision of United States during the 1950s and 1960s. This should come as no surprise; the same increased volume of metal per soldier that marked World War II continued in civil society. Today, the average American consumes about 350 pounds of metal a year. One of the essential realities of the world built since World War II is the overwhelming flow of metals, a flow controlled through the concerted attention of nation-states, including the United States.

In a recent RadioLab podcast, Jad Abumrad discussed his initial confusion about the Marvel Comics X-Men character Magneto in a way that frames the importance of metal in today's world. He didn't get it, Jad said. All the other X-Men had such cool powers – elasticity, fire, strength – but all Magneto could do was make metal do what he wanted. But then Abumrad watched the power at work and realized that Magneto "has the best power. Because the whole world is made of metal, he can control the world."[63]

---

[62] Brooke Adams, *The New Empire* (New York: MacMillan, 1903), 3.

[63] Jad Abumrad and Robert Krulwich, "More Perfect – One Nation, Under Money," podcast audio, *Radiolab,* January 31, 2018, www.wnycstudios.org/podcasts/radiolab/podcasts/7 (accessed August 5, 2019).

4

Fueling the "American Century"

Establishing the US Petroleum Imperative

Brian Black

> We must be the great arsenal of democracy.... I have the profound conviction that the American people are now determined to put forth a mightier effort than they have ever yet made to increase our production of all the implements of defense, to meet the threat to our democratic faith.
>
> – President Franklin Delano Roosevelt, December 29, 1940[1]

Americans proudly streamed to the 1939 World's Fair in New York City as World War II flared on the other side of the Atlantic. Not yet part of the conflict, Americans used the opportunity to escape the present and wax utopian. Although the dreams on display took many forms, they were synched together by an invisible hand – more specifically, by a basic assumption – concealed within each of the scenes: bountiful supplies of cheap energy.

Novelist E. L. Doctorow provides one of the most revealing descriptions of one of the fair's best-known attractions:

We rode across the Bridge of Wheels and got out, of course, at the General Motors Building. That was everyone's first stop.... In front of us a whole world lit up, as if we were flying over it, the most fantastic sight I had ever seen, an entire city of the future, with skyscrapers and fourteen-lane highways, real little cars moving on them at different speeds, the center for the higher speeds, the lanes on the edge for the lower.... This miniature world demonstrated how everything was planned.... It was a toy that any child in the world would want to own. You could play with it forever ... it was a model world.[2]

---

[1] Julian E. Zelizer, *Arsenal of Democracy: The Politics of National Security – From World War II to the War on Terrorism* (New York: Basic Books, 2010), 1–2.
[2] E. L. Doctorow, *World's Fair* (New York: Random House, 2007), 252–253.

Inside GM's Futurama, five million visitors rode on the "Magic Motorways" exhibit, which had been designed by Norman Bel Geddes, that led to the "Town of Tomorrow." Details of reality – such as grocery stores and gas stations – were left out of the vision, but the nation still grew abuzz with the futuristic glimpses, such as the flying sedans found on the model expressways of Ford's "Road of Tomorrow." Although the dream world clearly possessed iconic aspects that resonated for generations, its greatest appeal may have been its vision of a world in which basic aspects of everyday life occurred easily – encumbering consumers with neither care nor attention. Foremost among these unnecessary details, was the energy that made it all go – no mention of its source, method of acquisition, or the environmental implications of its rending. With their basic needs met in such a future, humans might occupy themselves with greater challenges or endless diversion.

Although utopian ideas grew distant from the minds of Americans once the nation entered the fighting in 1941, by the conclusion of World War II a basic regulative infrastructure had taken shape that all but assured an American future similar to the "Town of Tomorrow."[3] As President Franklin Roosevelt had forecasted, American industry powered the Allied war effort and dreams such as those seen in "Futurama" combined, by 1950, with the urgency of the Cold War to extend the "arsenal of democracy," eventually to be renamed the "military-industrial complex," beyond wartime. The United States set a new bar for the standards of human life, as mass consumption influenced patterns of everyday living from home heating to food preparation and from personal transportation to information exchange. Modern chemistry used raw materials, such as petroleum and coal or the energy made from them, to radically alter the basic materials and practices of everyday life. Many "hidden hands" allowed for this expansion; however, none was more essential than cheap energy (see Table 4.1).

As historian John G. Clark writes:

In the twentieth century, societies learned that modernization – urbanization, industrialization, and attendant socio-political change – did not come automatically but had to be planned and worked for. Efficient energy systems were fundamental to the process, indeed, modernization could not occur without them.[4]

Domestically, energy, particularly petroleum for transportation, was the common thread that enabled the formation of the postwar consumer

---

[3] See, for instance, Robert Rydell, *Designing Tomorrow* (New Haven, CT: Yale University of Press, 2010).
[4] Ibid., 2.

TABLE 4.1 *National-regional shares of world primary energy production.*
The period between 1925 and 1965 shows the dramatic shift in energy
production during the World War II era

	1925	1938	1950	1965
USA	49	39	44	31
Western Europe	34	32	19	10
USSR	2	9	11	18
Middle East	<1	1	5	11
Latin America	3	4	6	7
Eastern Europe	4	5	7	6
All others	7	10	8	17

Source: Adapted from John G. Clark, *The Political Economy of World Energy* (Chapel Hill:
University of North Carolina Press, 1990), 102.

landscape and lifestyle.[5] When the United States worked after the war to
reconstruct Western Europe and Japan, it also used the opportunity to
dictate global energy flows (see Table 4.2).[6]

For instance, when the United States transitioned to using more petroleum at home by 1950, it continued to mine coal but now sent it abroad as
an export. It was the domestic consumption of petroleum per person,
though, that proved to be truly transformative, rising after 1945 from less
than 10 to 20 BTUs in 1960, 40 in 1975, and more than 40 after 2000.[7]
A general high-energy existence for developed nations emerged as a
primary outcome of World War II; indeed, as we shall see, this insatiable
appetite for energy only grew in the face of competition between
developed nations.

As examined by other essays in this volume, environmental history
often concerns impacts on human health or on the environment; however,
larger patterns of resource management also constitute an important
avenue of inquiry for the field.[8] Energy is one of the basic exchanges that

[5] During the war, primary commercial energy use rose in the United States by 25 percent.
The trend continued in postwar America, when from 1950 to 1960 energy use rose by 55
percent.

[6] John G. Clark, *The Political Economy of World Energy* (Chapel Hill: University of North
Carolina Press, 1990), 99.

[7] These data are found in US Energy Information Administration, *Annual Energy Review
2009* (Washington, DC: US Energy Information Administration, 2009), xx.

[8] For more information on energy and environmental history, see, for instance, Brian Black
"Energizing Environmental History," in *A Field on Fire: The Future of Environmental
History*, ed. Mark D. Hersey and Ted Steinberg (Birmingham: University of Alabama
Press, 2018), 85–99.

TABLE 4.2 *Annual production of fuels in the United States, 1926–1950*

	Bituminous coal (million tons)	Anthracite coal (million tons)	Crude oil (million barrels)	Natural gas (billion cubic feet)
1926	573	84	771	1,336
1927	518	80	901	1,471
1928	501	75	901	1,596
1929	535	74	1007	1,952
1930	468	69	898	1,979
1931	382	60	851	1,722
1932	310	50	785	1,594
1933	334	50	906	1,597
1934	359	57	908	1,816
1935	372	52	997	1,969
1936	439	55	1,100	2,225
1937	446	52	1,279	2,473
1938	349	46	1,214	2,358
1939	395	51	1,265	2,538
1940	461	51	1,353	2,734
1941	514	56	1,402	2,894
1942	583	60	1,387	3,146
1943	590	61	1,506	3,516
1944	620	64	1,678	3,815
1945	578	55	1,714	4,042
1946	534	61	1,744	4,153
1947	631	57	1,857	4,582
1948	600	57	2,020	5,148
1949	438	43	1,842	5,420
1950	516	44	1,974	6,282

Source: Adapted from John G. Clark, *Energy and the Federal Government: Fossil Fuel Policies, 1900–1946* (Urbana: University of Illinois Press, 1987), 144. The production end of an energy transition within fossil fuels usage is reflected in this data. The primary change, however, was in overall energy capacity.

humans possess with the natural environment, and as energy historians seek to better illuminate and understand transitions in prime sources of power (often referred to as prime movers), none may be as striking as the shift to a high-energy existence during the mid-twentieth century. In general, the high-energy existence that defines what geologists and others now refer to as "the Anthropocene" after 1950 began during the interwar years, expanding widely during the 1920s and slowing during the worst of the Depression before accelerating once again just prior to the outbreak of World War II.[9] The definitive shift, however, occurred during World War II, when combatant nations committed substantial resources to securing fuel supplies sufficient to fight an industrial conflict. Every great power exerted extensive intervention in energy production and innovation.[10] This supplements the common assumption that it was America's domestic consumption that fueled the transition to a petroleum addiction. Set against the imperative for national security during World War II, the consumptive world of Tupperware, Hula Hoops, and Hemi engines becomes only a façade atop America's emerging ecology of oil.

Although energy made consumers' lives simpler, its use by the military fell into a different category entirely. Energy sources such as petroleum became the lifeblood of military forces and received their own administrative infrastructure at the highest levels of government during World War II.[11] The postwar era energy expansion is credited by historians such John R. McNeill and Robert Marks as the origin of the "great acceleration" in world history that defines the current "Anthropocene" epoch, when human impact takes on global ecological implications.[12]

PRIME MOVERS AND NATIONAL SECURITY

During and after World War I, energy production grew mostly from fossil fuels – coal and, ultimately, petroleum. When utilized in vehicles and ships, in fact, petroleum brought flexibility that powered new types of weapons – certainly a basic strategic and operational advantage. Within a few decades of its adoption for use in military equipment, oil and its acquisition took on the spirit of an international arms race. Even more significantly, the international corporations that harvested oil throughout the world acquired a level of significance heretofore extremely rare among other industries, earning the label "Big Oil." By the 1920s, Big Oil's product – unknown just decades prior – had become the lifeblood of national security to the United States and Great Britain. And from the start of this transition, the massive reserves held in the United States marked a strategic advantage that would last generations – and, indeed, continues today.

As impressive as American domestic oil production was from 1900 to 1920, however, the real revolution occurred on the international scene, as

---

[9] Clark, *The Political Economy*, 52.   [10] Ibid., 95–97.

[11] For a discussion of this terminology, see Joseph A. Pratt, *Exxon: Transforming Energy, 1973–2005* (Austin: Briscoe Center for American History University of Texas, 2013).

[12] John R. McNeill, *Something New under the Sun* (New York: Free Press, 2001); Robert Marks, *The Making of the Modern World* (New York: Rowman and Littlefield, 2007).

European powers used corporations, such as Shell, British Petroleum, and others, to begin extracting oil globally.[13] Colonialism became a primary method for securing access to petroleum, especially in the Middle East and Pacific regions. Remapping global geography based on resource supply, of course, was not new; however, doing so specifically for sources of energy sources was a striking change. The words of the young British First Lord of the Admiralty, Winston Churchill, reflected energy's new-found importance just prior to World War I:

As a coal ship used up her coal, increasingly large number of men had to be taken, if necessary from the guns, to shovel the coal from remote and inconvenient bunkers to bunkers nearer to the furnaces or to the furnaces themselves, thus weakening the fighting efficiency of the ship perhaps at the most critical moment in the battle.... The use of oil made it possible in every type of vessel to have more gun-power and more speed for less cost.[14]

By 1912 the new technology and policies had been put in place and, as Churchill recorded, in the world's greatest navy, "the supreme ships of the Navy, on which our life depended, were fed by oil and could only be fed by oil." Churchill and Britain's military leaders emphasized the great benefits for British naval superiority; however, their decision also marked a defining moment for a new era of the culture of petroleum. By association, committing the Royal Navy to petroleum meant that a consistent and reliable supply of petroleum had just become a national security imperative, making oil one of the most important commodities on Earth because the security of nations depended on petroleum reserves. By association, any nation wishing to compete with Great Britain had to follow suit. Naval power no longer relied on wind available to all or bulky and inefficient coal; now, oil was the key to military power.

The immediate needs of the World War I battlefield expanded experiments with the widespread use of petroleum and, specifically, the adoption of the internal combustion engine to power military equipment. The Great War was a transitional conflict, and the trucks, tanks, planes, and other petroleum-powered vehicles that emerged on its battlefields would profoundly alter the future of domestic living in the United States after the armistice.[15]

At this time, little knowledge existed about any hazards related to mining, refining, or burning oil. In fact, during this era of expansion in

---

[13] Brian C. Black, *Crude Reality: Petroleum in World History* (New York: Rowman and Littlefield, 2014), 140–141.
[14] Ibid., 156.   [15] Ibid., 125–128.

the petroleum industry, scant attention was applied to issues of environ-mental safety or pollution. Instead, the emphasis focused on reducing waste and on the innovation of new chemical products, such as high-octane fuels and thermo-plastics. Indeed, historian Hugh Gorman stresses that industrial engineers believed that many of these ancillary problems would be overcome through efficiency. From this perspective, he writes, "pollution-causing wastes from industrial facilities would cease to be a problem after they optimized the efficiency with which firms transformed resources into valuable products."[16] In one revealing example during the 1920s, chemists added lead to gasoline to reduce the "engine knock" that plagued many of the early internal combustion engines. Health activist Alice Hamilton and other medical investigators held public hearings to educate the public about the dangers to human health of this additive, which tainted vehicle exhaust. The data revealed a fairly clear, cause-and-effect relationship; however, Americans opted for improving engine per-formance over broader health concerns.[17] Gorman refers to this attitude as the industry's "governing ethic" of the era and during the lead debate the American Petroleum Institute (API) expertly presented it to the public as a positive virtue.[18] The urgency of World War II shifted the emphasis of the industry even further toward the supply imperative.

WORLD WAR II AND A "HIGH-ENERGY" MILITARY STRATEGY

Historian Keith Miller is succinct in his assessment of petroleum's import-ance to World War II when he writes:

The truth is – oil was the indispensable product, in all its forms, to the Allied campaigns around the world. Without it World War Two could never have been won. For oil, once processed or refined in various ways, became the source or indispensable material for laying runways, making toluene (the chief component of TNT) for bombs, the manufacturing of synthetic rubber for tires, and the distilling into gasoline (particularly at 100-octane levels) for use in trucks, tanks, jeeps, and airplanes. And, that is not to mention the need for oil as a lubricant for guns and machinery.[19]

---

[16] Hugh Gorman, *Redefining Efficiency: Pollution Concerns, Regulatory Mechanisms, and Technological Change in the US Petroleum Industry* (Pittsburgh: University of Pittsburgh Press, 2001), 269–271.

[17] See Black, *Crude Reality* and Gorman, *Redefining Efficiency*.

[18] Gorman, *Redefining Efficiency* , 137–149.

[19] Keith Miller, "How Important Was Oil in World War II?," *History News Network*, http://historynewsnetwork.org/article/339 (accessed July 16, 2019).

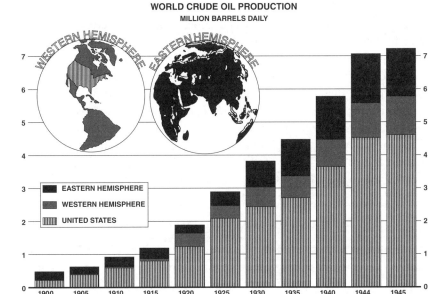

CHART 4.1 World crude oil production. World crude oil production grew rapidly during the early twentieth century.
Source: John W. Frey and H. Chandler Ide, eds., *A History of the Petroleum Administration for War, 1941-1945* (Honolulu, HI: University Press of the Pacific, 2005; reprint from 1946 edition), 172

Given its strategic importance, Daniel Yergin and other scholars refer to World War II as a "war for oil."[20] In particular, although the former World War I Allies had locked up the world's known supply, geologists promised that Saudi Arabia's potential as an oil-producing region was beyond any comprehension (see Chart 4.1).[21]

In general, the need to secure oil became one of the great imperatives among nations involved in the power brokering over the Middle East. This was particularly evident for European nations without their own reserves; however, American leaders refused to overlook US future interests as well. Although the US production of oil in 1941 stood at 64 percent of the world's supply, its consumption of energy had climbed at a similar rate. Even though the American population only grew from 106 to 133 million in the two decades before Pearl Harbor, annual consumption of oil and oil

[20] Daniel Yergin, *The Prize* (New York: Free Press, 2008), 303.
[21] Thomas McCarthy, *Auto Mania* (New Haven, CT: Yale University Press), 34.

products increased from 4.3 to 11.2 barrels per capita. On the eve of the war, writes David Painter, "the first 'Anglo-American petroleum order' had broken down under the impact of depression, world war, and the growing ability and desire of producing countries to control their economic destiny."[22] As each of the future Axis powers confronted its own energy needs, they sought drilling agreements with Saudi Arabia by lavishing its king with gifts and offers of huge payments, while also carrying out military expansion directed at oil producing nations, such as Romania. This early example of geo-political expansion ushered in conflicts over resources that contributed to the outbreak of World War II and in part defined international relations for the rest of the twentieth century.

FUEL FOR JAPANESE IMPERIALISM

Japan's quest for oil fueled the drive toward the resource-rich Dutch East Indies. The United States, which supplied approximately 80 percent of Japan's oil, joined other Western nations in condemning Japan's expansionist attacks on China in the 1930s and its expansion into Southeast Asia after the fall of France in the summer of 1940. In 1937, President Franklin Roosevelt began publicly discussing economic sanctions directed at halting Japanese expansionism. With this threat in the open, Japan tried to find ways of internally rationing petroleum so that it would still be available if the United States cut off its exports to the island nation. On July 2, 1940, Roosevelt signed the National Defense Act after the Wehrmacht overran France. This legislation provided him with the executive privilege to freeze economic activity to hostile nations. In response, Japanese forces pushed deeper into French Indochina to isolate China and position themselves to access additional supplies of crude in the Dutch East Indies if the United States cut off its exports. As American leaders argued over whether to completely cut off Japan's supply of oil, Japanese leaders assumed an embargo would occur. Unwilling to accede to US demands to reverse its expansion in Asia, Japanese military leaders devised a "southern strategy" to seize critical raw materials in the Pacific that would begin with a decisive attack on the US Pacific Fleet at its home base in Pearl Harbor, Hawaii.

Launched from aircraft carriers toward a distant, unprepared fleet at anchor, the Japanese attack on Pearl Harbor was made possible by oil

---

[22] David Painter, *Oil and the American Century* (Baltimore: Johns Hopkins University Press, 1986), 9.

and oil products. Ironically, though, the devastation was not as significant to the US Navy as it might have been with more careful, and thoughtful, planning. The Japanese attack sank or damaged a number of battleships and destroyed nearly two hundred aircraft while killing more than 2,400 US service personnel; however, the US fleet's stored supply of petroleum on Oahu remained largely unscathed, as did its maintenance facilities, its aircraft carriers, and its submarine fleet. Some scholars have credited the failure to target the US Navy's oil storage facilities to oversight; others suggest the opposite – that the Japanese hoped to put the supply to its own use following a full-scale invasion and occupation.[23]

HITLER'S BLITZKRIEG GUZZLES FUEL

Elected in 1933, the same year that Roosevelt came to power in the United States, Hitler's extreme goals and ideas faced practical limits as he implemented his plans.[24] Historians emphasize his diabolical ideas about assuring the success of the German race; however, a critical portion of his vision of an all-powerful Germany derived from what today we might call "energy independence." Synthetic fuels offered German scientists the ability to deliver new forms of energy to the Nazi state. These experiments, though, had begun earlier; in fact, some of them were carried out in the United States. I. G. Farben, the German chemical manufacturer, worked with Standard Oil to experiment with hydrogenation processes that synthetically derived additional fuel from petroleum. In 1931, the leader of I. G. Farben, Carl Bosch, shared the Nobel Prize in chemistry for the development of this important process.

With Hitler in power, such technical innovations became part of the German quest for resource autarky. Whereas the importance of energy resources had led to close relationships between oil companies and the governments in the United States and Great Britain, Hitler's Germany simply made I. G. Farben part of the Nazi state. In each situation, though, leaders identified energy from petroleum as a matter of national security. For Hitler, energy security meant expanding the production of synthetic fuels while also making the seizure of petroleum supplies a primary national security goal.

Hitler's basic military strategy, which Western journalists dubbed blitzkrieg or "lightning war," was organized around short, concentrated battles carried out by a largely foot mobile army with a spearhead of elite mechanized forces. A portion of his desire for rapidity derived from a

[23] Yergin, *The Prize*, 380.   [24] Ibid., 382.

need to secure victory before Germany's petroleum supplies ran out.[25] Although limited petroleum supplies constrained all of the Nazi commanders, General Erwin Rommel's Afrika Korps offensive across the wide expanse of Northern Africa most acutely demonstrates the importance of supply. His advance halted at El Alamein in the summer of 1942 when he outdistanced his logistical lifeline. Allied air and naval attacks on supply convoys crossing the Mediterranean from Italy to Tripoli crippled his lines of communication. In hindsight, Rommel recalled: "The bravest men can do nothing without guns, the guns nothing without plenty of ammunition, and neither guns nor ammunition are of much use in mobile warfare unless there are vehicles with sufficient petrol to haul them around."[26] In addition, Hitler's revolutionary use of rocket technology for attacks on England used devices (primarily manufactured by slave labor) powered by synthetic fuels. The realization of energy's importance had led him to create a formidable military force that ran roughshod over much of Europe from 1939 to 1942.

ALLIES WAGE ECONOMIC WAR THROUGH FUEL SUPPLIES

To defeat the Axis powers, the Allies harnessed their greatest resources, including access to abundant raw materials (with some exceptions, such as rubber), industrial capacity, the courage and innovative spirit of their soldiers, sound strategy, and, of course, a nearly endless-seeming supply of energy. This tremendous advantage was immediately transferred into leverage on the battlefield. At the peak levels of activity, American forces used one hundred times more gasoline in World War II than they had in World War I. Yergin estimates that the typical American division in World War I used 4,000 horsepower per day, while in World War II this rose to 187,000 horsepower per day. In total, the military used more than five hundred different types of products made from oil during World War II.[27] In 1942, US Army planners estimated that each soldier in the field required approximately 67 pounds of supplies and equipment to support him, of which half were petroleum products.[28] To supply this

[25] Henrietta M. Larson et al., *New Horizon: History of Standard Oil Company (New Jersey), 1927–1950* (New York: Harper and Row, 1971), 385.
[26] Ibid., 343.   [27] Ibid., 456.
[28] Ibid., 382. For a more itemized depiction, see "Logistics in World War II: Final Report of the Army Service Forces," https://history.army.mil/html/books/070/70-29/CMH_Pub_70-29.pdf. Many of these items included newly fabricated products, ranging from rubber canteen lids to nylon parachutes.

material and fuel, between 1939 and 1943 US oil consumption shot up by 28 percent.[29]

Although most of the Allies used American crude, the Soviets drew from supplies in Baku that they had started developing in the nineteenth century and then developed further between the wars. Because of growing requirements, oil workers in Baku reached a record level of oil extraction in 1941 – 23.482 million tons. As the hub of the Soviet oil industry, Baku became a prime target for Hitler.[30] His goal was to take the city in 1942 and develop the area's oil resources for export to Western Europe.[31]

On the battlefield, fuels made from petroleum altered nearly every activity. Using 100-octane gasoline, British Spitfires demonstrated a definite advantage over German Bf 109s (burning 87–octane gasoline) in air combat as early as 1940. Created in the United States and treated much like shipments of valuable gold, 100-octane gasoline was shipped through U-boat-infested waters under the strictest secrecy. Therefore, one of the greatest allied resources was the advanced US refining industry that utilized thermal cracking techniques to create fuels, such as 100-octane aviation gasoline, that significantly increased engine performance. Nothing demonstrates this new strategic importance as clearly as the invasion of Normandy. The delivery of fuel supplies presented a major component of the invasion. In fact, once the Allies moved through France, the difficulty facing General George Patton and others was the inability to rapidly transport fuel from the Normandy beaches across France to the front line near the Germany border. The fast-moving Allied armies simply outran their petroleum supplies. Yergin reports:

Down to a half-day supply of gasoline, Patton was furious. He appeared "bellowing like an angry bull," at the headquarters of General Omar Bradley, commander of the American forces. "We'll win your goddam war if you'll keep Third Army going," he roared at Bradley. "Dammit, Brad, just give me 400,000 gallons of gasoline, and I'll put you inside Germany in two days."[32]

In their seminal history of the Standard Oil Company, *New Horizons*, Henrietta Larson and colleagues write simply of World War II: "This was

---

[29] Painter, *Oil and the American Century*, 34.   [30] Yergin, *The Prize*, 387.

[31] Joel Hayward, "Hitler's Quest for Oil: The Impact of Economic Considerations on Military Strategy, 1941–42," *Journal of Strategic Studies*, 18, no. 4 (December 1995): 94–135.

[32] Yergin, *The Prize*, 387. The Wehrmacht, of course, was in even worse shape due to the targeting of German synthetic oil plants by the Eighth US Air Force and the Red Army's overrunning of the Romanian oil fields at Ploesti in the summer of 1944.

a war of mobility and speed, and oil was to supply the driving power."[33]
Even Stalin realized the critical importance of the American oil industry to
the war effort. At a dinner in Tehran in honor of British Prime Minister
Winston Churchill's birthday, Stalin rose to give one of his many toasts,
"This is a war of engines and octanes. I drink to the American auto
industry and the American oil industry."[34] With such strategic importance, oil's careful management had become a matter of national – and
international – security.

MANAGING THE ESSENTIAL ENERGY RESOURCE IN WARTIME

"Conservation" is a term that takes on alternative meanings at different
times in history, depending on variables including supply, waste, and
overproduction. Today, we often emphasize the term to mean limiting
use; however, during World War II, the conservation of energy resources
usually meant the careful *systemization* of supply. Although one aspect of
the domestic public policy to administer petroleum was rationing, federal-
izing its petroleum production and acquisition was the most pronounced
change during the war years. With a new imperative for abundant energy
supplies, the government enacted regulatory and policy methods for
administering critical energy resources during the war and to some degree
continued them afterward. These regulations provided little attention
to environmental or pollution concerns that would eventually become
well-known aspects of energy production and use. Indeed, streamlining
production and distribution stimulated additional use of petroleum across
society and, by extension, intensified the environmental impacts that
scientists would eventually attribute to the burning of fossil fuels.[35]

Unlike solid fuels, such as coal, petroleum received separate, specialized oversight during World War II. The petroleum industry proved much
more responsive to a centralized, structured administration. President
Roosevelt forced the industry into new methods of organization, including systematizing distribution, standardizing products, and even seemingly mundane matters such as using uniformly sized five-gallon gasoline

---

[33] Larson, *New Horizon,* 383.   [34] Yergin, *The Prize,* 364.
[35] The lack of attention to environmental considerations permeated the energy industry of
the mid-twentieth century as the effort for federal regulation was in its infancy. Environmental historians point to the "high energy" existence that compounded the burning of
fossil fuels and spread the use of petroleum throughout the economy as a major cause of
emissions and pollution. The influence of World War II in stimulating such activity
intensified the eventual implications that we now attribute to climate change.

cans – complete with a revolutionary, built-in, nozzle. To oversee these new standards and systems, Roosevelt created the post of Petroleum Coordinator for Defense and moved Secretary of the Interior Harold Ickes to the position. Eventually, this undertaking would become the Petroleum Administration for War (PAW).

One of Ickes's primary tasks was to alter the culture of those leading the petroleum industry, which was entirely organized to create production surpluses. Managing the supplies – conservation – and developing them strategically, it was believed, would better stabilize oil prices. Ickes was charged with obtaining "information as to (a) the military and civilian needs for petroleum and petroleum products and (b) any action proposed which will affect such availability of petroleum and petroleum products."[36] Ickes was viewed suspiciously by many oil companies. They feared that coordinated action would set them up for later difficulties with antitrust law.[37] To overcome this trepidation, Ickes in 1942 selected 72 leaders of America's oil industry for the Petroleum Industry Council for National Defense, which later became known as the Petroleum Industry War Council (PIWC). The first meeting of this group took place on the day after the attack on Pearl Harbor.[38]

The coordination effort involved every aspect of the oil business, with a particular emphasis on supply production and distribution and the manufacture of specific products of strategic military importance. Petroleum, in particular among energy resources, suffered under problems of distribution in the fall of 1941 that "intensified in 1942 and thereafter as the federal government struggled to balance legitimate civilian energy needs against the essential demands of burgeoning war industries."[39] Initially, the recalcitrance of industry insiders remained one of Ickes's primary nemeses – they did not wish to change and they resisted an outsider who sought to advise them. By early 1942, writes Clark, federal authority was paramount:

At one time or another, most sectors of the fuel industries required coercion [to adopt new management practices]. In addition to the imposition of sanctions, the government offered inducements. Whenever possible, the carrot was preferred to the stick, but one or the other was normally necessary.[40]

By 1943, however, Ickes won the support of many sectors of the industry that had grown frustrated by the number of federal agencies "meddling in

[36] Painter, *Oil and the American Century*, 11.   [37] Larson, *New Horizon*, 420.
[38] Harold Ickes, *Fightin' Oil* (New York: Alfred A. Knopf, 1943).
[39] Clark, *The Political Economy*, 320.   [40] Ibid., 317.

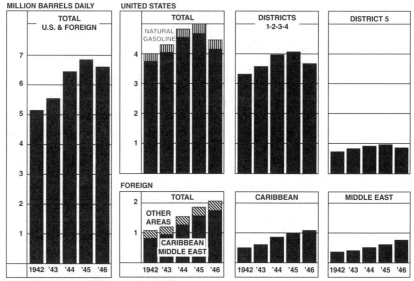

CHART 4.2 Petroleum production – world – excluding Axis and Russian areas. Petroleum production grew in many regions during World War II.
Source: John W. Frey and H. Chandler Ide, eds., *A History of the Petroleum Administration for War, 1941–1945* (Honolulu, HI: University Press of the Pacific, 2005; reprint from 1946 edition), 170

oil affairs." Ickes, at least, was someone with whom the industry could work. Although industry leaders remained wary of federal involvement that might "presage permanent involvement," they opened themselves to Ickes's management ideas.[41] With this acquiescence, the PAW implemented broad restructuring plans for the production, transportation, and refinement of petroleum during the war.

The PAW reported that global production of petroleum swelled from 3.9 million barrels daily (MBD) in 1941 to nearly 7 MBD after 1945 (see Chart 4.2).[42]

During this period, the United States produced at least four MBD and more than five MBD in 1945. The PAW estimated that prewar reserves in

[41] Ibid., 321–324.
[42] John W. Frey and H. Chandler Ide, eds., *A History of the Petroleum Administration for War, 1941–1945* (Washington, DC: Government Printing Office, 1946), 170.

the United States composed 39 percent of the world's supply. In 1941 approximately 50 percent of this production came from the American Southwest, particularly Louisiana, Arkansas, Mississippi, Texas, and New Mexico (see Table 4.3).

This region contributed mightily to the additional production needs during the war years, sending additional production by rail to refineries on the East Coast. Historian Dudley Hughes describes the "boom" of the war years for the South and notes the aggressive role of the federal government: "The government became dictatorial, even questioning the right of each state to manage its own oil business."[43] The production level of the war years exceeded agreements and state standards for "maximum-efficiency-rates." The PAW reported that such strain on supply brought pause to "thoughtful oilmen"; however, "war granted no freedom of choice. The Midwestern producers did what the Nation's needs demanded; they operated the wells at excessive rates, and they sent the crude oil eastward that war plants might turn out the military petroleum products that had to be made."[44]

In the oil fields, extreme measures helped meet the production needs. For instance, Carl Coke Rister writes:

Men and engines worked as a team, the huge ditchers, like waddling monstrous turtles, plowing mile after mile of deep trenches for the twenty-four-inch pipe, over hills, through the swamps of Arkansas, across Missouri and southern Illinois, across rivers and over mountains, until the task was done. Arkansas and Mississippi river floods washed away sections of the pipe, but repairs were hastily made and the work went on.[45]

Efforts were made to maximize the efficiency of technology that was currently in use. Much like soil conservation officers, PAW representatives instructed oil workers on practices based in "conservation," including the encouragement of pressure maintenance by natural or artificial means, repressuring, and the application of secondary recovery

---

[43] Dudley J. Hughes, *Oil in the Deep South: A History of the Oil Business in Mississippi, Alabama, and Florida, 1859–1945* (Jackson: University Press of Mississippi, 1981), 188.

[44] Frey and Ide, *A History of the Petroleum Administration*, 176.

[45] Carl Coke Rister, *Oil! Titan of the Southwest* (Norman: University of Oklahoma Press, 1949), 359–362. Rister also includes a footnote (note 28, p. 362) that reads: "River and large creek crossings were difficult and required separate contracts. Ditchers moved through swampland, as much as fifteen miles on a stretch, roaring and plunging; and tractors followed over corduroyed roads to deliver two-ton joints of pipe to the workmen."

TABLE 4.3 *Annual proved discoveries for United States and PAW districts for indicated year (thousands of barrels)*

Year	District 1	District 2	District 3	District 4	District 5	United States
1900	15,398	22,975	–	205	180,807	219,385
1901	1,016	45,855	172,490	700	614,535	834,596
1902	9,940	–	135,638	5,010	–	150,588
1903	3,450	387,065	155,500	–	29,255	575,270
1904	9,261	258,376	–	–	21,999	289,636
1905	6,572	342,102	152,500	–	–	501,174
1906	1,715	152,313	204,948	285	11,000	370,261
1907	56,987	33,161	–	–	–	90,148
1908	5,345	57,195	110,898	371,242	34,993	579,673
1909	4,565	20,329	–	–	550,000	574,894
1910	13,926	14,367	51,000	–	98,443	177,736
1911	19,499	31,192	550,330	–	139,674	740,695
1912	2,702	651,588	11,535	3,393	86,897	756,115
1913	–	292,454	51,331	–	–	343,785
1914	9,131	118,087	59,150	32,185	–	218,553
1915	1,976	296,656	245,225	14,105	29,089	587,051
1916	296	222,828	167,558	59,691	300,000	750,373
1917	2,956	280,830	258,618	543	141,370	684,317
1918	–	132,279	156,793	160,657	1,957	451,686
1919	3,398	176,427	93,571	8,402	1,157,910	1,439,708
1920	4,083	344,579	122,090	27,345	313,353	811,450
1921	2,229	217,159	1,121,205	1,920	813,887	2,156,400
1922	–	79,404	605,439	933,459	134,952	913,254
1923	434	343,394	253,475	31,912	180,391	809,606
1924	4,392	167,151	58,799	42,194	331,239	603,775

Year						
1925	–	41,243	232,475	334	66,523	340,575
1926	–	553,099	1,338,181	8,400	99,988	1,999,668
1927	–	511,314	584,664	127,850	180,583	1,404,411
1928	–	873,561	566,908	23,224	641,304	2,104,997
1929	–	291,585	962,420	2,818	100,336	1,357,159
1930	–	75,807	5,275,631	130,663	–	5,482,101
1931	–	325,881	1,531,845	142,464	79,331	2,079,521
1932	–	91,663	192,586	490	255,222	539,961
1933	–	224,033	279,169	30,030	93,266	626,498
1934	–	199,385	1,429,967	21,496	229,062	1,879,910
1935	–	173,578	1,847,085	71,796	23,017	2,115,476
1936	–	82,101	1,226,384	5,736	312,588	1,626,809
1937	–	457,030	1,522,928	39,000	435,174	2,454,132
1938	–	410,042	918,250	16,495	770,683	2,115,470
1939	–	152,769	551,402	–	113,604	817,775
1940	–	275,601	1,195,821	118	67,478	1,539,018
1941	–	193,890	993,274	4,180	77,961	1,269,305
1942	–	150,796	480,634	164,671	43,665	839,766
1943	–	311,324	547,483	51,312	25,741	935,860
1944	–	48,466	454,670	65,937	89,714	658,787

Note: This table breaks American annual proved discoveries into US total and then the PAW districts between 1900–1944.
Source: Adapted from Frey and Chandler *A History of the Petroleum Administration*, 443.

methods.[46] Once these "stripper" wells had expired, these regions sought exploratory and development drilling programs to locate new supplies. Although the industry's existing reserves initially proved adequate, Larson and colleagues write that: "During the last two war years, the industry had to drive hard to provide enough raw materials to keep its refineries supplied."[47]

Increased production efforts could only succeed in cooperation with new attention to the more effective distribution of crude. The PAW noted that when the United States was attacked in 1941, "the problem was not producing enough crude oil; it was getting that crude moved."[48]

The PAW facilitated the construction of new infrastructure that would benefit the oil industry for the long term (see Map 4.1). Tanker loans to the Allies quickly replaced much of what had been lost to enemy action and, for domestic shipping of oil, railroads replaced ships whenever possible. This helped to stabilize the flow of crude to overseas theaters. More importantly, the PAW emphasized pipeline construction.[49] Most famously, it oversaw the construction of the "Big Inch" (for crude) and the "Little Inch" (for product) pipelines that connected the oil fields of Texas to the Northeast. Construction of the Big Inch began in August 1942 and was completed in 1943.[50] These pipelines became instrumental in making the industry function more reliably during the war and afterward. The main purpose of the infrastructure was to connect production sites to refineries, of course; however, an additional focus was to bring supplies of crude to specialized processing sites that contributed essential products to the war. As oil production grew in the South, refining and processing sites centered on Baton Rouge and Baytown, Louisiana, and Houston, Texas. In these sites, extended workweeks helped to solve the manpower problems and also trained thousands of workers who were then employed throughout the industry (see Chart 4.3).[51]

Petroleum served as the raw material for many products besides just gasoline. Breakthroughs in chemistry placed the petrochemical industry as a central element in the production of toluene, synthetic rubber, and gasoline of all types – but most importantly 100-octane grade aviation fuel. For years, toluene and butadiene, which were used in the

---

[46] Frey and Ide, *A History of the Petroleum Administration*, 188. These efforts to wring oil from existing wells that had previously been abandoned was one of the most efficient changes in the industry that came out of World War II.

[47] Larson, *New Horizon*, 470.

[48] Frey and Ide, *A History of the Petroleum Administration*, 176.

[49] Larson, *New Horizon*, 403–405.   [50] Ibid., 333–334.   [51] Ibid., 496.

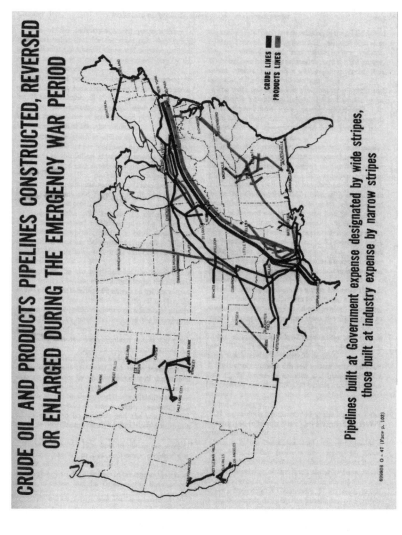

MAP 4.1 Crude oil and products pipelines constructed, reversed, or enlarged during the emergency war period. During the emergency war period, the PAW also needed to control the methods for moving crude and oil products throughout the nation. This map shows the changes in pipeline use during World War II.

Source: John W. Frey and H. Chandler Ide, eds., *A History of the Petroleum Administration for War, 1941–1945* (Honolulu, HI: University Press of the Pacific, 2005; reprint from 1946 edition), 103

WAR CHANGES IN REFINERY RUNS – BY AREAS

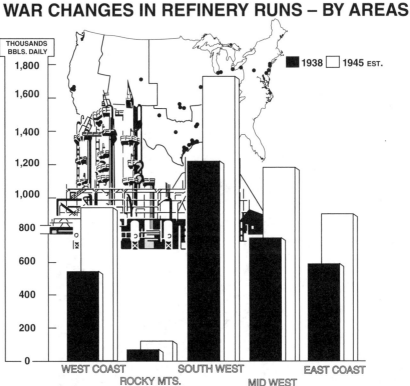

CHART 4.3 War changes in refineries runs – by areas. During the emergency war period, the PAW also needed to control the methods for refining crude. This diagram reveals the changes in refining by region between 1938–1945.
Source: John W. Frey and H. Chandler Ide, eds., *A History of the Petroleum Administration for War, 1941–1945* (Honolulu, HI: University Press of the Pacific, 2005; reprint from 1946 edition), 217

manufacture of explosives, had come as by-product of coke-oven oper-ations, but in 1933 the Standard Oil Development Company announced a laboratory method for producing it from oil.[52] As hostilities grew, Stand-ard faced severe challenges over how to proceed with chemical processes that it had patented through its relationship with the German company I. G. Farben. Following extensive negotiations through 1939, Farben agreed to divide the rights on a "territorial basis."[53]

By World War II, the process had been perfected, and Humble Oil & Refining Company, a subsidiary of Standard Oil of New Jersey, through

[52] Ibid., 321–322.   [53] Ibid., 407–408.

the operation of the government-owned Baytown Ordinance Works, produced almost half of the US supply of toluene. From 1940 through 1945, the total production of toluene by American oil companies equaled 484,282,000 gallons, with 239,282,000 from the Baytown Ordnance Works (49.4 percent of the total) and 72,735,000 gallons from Shell (15.0 percent).[54] In the case of rubber, in 1941 Japan controlled 90 percent of the world's natural supplies of rubber. To produce synthetic rubber required the making of butadiene, a derivative of petroleum. Standard Oil Company of Louisiana and Humble Oil & Refining Company, both subsidiaries of Standard Oil of New Jersey, built plants at Baton Rouge and Baytown, respectively. Other companies produced butadiene during the war, but none were more important than these two, which together provided 29.1 percent of the total US yield of butadiene from 1943 through 1945 (see Chart 4.4). When the supply of rubber from Southeast Asia was lost to Japanese offensives, American oil companies filled the gap by manufacturing synthetic rubber so that Allied forces did not routinely suffer from shortages.[55]

Finally, the overall gasoline production by American oil companies exceeded even US government expectations. Clark reports that by mid-1943, producers and refiners were operating at 90 percent capacity and crude oil production rose from 1.6 MBD in 1932, to 3.7 MBD in 1940, and to 4.6 in 1945. In particular, the production of 100-octane fuel needed for airplanes was produced in 1945 at six-times the level achieved in 1943 (see Table 4.4).[56]

Unlike other energy industries, petroleum supplies also directly touched the lives of consumers. Spring 1942 brought the first episodes of consumer rationing in the United States. Throughout World War II, rationing or conservation on the US domestic front spurred the first recognition of how critical ensuring a consistent supply of petroleum had become. Initially, the use of gasoline for auto racing was banned. In May, rationing cards, which would be punched when a driver filled up at a gas station, were put into service on the East Coast. Eventually, the cards gave way to the widespread use of coupons for gasoline. In general, the rationing of gasoline focused on the more densely populated Northeast and allowed westerners and others to pump gasoline largely at will. Other measures implemented a 35 mile-per-hour speed limit and

---

[54] Keith Miller, "How Important Was Oil in World War II?" See also Larson, *New Horizon*, 408.
[55] Larson, *New Horizon*. [56] Ibid., 325.

100-OCTANE AVIATION FUEL
SOURCES OF PRODUCTION

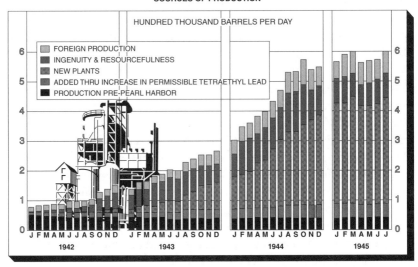

CHART 4.4 100-octane aviation fuel – sources of production. A decisive tool in fighting World War II was air power, which required the world's greatest supply of aviation fuel. This table breaks down how the United States was able to meet this massive need.

Source: John W. Frey and H. Chandler Ide, eds., *A History of the Petroleum Administration for War, 1941–1945* (Honolulu, HI: University Press of the Pacific, 2005; reprint from 1946 edition), 193

also sought to restrict "nonessential driving." This latter effort resulted in a rationing system of five separate grades of driving (essential, including doctors and clergy, to nonessential) to be demarcated by stickers that drivers displayed in their automobile windows. Typically, those at the basic level of nonessential driving received one to four gallons per week, while the essential drivers received as much as needed. Of course, driving was also influenced by other forms of rationing, including of rubber.[57]

Finally, new chemistry methods pioneered during the war forever altered domestic living by transforming petroleum into such materials as nylon and the resins to make plastics, which are today found in nearly every American home. During the war, plastic production tripled to satisfy wartime needs but also because American manufacturers found it to be a good substitute for materials that had been diverted from the home

[57] Black, *Crude Reality*, 140–141.

TABLE 4.4 *Daily average production, refinery runs, and requirements in Allied and neutral countries (excluding the USSR and certain others), 1942 to July 1, 1943 (in thousands of 42-gallon barrels)*

	1942	1943	1944	1945 (1st half)
Crude Oil Production				
United States	3,795	4,117	4,583	4,806
Caribbean	494	584	822	926
(Venezuela, Trinidad, Colombia, and Dutch West Indies)				
Eastern Mediterranean	73	99	113	121
(Iraq, Egypt, Syria, and Palestine)				
Persian Gulf and India	246	241	329	385
(Iran, Bahrain, Saudi Arabia, Kuwait, and India)				
Canada	28	26	23	23
Mexico	96	96	104	116
Other Latin American countries	112	116	115	111
UK and Western Europe	-	2	2	2
Total	**4,844**	**5,281**	**6,091**	**6,490**
Refinery Crude Runs				
United States	3,654	3,916	4,551	4,815
Caribbean	401	500	626	684
(Venezuela, Trinidad, Colombia, and Dutch West Indies)				
Eastern Mediterranean	83	104	119	120
(Iraq, Egypt, Syria, and Palestine)				
Persian Gulf and India	254	260	330	392
(Iran, Bahrain, Saudi Arabia, Kuwait, and India)				
Canada	149	162	179	168
Mexico	82	90	94	98
Other Latin American countries	119	119	118	118
UK and Western Europe	1	3	3	3
Total	**4,743**	**5,154**	**6,020**	**6,398**
Requirements of Major Products by Product				
Aviation gasoline (100-octane)	165	310	566	640
Motor gasoline	1,817	1,673	1,782	1,961
Kerosene	249	253	259	288
Distillates and diesels	723	768	852	980
Residual fuels	1,607	1,784	2,084	2,318
Total	**4,561**	**4,788**	**5,543**	**6,187**

(*continued*)

TABLE 4.4 (*continued*)

	1942	1943	1944	1945 (1st half)
Requirements of Major Products by Consumers (Civilians)				
United States	3,074	2,833	2,904	3,100
Other Western Hemisphere	402	390	412	429
United Kingdom and Neutral Europe	137	133	143	156
Middle East and Far East and Africa	141	137	143	149
Total	3,754	3,493	3,602	3,834
Indirect military bunkers, ocean vessels at US ports	90	162	235	322
Indirect military bunkers, ocean vessels at non-US ports	185	160	230	267
Direct military, worldwide	532	963	1,476	1,764
Total	4561	4788	5543	6187

Note: Breaking down each of the primary years of US involvement in the war, this chart shows the production of oil with its source, where it was refined, and the output to which barrels were put.
Source: Henrietta M. Larson et al., *New Horizons: History of Standard Oil (New Jersey), 1927–1950* (New York: Harper and Row, 1971), 458.

front.[58] Historian Susan Frankel writes of the remarkably rapid integration of plastics into domestic life after the war:

Just months after the war's end, thousands of people lined up to get into the first National Plastics Exposition in New York, a showcase of the new products made possible by the plastics that had proven themselves in the war. For a public weary of two decades of scarcity, the show offered an exciting and glittering preview of the promise of polymers. There were window screens in every color of the rainbow that would never need to be painted. Suitcases light enough to lift with a finger, but strong enough to carry a load of bricks. Clothing that could be wiped clear with a damp cloth. Fishing line as strong as steel. Clear packaging materials that would allow a shopper to see if the food inside was fresh. Flowers that looked like they'd been carved from glass. An artificial hand that looked and moved like the real thing. Here was the era of plenty that the hopeful British chemists had envisioned. "Nothing can stop plastics," the chairmen of the exposition crowed.[59]

[58] Jason P. Theriot, "World War II," *Encyclopedia of American Environmental History*, 3; Joseph L. Nicholson and George R. Leighton, "Plastics Come of Age," *Harper's*, August 1, 1942, 306.
[59] Susan Freinkel, *Plastics: A Toxic Love Story* (New York: Houghton Mifflin, 2011), 26.

Events such as this Exposition extended the vision that had begun to emerge at the 1939 World's Fair with the added influence of technologies that had emerged during the war.

Overall, in 1939, American companies produced 213 million pounds of synthetic resins. By 1945, this production had reached 818 million pounds; by 1951, 2.4 billion pounds of synthetic resins were produced in the United States. It was staggering growth sufficient to remake a civilization. And in the 1950s, writes historian Jeffrey Meikle, that is exactly what happened as "the plastic industry shifted from thermosets to such thermoplastics as polyethylene that contributed to a flood of new uses – garbage pails, squeeze bottles, hula hoops – lighter, more flexible, less permanent than objects made from thermosets." The use of petroleum, in particular, allowed plastics to become "infinitely shape-shifting."[60] Infinite shapes and possibilities would become a commodity in its own right if combined with basic human needs.

However, such dramatic shifts in patterns of consumption did not simply occur on their own. The structure of the bureaucracies and systems to oversee petroleum reflected the unique aspects of its production and its role in producing many other necessary products. As the PAW reports, the war effort "brought about the increase of a million barrels per day that had to be brought about without enough material, without enough manpower, without enough time – without practically everything but courage, determination, resourcefulness, skill, and the willingness to put the national welfare ahead of the individual interest."[61] While it was most often referred to as "conservation" during this era, much of the strategic oversight would continue to some degree after the war. When interest in environmental regulation grew during the 1960s, the API "took seriously" calls for the industry to ensure clean water and air. Enforcement of such measures, however, would largely be carried out within the industry until the establishment of federal regulatory agencies after 1969.[62]

FROM A "WRANGLE OVER OIL" TO THE ERA OF GEOPOLITICS

The acute energy imperative of World War II spurred a growing awareness for the United States to access foreign supplies of petroleum to

[60] Jeffrey Meikle, *American Plastic: A Cultural History* (New Brunswick, NJ: Rutgers University Press, 1995), 176–177.
[61] Frey and Ide, *A History of the Petroleum Administration*, 189.
[62] Gorman, *Redefining Efficiency*, 271–273.

supplement its own reserves – part of what today has become known as "geopolitics." By the war's end, the United States had developed a diplomatic strategy to at least consider the flow of and access to petroleum supplies in its affairs with other nations. This strategy focused on the Middle East more than any other region. While the American public spent the postwar years basking in supplies of cheap petroleum – finding ways of using it for even the most frivolous everyday tasks – military and political leaders began the process of fully incorporating the resource into the strategic planning of the nation's future. Specifically, they followed the model of Britain and France to increase their strategic connectivity in the oil-rich northern areas of the African continent. As early as 1943, Ickes had written: "We're Running Out of Oil!" He went on to stress that World War III would have to be fought with someone else's petroleum because the reserves of the United States were dwindling.[63]

As a national priority, the American effort to reach out to King Ibn Saud and other Middle Eastern leaders was carried out by government officials and American oil companies. Even during World War II, this effort was viewed by some American officials as a competition for favor with US allies, particularly Britain. During the war, Ickes's efforts resulted in Roosevelt's creation of the Petroleum Reserves Corporation, which was cast as a war-related Lend-Lease policy with Saudi Arabia. Before the end of World War II and prior to Roosevelt's death in 1945, Churchill looked with concern on the ongoing efforts by Ickes and others, it seemed, to compete with the British to secure Middle Eastern oil. On February 20, 1944, Churchill wired Roosevelt to say that he had been watching the telegrams from the United States about oil with "increasing misgivings." "A wrangle about oil," he continued:

> Would be a poor prelude for the tremendous joint enterprise and sacrifice to which we have bound ourselves. . . . There is apprehension in some quarters here that the United States has a desire to deprive us of our oil assets in the Middle East on which, among other things, the whole supply of our Navy depends.[64]

He concluded that some British officials felt they were being "hustled" by the United States. Roosevelt did not back down and their exchange went back and forth before, finally, concluding with mutual assurances that each nation would give way to the efforts of the other in specific areas:

---

[63] Yergin, *The Prize*, 395. Ickes was, of course, wrong; the use of hydraulic fracturing techniques has dramatically expanded the US supply of oil in the twenty-first century.

[64] Ibid., 401.

British *entrée* into Iran and Iraq; and the United States into Saudi Arabia. The result was the Anglo-American Petroleum Agreement, which was signed on August 8, 1944, which assured the equity of all parties and the cooperative application of technology and developmental systems to extract petroleum from the Middle East and to bring it to the great Allied powers.[65]

Before Roosevelt could meet with Ickes to discuss the new arrangements for Saudi oil, however, the president died in Warm Springs, Georgia. Ickes went to work with President Harry Truman to make the Petroleum Agreement acceptable to the US Senate. Very quickly, though, the urgency of the moment diminished. With the end of World War II, the overt concern over supply largely vanished, and few policy makers would openly discuss the idea of conserving natural resources – particularly petroleum. Petroleum's management remained tantamount, but now it was carried out more covertly. In a moment of frustration, Ickes submitted his letter of resignation, which the no-nonsense Truman accepted. Without Ickes's influence, public sentiment over the Petroleum Agreement focused on the perceived impact that importing foreign oil would have on American production. Therefore, any agreements to organize oil imports would need to occur in a different, less-public forum.

Within 24 hours of the Japanese surrender in August 1945, domestic gasoline rationing ended. Consumers rebounded by designing their postwar lives around energy abundance and "conspicuously" flaunted the successful middle-class lifestyle produced by consumer capitalism. to support this lifestyle, however, Standard Oil of New Jersey and other companies discussed behind the scenes a strategy to divvy up the opportunity to develop Saudi oil. By applying the concept of "supervening illegality" that Britain had used to seize shares and properties of any owner associated with the Axis powers, the oil executives voided the IPC agreement that had created the "red line" and divided up Middle Eastern oil among themselves. Forcing their way to the table, American oil executives demanded to be officially granted access to Middle Eastern reserves. Although Aramco and British leaders eventually agreed to proceed with a new arrangement, France refused. When the parties approached Ibn Saud (possibly recalling his meeting with President Roosevelt at the close of World War II), he demanded only that the Americans be included. Ultimately, the Group Agreement of November

[65] Ibid., 400.

1948 laid out a new worldwide oil structure. This initiative grew from the imperative for oil and, particularly, the massive reserves that remained undeveloped.

The energy imperative initiated during World War II had clearly become an organizing mechanism for a new world order. Between 1948 and 1972, oil consumption in the United States grew from 5.8 to 16.4 MBD. This threefold increase was surpassed by other parts of the world: Western Europe's use of petroleum increased by 16 times and Japan's by 137 times, albeit from lower baselines.

CONCLUSION: ORGANIZING THE MODERN WORLD AROUND ENERGY

Although American life in 2017 may not quite have reached the ideal that was on exhibit at the 1939 World's Fair, humans after 1945 would never live the same after integrating inexpensive energy into their everyday lives. Today, it is difficult to reconstruct the extent to which limitless crude shaped the expectations of Americans in the early twentieth century. Oil discoveries, such as those at Spindletop, Texas, in 1901 launched this era by providing a growth in supply that predated many of the actual applications for its use. "The [1910s–1920s] thus had an energy crisis of its own," writes historian Stephen Kern, "– a crisis of abundance.... It was the reverse of the [1970s] ... energy crisis.... There was little talk of running out."[66] The era of conspicuous consumption that followed World War II became a showcase for the new war-inspired technologies, particularly clothing made from artificial fibers and other everyday products that put cheap petroleum to use.

Fundamentally, World War II enabled – some would argue that it required – a new, fuller understanding of the importance of energy to developed societies. Overlooked or simply undeveloped prior to World War II, energy was the essential ingredient to the world of Futurama that Americans dreamed of in 1939. In *Fightin' Oil*, Ickes considered the various implications of oil in World War II when he wrote:

It becomes more evident, as distances are annihilated, that this organized human slaughter in which the world is now engaged, is moving to a tempo that petroleum may, in a sense, be said to have set. Had there been no such thing as oil, I doubt if

[66] Stephen Kern, *The Culture of Time and Place* (Cambridge, MA: Harvard University Press, 2003), 9.

there would have been a world war. Without oil, I don't see how we could now be fighting on all sides of the earth.[67]

In the crucible of war from 1941–1945, energy supplies – particularly petroleum – emerged as both a necessity as well as a manageable commodity. An awareness of the methods, applications, and business involved in acquiring sources of power became an essential aspect of "the arsenal of democracy" begun in World War II that would extend through the Cold War and into the twenty-first century. In his administrative role during World War II, Ickes personified this growing awareness of the importance of energy, generally, and petroleum, specifically.

During World War II, observes historian John Clark, Ickes "employed the rhetoric of cooperation, but believed in the necessity of coercion just as he had during the Depression. He was, however, forced by the steady state of emergency that accompanied his long tenure in office to concede more to the larger units of the oil industry than he, perhaps, wished."[68] In short, Ickes represents an awareness of the connection between national political power and energy interests. His awareness of the need for conservation and careful management foreshadows federal efforts to regulate supplies again during the 1970s energy crisis. The difference between the 1940s and 1970s, of course, is that the imperative of managing and regulating Big Oil originally emerged to fulfill the emergency needs of an existential national security crisis and not to fulfill the cultural aspirations of the American people. Big Oil's power today is reflected in the naming of ExxonMobil's former chief executive as US Secretary of State in 2017.[69]

At the root of this story of oil's importance is a historical quandary: Was American dependence on cheap energy an organic product of the growth of the middle class in a surging capitalist economy as historians have often argued? Or was that construct of drive-in theaters, muscle cars, and electric kitchen blenders only the façade fronting an elaborate political and industrial scheme that reorganized the politics of the entire globe to ensure stability and security for developed nations? While it can be

[67] Ickes, *Fightin' Oil*, 200. Ickes was clearly not a historian, as the Seven Years' War and the Napoleonic Wars were clearly fought "on all sides of the earth" without the use of oil-powered engines.

[68] Clark, *The Political Economy*, 347.

[69] Meg Jacobs, *Panic at the Pump*; Brian Black, "Exxon's Rex Tillerson and the Rise of Big Oil in American Politics," *The Conversation*, January 9, 2017, https://theconversation.com/exxons-rex-tillerson-and-the-rise-of-big-oil-in-american-politics-70260 (accessed October 26, 2019).

argued that the conspicuous consumption of the post–World War II era may have occurred without the energy that these arrangements ensured, it is highly unlikely. Therefore, one can clearly hypothesize that without first fulfilling the petroleum needs of national security, conspicuous consumption would have been lessened if not impossible. In the formation of the "arsenal of democracy," the need for energy to support national security provided the essential foundation that allowed for abundant supplies to support ancillary social and cultural changes on the domestic front once the crisis had passed.

PART III

MILITARY MATERIALS II (FOODS AND PLANTS)

5

Soldiers of the Soil

Labor, Nature, and American Agriculture during World War II

Kendra Smith-Howard

World War II sparked cultural and material transformations to American food and agriculture. Indeed, even before the United States formally entered the war in December 1941, American farmers played a critical role in supplying its Allies with foodstuffs. The war recast farming as an act of national security, for the animals and plants raised on American farms were critical to the war effort. Some wartime changes were short-lived. But others, such as the movement of farm laborers to industrial work in the West and North, and the technological developments facilitated by war-funded research, would have long-lasting effects. The war induced demand for farm crops and created labor shortages that required farmers to make new choices about how they tilled soil and which technologies they used to do it. Further, the higher farm prices farmers earned during the war years made it possible for them to invest in new technologies. By familiarizing farmers with new crops and technologies, the effects of World War II on the nation's rural environment were profound, and they unfolded for decades after the Axis powers surrendered.

World War II triggered two key changes that mirrored those of World War I. First, as was the case during the Great War, the conflict of 1939–1945 created increased demand for agricultural products. Federal officials asked American farmers to produce more grain and meat and also to produce homegrown versions of products like rubber and hemp, to which access was cut off by wartime activities. As an incentive, Congress passed legislation to guarantee farmers high commodity prices, increasing production so much that farm income more than doubled between 1940 and 1945.[1] Second, as in World War I, the war drew agricultural workers away from the farm through military conscription and by stimulating industrial development in northern and western cities.[2] In broad strokes, then, the agricultural history of World War II resembled that of its immediate predecessor.

But on closer examination, World War II had a distinctive effect on agricultural environments and communities. The expanded scale and extended duration of American involvement in World War II intensified the labor shortages and the variety of demands for foodstuffs. Farmers' response also exceeded that of their World War I predecessors: despite a reduced labor force, American farmers produced more for civilians at home as well as twice as much food for military needs abroad as in World War I.[3] Furthermore, experiences with ecological crises – including sustained soil loss in the South and the Dust Bowl, as well as the agricultural economic depression in the immediate aftermath of World War I – made policy makers plan cautiously both for wartime buildup and for postwar peace. Finally, bolstered by experience organizing and directing the agricultural economy through the New Deal, the federal government more actively intervened in the agricultural economy in World War II. For instance, whereas in World War I, the Food Administration relied upon

---

[1] Sarah Phillips, *This Land, This Nation: Conservation, Rural America, and the New Deal* (New York: Cambridge University Press, 2007); R. Douglas Hurt, *Problems of Plenty: The American Farmer in the Twentieth Century* (Chicago: Ivan R. Dee, 2004), 100–101.

[2] Katherine Jellison, *Entitled to Power: Farm Women and Technology, 1913–1963* (Chapel Hill: University of North Carolina Press, 1993), 131–148; Stephanie Carpenter, "'Regular Farm Girl: The Women's Land Army in World War II," *Agricultural History* 71, no. 2 (Spring 1997): 162–185; Stephanie Carpenter, *On the Farm Front: The Women's Land Army in World War II* (Dekalb: Northern Illinois University Press, 2003); Cindy Hahamovitch, *No Man's Land: Jamaican Guestworkers in America and the Global History of Deportable Labor* (Princeton, NJ: Princeton University Press, 2012); Erasmo Gamboa, *Mexican Labor and World War II: Braceros in the Pacific Northwest, 1942–1947* (Seattle: University of Washington Press, 2000); Wayne Rasmussen, *History of the Emergency Farm Labor Supply Program, 1943–1947* (Washington, DC: US Department of Agriculture, 1951). Jack Temple Kirby, *Rural World Lost: The American South, 1920–1960* (Baton Rouge: Louisiana State University Press, 1986); Gavin Wright, *Old South, New South: Revolutions in the Southern Economy since the Civil War* (Baton Rouge: Louisiana State University Press, 1997); Nicholas Lemann, *The Promised Land: The Great Black Migration and How It Changed America* (New York: Vintage, 2011); Isabel Wilkerson, *Warmth of Other Sons: The Epic Story of America's Great Migration* (New York: Vintage, 2010); James Gregory, *The Southern Diaspora: How the Great Migrations of Black and White Southerners Transformed America* (Chapel Hill: University of North Carolina, 2005).

[3] Walter Wilcox, *The Farmer in the Second World War* (Ames: Iowa State University, 1947), 51–52.

voluntary actions to guide Americans food habits, during World War II, the Office of Price Administration and the War Food Administration passed mandatory food rationing guidelines and also rationed other materials, including gasoline and steel used for farm equipment.[4]

Agricultural and environmental historians most often comment on World War II's significance not by contrasting it to World War I, but by emphasizing the changes it sparked in the post–World War II era.[5] For instance, longtime US Department of Agriculture (USDA) historian Wayne Ramussen identified two key "revolutions" in American agriculture: the first, prompted by the Civil War, replaced human power with animal power; the second, stimulated by World War II, substituted mechanical power and chemical inputs for the work and manure once provided by animals.[6] While World War II set off a "revolution" in American agriculture, that revolution only unfolded fully after peace treaties were signed. World War II provided the funding for research and impetus for mass production of many technologies (e.g., synthetic fertilizers, herbicides, insecticides, irrigation equipment, and antibiotics) that facilitated intensification of large-scale agriculture in the postwar era. While some of these technologies, such as synthetic fertilizers and herbicides, had nineteenth- and early-twentieth-century roots, many were expensive or ineffective to use in practice, and so not readily adopted before the war. In many cases, that did not change during the war. As one Kentucky farmer noted, "an observer would not have noticed many overt changes in the local farm economy during the war."[7] However, the research and

[4] For World War I, Helen Zoe Veit, *Modern Food, Moral Food: Self-Control, Science, and the Rise of Modern American Eating in the Early Twentieth Century* (Chapel Hill: University of North Carolina, 2013). For rationing, see Amy Bentley, *Eating for Victory: Food Rationing and the Politics of Domesticity* (Urbana: University of Illinois Press, 1998); Barbara McLean Ward, ed., *Produce and Conserve: Share and Play Square: The Grocer and Consumer on the Home-Front Battlefield during World War II* (Portsmouth, NH: University Press of New England, 1994); Tracey Deutsch, *Building a Housewife's Paradise: Gender, Politics, and American Grocery Stores in the Twentieth Century* (Chapel Hill: University of North Carolina Press, 2010).

[5] Wayne Rasmussen, "Twenty-Five Years of Change in Farm Productivity," *Agricultural History* 49, no. 1 (January 1975): 84–86; J. L. Anderson, *Industrializing the Corn Belt: Agriculture, Technology, and Environment, 1945–1972* (DeKalb: Northern Illinois University Press, 2009), 8–9: Mark Finlay, "Hogs, Antibiotics, and the Industrial Environments of Postwar Agriculture," in *Industrializing Organisms*, ed. Susan Schrepfer and Philip Scranton (New York: Routledge, 2004), 237–260.

[6] Wayne D. Rasmussen, "The Impact of Technological Change on American Agriculture, 1862–1962," *Journal of Economic History* 22, no. 4 (December 1962): 578, 588.

[7] Paul Conkin, *A Revolution Down on the Farm: The Transformation of American Agriculture since 1929* (Lexington: University Press of Kentucky, 2008), 78.

development conducted during the war years, combined with labor short-ages and high commodity prices, set the stage for massive technological changes in the postwar era.

Only in a few, unique situations did agriculture change markedly during the war. For instance, Japanese internment of agricultural laborers altered land and labor in California, and farmers grew new crops to compensate for lost imports of rubber, tropical oils, and abaca. Entrenched patterns in the American agriculture, and uncertainty about the future of wartime production directives discouraged farmers from radically transforming their farming techniques. But the war was none-theless significant, for the experience of operating with fewer laborers, combined with the high prices that farmers garnered during the war years, made farm families eager to adopt newly available labor-saving technolo-gies and enabled many to afford them afterward.

This chapter examines three facets of the environmental history of agriculture in the World War II era. First, the chapter narrates the technological innovations developed during the war that were imple-mented in the decades after the war concluded. Second, it examines how World War I and the New Deal conditioned farmers' responses to the demands of intensified production and high commodity prices of the war years, particularly as relevant to soil conservation. Finally, it considers the unique situations in which agriculture *did* change markedly during the war – through Japanese internment and the development of new crops.[8]

TECHNOLOGIES IN WAITING

Many significant wartime developments that reshaped agricultural envir-onments took place in boardrooms and laboratories rather than farm fields. One area of expansion was chemical research. Leaders of the US military paid special attention to research on the use of growth-regulating chemicals, such as herbicides. For instance, by 1943, University of Chicago plant pathologist E. J. Kraus received funding for his research on the growth-regulating chemical 2, 4-D from the US Army. The next

---

[8] Mark R. Finlay, *Growing American Rubber: Strategic Plants and the Politics of National Security* (New Brunswick, NJ, and London: Rutgers University Press, 2009); Smith-Howard, *Pure and Modern Milk: An Environmental History since 1900* (New York: Oxford University Press, 2014); Bartow J. Elmore, *Citizen Coke: The Making of Coca-Cola Capitalism* (New York: W. W. Norton & Company, 2015); Andrew P. Duffin, *Plowed Under: Agriculture and Environment in Palouse* (Seattle: University of Washington Press, 2007).

year, Kraus expanded his herbicide research with experiments at the army's biological warfare research and testing site, Maryland's Camp Detrick. By that time, agricultural researchers found the herbicide 2, 4-dichlorophenoxyacetic acid (2,4-D) effectively eradicated bindweed and dandelions. In 1946, California researchers deemed it useful against 49 broad-leaved weeds, and as results of the experiments became public, farmers clamored for the weed killer. Production rapidly expanded – from 917,000 pounds in 1945 to 5,466,000 pounds in 1946.[9]

Similarly, funding from the Chemical Warfare Service fostered research on insecticides. The use of DDT as a delousing agent to control typhus among American soldiers and to prevent malaria in the South Pacific generated popular interest in practical applications of the chemical in agriculture. With War Production Board funding, chemical companies like DuPont and Geigy could expand their manufacturing capacities to produce it.[10] In the postwar era, farmers eager to give up chopping thistles with scythes turned to 2, 4-D as an effective labor-saving weed killer. Air force veterans applied their battle-tested aerial skills to piloting crop-dusting aircraft and dropping insecticides on boll worms, flies, mosquitos, and fire ants.[11]

Wartime pharmaceutical research also saw big gains that would fuel changes in animal husbandry. By perfecting methods and building infrastructure to manufacture penicillin at an industrial scale, teams of British and American researchers converted Alexander Fleming's 1928 discovery of the bacteria-arresting properties of penicillin mold into a miracle drug. Large-scale production began in 1943 under the auspices of the War Production Board, which contracted with commercial pharmaceutical firms including Lederle, Merck, Pfizer, Squibb, and Abbott Laboratories. The wartime emergency energized production of this critical antibiotic; between 1943 and 1945 production increased from 21 billion to 6.8 *trillion* units.[12] The drug healed both battlefield wounds and chronic conditions that sapped troops' strength. By the war's end, civilians benefited. Antibiotics

[9] Gale Peterson, "The Discovery and Development of 2, 4-D," *Agricultural History* 41, no. 3 (July 1967): 246–252.

[10] Edmund Russell, *War and Nature: Fighting Humans and Insects with Chemicals from World War I to Silent Spring* (New York: Cambridge, 2001), 126–131, 145–150.

[11] Pete Daniel, *Toxic Drift: Pesticides and Health in the Post–World War II South* (Baton Rouge: Louisiana State University Press, 2005), 49–55.

[12] "Discovery and Development of Penicillin," American Chemical Society, www.acs.org/content/acs/en/education/whatischemistry/landmarks/flemingpenicillin.html#us-penicillin-production (accessed March 20, 2017).

also revolutionized animal health, providing farmers and veterinarians with a powerful tool to treat a host of livestock ailments. Over the next two decades, antibiotics in animal feed facilitated the enclosure of domesticated animals in larger numbers, and enabled hogs and beef cattle to reach market weights more quickly. By the 1950s, nearly a quarter of the antibiotics produced in the United States were directed to agricultural purposes.[13]

EXPAND PRODUCTION, MAINTAIN THE SOIL

Food constituted an essential material contribution to the American war effort and fueled the Allies to victory. Even before American leaders called on American GIs, they turned to American farmers and the fields and forests in which they labored for food as a tool of war. American farmlands, and the people who tended them, staved off hunger in Britain with Lend-Lease exports. Once American troops entered the war, their GI rations – far more generous than those of the British – kept American troops fed, and even indirectly provided vital nutrients to British women and children subject to strict rationing to supply British servicemen.[14] And in the war's waning days and afterward, American-supplied foodstuffs nourished civilians in Belgium and France. It's no wonder that Secretary of Agriculture Claude Wickard, in his 1943 appeal to urge farmers to produce more food, called war "a Healthy Eater."[15] American farmers, and the plants and animals they tended, rose to the challenge, producing 15 percent more grain crops, 37 percent more beef, and 63 percent more pork during the war years.[16]

---

[13] Robert Bud, *Penicillin: Triumph and Tragedy* (New York: Oxford University Press, 2007); Claas Kirchhelle, "Pyrrhic Progress: Antibiotics and Western Food Production (1949–2013)" (PhD diss., University of Oxford, 2015); Kendra Smith-Howard, "Antibiotics and Agricultural Change: Purifying Milk and Protecting Health in the Postwar Era," *Agricultural History* 84, no. 3 (Summer 2010): 327–351; William Boyd, "Making Meat: Science, Technology and American Poultry Production," *Technology and Culture* 42, no. 4 (October 2001): 631–664; Finlay, "Hogs, Antibiotics, and the Industrial Environments of Postwar Agriculture," 237–260; Terry Summons, "Animal Feed Additives, 1940–1966," *Agricultural History* 42, no. 4 (October 1968): 305–313; Alan Marcus, *Cancer from Beef: DES, Federal Food Regulation and Consumer Confidence* (Baltimore: Johns Hopkins University Press, 1994).

[14] Williamson Murray and Allan R. Millett, *A War to Be Won: Fighting the Second World War* (Cambridge, MA: Belknap Press of Harvard University Press, 2000), 529–533.

[15] Claude Wickard, "War Is a Healthy Eater," *Farm Journal and Farmer's Wife* 67 (January 1943): 13.

[16] Clayton Koppes, "USA," in *The Oxford Companion to World War II*, ed. I. C. B. Dear (Oxford: Oxford University Press, 1995), 1182.

Given the ravenous demands World War II created for food, one might expect that farmers, rushing to take advantage, quickly denuded soils. After all, during World War I, farmers expanded wheat fields at the expense of native prairie grasses, using tractor-drawn disk plows and harvester-threshers that accelerated erosion.[17] But increased wartime production did not exactly mirror the effects of World War I. When the United States began supplying the war effort in 1941, the nation still had surplus of wheat and cotton stored from the 1930s, and so the USDA did not immediately promote expansion those soil-depleting crops. Soil conservation programs discouraged the use of submarginal lands. Not until 1944 did the USDA ask wheat farmers to grow as much wheat as possible for harvest.[18] Hence, despite the push to produce more food, American farmers did *not* cultivate a much larger number of acres during the war. While the amount of land in cultivation increased between 1942 and 1943 from 349.7 to 360 million acres, the nation still had 13 million fewer acres under cultivation than it had a decade earlier, at the height of the Dust Bowl in 1933.[19] More efficient farming, not more acreage, helped supply Uncle Sam.

Two factors discouraged rapid expansion of soil-depleting crops. First, agricultural planners and soil conservation officials were determined not to match the deleterious soil erosion unleashed by intensified agricultural production during World War I. "If necessary to win the war," the midwestern farm journal *Wallace's Farmer* editorialized in January 1942, "farmers will plow up the pastures again and wreck hillsides that have been seeded down. But chances are it won't be necessary. We can grow less wheat, cotton, and tobacco, shift to feed crops on those acres, and leave the pastures alone."[20] Farm people, not just editorialists, identified World War I as a driver of soil erosion. Missourian Gilbert Kimbrough noted in a letter to *Farm Journal and Farmer's Wife*, "I think you will agree that most of the loss in fertility was caused from the effects

---

[17] Donald Worster, *Dust Bowl: The Southern Plains in the 1930s* (New York: Oxford University Press, 1979), 87–92.

[18] Wilcox, The *Farmer in the Second World War* (Ames: Iowa State College Press, 1947), 161; R. Douglas Hurt, *The Great Plains during World War II* (Lincoln: University of Nebraska Press, 2008), 161, 168.

[19] Bela Gold, *Wartime Economic Planning in Agriculture: A Study in the Allocation of Resources* (New York: Columbia University Press, 1949), 87. Comparing land in acreage between 1935–1939 and 1943–1944, George Collier, director of the Soil Conservation Service Economic section called it "practically unchanged." Collier, *Soil Conservation during the War*, US Department of Agriculture, War Records Monographs (Washington, DC: Soil Conservation Service, 1946), 2.

[20] "Odds and Ends," *Wallace's Farmer*, January 10, 1942, 7.

of the last war when farmers seemed to think the good prices and soil fertility would last forever."[21] Such cautionary advice circulated widely, because by the late 1930s, local farmers began to establish soil conservation districts as part of federal soil conservation programs. As Joel Bius explains in this volume, at the very moment when American farmers began increasing production for the war effort, they were simultaneously seeking out technical advice from the Soil Conservation Service (SCS). Indeed, whereas in 1939, only 187 conservation districts had been established nationwide, by 1945, soil conservation districts numbered 1,346.[22] Second, rationing of steel, gasoline, and rubber limited the adoption of new technologies. Farmers produced more on the acres they had in cultivation rather than converting marginal lands to croplands.

The war's demands for resources, though, put pressure on the burgeoning efforts of soil conservation service districts to protect soils. As military service and wartime employment opportunities sapped the agricultural labor force, both farmers and the soil conservation service had fewer workers to implement labor-intensive methods. In some cases, the Soil Conservation Service turned to conscientious objectors for soil conservation projects. Members of the Church of the Brethren, Mennonite, and Quaker denominations applied their expertise and time to terracing, planting crops, and mending gullies in lieu of military service. In Idaho, conscientious objectors hoisted picks and shovels to dig irrigation ditches to help put dry-farming areas under cultivation and drainage ditches for soggy soils.[23]

A second challenge was convincing farmers to continue to heed warnings about soil conservation, particularly at a time when prices for agricultural commodities ticked upward due to rising demands. While more conservation districts existed in 1945 than in 1939, membership and involvement in such organizations was voluntary, limiting their ability to dictate how land was used.[24] The 1942 annual report of the county

---

[21] Gilbert Kimbrough, "Letter to the Editor," *Farm Journal and Farmer's Wife* 67 (May 1943): 10.

[22] Walter Wilcox, *The Farmer in the Second World War* (Ames: Iowa State College Press, 1947), 27; Collier, *Soil Conservation during the War*, 6–7.

[23] Charles Hirsch, "The Civilian Public Service Camp Program in Indiana," *Indiana Magazine of History* 46 (1950): 259–281; John Olinger, "They Called It Camp Downey," *Idaho Yesterdays* 31 (March 1988): 15–23; Patricia Ourada, "Reluctant Servants: Conscientious Objectors in Idaho during World War II," *Idaho Yesterdays* 31 (March 1988): 2–14.

[24] Duffin, *Plowed Under*, 94–95.

agent in western Wisconsin's Trempeleau County reveals the challenge. Hilly Trempeleau County was prone to erosion, and its agricultural agent, Charles Nelson, promoted the importance of soil conservation, even turning to capital letters to underscore its importance: "WE HAVE TO GUARD AGAINST DESTRUCTION OF SOIL RESOURCES THAT MIGHT CATCH US SHORT BEFORE THE END OF THE WAR." By 1942, the county's farmers had ample opportunity to learn about conservation methods, for it sat adjacent to the nation's first soil conservation project, in the Coon Valley watershed, where conservation efforts began in the early 1930s. Still, only 400 Trempeleau County farms had established conservation plans with the Soil Conservation Service by 1942; 3,100 of them had not.[25] Thus, in Trempeleau County, and throughout the country, soil conservationists had to persuade farmers of the merits of soil conservation. Hugh Hammond Bennett, head of the Soil Conservation Service, reminded those who would abandon conservation measures for the duration of the war that it was unknown how long the war emergency would last, and that soil fertility was the key to producing for the entire duration of the war and for reconstruction.[26] Although in some regions and agricultural sectors, such as among the tobacco farmers that Joel Bius discusses in this volume (Chapter 7), farmers readily embraced soil conservation, other farmers were ambivalent or reluctant to adopt conservation methods. As historian Andrew Duffin explains in his study of the Washington Palouse, although agronomists suspected erosion and soil loss would lead to lower wheat yields, they could not definitively demonstrate erosion's effects on yields and, at times, high yields from eroded fields seemed to suggest otherwise. Further, the short-term economic rewards of intense production, and desire to use one's own property as one saw fit tempered some farmers' receptivity to soil conservationists' moral suasion.[27]

Within this context, farmers sought out methods of soil conservation that could be readily applied without lots of technical assistance, and that would have short-term results that could boost their yields to meet production demands.[28] Generally, three kinds of soil conservation practices – improving pastures, liming the soil, and contour plowing – received

[25] Charles Nelson, "Annual Report of Agricultural Agent of Trempealeau County, 1942," November 10, 1942, University of Wisconsin Digital Collections, http://digital.library .wisc.edu/1711.dl/WI.AATrempCo (accessed December 1, 2018).
[26] "Plowing Hill Slopes Won't Help Win War," *Wallace's Farmer*, November 28, 1942, 716.
[27] Duffin, *Plowed Under*, 94–100.   [28] Collier, *Soil Conservation*, 11–12.

the bulk of the agency's attention and had the biggest impact during the war years.

One facet of the wartime soil conservation program was to improve pastures, simultaneously conserving soil and also boosting milk and meat production. Agricultural magazines and USDA agricultural extension workers extolled various pasture grasses that thrived on worn-out lands and provided fodder for livestock, such as lespedeza, birdsfoot trefoil, and Johnson grass. Legumes like lespedeza and alfalfa not only covered worn-out soils and prevented them from washing away but also improved the soil for future use. Just at the point in the summer when bluegrasses withered and dried, lespedeza thrived. Converting cornfields to pasture grasses like lespedeza saved soil and labor alike – important at a time of acute labor shortages.[29]

In the South, the government encouraged farmers to plant quick-growing kudzu, the bane of many of today's native plant enthusiasts and gardeners, with payments up to eight dollars an acre. Hence, even after the war cut off access to kudzu seed from Japan, Soil Conservation Service nurseries in states across the South kept farmers supplied with kudzu.[30] Kudzu and lespedeza took on new significance during the war. Because nitrate factories produced bombs as well as fertilizers, enriching soils with nitrogen-fixing crops meant more artificial nitrogen could go to munitions. As one 1942 booster of legumes put it, "Oregon's 200,000,000 pound crop of Austrian winter pea, vetch, and crimson clover seed this year is the equivalent of 24,000,000 100-pound bombs."[31] The crops' use as animal feed also took on new wartime meaning. Legumes like kudzu made protein-rich hay that could replace the protein-rich components of animal fodder cut off by the war, like fish meal, which were seen as essential to maintaining and boosting meat production.[32]

[29] "They Like Lespedeza," *Farm Journal and Farmer's Wife* 67 (March 16, 1943), 28; "Lespedeza for Pasture," *Wallace's Farmer*, February 4, 1944: 17.
[30] *Kudzu for Erosion Control in the Southeast,* US Department of Agriculture Farmers' Bulletin 1840 (Washington, DC: Government Printing Office, 1939): 1–31; Mart A. Stewart, "Cultivating Kudzu: The Soil Conservation Service and the Kudzu Distribution Program," *Georgia Historical Quarterly* 8, no. 1 (Spring 1997): 157–159; John Winberry and David Jones, "Rise and Decline of 'The Miracle Vine': Kudzu in the Southern Landscape," *Southeastern Geographer* 13, no. 2 (November 1973): 64–67; Derek Alderman, "Channing Cope and the Making of a Miracle Vine," *Geographical Review* 94, no. 2 (April 2004): 163–166.
[31] "Cover Crops Save Nitrogen," *Farm Journal and Farmer's Wife* 66 (November 1942): 31.
[32] R. W. Howard, "A Protein Shortage in '43," *Farm Journal and Farmer's Wife* 67 (February 1943): 19; Smith-Howard, *Pure and Modern Milk,* ch. 3.

Second, American farmers also improved soils with fertilizer, applying 6.5 times more tons of ground limestone and 16 times more fertilizer to their farms in 1944 than in 1936. The government made it easy to adopt this technology. Farmers ordered ground limestone through the local AAA committee, and local quarries supplied it to farmers. Farmers also could arrange for triple-superphosphate, supplied by the Tennessee Valley Authority, to be delivered to local railyards. Farmers had the costs for these soil amendments deducted from their AAA conservation payments. By 1943, 35 percent of all conservation payments to farmers were to carry out liming and fertilizing – more than any other conservation measure.[33] Generally, fertilizer use – in terms of nitrates, phosphate, and potash – was 95 percent higher in 1945 than in the period 1935–1939.[34] In the 1930s and during the early 1940s, the bulk of fertilizers farmers applied to the soil were phosphate based.[35] But the war prompted the creation and expansion of a number of ammonia-produced nitrogen plants for the manufacture of explosives – plants with the capacity in the postwar era to supply farmers with ammonia-based nitrogenous fertilizers.[36]

A third element of the wartime conservation was contour farming, which expanded dramatically. By 1944, the Soil Conservation Service counted more than 10 million acres that had been contour furrowed (an eightfold increase from 1936), 1.7 million acres in terraces (more than twice as many as in 1936), and nearly 18 million acres on which small grain crops were intertilled on the contour. Like liming soils and planting legumes, contour cropping was by no means a new soil conservation technique. But attention to contour farming crested as the USDA set increasingly higher targets for corn and soybean production. Farmers

---

[33] Collier, *Soil Conservation*, 13–14; "They Spread More Lime Now: Farmers Build Up Soil thru Lime and Charge Expense against Next AAA Check," *Wallace's Farmer*, March 21, 1942, 183.

[34] US Congress, House Committee on Appropriations, Hearings on Agriculture Department Appropriation Bill, 1947 (Washington, DC: US Government Printing Office, 1946), 248.

[35] "Keep Crushers Turning Out Limestone," *Wallace's Farmer*, September 5, 1942; Joseph Mahoney to *Wallace's Farmer*, October 3, 1942; "The Soil," *Farm Journal and Farmer's Wife* 66 (November 1942); "Dollar Corn Makes Fertilizer Pay," *Wallace's Farmer*, January 15, 1944, 18–19.

[36] Hugh Gorman, *The Story of N: A Social History of the Nitrogen Cycle and the Challenge of Sustainability* (New Brunswick, NJ: Rutgers University Press, 2013), 88–92; Lewis Nelson, *History of the US Fertilizer Industry* (Muscle Shoals, AL: Tennessee Valley Authority, 1990), 323–327, 331–333.

who were determined to meet these production targets without ruining soils contoured their fields.[37]

The end of the war ended wartime urgency for expanded production, and also lessened the intensive attention to conservation practices. Corn Belt farmers could boost corn and bean yields with ammonia-based fertilizers, and the factories constructed to synthesize ammonia into explosives in the 1940s were eager to supply them. Synthesized ammonia, not crushed lime or leguminous crops, enriched soils.[38] But this general trend should not prevent us from seeing the more diverse agricultural landscape of the war years – in which farmers turned to lime crushers and lespedeza, rather than anhydrous ammonia – to sweeten the soil.

WARTIME CROPS: SOYBEANS, HEMP, AND GUAYULE

Besides maximizing production of corn, soybeans, wheat, and livestock, American agriculture stepped up to supply imported raw materials like palm oil, rubber, or abaca, which Axis aggressions prevented from reaching the United States. Some import-replacement crops, such as hemp and guayule, had a short-lived impact. Others, like soybeans, reshaped American agriculture for years to come. Studying the fate of these crops helps reveal both the power and limitations of the federal government's organization of natural resources in wartime. On one hand, the war empowered the federal government to authorize spending to help ensure that the US military had sufficient supplies. On the other hand, the federal government's efforts to exert influence always relied on farmers' willing participation to alter their planting and harvesting activities on private lands. Farmers did not always realign their farms' activities to meet federal directives.

Federal officials often conceptualized the need for particular commodities in isolation – they wanted more hemp or more oil-bearing raw materials. But farmers' decisions about whether and how to cultivate a new crop required them to consider the relationship between all the plants and animals on the farm. Changing the mix of crops raised meant reallocating lands grown for something else and calculating the value of that new crop versus the worth of the old one. Swapping out some acres of

---

[37] "Four Inches of Soil," *Wallace's Farmer*, March 7, 1942, 158.
[38] Vaclav Smil, *Enriching the Earth: Fritz Haber, Carl Bosch, and the Transformation of World Food Production* (Cambridge, MA: Massachusetts Institute of Technology Press, 2001), 115–116.

rich cornfields for hemp, for instance, might mean having to pay a neighbor to provide enough grain for the farm's chickens and hogs. Planting guayule rubber meant forgoing profits for vegetables that could be cultivated on the same land.

Hemp was one wartime crop grown to replace imported goods. Japanese occupation cut off Americans' access to abaca and hemp grown in the Philippines and Dutch Indies, used by the US military for rope and cordage. Hence the military convinced American farmers to grow it. Switching crops involved risk, and so the federal government had to overcome resistance from those for whom corn seemed a surer bet. To convince farmers to grow hemp instead of corn, the USDA engaged in all-out promotional efforts. Illinois farmers who were prospective hemp growers gathered in high school gyms to hear presentations by experienced hemp horticulturalists.[39] In neighboring Iowa, residents settled into their seats in movie theaters to watch the USDA film "Hemp for Victory."[40] But farmers were reluctant. In January 1943, just months before the planting season, one Illinois extension agent had only convinced farmers in his district to plant 20 percent of the acreage needed to supply the nearby processing plant.[41] For those farmers in Wisconsin, Kentucky, Minnesota, and Illinois who were willing to grow hemp, the federal government furnished seed to growers, provided loans for equipment and labor, and financed the construction of 71 hemp mills to dry, crush, untangle, and bale the crop.[42] Attention to hemp was short-lived. A year later, in the spring of 1944, with fewer submarines blocking the paths to Central American hemp and Mediterranean jute, the US government needed less hemp and asked farmers to seed grains instead.[43]

A second newly homegrown crop was rubber. Before Pearl Harbor, the United States imported 97 percent of its rubber from Southeast Asia.

---

[39] Robert Marsh, "The Illinois Hemp Project at Polo in World War II," *State Historical Society of Illinois* 60, no. 4 (1967): 394–397.

[40] Lisa Lynn Ossian, "The Home Fronts of Iowa, 1940–1945" (PhD diss., Iowa State University, 1998), 64.

[41] "Corn Land Produces Fiber for Rope," *Wallace's Farmer*, October 2, 1943.

[42] C. P. Wilsie, E. S. Dyas, and A. G. Norman, *Hemp: A War Crop for Iowa* (Ames: Iowa State University, October 1942), 589–598.

[43] "War Demands More Hemp," *Farm Journal and Farmer's Wife* 66 (June 1942): 17; "Home-Grown Twine," *Farm Journal and Farmer's Wife* 66 (November 1942), 86; "Corn Land Produces Fiber for Rope," *Wallace's Farmer* October 2, 1943, 22; "Hemp Acreage to Be Cut," *Wallace's Farmer*, February 5, 1944, 15; John Frederick Zwicky, "A State at War: The Home Front in Illinois during the Second World War" (PhD diss., Loyola University of Chicago, 1989), 265–267.

At the very moment the nation required more rubber for gas masks, truck and airplane tires, medical supplies, and telegraph wire insulation, the nation was cut off from its supply of this essential resource.[44] As rubber rationing began and tires thinned, Americans looked to the pithy plants that grew near them as potential rubber alternatives. Domestic rubber enthusiasts especially promoted a deep-rooted desert shrub called guayule. But even as a rubber shortage loomed, Congress rebuffed a funding request from the Intercontinental Rubber Company (IRC), a California firm that sought to process guayule into domestic rubber. After Pearl Harbor, Congress reversed course and supported domestic rubber production, launching the Emergency Rubber Program in early March 1942. The program transferred the processing machinery, employees, and guayule seed of the IRC to the US Forest Service and provided millions of dollars to rubber research. By April 1942, test plots of guayule had been planted not just in California but also Texas, Arizona, and New Mexico.[45]

Growing guayule demanded lots of labor. California guayule growers relied on women, German and Italian POWs, and, most importantly, Mexican workers. By 1943, 40 percent of the workers in the California rubber fields were Mexican nationals.[46] The federal government even tapped interned Japanese American citizens, who developed hybridization techniques to cultivate guayule on unirrigated soils and new methods to extract rubber from guayule's roots.[47]

Demand for land – including irrigated land – posed the biggest challenge to homegrown rubber and proved to be a flash point between the federal government and private landholders. Because the crop took four to five years for its roots to produce the pithy extract used to make rubber, farmers cultivated large acreages of varying ages, harvesting a different field annually.[48] In September 1942, a presidential-appointed committee recommended that guayule production be extended far beyond the 75,000 acres under cultivation through the Emergency Rubber

[44] Finlay, *Growing American Rubber*, 1.
[45] Ibid., esp. chs. 2 and 4; "Plant Guayule in Test Areas of Four States," *Chicago Daily Tribune*, April 9, 1942.
[46] "Workers Wanted in Guayule Fields," *Los Angeles Times*, May 3, 1942.
[47] Neil Naiden, "Two Jap Nurserymen Experiment to Solve Rubber Shortage by Guayule Production," *Washington Post*, September 6, 1942; "Rubber Substitute Program Aided: Guayule Seedlings Put Out by Manzanar Japs," *Los Angeles Times*, May 2, 1942; Finlay, *Growing American Rubber*, 152–157, 199–201.
[48] Finlay, *Growing American Rubber*, 13, 17.

Program.[49] The federal government sought to lease land from private landholders – particularly where rich soil conditions and climate could hasten guayule shrubs' growth.[50]

In Kern and Santa Maria counties, farmers balked. Like midwestern farmers reluctant to take the risk of growing hemp on fields fertile for corn planting, Kern County farmers hesitated to shift lands cultivated for melons, hay, sorghum, cotton, and potatoes for an unfamiliar desert shrub.[51] To such farmers, *food* for freedom seemed just as patriotic as growing rubber – and probably more lucrative as well.[52] Expressing his disgust at replacing food with guayule production, agricultural journalist Ernest Broughton resorted to all caps to exclaim, "ONE GUAYULE PLANT FOR SEVEN HILLS OF POTATOES, AND EACH HILL OF POTATOES IS WORTH AS MUCH OR MORE THAN ONE GUAY-ULE PLANT."[53] California growers protested that the wages paid to guayule workers made it more difficult for them to recruit laborers for the vegetable crop.[54] Ultimately, 800 acres of Kern County lands leased for guayule production were released back to owners.[55]

Critics who challenged the guayule industry's place relative to other farm crops proved prescient by stating that "So soon as rubber resumes its prewar level of values, the guayule industry will drop with a bang."[56] Indeed, victory in the Pacific and restoration of regular trade with Southeast Asian rubber-growing districts brought an end to American sources of natural rubber. Resumption of trade, combined with the development of a synthetic rubber industry based on chemical and petroleum products, doomed guayule. By 1946, fields full of guayule bushes whose xylem bulged with rubbery pith smoldered or were

[49] James B. Conant, Karl Compton, and Bernard Baruch, *Report of the Rubber Survey Committee, September 10, 1942.*

[50] "New Guayule Land Sought: Planting to Start on 15,000 Acres Rich Kern Farms," *Los Angeles Times* December 5, 1942, A7; "Guayule Land Demand Stirs Farmer Protest," *Los Angeles Times*, December 7, 1942.

[51] "Guayule Plan Protest Field," *Los Angeles Times*, February 23, 1943.

[52] "Guayule Land Row Spreads: Secretary Wickard Promises Study of Kern County Protests," *Los Angeles Times*, December 12, 1942; "Farmers Carry Guayule Fight to Washington," *Los Angeles Times*, March 1, 1943.

[53] Ernest Broughton, "What about This Guayule Rubber Anyway," *Los Angeles Times*, March 1, 1943, A4.

[54] Lorania Francis, "Bewilderment Stirred by Split over Guayule," *Los Angeles Times*, March 8, 1943, 10.

[55] "Kern Guayule Land Released," *Los Angeles Times*, April 3, 1943.

[56] Broughton, "What about This Guayule Rubber Anyway?"

plowed under. Guayule seeds, once treated as precious keys to national security, became cattle feed.[57]

Federal government and landholder objectives met most neatly in the case of oil-producing crops, and particularly soybeans. Axis aggressions also cut off access to tropical oils, which were raw materials for soap, paint, plastic, and munitions manufacture. These oils also constituted a key ingredient in foods used as dairy substitutes, such as margarine, and were important components of livestock rations. In place of imported coconut, palm, tung, and rapeseed oils, federal officials encouraged farmers to grow soybean and peanuts for crushing.[58]

Midwest farmers loosened their corn belt to add soybeans to their fields. Farmers did not enter the war entirely unfamiliar with soybean cultivation. During the 1930s, the Soil Conservation Service recommended soybeans as a soil-saving legume, and nationally soybean cultivation saw a sharp boost in acreage in 1935.[59] But wartime demands, combined with price supports, brought vastly more land than ever into soy production. In 1942, federal government guarantees doubled the average price and increased it again through the war. Farmers responded. Just in the years between 1939 and 1942, the land cultivated to soybeans increased from roughly 4 million to more than 10 million acres. Most of the expansion in soybean production took place in the midwestern states of Ohio, Illinois, Iowa, Indiana, and Missouri, which together produced more than 85 percent of the nation's soybean crop. Unlike hemp or guayule, the reorientation toward soybean production outlasted the war, so that soybean fields became as common as cornfields, reducing the acreage in hay.[60]

As soybeans took root, their role on the farm changed. Before the war, farmers prized soybeans for the plant's leaves and stems, which provided forage for cattle and hogs. But wartime shortages of other protein sources (like fish meal) turned scientists' attention to the seed of a soybean as a

[57] Ibid.
[58] Robert D. McMillen, "We've Got to Pump Oil," *Farm Journal and Farmer's Wife* 66 (February 1942); Bureau of Agricultural Extension, *Soybeans Go to War* (Washington, DC: Government Printing Office, 1943); R. W. Howard, "Little Beans, Big Business: New American Crops" *Farm Journal and Farmer's Wife* 65 (November 1941): 18–19, 24.
[59] Merle Prunty, "Soybeans in the Lower Mississippi Valley," *Economic Geography* 26, no. 4 (October 1950): 303–304.
[60] Smith-Howard, "Ecology, Economy, Labor: The Midwestern Farm Landscape since 1945," in *The Rural Midwest since World War II*, ed. J. L. Anderson (DeKalb: Northern Illinois University Press, 2014), 46.

readily digestible alternative protein source. Crushed as soybean meal, these seeds provided the material underpinnings for more intensive animal agriculture in which farmers delivered feed to animals in confinement, rather than turning animals out to graze. Whether fed to cattle on feedlots or chickens in broiler houses, soybean-enriched feeds helped usher in a new kind of agriculture. World War II provided the impetus for thinking of soybeans differently.[61]

Equally important, soybeans became a crop to be fertilized, rather than a fertilizing crop. With more of the biomass in its bean than its roots, modern soybean cultivars take more nitrogen out of the soil than they fix.[62] Hence, by the 1960s, farmers began fertilizing not just corn, but bean crops with additional nitrogen, rather than turning to them to enrich their soil. Excess nitrogen from heavily fertilized soils flowed into rivers, such as the Mississippi, so that the average mean concentration of nitrate in the lower Mississippi doubled between 1955 and 1990. Because bacteria are unable to take up the excess nitrogen, it fuels algal blooms and the growth of zooplankton in greater numbers than fish can consume. When the zooplankton die, their decomposition takes up the oxygen in the water, leading to a hypoxic state that kills any marine animals that cannot swim away quickly enough. While fertilizer is not the *only* contributor to an increased nitrogen load in the Mississippi River, the sixfold increase in fertilizer use – spurred in part by wartime developments – has spelled ecological consequences not simply on farmlands but also on the Gulf of Mexico downstream.[63]

INTERNMENT AND AGRICULTURAL CHANGE IN THE PACIFIC WEST

The federal government's actions on farm labor, like its efforts to promote wartime crops, demonstrated an active state hand in organizing resources. The *bracero* program, authorized in 1942, brokered relations between growers and Mexican workers, bringing 219,000 Mexicans to the United States as farm workers between 1943 and 1947, and setting in motion

---

[61] Boyd, "Making Meat," 645–646.
[62] Vaclav Smil, "Magic Beans," *Nature* 407 (2000): 567; Anderson, *Industrializing the Corn Belt*, 164–165.
[63] Dan Farber, "Keeping the Stygian Waters at Bay," *Science* 291 (February 9, 2001): 968–973; R. Eugene Turner and Nancy Rabalais, "Changes in Mississippi River Water Quality This Century," *Bioscience* 41, no. 3 (March 1991): 142–144.

reliance on guest workers that continued after the war.[64] Other wartime developments seemed, on the face of it, to have little to do with reorganizing agricultural resources, but in fact held important implications for rural land use and labor – including Japanese American internment. As internment assaulted Japanese Americans' civil liberties, it also uprooted agricultural communities and fostered the consolidation of fruit and vegetable production on the West Coast.

The Japanese attack on Pearl Harbor inflamed long-standing racial prejudices. On February 19, 1942, Executive Order 9066 empowered the secretary of war to designate sensitive "military areas" and exclude "any and all" persons from them. In practice, this act prompted the removal and imprisonment of Japanese American residents, including US citizens, who resided in western Washington, Oregon, and California, and southern Arizona to 10 concentration camps in remote areas throughout the West and the South. Many were Japanese American farmers and fruit growers who had spent half a century toiling in American agriculture. First hired to clear or reclaim land and bring it under cultivation in the late nineteenth century, many Japanese Americans continued to live in rural areas as farm laborers, tenants, and owners.

Japanese internment is more often considered from the perspective of civil liberties and immigration than environmental history, but the internment had key environmental dimensions.[65] First, while wartime context and concerns about national security added a new urgency to anti-Japanese prejudice, much of the resentment about Japanese settlers had long been framed around control over land. The long history of land laws, including alien land laws, at root were legislation governing who shall have access to environmental resources and in what circumstances. Second, anti-Japanese actors enacted violence not simply against Japanese Americans but also against their land. Burning a barn or orchard was simultaneously an environmental and a political act: attacking the land sent a nativist message.

Finally, and perhaps most importantly, knowledge of natural systems and agricultural work shaped the experience of internment for Japanese Americans. For Japanese American farming communities, social and political exclusion that the war inflamed was felt in environmental terms. Connections to land exacerbated the emotional and economic losses

---

[64] Hurt, *Problems of Plenty*, 102–103; Hahamovitch, *No Man's Land*, 6–7.
[65] The exception here is Connie Chiang, *Nature behind Barbed Wire: An Environmental History of Japanese American Incarceration* (New York: Oxford University Press, 2018).

internees experienced as part of their displacement. Wartime imprisonment removed the Issei and Nikkei from the farms and orchards in which they had toiled, cut off Japanese immigrants' access to agricultural credit, and prevented them from managing their lands. Often it precipitated land loss. Indeed, some of the strongest existing literature on the environmental dimensions of Japanese internment has documented the ways that internees utilized gardening and natural resources to challenge their imprisonment.[66]

For decades prior to World War II, anti-Japanese nativists restricted Japanese immigrants' freedom by limiting their access to land. California's 1913 Alien Land Act restricted Japanese immigrants from purchasing agricultural lands or leasing land for a period over three years. In 1922 and 1923, respectively, Washington and Oregon also restricted landownership for noncitizens. In 1922, the Supreme Court ruled in *Ozawa vs. US* that Japanese immigrants were not eligible for citizenship, and the 1924 Immigration Act further prohibited the entry of Japanese immigrants. To circumvent these laws, many Japanese American families purchased land in the name of corporations, or in the names of their American-born daughters and sons once they reached legal age. By the time of the 1942 evacuation, 30 percent of the 6,000 Japanese farm operators interned were landowners.[67]

Even after state restrictions on landownership, Japanese American agrarian communities took root in the interwar period in eastern Multonomah County and the Hood River valley of Oregon, on Bainbridge Island, and in Bellevue, Washington, and in the San Joaquin and Santa Clara Valleys of California, as well as in the outskirts of Los Angeles and San Francisco. In California, Kyutaro Abiko facilitated the purchase of land in the central valley of California in three agricultural settlements.[68] Japanese agricultural communities focused on crops deemed too labor intensive or merely disregarded by white farmers, such as asparagus, celery, and strawberries. They formed cooperatives to market and pack the crops to supply distant markets. By 1941, Japanese Americans grew 42 percent of California's commercial truck crops (a term used to describe vegetables and fruits to be "trucked" to

---

[66] Russell, *War and Nature*, 132–133; Connie Chiang, "Imprisoned Nature: Toward an Environmental History of the World War II Japanese American Incarceration," *Environmental History* 15, no. 2 (April 2010): 236–267.

[67] Valerie Matsumoto, *Farming the Home Place: A Japanese-American Community in California, 1919–1982* (Ithaca, NY: Cornell University Press, 1993), 89.

[68] Matsumoto, *Farming the Home Place*, 30.

consumers). When California consumers reached for snap beans, celery, peppers, or strawberries, there was a 9 in 10 chance that those fruits and vegetables had been cultivated by Japanese American farmers. Nearly 50,000 acres of the state's vineyards and orchards were operated by Japanese American growers.[69]

In the immediate aftermath of the attack on Pearl Harbor, Japanese American farmers faced acts of retribution exacted on their land. In Santa Cruz County, California, arsonists set ablaze the trees on Japanese farms.[70] In King County, Washington, Japanese-owned barns and warehouses were torched.[71] Farm residents within close range of sites chosen for relocation camps expressed fears of sabotage, believing Japanese Americans might burn their crops. War inflamed long-existing racial animosity. Immigration restrictionists hoped to take advantage of the war to target long-desired Japanese-owned landholdings.[72] Farmers in the interior opposed the relocation camps because they wanted to preserve the landholding privileges that Caucasians held in those districts.[73]

By the spring of 1942, Japanese farmers lived in limbo, planting crops they knew they might not harvest. Dorothea Lange's photographs capture these Japanese American families in the weeks immediately prior to evacuation (see Figures 5.1 and 5.2). The images of cartons brimming with strawberries or Japanese American women watering tomato plants are poignant for they demonstrate a faith in the land to provide even as stability and security of agricultural life crumbled. Or perhaps keeping busy with agricultural tasks helped these women maintain a sense of normalcy at a time of great change.

As many Japanese Americans continued to work in the field, others hoped to avoid forced eviction and internment, by voluntarily moving from where evacuation was imminent to the interior. Others took offers from friends, former employees, or tenants to take over the lands, including

---

[69] Masakazu Iwata, "The Japanese Immigrants in California Agriculture," *Agricultural History* 36, no. 1 (January 1962): 32–33.

[70] Timothy Lukes and Gary Okihiro, *Japanese Legacy: Farming and Community Life in California's Santa Clara Valley* (Cupertino: California History Center, 1985), 116.

[71] Stan Flewelling, *Farmlands: The Story of Thomas, a Small Agricultural Community in King County, Washington* (Auburn, WA: Erick Sanders Historical Society, 1990), 116.

[72] Lukes and Okihiro, *Japanese Legacy*, 117.

[73] Robert M. Wilson, "Landscapes of Promise and Betrayal: Reclamation, Homesteading, and Japanese American Incarceration," *Annals of the Association of American Geographers* 101, no. 2 (March 2011): 434–435.

FIGURE 5.1 Dorothea Lange, San Leandro, CA. Watering young plants on a farm in Alaeda County, California, prior to evacuation, April 26, 1942.
Source: Central Photographic File of the War Relocation Agency, 1942–1945. Record Group 210. Records of the War Relocation Authority. National Archives Identifier: 536437. Local Identifier: 210-G-A546. Image in the public domain

equipment and greenhouses.[74] Hood River Oregon's Noji entrusted the land to caretakers for little compensation, with parting words to "take good care of our orchard."[75] In the California Abiko colonies, Japanese Americans in the growers' associations appointed an advisory board and

[74] Mary Tsukamoto, "Jerome," in *And Justice for All: An Oral History of the Japanese American Detention Camps*, ed. John Tateishi (Seattle: University of Washington, 1984), 10–11.
[75] Linda Tamura, *Nisei Soldiers Break Their Silence: Coming Home to Hood River* (Seattle: University of Washington Press, 2012), 64.

FIGURE 5.2 Dorothea Lange, Florin, Sacramento County, California. A soldier and his mother in a strawberry field. May 11, 1942.
Source: Central Photographic File of the War Relocation Agency, 1942–1945. Record Group 210. Records of the War Relocation Authority. National Archives Identifier: 536475. Local Identifier: 210-G-A585. Image in the public domain

hired a manager to ensure the lands be kept in production so they would not have to liquidate their homes and businesses.[76]

Many had to sell. In the Hood River, Oregon, for instance, Masuo Yasui had been a pillar of the agricultural community since 1908, starting a general store, purchasing land and leasing it to Japanese immigrants, and helping to finance others' purchases. By the 1930s, Yasui served on the Board of Directors of the Apple Growers' Association, the Rotary Club, the Chamber of Commerce, and even the selective service board. But in 1942, Masuo Yasui was deemed an enemy alien and imprisoned in Santa Fe, New Mexico. Like many of the Japanese Americans who had toiled for years to become landowners, Yasui sold off properties at bargain prices, agreeing to sell one 160-acre track for less than a third

---

[76] Matsumoto, *Farming the Home Place*, 99–101.

of what he had paid, and another for less than half of the purchase price.[77] Yasui was not alone. Many were not compensated or were compensated poorly for the land turned over due to internment.[78]

An important dimension of the experience of internment, then, was not simply being ostracized by the broader community, but being torn from beloved environments. Recalling the morning of her evacuation, Mary Tsukamoto remembered that how sad her daughter was to leave her dog. Other family members lingered with the plants they'd so long tended. "Grandma couldn't leave her flowers, and Grandpa looked at his grape vineyard." Tsukamoto's farming experience made the dehumanizing experiences of internment hit home: "Suddenly you realized that human beings were being put behind fences just like on the farm where we had horses and pigs in corrals."[79] While gardening and farming skills proved to be resources used to sustain both bodies and spirits while interned, Japanese Americans' environmental relationships also colored the experiences of forced removal.

The federal officials charged with overseeing internment prioritized fulfilling the nation's insatiable needs for agricultural products during wartime over the concerns of individual farm owners. What mattered most to government officials was not who operated farms once operated by Japanese Americans, but that the land remained in production. Fearing that productive land might lie fallow, the War Relocation Department sought out substitute farm operators and even provided production credits and financial assistance to help non-Japanese farmers take over Japanese-operated farms.[80] Further, they helped broker connections between labor-short sugar-beet farmers in the interior with Japanese Americans who could serve as agricultural laborers.[81] Within the camps, internees toiled in lands ill-suited for farming to raise food crops to support their own incarceration, and even to contribute to the war effort.[82]

Once interned, Japanese Americans had little leverage to ensure that the terms of the agreements that they had established to manage their lands were respected. Some generous neighbors tended the lands

---

[77] Lauren Kessler, *Stubborn Twig: Three Generations in the Life of a Japanese-American Family* (New York: Random House, 1993), 104–105, 107, 123–124.

[78] Chiang, *Nature behind Barbed Wire*, 17.   [79] Tsukamoto, "Jerome," 11–12.

[80] Adon Poli and Warren Engstrand, "Japanese Agriculture on the Pacific Coast," *Journal of Land and Public Utility Economics* 21, no. 4 (November 1945): 359.

[81] Louis Fiset, "Thinning, Topping, and Loading: Japanese Americans and Beet Sugar in World War II," *Pacific Northwest Quarterly* 90, no. 3 (Summer 1999): 123–139.

[82] Chiang, *Nature behind Barbed Wire*, 93–121.

carefully. But other tenants stopped paying rent to Japanese owners. A few lessees claimed that the harvests from Japanese-owned tracts were smaller than they were, dishonestly withholding the owners' share of earnings from imprisoned landlords.[83] Despite being unable to exert their direct authority over management, landowners remained liable for taxes and mortgages on those properties.

The end of internment brought new challenges. Once again, Japanese properties were vandalized, and Japanese Americans were refused service and shunned in rural districts.[84] Even families of Japanese American soldiers were targeted. In Placer County, California, angry citizens attempted to dynamite and burn the packing shed at the orchard where Shig Doi, who served with the 442nd Regimental Combat Team, grew up.[85] Arsonists destroyed the farmstead of Wilson Makabe, a fellow Placer County orchard grower's son who served with the 442nd.[86] In more than one case, white farmers to whom Japanese American families had entrusted their lands refused to relinquish them. Many returnees found fields choked with weeds and orchards that hadn't been pruned or tended. Even if one was able to get access to lands and grow a crop, the Teamsters Union and Produce Dealers' Associations organized boycotts of vegetables grown by Japanese American farmers.[87] It's no wonder that two social scientists concluded in 1945, "There is now little evidence that the Japanese American will soon regain any prominence in the agriculture of the West Coast."[88]

Besides these immediate challenges, broader demographic and economic trends made it especially difficult for Japanese American truck farmers to return. As white families abandoned West Coast cities for suburban neighborhoods, they drove up land values on the urban fringe, often in the very areas where truck farms had once prospered. King and Kitsap counties, bordering Seattle, lost half their farms between 1940 and 1960. More than 60 percent of Los Angeles County California's farms foundered during the same period.[89] In the San Jose valley, where defense

[83] Kessler, *Stubborn Twig*, 227–228.
[84] Poli and Engstrom, "Japanese Agriculture on the Pacific Coast," 362; Kessler, *Stubborn Twig*, 239–241.
[85] Shig Doi, "Shule Lake," in Tateishi, *And Justice for All*, 157–159.
[86] Wilson Makabe, "442nd Regimental Combat Team, Italy," in Tateishi, *And Justice for All*, 255.
[87] Dillon Myer, *Uprooted Americans: The Japanese American and the War Relocation Authority during World War II* (Tucson: University of Arizona Press, 1971), 200–201.
[88] Loki and Engstrom, "Japanese Agriculture on the Pacific Coast," 364.
[89] US Bureau of the Census, *Sixteenth US Census of Agriculture – Volume I – Part 48: California* (Washington, DC: US Government Printing Office, 1942), 91; US Bureau of

industries thrived, land prices skyrocketed. One Issei farmer found that lands he sold for $650 per acre now cost $1,500 per acre, so he had to work as a laborer to earn sufficient funds to begin to recoup even part of what he had earned.[90] Centralized produce buying for supermarkets favored farms that produced uniform vegetables in quantity. Japanese vegetable growers, by contrast, had made their mark by growing high-quality vegetables.[91] Further, supermarkets weakened the place of Japanese American retailers, who had previously relied on Japanese American truck farmers for their goods.[92] As supermarkets favored larger produce growers, it became ever-more challenging for Japanese American growers to find markets.

CONCLUSIONS

World War II was a watershed in twentieth-century American environmental history, but when examined from the perspective of the farm field during the war, it is striking to see how the period paired continuity with change. Even as the war created intense demands for food, fiber, and raw materials, farmers used time-tested methods to produce it during the war. The methods by which farmers achieved higher yields – contour cropping, planting legumes, and liming soils – were expanded and intensified, but not introduced. Farmers eagerly awaited, but had yet to experience the pesticides, antibiotics, and herbicides that would transform American agriculture in the years ahead. Given the tendency to view the agricultural system as widely transformed after World War II, it can be surprising to see that Walter Wilcox, the economist charged with summing up the effects of the war on agriculture in 1947, would conclude that there was "no revolutionary technology adopted in war years."[93]

the Census, *Sixteenth US Census of Agriculture – Volume I – Part 46: Washington* (Washington, DC: US Government Printing Office, 1942), 548; US Bureau of the Census, *US Census of Agriculture – Volume I – Part I: California* (Washington, DC: US Government Printing Office, 1961), 165; US Bureau of the Census, *US Census of Agriculture – Volume I – Part 46: Washington* (Washington, DC: US Government Printing Office, 1959), 143.

[90] Lukes and Okihiro, *Japanese Legacy*, 120.

[91] Eiichi Sakauyu, interview by Jiro Saito, San Jose California, February 8, 2005, Densho Digital Repository, https://ddr.densho.org/media/ddr-jamsj-2/ddr-jamsj-2-7-transcript-24b27a5feb.htm (accessed August 15, 2016).

[92] Chiang, *Nature behind Barbed Wire*, 191.

[93] Wilcox, *The Farmer in the Second World War*, 289.

World War II made plain the importance of the federal state in organizing agricultural environments. The federal government funded research, guarded seed stock, built processing capacity, and fostered new ways of conceiving of environmental resources – from kudzu to skim milk. Evicting and housing Japanese American farmers also demonstrated federal power. Price incentives, target production levels, and appeals to patriotism exerted enough pressure to organize major changes in agriculture.

Two federal interventions were especially critical: building processing facilities and channeling funds into research. First, when cultivation patterns did change during the war, they did so due to changes in processing capacity. The state was able to obtain ample hemp production by ensuring sufficient plants to process it. Soy and peanut cultivation, similarly, flourished because it was accompanied by the construction of crushing mills. Farmers were willing to lime their fields but needed a ready capacity for grinding the stone. Defense industry investments in skim milk dryers enabled the product to reach soldiers on naval ships in the Pacific. After the war, policy makers would have to look for alternative outlets for the increased amounts of vegetable oils and dried milk that farmers produced in abundance. By the 1950s, agricultural goods once destined for soldiers' rations or billed as war-ready bargains would be recast as foods to send to war-torn or suffering nations or would be modified in the era of would be modern food chemistry.

Second, wartime spending fostered the development of farm chemicals and pharmaceuticals. After the war, farmers were primed to purchase these products, as high wartime farm prices allowed farmers to climb out of debt and save money for farm improvements. Such technological investments appealed to farmers as farm laborers relocated to cities with burgeoning defense industries and returning veterans migrated to urban and suburban districts, rather than returning to rural areas.

If World War II made plain the importance of the federal state, it also revealed limitations. The resistance and failures of some new agricultural sectors to take root and the organized opposition of farm groups to state production in a time of war are also worth noting. Coming after a decade of deep federal involvement in agriculture (the New Deal), farmers weary of federal involvement challenged federal authority over wartime agricultural projects. They balked at growing hemp and guayule. Fear of rural resistance led soil conservation officials to keep its programs voluntary. Conservationist Aldo Leopold reminded landowners that individual action limited government's power, writing in a 1942 essay "Democracy and Land-Use," "government, no matter how good, can only do certain things. Government can't raise crops, maintain small scattered structures, administer small scattered areas, or bring to bear on small local matters that combination of solicitude, foresight, and skill we call husbandry."[94] Even as World War II encouraged farmers to remake private lands to meet public obligations, it left unresolved how exactly the balance between citizens' individual responsibilities and collective security and safety would be carried out. Determining that balance would have great significance not just for rural environments during war, but in many environmental battles in the years to come.

[94] Aldo Leopold, "Land-Use and Democracy," *Audubon* 44 (September–October 1942): 152.

6

When Meals Became Weapons

American Food in World War II

Kellen Backer

In World War II, food became a weapon. This metamorphosis was at the center of the US propaganda film *Food and Magic*. The film follows a trick-performing magician who teaches an audience about the new significance and transformations of American food from plow to table. While the magician praised farmers – and the new workers on farms – for creating abundance, he also stressed that food was a limited resource, one that was constantly being wasted. The magician shrank a tomato, telling the audience, "by waste ... we've shrunk our available food supply ... that's like throwing victory into the garbage can." The film promised hope, though, if Americans could learn to conserve food. As the film concludes, "Food fights for freedom ... it is the weapon in our hands at home."[1]

Food helped determine the war's outcome: from the outset, when concern over *Lebensraum* ("living space") pushed Hitler to invade Poland and the Soviet Union, to the close, when American farmers kept US and Allied troops and populations fed and content while enemy armies and populations slowly starved. Overall, the United States was able to supply its soldiers – and to supply other Allied nations – with ample food. While famine plagued many areas during the war, America and its soldiers were well fed. In this arena, America's food strategy worked quite well. But this wartime strategy also significantly changed American food production for decades to come.[2]

[1] *Food and Magic*, directed by Jean Nugulesco (Washington, DC: Office of War Information, 1943), http://archive.org/details/FoodAndMagic (accessed July 14, 2017).
[2] For a full discussion of food as a weapon of war, see Lizzie Collingham, *The Taste of War: World War II and the Battle for Food* (London: Allen Lane, 2011).

The war had paradoxical consequences. On the one hand, it fashioned a food system that was more highly industrialized. Moreover, this system emphasized processed products, such as canned, frozen, and dehydrated foods, that were more removed from farms and were capable of being consumed outside of traditional harvesting seasons. At the same time, the war also helped many Americans become more involved in agriculture. As Americans established "victory gardens" and conserved food, people learned more about agricultural production. Ultimately, however, the war's legacy had more to do with industrializing American food production, as the research and infrastructure supporting processed foods persisted into peacetime, while victory gardens and conservation campaigns disappeared.

We can see these widespread changes in the three main themes that government wartime propaganda emphasized: produce, conserve, and share and play fair.[3]

As the war transformed food into a strategic resource that could help the United States and its allies win the war, food production changed, hence the wartime emphasis to *produce*. Much like car factories were remade to make tanks, food production shifted, especially because of the growth of food processing. To meet the war's demands, the US military turned to processed foods that aimed to liberate food from typical environmental restraints. To prevent food spoilage, the military wanted long-lasting products not subject to seasonal and geographic constraints. To *produce* also meant encouraging many people – including large numbers of urban women and international laborers – to play a new role in American agriculture. It also meant the development of "victory gardens." Farming and agricultural also changed during the war, as Kendra Smith-Howard shows in this book (Chapter 5).

Conserve meant utilizing resources efficiently. Wartime propaganda encouraged Americans, particularly women – who theoretically did the most domestic cooking, to avoid waste. *Food and Magic* claimed that food waste equaled the total food needs of the armed forces. This propaganda campaign focused on the home, where spoiled foods and thrown away

---

[3] The full slogan was "produce and conserve, share and play fair." For more on these wartime themes, see Barbara McLean Ward, ed., *Produce and Conserve, Share and Play Square: The Grocer and the Consumer on the Home-Front Battlefield during World War II* (Portsmouth, NH: University Press of New England, 1994); Amy Bentley, *Eating for Victory: Food Rationing and the Politics of Domesticity* (Urbana: University of Illinois Press, 1998); and Kellen Backer, "World War II and the Triumph of Industrialized Food" (PhD diss., University of Wisconsin – Madison, 2012).

leftovers represented wasted weapons. The kitchen became imbued with newfound significance. Conservation transformed American relationships with food, as did the increasing importance of nutrition during the war, though these values, especially conservation, diminished after the war.

Sharing emphasized the importance of selflessness; *playing square* meant following wartime regulations. To discourage hoarding, government propaganda reminded Americans of food shortages around the world and of the needs of the armed forces. Being patriotic also meant following rules about rationing, price controls, and a host of regulations aimed at improving production and ensuring a fair distribution of food. Following regulations helped to reshape the kind of food that companies produced and citizens ate. That said, state policy did not always create a level playing field. Regulations benefited products that helped the war effort, especially those that large-scale industrialized food processors created.

As food became a weapon, World War II created massive shifts in the American food system and America's food culture. To better understand the scope of these changes, the following sections examines what it meant to *produce*, *conserve*, and *share* and *play square* as food transformed into a weapon.

PRODUCING MILITARY FOOD

During World War II, the United States had tremendous food needs. It needed to feed the largest army in its history across multiple distant theaters, while also helping far-flung allies. The military stood at the center of production, with the army's Quartermaster Corps playing the biggest role in designing and procuring food and setting requirements. Although the navy also procured food, it was smaller and often relied on the army's distribution networks and rations.[4]

More so than ever before, the US government's food strategy relied on processing and standardization. This meant creating uniform products. World War I had revealed the shortcomings of older strategies surrounding "subsistence," the military's term for food. During the war, rations were shipped in awkwardly sized containers – sometimes with different portion sizes for each part of a meal, which increased leftover food waste. In addition, the containers often fell apart during overseas transit. In the

---

[4] For more on the army versus navy, see Backer, "World War II and the Triumph of Industrialized Food"; and Julius Augustus Furer, *Administration of the Navy Department in World War II* (Washington, DC: US Government Printing Office, 1959), 454 and 594.

1920s and 1930s, through slow but steady research and training, the Quartermaster Corps created new ways of procuring, distributing, and serving food – methods emphasizing standardization.[5]

The first way the military improved its food strategy came through improved education. After World War I, the Corps started a small school that trained officers from throughout the military, including the navy. The school developed textbooks and manuals for training new cooks, such as *The Army Cook*, which became the main guidebook for World War II. Importantly, the Quartermaster Corps understood that, historically, cooks had rarely followed recipes in the field. The new manuals aimed to standardize and improve recipes and practices, so that cooks would follow instructions. When the school closed in 1936, it was turned into a laboratory – the Subsistence Research Laboratory – where officers and civilians worked to standardize foods and develop new rations.[6]

The lab was the second, and more important, way the army worked to improve its food strategy between the world wars. Quartermaster Corps researchers at the lab worked closely with experts in industry and academia to devise ways to standardize foods and develop new rations. For academics, such research highlighted the possibilities of using new techniques, such as freezing, canning, and dehydrating, as well as new nutritional knowledge, to transform food. For industry, such research helped to create close ties with the military that in later years would prove very profitable. For example, in the late 1930s, Hershey helped develop the D ration, a compact chocolate bar that could sustain a soldier in an emergency. However, because of the technologies used to produce the bar, only a handful of companies could manufacture it, giving Hershey a substantial advantage in selling to the military when production increased during World War II.[7]

---

[5] For World War I, see Walter Porges, *The Subsistence Research Laboratory* (Chicago: Chicago Quartermaster Depot, 1943); Harold W. Thatcher, *The Development of Special Rations for the Army* (Washington, DC: Office of the Quartermaster General, 1944); and Erna Risch, *The Quartermaster Corps: Organization, Supply and Services* (Washington, DC: Center of Military History, 1995).

[6] For the history of the school, see Porges, *The Subsistence Research Laboratory*; for later research see also, Backer, "World War II and the Triumph of Industrialized Food"; and Thatcher, *The Development of Special Rations for the Army*.

[7] See Porges, *The Subsistence Research Laboratory*; Backer, "World War II and the Triumph of Industrialized Food"; and Thatcher, *The Development of Special Rations for the Army*. For information on Hershey's role in developing the D ration, see Paul P. Logan to Rohland A. Isker, April 26, 1943, reprinted in Porges, *The Subsistence Research Laboratory*, Appendix IV.

During World War II, the army implemented its new subsistence strategy, using standardized field rations away from camps and standardized menus at camps. For field rations, the C ration replicated a standard meal, like a meat stew. For emergencies, when soldiers lacked other foods, the army used D rations and later developed K rations. At bases, cooks used standardized cookbooks and menus. In earlier wars, cooks had freedom to use foods as they saw fit. In World War II, however, the Quartermaster Corps sent specific foods to bases along with menus and recipes. This strategy gave the Quartermaster Corps control over soldiers' food, but the strategy also required processed and standardized foods.[8]

The military shipped processed foods from the United States to troops on the front lines. Rather than rely on an unpredictable supply of local or seasonal foods, the army worked to create a seamless network that could transport foods around the globe, providing products independent of growing seasons. New technologies and industries allowed for many more foods to be canned, frozen, and dehydrated. The Quartermaster Corps worked with civilian regulatory agencies to increase the infrastructure supporting these industries. For frozen foods, for example, the war brought an increase in refrigerated warehouse space, which allowed many more products to be stored. For all these industries, the US government worked to improve production, transportation, and storage, ultimately creating a global distribution network for processed foods.[9]

In addition to using the latest processing technologies, the army's new subsistence strategy meant standardizing food. This was a tricky task, as

[8] For a detailed look at this strategy, see Kellen Backer, "Constructing Borderless Foods: The Quartermaster Corps and World War II Army Subsistence, in *Food across Borders*, ed. Matt Garcia, E. Melanie Dupuis, and Don Mitchell (New Brunswick, NJ: Rutgers University Press, 2017), 121–139.

[9] See Porges, *The Subsistence Research Laboratory*; Backer, "World War II and the Triumph of Industrialized Food"; and Thatcher, *The Development of Special Rations for the Army*. For a more transnational look at food as a weapon in World War II, see Collingham, *The Taste of War*. For more on the history of canned foods in the 1920s and 1930s see Anna Zeide, *Canned: The Rise and Fall of Consumer Confidence in the American Food Industry* (Oakland: University of California Press, 2018). For an older history, of canned foods, see C. Anne Wilson, ed., *Waste Not, Want Not: Food Preservation from Early Times to the Present Day* (Edinburgh: Edinburgh University Press, 1991). For frozen foods, see Oscar Edward Anderson, *Refrigeration in America* (Princeton, NJ: Princeton University Press, 1953); and Jonathan Reese, *Refrigeration Nation: A History of Ice, Appliances, and Enterprise in America* (Baltimore: Johns Hopkins University Press, 2013). See also Gabriella M. Petrick, "The Arbiters of Taste: Producers, Consumers, and the Industrialization of Taste in America, 1900–1960" (PhD diss., University of Delaware, 2006).

many products are inherently different. Indeed a 1944 Quartermaster manual on grading noted "no two heads of cabbage are identical." In addition, even processed products – ranging from bologna to salami to canned fruit cocktail – varied from manufacturer to manufacturer. Nonetheless, the Quartermaster Corps worked with experts in industry – usually from larger food production companies – to develop standards. The army's purchasing power pressured companies to conform to these requirements.[10]

Standards, in turn, reshaped the growing and production of foods. During World War II, Frederick Stare, the president of the Columbus Canning Company and president of the National Canners Association, began to notice something odd about the grading of peas. Ostensibly, peas were supposed to be graded on a number of different criteria that included things like color, flavor, and tenderness. The sudden expansion of grading during the war, however, meant new inspectors seemed to be relying on a more specific criterion. Frederick Stare wrote that "inspectors ... simply see whether the can is full and then put some of the peas in a salt solution, and then if the majority of them float almost immediately, they are O.K." The war helped turn peas into something that floated, an easily graded canned food, rather than something consumers might want to eat.[11]

The war also spurred research in technologies that improved food production. While there was nothing quite as dramatic as the atomic bomb in terms of food research, the Quartermaster Corps and academic and

[10] For some of the challenges of standardizing food, see *Inspection Handbook, Subsistence, QMC 25-1 November 1944*, pp. 2 and 7; QMC Manual 23-5 thru QMC Manual M608–3; Record Set of Publications: 1944–61; Office of the Quartermaster General, Record Group 92; National Archives and Records Administration, College Park, MD. Henceforth, this record group and archive will be referred to as OQG. The entry General Correspondence Relating to Research and Development, 1928–1954 contains hundreds of boxes related to the development of army specifications. For an example of a specification, see PP-S-96 in 400.1141 Sausage, Salami PP-S #96 1943; General Correspondence Relating to Research and Development, 1928–1954; OQG.

[11] Quotation from Stare to Office of Production Management, July 12, 1941, Reel 9. See also Stare to Office of Production Management June 20, 1941, Reel 10; Stare to Office of Production Management June 27, 1941, Reel 10; and Stare to Office of Production Management, July 3, 1941, Reel 10; and Stare to Quartermaster Corps, July 9, 1941, Reel 9. In Stare to USDA, March 17, 1943, Reel 9, Stare lists individuals qualified for grading. All these letters are located in Records, 1901–1946, Columbus Food Corporation, Wisconsin Historical Society Archives, Madison, WI. For an analysis of why density mattered to peas, see L. S. Fenn, "Specific Gravity of Canned Peas as an Index of Maturity," *The Canner*, March 28, 1942, 18.

industry experts made myriad small improvements. Cans became stronger and used less tin. Dehydrated food packaging improved. Experiments tested the use of insecticides in packaging. The Subsistence Research Laboratory evaluated new processed foods, such as canned bread and dehydrated foods. Wartime research also yielded several spin-off technologies, such as DDT and frozen-concentrated orange juice.[12]

All this research supported military food, which meant developing highly processed foods that could be distributed globally. Such changes reverberated through the civilian food industry, as regulators worked to create networks to distribute industrialized foods throughout the country.

PRODUCING CROPS AND GARDENS

Increasing production required solving labor shortages. As many young men left for war, farms needed new workers. In response, women took on jobs traditionally reserved for men. Rural schools enlisted teenagers to do farm work. Government agencies brought international workers to the countryside to help work; one Wisconsin canning company, for example, employed Jamaican workers for part of the war. The government even allowed some German prisoners into the paid agricultural workforce. Finally, urban women directly joined the war effort by farming.[13]

Just as Rosie the Riveter entered factories, women who had never farmed before worked on farms, particularly through the work of the Women's Land Army, which transported predominantly urban women to rural areas to work on farms. Growing foods provided these women new opportunities to understand agriculture and women's new roles within the workforce. Farm women had done agricultural work, such as raising poultry, throughout the nation's history. However, women's new wartime roles were much more prominent. In 1942, the Department of

---

[12] See Backer, "World War II and the Triumph of Industrialized Food"; for cans, see "Metal Container Changes in the Interest of Tin Conservation," *The Canner*, August 1, 1942, 11 and 24; "Extension of Electrolytic Tinplating Will Help Alleviate Tin Shortages," *The Canner*, October 10, 1942, 18. For DDT, see Edmund P. Russell, "The Strange Career of DDT: Experts, Federal Capacity, and Environmentalism in World War II," *Technology and Culture* 40, no. 4 (1999), 770–796; and Edmund P. Russell, *War and Nature: Fighting Humans and Insects with Chemicals from World War I to Silent Spring* (New York: Cambridge University Press, 2001). For orange juice, see Alissa Hamilton, *Squeezed: What You Don't Know about Orange Juice* (New Haven, CT: Yale University Press, 2009).

[13] For a more comprehensive look at these changes, see Backer, "World War II and the Triumph of Industrialized Food."

Agricultural approved funds to create the Women's Land Army, which served as a very visible example of women doing work that even included uniforms to identify "troops." In total, about three million women joined the Women's Land Army, making it the largest group helping fill agricultural labor shortages. World War II increased women's involvement in agriculture, a trend that extended into the postwar era.[14]

No agricultural labor program that emerged from the war was better known than the Bracero Program. Mexican immigrants had moved across the US border for work long before World War II. In 1942, however, the US and Mexican governments agreed to allow Mexican workers to enter America. The War Manpower Commission worked with companies in the United States and with Mexican immigrants to fill labor shortages. As part of the program, more than 100,000 Mexicans moved to the United States during World War II, and over four million by 1962.[15]

Americans also increased food production at home. According to government propaganda, "victory gardens," as they came to be known, were an essential part of the war effort. Posters encouraged individuals to remember that "our food is fighting" and gardens could help "rations go further." Other posters were more blunt and encouraged individuals to "be sure" of their food supply by growing "your own." Victory gardens were described as both a "public duty" and a "private necessity."[16]

Victory gardens changed gardening. First, the war increased the number of people who gardened. Women in garden clubs found new audiences for their expertise, giving classes to teach more people how to cultivate foods. Colleges, botanical gardens, and extension services

[14] See Cecilia Gowdy-Wygant, *Cultivating Victory: The Women's Land Army and the Victory Garden Movement* (Pittsburgh, PA: University of Pittsburgh Press, 2013); and Stephanie A. Carpenter, *On the Farm Front: The Women's Land Army in World War II* (DeKalb: Northern Illinois University Press, 2003). For a look at how rural communities persuaded men to stay on the farm, see Katherine Jellison, "Get Your Farm in the Fight: Farm Masculinity in World War II," *Agricultural History* 92, no. 1 (2018): 5–20.

[15] See Deborah Cohen, *Braceros: Migrant Citizens and Transnational Subjects in the Postwar United States and Mexico* (Chapel Hill: University of North Carolina Press, 2011); Erasmo Gamboa, *Mexican Labor and World War II: Braceros in the Pacific Northwest, 1942–1947* (Austin: University of Texas Press, 1990); and Don Mitchell, *They Saved the Crops: Labor, Landscape, and the Struggle over Industrial Farming in Bracero-Era California* (Athens: University of Georgia Press, 2012).

[16] For posters, see "Plant a Victory Garden: Our Food Is Fighting: A Garden Will Make Your Rations Go Further" and Grover Strong, "Grow Your Own: Be Sure!; Be Sure." All posters come from Northwestern University Library's World War II Poster Collection. The final quotation comes from Victor R. Boswell, *Victory Gardens* (Washington, DC: US Department of Agriculture, 1943), 3.

increased their outreach as well. One estimate suggested that 21 million gardens in 1943 produced more than 10 million pounds of food. This estimate comes from government literature, which tended to overstate the success of wartime programs, but if the numbers were true, there were at least twice as many people gardening as there were people working on farms. Moreover, as Anastasia Day notes, this estimated production represents more than 40 percent of the annual civilian consumption of fresh fruit and vegetables.[17]

Second, gardening introduced new values, reshaping people's attitudes toward the environment. For example, pamphlets described food as a weapon, with the enemy being animals and insects that might disrupt the garden. Such analogies encouraged gardeners to understand their task in military terms, where insects became invaders to be killed using insecticides. Decades later, Rachel Carson noted the relentless military nature of the fight against insects, which she dubbed a "war against nature." Many of the chemicals used in this war, and the accompanying attitudes, emerged from World War II. The pamphlets pushing victory gardens also carried alternative agendas. One gardening pamphlet in New York specifically described the best place to garden as being "the home," which gave "pride in ownership," and allowed individuals to protect against "all enemies, including suburban marauders." Here, neighbors became enemies and the pamphlet eschewed any promotion of community gardens.[18]

As gardening became linked to warfare, people's understandings of food began to change, particularly because of the government's emphasis on efficiency. Victory gardeners, for example, needed to decide what

[17] For examples of the growth of gardening and garden outreach, see Clement G. Bowers, "Garden Clubs Provide Training Useful in This Time of Emergency," *New York Times*, January 17, 1943; and "Victory Garden Courses Start," *New York Times*, March 22, 1942. For figures on gardening, see Office of Program Coordination, Office of War Information, and the War Food Administration, in cooperation with Office of Price Administration, *Food Fights for Freedom* (Washington, DC: US Government Printing Office, 1943). The quotation comes from Anastasia Day and Timothy Johnson, "Rethinking American Agriculture: Fertilized Farms and Victory Gardens," *Edge Effects*, January 10, 2017, http://edgeeffects.net/rethinking-agriculture/ (accessed June 20, 2017). See also Anastasia Day, "The Industrial Gardener: Management of World War II Victory Gardeners within a Factory Paradigm," in *The Good Gardener? Nature, Humanity and the Garden*, ed. Annette Giesecke and Naomi Jacobs (London: Artifice Books on Architecture, 2015), 114–127.

[18] See New York State College of Agriculture, *Victory Gardens in Greater New York* (New York: Greater New York Victory Garden Council, 1943), 4; and Rachel Carson, *Silent Spring*, 40th Anniversary Edition (Boston: Mariner, 2002), 7. For more on the broader history of insecticides, see Russell, *War and Nature*.

kinds of foods to plant. Such decisions involved values such as taste, health, and efficiency. Government propaganda suggested that the ideal foods would be easy to grow, nutritious, and appetizing. In pamphlets, taste lost out, as writers described fruits and vegetables exclusively in terms of their growing efficiency and nutritional content.[19]

Paradoxically, victory gardens also seem to have taught consumers about processed foods. During peak growing seasons, gardeners produced more than they could eat. To save food for the war, people needed to preserve their harvest. Home canning offered one option; in trade journals, however, industry experts argued that people would struggle with the process and that home canning would ultimately lead consumers to better appreciate the quality of commercially canned goods.[20]

Freezing was also a viable and increasingly used option for preserving garden foods. As few consumers had freezers at home, the War Production Board approved the construction of numerous community freezing facilities, where consumers could rent individual lockers to freeze foods. Though commercially frozen foods started to be sold in the late 1920s, they were still a rarity at the start of World War II. Preserving homegrown vegetables allowed many consumers to taste frozen foods for the first time; companies argued that this process ultimately helped consumers accept their frozen products.[21]

The wartime call to "produce" meant growing more, producing more, and making food fit the needs of the war. This work on production was important, but there were limits to increasing outputs. The war required more: it required conservation, which put added pressures on individuals and transformed meals into a patriotic duty.

CONSERVE: TURNING FOODS INTO NUTRIENTS

A 1943 Betty Crocker cooking pamphlet proudly declared: "Hail to the women of America! You have taken up your heritage from the brave women of the past. Just as did the women of other wars, you have taken your position as soldiers on the Home Front.... But whatever else you

---

[19] See New York State College of Agriculture, *Victory Gardens in Greater New York* for an example of how taste gets ignored in describing Victory Gardens.

[20] See "The Candid Canner," *The Canner*, July 17, 1943, 11.

[21] See S. T. Warrington, "Local Food Processing and Frozen Storage – Its Contribution to the War Food Program," *Ice and Refrigeration*, November 1943, 245; Helen E. Kimball, "Wartime Refrigeration," *Ice and Refrigeration*, February 1943, 211; and "Locker Plants Help Promote Victory Gardens," *Ice and Refrigeration*, June 1943, 337.

do – you are, first and foremost, homemakers – women with the welfare of your families deepest in your hearts." Above all, the pamphlet emphasized women's new responsibility to help win the war by providing nutritious meals at home. But this was a difficult task: "you must make a little do where there was abundance before.... You must heed the government request to increase the use of available foods, and save those that are scarce – and, at the same time, safeguard your family's nutrition." In sum, the pamphlet concluded, "Never has there been such an opportunity, and a need, for what American women can contribute."[22]

Women had been told before World War II that making meals was an essential part of taking care of a family; wartime rhetoric, however, linked meals to both family and nation. During World War II, government propaganda suggested that preparing proper meals was a duty and wasting foods hindered the war effort. Moreover, new rhetoric equated food with nutrients that were important for keeping bodies healthy, preserving resources, and helping to win the war.[23]

During the war, rationing limited the availability of certain foods, yet the pressure to make nutritious meals grew. Nonnutritious meals wasted agricultural resources and medical resources. In World War I, hundreds of thousands of men were turned away from the military for poor health; more nutritious meals would help to remedy this problem. Consumers could also use different products. World War II slogans suggested that "[i]t's a part of patriotism to be ready to shift our cooking and our eating habits on short notice." Instead of using high demand foods, like prime cuts of meat, consumers were encouraged to utilize substitutes and lesser-valued alternatives. Americans could also save food by making "the most of every pound of food we have."[24]

---

[22] Betty Crocker, *Your Share: How to Prepare Appetizing, Healthful Meals with Foods Available Today* (Minneapolis, MN: General Mills, 1943), inside cover. This pamphlet comes from Folder 12, Box 20, Series 13 [pamphlets], Cecily Brownstone Papers, Fales Library, New York University.

[23] For examples of pressures on mothers before World War II, see Katherine J. Parkin, *Food Is Love: Advertising and Gender Roles in Modern America* (Philadelphia: University of Pennsylvania Press, 2007); and Ruth Schwartz Cowan, *More Work for Mother: The Ironies of Household Technologies from the Open Hearth to the Microwave* (New York: Basic Books, 1983). For World War II, see Bentley, *Eating for Victory*; Charlotte Biltekoff, *Eating Right in America: The Cultural Politics of Food and Health* (Durham, NC: Duke University Press, 2013); and Backer, "World War II and the Triumph of Industrialized Food."

[24] Quotations from Bureau of Home Economics, "Cheese in Your Meals," (Washington: US Department of Agriculture, 1943), https://naldc.nal.usda.gov/download/1789382/PDF (accessed July 29, 2019). For World War I, see Sanders Marble, "Origins of the Physical

As wartime propaganda placed new pressures on consumers, food companies offered to help with conserving food. For example, a Betty Crocker pamphlet suggested tactics for stretching ingredients. To save butter, the pamphlet suggested adding it to the serving dish, rather than to cooking dish, where some would be lost. An enterprising cook could also make a butter substitute by using gelatin, milk, butter, and food coloring. But the pamphlet's main message was about how General Mills could aid wartime conservation efforts: cake mixes could spare cooks from making sugar substitutions, while Bisquick contained shortening and again saved ingredients. Commercial products thus offered a way to conserve critical food materials.[25]

World War II created a new discourse surrounding nutrition. For example, a World War II booklet warned women that in 1936–1937 "only one-fourth of the families in the United States were getting what nutritionists call 'a good diet.'"[26] The war increased the importance of a good diet, and women were pressured to improve family diets, while spending less money and navigating wartime rationing.

Home economists, nutritionists, and other experts emphasized the newfound importance of nutrients. The Bureau of Home Economics told women that they had "a great advantage over women in World War I. Information on calories, proteins, vitamins, and minerals has been increased until it is possible to set up charts" that would detail exactly what humans needed. Nutrient charts were a common part of wartime cooking manuals. One manual listed a number of ingredients that could be substituted for proteins. Nuts, for example, could replace meats. There were recipes for "walnut sausage" and "mock meat loaf" consisting of bread and peanut butter.[27]

Governmental rhetoric about food and conservation, then, helped to transform foods into nutrients. Nutrients allowed walnuts to equal sausages, though of course the foods tasted completely different. Recently,

Profile," *Military Medicine* 178, no. 8 (2013): 887–892. See also, Bentley, *Eating for Victory*; Biltekoff, *Eating Right in America*; and Backer, "World War II and the Triumph of Industrialized Food." For more on rationing, see the discussion of the Office of Price Administration later in this chapter.

[25] Crocker, *Your Share*.

[26] Helen Dallas, *How to Win on the Home Front* (New York: Public Affairs Pamphlet, 1942), 17.

[27] The first quotation is from ibid., 17. For substitution recipes, see Corrinne Bush, Ina Gerritt, Esther T. Long, and Claude Steen, eds., *Victory Proteins* (Fullerton, CA: Nutrition Committee of the Fullerton Civilian Defense Council, 1943).

Gyorgy Scrinis and Michael Pollan have critiqued "nutritionism." Scrinis, who created this term, argues that in this worldview, "a focus on nutrients has come to dominate, to undermine, and to replace other ways of engaging with food and of contextualizing the relationship between food and the body." Moreover, nutritionism is often "co-opted by the food industry and has become a powerful means of marketing their products." Looking at World War II shows the historical roots of contemporary nutritionism.[28]

Indeed, foods were so reduced to their bare essentials in World War II that, in the name of conservation, some even equated food with explosives. To conserve resources, the US government organized drives that would allow Americans to recycle materials. Because tin and aluminum were scarce, reusing these materials would extend existing resources. During the war, the government organized drives to collect and reuse different materials, including kitchen fats. Meat dealers would collect kitchen fats, which would then be turned into explosives. The abstraction of food as nutrients meant understanding how the molecular composition of foods could aid the war, whether through creating meals with proper nutrients or transforming leftover waste into a weapon.[29]

The wartime emphasis on conservation thus helped to reshape how people thought about foods. Conservation efforts were widespread during the war. In 1942, "an army of a million and half women" pledged to "buy carefully ... take care of the things I have ... [and] waste nothing."[30] As millions of Americans thought about conservation, their ideas about food changed. Nothing should be wasted and substitutions needed to be made. Ideas about substitutions and health helped consumers conceptualize foods as merely nutrients. Such transformations also opened the door for food companies to sell new products. Production pushed industrialized foods and conservation helped to reshape food cultures to accept these foods. The final wartime themes, "share and play square" further helped to reshape American food.

---

[28] Gyorgy Scrinis, "On the Ideology of Nutritionism," *Gastronomica* 8, no. 1 (2008): 39–48, quotation from 39. See also Gyorgy Scrinis, *Nutritionism: The Science and Politics of Dietary Advice* (New York: Columbia University Press, 2013), and Michael Pollan, *In Defense of Food: An Eater's Manifesto* (New York: Penguin Press, 2008).

[29] For more on fat drives, see Susan Strasser, *Waste and Want: A Social History of Trash* (New York: Holt, 1999).

[30] Dallas, *How to Win on the Home Front*, 3.

SHARE AND PLAY SQUARE: HOW REGULATIONS RESHAPED AMERICAN FOOD

The war also raised important questions about fairness in the food production and distribution systems. Would individuals or companies try to take advantage of the unusual wartime situation? Here, the government stressed "share and play square." Sharing meant being willing to share foods through both literal sharing and through not taking more than one's fair share. Playing square meant following the rules. Companies were also expected to share and play square, though companies competed on an uneven field in the wartime regulatory environment, as those firms whose work could be tied to war production had advantages. Larger food-processing companies benefitted the most from wartime regulations.

For consumers, the government encouraged sharing and playing square through the regulations of the Office of Price Administration (OPA), which worked to protect consumers and ensure a fair division of products with price ceilings and rationing. Price ceilings combated the inflation that wars often bring. As Depression-weary Americans had more money from a suddenly vibrant economy, they clamored for more food. Price ceilings helped to allow everyone a chance at purchasing goods. To ensure access, OPA rationed certain foods, including sugar and popular cuts of meat.[31]

The government also organized rationing as a response to shortages caused by several factors. First, the military limited what was available for the civilian market. Second, fewer international products came into the United States – and virtually no products from regions with significant fighting. Third, through a process known as Lend-Lease, the United States delivered food to its allies. While American farms managed to increase production, labor shortages and scarce materials still threatened to derail production. Furthermore, the military wanted to create a stockpile that would ensure continued supply.[32]

---

[31] For more on the history of OPA, see Laurence E. Tilley, *Chronology of the Office of Price Administration* (Washington, DC: US Government Printing Office, 1946); *The Beginnings of OPA* (Washington, DC: Office of Temporary Controls, Office of Price Administration, 1947); Harvey Mansfield, *A Short History of OPA* (Washington, DC: Office of Temporary Controls, Office of Price Administration, 1946); Meg Jacobs, "'How about Some Meat?': The Office of Price Administration, Consumption Politics, and State Building from the Bottom Up, 1941–1946." *Journal of American History* 84, no. 3 (1997), 910–941; and Bentley, *Eating for Victory*.

[32] For a more detailed look at these trends, see Backer, "World War II and the Triumph of Industrialized Food."

Military stockpiles also shaped rationing policy when stored materials were released to the public. The military requested a large stockpile of frozen foods, though it rarely drew from this stockpile. In the subsequent year, when crops were being harvested, warehoused frozen foods were released to the civilian market. Because of the large stockpile, OPA lowered the ration point cost of frozen foods, which in turn helped frozen foods began a part of everyday life, though a lack of freezer space in the home meant consumers purchased products for daily use. Clarence Birdseye, a man whose name was nearly synonymous with frozen foods, argued that wartime rationing had "broken down the housewife's reluctance to shop around for new products." Another expert observed after the close of the war that "consumer acceptance of frozen foods was hastened during the war by the elimination from the ration list of frozen fruits and vegetables. Many consumers, who otherwise would have hesitated to try a new product, became acquainted with and found they liked frozen foods."[33]

Price ceilings and rationing also helped to introduce new meats, particularly chicken, to the American diet. The government reserved large quantities of beef and pork, long staples of the American diet, for soldiers. The military valued these meats for their cultural importance, as well as for the infrastructure available to process them. Well-established industries, like beef and pork, had ties to butchers and processors who could make these meats useful for the military. This left other meats, like poultry, for the civilian market. Indeed, chicken production and consumption soared during the war. In the decade before World War II, poultry production rose about 1 percent a year. After World War II, the industry grew by 7 percent annually. All meat production increased during the war, but the poultry industry could expand rapidly, as chickens matured quickly and required less processing. For these reasons, government regulators pushed increased chicken production.[34]

The poultry industry was not an isolated example: new government regulations, especially rules from the War Food Administration and the War Production Board, encouraged many other specific industries during

[33] See "Rationing Helps Frozen Food Sales," *Ice and Refrigeration*, March 1944, 156; "Food Processing and Marketing Outlook Indicates Expansion of Refrigeration Industry," *Ice and Refrigeration*, February 1946, 25.

[34] For production figures before World War I, see Walter Wilcox, *The Farmer in the Second World War* (Ames: Iowa State College Press, 1947), 135. For after World War II, see William Boyd, "Making Meat: Science, Technology, and American Poultry Production," *Technology and Culture* 42, no. 4 (2001): 631–664.

the war. The War Production Board controlled critical materials, such as gasoline, tin, and farm machinery. For food companies, expanding facilities required regulatory approval. Companies that did not sell foods to the armed forces could not access critical materials. The war brought very high corporate tax rates, while also bringing a boom in sales. Instead of paying a high tax rate, companies wanted to use profits to expand. However, the War Production Board only allowed certain companies to expand, favoring companies that produced processed foods that could be shipped around the world.[35]

The War Food Administration (WFA) regulated food. Government officials from the military, regulatory, and agricultural agencies related to food production gave the WFA benchmarks. To encourage production, the WFA guaranteed prices, so that farmers knew how much money they would make. It also worked to prevent bottlenecks in processing and distribution, by helping to expand factories, storage space, and transportation infrastructure. For many of these tasks, the WFA depended on the War Production Board to release certain critical materials.[36]

The rules of these two agencies reshaped food production for the military. Consider, for example, food canners. Food canners had to orient production toward the military to be able to get cans, a key element of their business. Tin was in short supply during the war, so the War Production Board issued regulations that specified exactly what materials could be canned. Foods had to be on a specific list – a list that excluded many regional specialties or foods of immigrant communities that the

---

[35] A useful overview of the administrative history of these agencies is *The United States at War: Development of the War Program by the Federal Government* (Washington, DC: US Government Printing Office, 1946). Additionally, the National Archives, *Federal Records of World War II* (Washington, DC: US Government Printing Office, 1950) is a critical resource for exploring the size and scope of many wartime agencies. For more on the War Production Board, see US Civil Production Administration, *Industrial Mobilization for War; History of the War Production Board and Predecessor Agencies, 1940–1945* (Washington, DC: US Government Printing Office); and Paul Koistinen, *Arsenal of World War II: The Political Economy of American Warfare, 1940–1945* (Lawrence: University Press of Kansas, 2004). For how these agencies related to small businesses, see Jonathan J. Bean, *Beyond the Broker State: Federal Policies toward Small Business, 1936–1961* (Chapel Hill: University of North Carolina Press, 1996), 92–95; and Jim F. Heath, "War Mobilization and the Use of Small Manufacturers, 1939–1943," *Business History Review* 46, no. 3 (1972): 295–315. For a look at how food canners responded to taxes, see "The Candid Canner," *The Canner*, November 27, 1943, 9, and "The Candid Canner," *The Canner*, June 5, 1943, 9.

[36] For a general overview of this agency, see *Final Report of the War Food Administrator* (Washington, DC: US Government Printing Office, 1945).

army did not procure. LaChoy, a food canner that had historically focused on Chinese foods, found it could not get access to cans for most of its products, so it decided to shift production to canning only fruits and vegetables during the war.[37]

In general, government regulators found larger companies easier to work with. OPA, for instance, favored chain stores and larger retailers to implement rationing and price controls. Foods were sold at all sorts of locales, ranging from small farm stands to supermarkets. Such variety presented logistical and administrative challenges. Because chain stores were easier to regulate and did more to comply with price ceilings, OPA created special policies that often favored these stores. This was about playing fair – that is, it was about following wartime rules, but larger and more sophisticated organizations were better equipped to keep up with changing regulations. Smaller retailers never had a fair chance to keep up with regulations. OPA eventually even imposed policies that effectively closed some small retailers.[38]

Because of these wartime regulations, the number of small food manu- facturing businesses fell significantly. In the food industry, the overall number of food-processing businesses during the war fell from 46,300 to 34,800. Moreover, the companies with more than 10,000 workers increased their share of the total industry workforce from 11 percent to 15.4 percent. The war also left larger businesses bigger and better pre- pared to take advantage of the return to peacetime.[39]

---

[37] This order is known as M-81, for more information on it, see E. Vogelsang to Donald D. Davis, April 15, 1943; 565.35, Metal Food Containers – Orders; Policy Documenta- tion File; War Production Board, RG 179; NARA, College Park, MD. For more on this order, see various letters and reports in 517.126 Tin Plate Metal-Requirements-Industry Branches and Divisions in this same record group. For LaChoy, see "LaChoy Moves from Detroit to Archbold, O. [Ohio], Will Resume Production in August," *The Canner*, June 27, 1942, 16.

[38] For grocery stores, see Tracey Deutsch, *Building a Housewife's Paradise: Gender, Polit- ics, and American Grocery Stores in the Twentieth Century* (Chapel Hill: University of North Carolina Press, 2010); for a broader look at government policies and smaller food businesses, see Backer, "World War II and the Triumph of Industrialized Food."

[39] For figures, see John M. Blair, Harrison F. Houghton, and Matthew Rose, *Economic Concentration and World War II: Report of the Smaller War Plants Corporation to the Special Committee to Study Problems of American Small Business, United States Senate* (Washington, DC: US Government Printing Office, 1946), 57 and 213. For more on the challenges facing small businesses, see Bean, *Beyond the Broker State*; and Heath, *War Mobilization and the Use of Small Manufacturers, 1939–1943*. For a more comprehen- sive look at the US government and business during World War II, see Mark R. Wilson, *Destructive Creation: American Business and the Winning of World War II* (Phila- delphia: University of Pennsylvania Press, 2016).

Coca-Cola, for example, used World War II to grow from a popular drink in the South into the national beverage of the country. While Coca-Cola lobbied for a variety of benefits, it gained importance to the armed forces through chance. Letters from the army, especially from Army Chief of Staff Gen. George C. Marshall, who was personally fond of Coca-Cola, helped Coca-Cola gain unlimited access to sugar to sell drinks to the commissary and permission to set up new factories to better deliver soda to the front lines. While other companies had to "play square" by going without critical materials, Coca-Cola was able to vault to national prominence.[40]

Because of the importance of sharing the burden, companies disadvantaged by this regulatory framework had little recourse. To complain about a lack of profits appeared unpatriotic. Sharing and playing square thus combined to create a system that benefitted industrialized foods and large companies. Overall, the war was a time that remade food to fit the needs of the war. Sharing, playing square, producing, and conserving all helped to remake the structure of the food system and cultural attitudes toward food.

THE LEGACY OF WORLD WAR II

Although World War II helped to transform the way that Americans ate, most of the changes came from small shifts. There was no radical breakthrough for food technology that reshaped food processing overnight. Instead, minor improvements and small shifts incrementally changed America's food system and food cultures. There were, however, two very notable technologies that emerged from wartime research, which can help to sum up World War II's food legacy.

The first innovation, DDT, profoundly changed the country's agriculture and ecology. During World War I, insect-borne diseases had killed as many soldiers as had actual combat. In World War II, typhus and malaria posed as much of a danger as did enemy bullets in areas where they were prevalent, such as in the South Pacific. In October 1942, the US Bureau of Entomology found a solution to insect-borne diseases, after a Swiss company suggested trying DDT. Bureau researchers found that DDT

---

[40] For more on Coca Cola, see Mark Pendergrast, *For God, Country, and Coca-Cola* (New York: Scribner, 1993); J. C. Louis and Harvey Yazijian, *The Cola Wars* (New York: Everest House, 1980); and Bartow J. Elmore, *Citizen Coke: The Making of Coca-Cola Capitalism* (New York: W.W. Norton & Company, 2015).

could keep troops safe, as it appeared to have relatively little short-term toxicity – other insecticides might make soldiers immediately sick if swallowed. Furthermore, DDT broke down slowly, so it would not need to be sprayed as often. To keep soldiers safe, these were ideal qualities. But they made DDT especially problematic for use in agriculture. At the end of the war, DDT moved beyond the military to become widely used in civilian markets. For agriculture, DDT's slow breakdown meant that the pesticide could aggregate in the products that consumers ate and in the environment. Other pesticides had greater toxicity, but these products broke down quickly, in theory before consumers would eat them or before the pesticides would accumulate to cause environmental damage. DDT, however, remained unchanged, leading to devastating consequences to the ecosystem, especially to birds at the top of the food chain.[41]

DDT serves as a cautionary tale, often used to highlight the dangers of new technologies in food production. But a closer look at the history of DDT reveals a different cautionary tale. In DDT, a product was developed for particular circumstances in a war. To produce this insecticide, a new industry arose – an industry in search of a market after the war. After the war, DDT became a widely used agricultural pesticide, one so harmful to the environment that its use in the United States was eventually banned.

The second innovation, frozen concentrated orange juice, came from research that sought to get soldiers more vitamin C. Researchers made a breakthrough in preserving citrus through freezing during the war; after the war, this technique allowed businesses to produce frozen concentrated orange juice. Canned orange juice tasted bad; fresh orange juice required a great deal of labor in squeezing oranges. The convenience and taste of frozen concentrate made it a popular product among consumers. This new product, however, was only made possible because wartime regulations had improved every aspect of frozen food production and distribution. Without wartime changes expanding production facilities, improving refrigerated warehouses and transportation, and adding new freezer space in grocery stores, frozen concentrated orange juice would not have thrived after the war.[42]

---

[41] See Russell, "The Strange Career of DDT"; Russell, *War and Nature*; and David Kinkela, *DDT and the American Century: Global Health, Environmental Politics, and the Pesticide that Changed the World* (Chapel Hill: University of North Carolina Press, 2011).

[42] See Hamilton's *Squeezed* for the history of orange juice. For more on how the war improved the frozen food industry, see "Frozen Foods Expect to Hold Gains Made during War," *Ice and Refrigeration*, April 1946, 49; and "Food Processing and Marketing Outlook Indicates Expansion of Refrigeration Industry," *Ice and*

Many other processed foods flourished after the war. "Of all the violent upheavals that have shaken and transformed the American market," a 1953 *Fortune* article noted, "none have been bigger, or more baffling, than those affecting food." The author examined the increase in consumer spending: "Back in 1941, Americans spent $20 billion for food. In 1953, to the stupefaction of just about everyone who thought he understood the food market, they are spending $60 billion." World War II started this transformation; it continued after the war, when consumers bought more processed and convenience products and paid more for each item. By 1953, prepared cake mixes sold about six times the amount they did in 1941, as did frozen fruits, juices, and vegetables. The era also brought the rapid expansion of other processed products, such as soluble coffee and canned baby foods. Likewise, rather than buying whole chickens, consumers were purchasing increasing quantities of "frozen chicken livers, canned breast of chicken, and dehydrated chicken soup." In all, the rapid growth of spending on food owed much to the increased sales of processed products. World War II had prepared the infrastructure and the new food values that enabled this revolution.[43]

During the war, Americans remade their food system to fight a global war. Processed foods offered a solution to wartime logistical challenges, as these products could be preserved for a long time and many of them could be shipped easily. The war also meant expanding production in particular ways. To boost production, farms relied on new labor sources, such as immigrant laborers. Businesses needed to work closely with the government to figure out food requirements and how to achieve production goals. In this process, larger companies tended to do much better, often because they worked more closely with regulators and military planners. There was a wartime logic to the decisions that created this system. But food systems involve many pieces and the close of the war did not return business practices to the prewar normal. Businesses that had created products for the armed forces now sought to use their expanded facilities to feed consumers.

Refrigeration, February 1946, 25–26. For examples of the critical bottlenecks facing the industry before the war, see Robert E. Ottenheimer, "The 'Bottle Neck' of Frosted Food Distribution," *Ice and Refrigeration*, September 1939, 181–182.

[43] See "The Fabulous Market for Food," *Fortune*, October 1953, 135 and 138. For more on the growth of processed foods after the war, see Shane Hamilton, "The Economics and Convenience of Modern-Day Living: Frozen Foods and Mass Marketing, 1945–1965," *The Business History Review* 77, no. 1 (2003): 33–60; and Laura Shapiro, *Something from the Oven: Reinventing Dinner in 1950s America* (New York: Viking, 2004).

CONCLUSION

In the second half of the twentieth century, American foods moved along several distinct trajectories. The end of the century gave rise to movements emphasizing seasonal food, grown locally, where consumers knew about the foods they ate. At the same time, American food also became more homogenized and more processed, as large companies rolled out product after product in a way that disconnected consumers from the environments in which foods were grown.[44]

The war shaped both of these trajectories of American food. Through victory gardens and thinking about conservation, Americans gained new knowledge about the foods they ate. At the same time, demand shifted to industrialized foods and wartime rules favored the production of uniform industrialized foods that could be moved seamlessly around the world without spoiling.

While World War II opened a number of possibilities, American food left the war more highly industrialized than it had been at the start. Food became a potent weapon during the war, but the changes that made it so remained in place after the war. Victory gardens and conservation campaigns disappeared but Coca-Cola and other large companies used the war to vault to prominence. The ultimate legacy of World War II for American food was to create a highly industrialized, homogenous food system that disconnected consumers from the foods they ate.

---

[44] The latter half of the twentieth century also gave rise to a growing global influence on foods in America. See Donna R. Gabaccia, *We Are What We Eat: Ethnic Food and the Making of Americans* (Cambridge, MA: Harvard University Press, 1998); and Matt Garcia, E. Melanie Dupuis, and Don Mitchell, eds., *Food across Borders* (New Brunswick, NJ: Rutgers University Press, 2017). For two general histories of late twentieth-century American food, see Harvey Levenstein, *Paradox of Plenty: A Social History of Modern America* (Berkeley: University of California Press, 2003); and David Kamp, *The United States of Arugula* (New York: Broadway Books, 2006).

7

From Field to Foxhole

Cigarettes and Soldiers in World War II

Joel R. Bius

In the fall of 1944, while the Allied Armies broke out of Normandy and fought toward Germany, a small, select committee of US Senators met to discuss an emerging resource crisis that could possibly grind the Allied war effort to a halt.[1] Affecting both the fighting overseas as well as the war production effort at home, the crisis carried strategic consequences.[2] The issue was not gasoline, armor, or ammunition – it was cigarettes. Tobacco in the form of cigarettes had become a staple of American life by World War II, and the trend expanded dramatically with America

---

[1] Some may disagree with the term "halt" as used here. However, anyone who has served in a combat environment will readily recall the place of hot food, dry clothes, and morale items like mail and cigarettes – even more so among a draft/conscripted force. As Clause-witz says in *On War*, "when an army lacks military virtues [i.e. the professionalism of regulars], every effort should be made to keep operations as simple as possible, or else twice as much attention should be paid to *other aspects* of the military system.... Military spirit, then, is one of the most important moral elements in war." In this essay, I argue that cigarettes constituted the *other aspect* of the war-fighting, military spirit mentioned here by Clausewitz. See Carl Von Clausewitz, *On War*, ed. and trans. Michael Howard and Peter Paret (Princeton, NJ: Princeton University Press, 1976), 188–189.

[2] For example, historian Lee Kennett describes how a shortage in cigarettes during the Salerno landings was considered so worrisome that it became a planning factor during subsequent landings. See Lee Kennett, *G.I.: The American Soldier in World War II* (Norman: University of Oklahoma Press, 1987), 97. In more recent times, Russian Defense Minister Sergei Shoigu found out the strategic significance of cigarettes as he brought the massive Russian field forces to near riot with his attempt to cut the 10 cigarette a day ration. Troops, "not able to handle losing their free smokes," were supported by the Union of Soldiers' Mothers' Committee as they advanced a prosmoking agenda based on the harmful effects on the "psychology of smokers" if the ration was cut. See Robert Beckhusen, "Russia Fears Its Troops Will Riot If Cigarette Rations End," *Wired* (March 5, 2013), www.wired.com/2013/03/russian-cigarettes/ (accessed August 28, 2017).

embroiled in war. When soldiers fought, they smoked. When workers worked in the war factories, they smoked. Indeed, nicotine was actively encouraged by the military because it calmed nerves, steadied the hands, assuaged boredom, and demonstrated a commander's care for his soldiers. Any interruption to this cycle of working, fighting, and smoking, could yield severe consequences.

Thus, the question at hand for the Senate committee: To what extent should the nation go to meet the need for nicotine? More directly, how would the long shadows of the Great Depression and the New Deal affect efforts to mobilize the resource central to the cigarette: Tobacco? It is not possible to talk about the environmental history of World War II without talking about political economy in general and, more specifically, the impact of environmental policies that emerged during the period immediately prior to World War II. The tobacco economy in America had grown to immense proportions in the decades leading up to the war. Quantified in terms of weight and taxes, cigarettes were a substantial aspect of the American economy immediately prior to the war. Tobacco production by pound had increased fivefold since 1880 and increased to nearly 1.2 billion pounds in 1930. In what historian Robert Proctor calls the "tax addiction" and the cigarette "cash cow," by the mid-1930s, cigarettes brought the federal government in taxes nearly the same amount it was reaping from the entire population in individual income taxes.[3] Thus, the implications in terms of political economy, and by extension environmental policy, are profound.

During the war, the soaring demand for cigarettes and the large economic benefits of tobacco generated pressure on New Deal land use, soil conservation, and agricultural policies designed to restrain tobacco overproduction. FDR's New Deal had successfully stabilized tobacco prices and conserved soil, but also pulled tobacco land out of production and positioned the federal government, not the free hand of capitalism, as a main actor in the agro-economy. As war approached and the demand for cigarettes and tax receipts mounted, some Senators and Congressman

---

[3] Robert Proctor, *Golden Holocaust: Origins of the Cigarette Catastrophe and the Case for Abolition* (Los Angeles: University of California Press, 2011), 50; Allan Brandt, *Cigarette Century: The Rise, Fall, and Deadly Persistence of the Product That Defined America* (New York: Basic Books, 2006), 96–98; David M. Burns et al., *Smoking and Tobacco Control Monograph No. 8*, "Cigarette Smoking Behavior in the United States" (December 1996), 13, https://cancercontrol.cancer.gov/brp/tcrb/monographs/8/m8_complete.pdf (accessed August 28, 2017). In 1950, cigarettes GNP contribution stood at 1.4 percent and at 3.5 percent of all consumer spending on nondurables.

pushed hard to reverse aggressive federal agricultural and environmental policies limiting tobacco production.

Ultimately, these regulations withstood the pressure. When America entered the war and strained to supply the resources and labor needed for victory, the federal government maintained its strong position as arbiter over production and consumption, despite the hopes of some to roll back New Deal policies. This was a case in which the drive for greater production, and greater manipulation of the environment, had limits. Farmers and policy makers did not so easily forget past problems with runaway production and dramatic price fluctuations. Yet another problem emerged as part and parcel to the government's successful campaign to retain control over the production problem and supply cigarettes to soldiers: the destructive impact of cigarette consumption on the human ecosystem. Thus, federal policy toward cigarettes and tobacco during World War II generated a mixed legacy, revealing a growing federal government's ability to manage land use for the greater enviro-economic good while subsidizing a deadly habit that seared the lungs of America's fighting men and their families for generations.

Understanding this apparently paradoxical moment in history is an important component of American environmental history. Albert E. Cowdrey defines *environmental history* as "the interface between culture and nature."[4] Cowdrey's enviro-cultural framework is a useful lens to examine World War II policies regarding tobacco production, soil conservation, agricultural allotments, and Americans' demand for cigarettes and nicotine. What is valued defines culture and shapes landscapes, and Americans valued cigarettes, tobacco, and nicotine during World War II, producing a prolific cigarette culture. This demand for cigarettes and other resources extracted from the land subsequently levied immense pressure on nature's soil and the New Deal regulations enacted to protect it. When the smoke cleared and the war was over, New Deal agricultural allotments and soil conservation survived, as did an expanded national addiction to nicotine. However, this political struggle highlights one of the most tragic mixed environmental legacies of the twentieth century: solid agro-enviro-economic policy existing hand in hand with lucrative tax policy, as well as terribly costly public health policy.

---

[4] Albert E. Cowdrey, *This Land, This South: An Environmental History* (Lexington: University of Kentucky Press, 1996), 7.

TOBACCO COUNTRY AND THE FEDERAL GOVERNMENT
BEFORE WORLD WAR II

Students of American agricultural history recognize the Soil Conservation
and Domestic Allotment Act, passed on the eve of World War II, the main
New Deal intervention into the tobacco economy, as a dramatic policy
shift long in the making. Ever since the founding of the Republic, farmers
and agrarians had bitterly resisted governmental regulation of land and
production. During the colonial years, when land was abundant, conservation received little thought. When they depleted and leached the soil,
growers simply moved to other land. The nation expanded one field at a
time. This pattern of land use continued after the Revolution and
throughout the westward expansion.[5]

As markets expanded and the scale of production increased, farmers
continued to resist governmental intervention. Farmers transitioned
from largely communal and subsistence operations to market-based
agriculture, becoming more and more sensitive to market prices and
the productivity of their land. Prior to the Civil War, Southern politicians in particular, influenced by agrarian and classically liberal
ideals, resisted federal intervention or any scheme to centralize planning for agricultural production. However, in 1862, after the entire
Southern delegation left Congress to form a new Confederate States
delegation, a wartime Congress seized the opportunity to outflank
traditional resistance to federal activism in the agricultural sector.[6]
Minus the Southern caucus, this new Congress passed the Morrill
Land Grant Act and created the US Department of Agriculture. With
these two measures, the federal government made its first forays into

---

[5] Jack P. Greene, *Pursuits of Happiness: The Social Development of Early Modern British Colonies and the Formation of American Culture* (Chapel Hill: University of North Carolina Press, 1988), 36–37, Gloria Main, *People of a Spacious Land: Families and Cultures in Colonial New England* (Cambridge, MA: Harvard University Press, 2001), 28; Joyce Appleby, *Capitalism and a New Social Order: The Republican Vision of the 1790s* (New York: New York University Press, 1984), 7–8; James Lemon, *The Best Poor Man's Country: A Geographical Study of Early Southeastern Pennsylvania* (New York: W. W. Norton & Co. 1976), 27; Charles Sellers, *The Market Revolution: Jacksonian America, 1815–1846* (New York: Oxford University Press, 1991), 16–19; Cowdrey, *This Land, This South*, 30–33. Tobacco was particularly destructive to the land: after only three or four years of use, tobacco land required 20 fallow years to replenish.

[6] Paul S. Sutter, *Let Us Now Praise Famous Gullies: Providence Canyon and the Soils of the South* (Athens: University of Georgia Press, 2015), 26.

the business of governing land use and agricultural practices.[7] Nothing, however, was settled.

After the Civil War, Southern farmers struggled to remain solvent and worked hard to keep land in production. As dependence on agricultural markets and commodity prices deepened, a disturbing pattern emerged. When prices dropped, farmers reacted by placing more and more land under the till, including lands not well suited for agriculture. In time, prices eventually recovered, only to drop again at some point, resulting in a harrowing boom-and-bust cycle.[8] Despite this troubling pattern, from 1862 to 1900, the government skirted direct control of production and prices, and certainly did not address exhaustion or advance an aggressive long-term soil conservation plan. In fact, the government's chief soil scientist during this period, Milton Whitney, emphatically insisted, "There was no such thing as soil exhaustion."[9] Whitney went as far as claiming: "The soil is the one indestructible, immutable asset that the Nation possesses ... it cannot be exhausted [or] used up."[10] When a department researcher dared to challenge Whitney's "inexhaustible soil" thesis in 1904, he was labeled an apostate and forced to resign.[11] Despite the late-nineteenth-century push by the Populists and the Grange movement toward more federal activism, agricultural education, and collectivist programs, deep into the twentieth century, farmers, wholesalers, and manufacturers as a broad sector continued a stubborn commitment to maximum land usage and unfettered production.[12]

Yet there were economic and environmental risks to this entrenched resistance to rationalized planning and soil conservation. Because of the boom-bust cycle, those engaged in commercial agriculture, whether tobacco, cotton, or any other commodity, were forced to borrow,

---

[7] Paul K. Conkin, *A Revolution Down on the Farm: The Transformation of American Agriculture since 1929* (Lexington: University of Kentucky Press, 2009), 19.

[8] Sellers, *The Market Revolution*, 12–16; Appleby, *Capitalism and a New Social Order*, 39–40; Sutter, *Let Us Now Praise Famous Gullies*, 152–153.

[9] Sutter, *Let Us Now Praise Famous Gullies*, 41.   [10] Ibid., 53.

[11] Ibid., 42–43. In response to this seemingly regressive federal soil policy, one critic commented: "Other peoples have ruined their lands, but in no other country has the powerful factor of government influence ever been used to encourage the farmers to ruin their lands." Despite these critiques, Whitney received the full support of the US Department of Agriculture.

[12] Drew Swanson, *A Golden Weed: Tobacco and Environment in the Piedmont South* (New Haven, CT: Yale University Press, 2014), 7, 235–238; Conkin, *A Revolution Down on the Farm*, 19–30, 62. Conkin says that by 1932, the game was up and what farmers "had long resisted-bureaucratic control over their production" was now supported.

leverage farm assets, and cultivate even more land to compensate for price drops. Sadly, in the case of tobacco, this only created greater surpluses and even lower prices, as well as a scarred, depleted landscape.[13] Tobacco was particularly destructive to the land: after only three or four years of use, tobacco land required 20 fallow years to replenish. Neither conservation nor monitoring of demand received attention. Staunchly "unconcerned with soil erosion as an agricultural and environmental problem for the duration of his career," as one historian put it, Whitney remained in office as the government's chief soil scientist until his retirement in 1927. Thus, the government's annual "state of the soil" report never mentioned soil erosion as a chief concern until the year after Milton Whitney stepped down from his post.[14] Soil conservation never gained traction at the US Department of Agriculture as official policy until FDR's New Deal in 1933 (see Figures 7.1 and 7.2).

When combined, these economic and policy conditions underpinned a substantial problem: massive soil erosion. Along with two other looming issues, stagnant consumption and destruction of middle-class purchasing power, the combination of these factors created a desperate situation during the period immediately prior to World War II.[15]

THE RESPONSE TO DEPRESSION AND DUST BOWL

What happened in the war was a big struggle over the tobacco conservation policies that emerged during the Depression. During the 1930s, economic and environmental conditions led to crippling poverty and devastating dust storms, spurring unprecedented federal economic and environmental activism. In addition to the economic recovery most are

---

[13] See Gavin Wright, *Old South, New South: Revolution in the Southern Economy since the Civil War* (Baton Rouge: Louisiana State University Press, 1986).

[14] Sutter, *Let Us Now Praise Famous Gullies*, 46, 59–60; Swanson, *A Golden Weed*, 235–237.

[15] The literature on the New Deal and the Great Depression is immense. For America's shift to a consumption economy and the Great Depression as a downturn rooted in the production-consumption conundrum, see Sellers, *The Market Revolution*; Alan Brinkley, *The End of Reform: New Deal Liberalism in Recession and War* (New York: Vintage Books, 1995) as well as *Liberalism and Its Discontents* (Cambridge, MA: Harvard University Press, 2000); Steve Fraser and Gary Gerstle, eds., *The Rise and Fall of the New Deal Order, 1930–1980* (Princeton, NJ: Princeton University Press, 1989); David Kennedy, *Freedom from Fear: The American People in Depression and War, 1929–1945* (New York: Oxford University Press, 1999); and Michael Lind, *Land of Promise: An Economic History of the United States* (New York: HarperCollins, 2013).

FIGURE 7.1 Tobacco farm, erosion, and cigarette advertising, Person County, NC, 1939. General view of a hillside farm which faces the road showing owner's house, outbuildings, and tobacco field showing erosion. Notice the three tobacco advertisements on the outbuilding: Prince Albert, Bull Durham, and Camel.
Source: Library of Congress Public Use Image 2017772389

familiar with, soil erosion was a major policy issue as well. As Conkin says, "[S]oil conservation became a national obsession."[16] This economic recovery and "soil obsession" were ubiquitous issues in tobacco country, where farmers and land suffered, yet cigarette industry executives swam in prosperity. Tobacco was at the center of North Carolina's economy, with the cigarette industry its most lucrative enterprise. In 1900, only 2 percent of the tobacco produced in America was used for cigarettes, the remainder used for chewing tobacco (48 percent), cigars (27 percent), pipe tobacco (19 percent), and snuff (4 percent). By 1930, cigarette production had increased by 1,300 percent, and the majority of leaf harvested from the soil found its way into cigarettes. Most of the 1920s was very kind to the tobacco industry. North Carolina produced more than 70 percent of the nation's flue-cured tobacco, and 4 out of every 10 workers still resided on the farm. The

---

[16] Conkin, *A Revolution Down on the Farm*, 72.

FIGURE 7.2 Small tobacco farm with erosion, Person County, NC, 1939.
Story-and-a-half weatherboard house. Note chinaberry tree, common for shade.
Note soil erosion in foreground and corner of tobacco field.
Source: Library of Congress Public Use Image 2017772429

average tobacco farm covered seven acres, and farmers earned consistent, good prices for their leaf.[17]

Late in the decade, however, old problems led farmers back into overproduction. As in the past, when prices were good, farmers produced more
to capitalize on the good market. This surplus eventually resulted in a price
drop, and farmers responded by planting more. No matter which way the
market turned, farmers reacted by increasing acreage and production.
Grassroots efforts at the local and state level to get farmers to cut production and achieve long-term price stability failed. Essentially, farmers refused
voluntary acreage reduction if they could not verify that all their neighbors,
near and far, were doing the same. In due course, the bottom fell out, with
prices dipping as low as 8.4 cents per pound in 1931, after an entire decade
of never dropping below 20 cents per pound, a 65 percent drop in prices.[18]

---

[17] Anthony J. Badger, *Prosperity Road: The New Deal, Tobacco, and North Carolina*
(Chapel Hill: University of North Carolina Press, 1980), xvi, 4, 17, 11; Brands, *Cigarette
Century*, 97.

[18] Badger, *Prosperity Road*, 21, 25, 33.

At ground level, the scene was dire as FDR took office in 1933. Down in southern tobacco land and out on the western plains, the farmers and the soil suffered.[19] Though the Dust Bowl associated with the Midwest looms large in historical memory as the most severe soil catastrophe, historian Paul Sutter argues that soil loss in the tobacco and cotton lands of the South was arguably a "more substantial disaster."[20] Hugh Hammond Bennett estimated that by 1934, more than half of two billion acres surveyed in the South was scarred by human accelerated erosion.[21] To these tobacco belt and plains farmers, as well to their land, the New Deal was a new lease on life. Legend has it that as Hugh Hammond Bennet, the first chairman of the federal Soil Erosion Service (SES), was struggling in congressional meetings to obtain permanent funding for soil conservation and erosion research, he paused the 1935 hearings so legislators could go to the window and see the arrival of the great dust storms.[22] As they looked out the windows at eroded soil lifted from the earth in Oklahoma, they quite possibly noticed the unemployment lines and hopeless men milling about with nothing to do. As was the case with most of FDR's unprecedented early New Deal programs, this scene of dust and depression pushed Congress to allow further expansion of federal power over the agro-economy.

Yet as their initial fears of revolution and chaos subsided and FDR moved into his second term, many pre–World War II conservative legislators of all regions and party affiliations, industry executives, and even groups of farmers remained suspicious of federal intervention in local affairs. They grew increasingly suspicious of FDR's New Deal and continued centralization, especially after the court packing affair of 1937. Conservatives, many who initially lined up behind FDR in 1933, were now voicing fears that his agricultural and conservation programs were a dangerous break with long-standing precedent. Some labeled these an alarming foray "counter to every principle of American Liberty" in the words of Senator Josiah Bailey's (D-NC), or "undemocratic and

---

[19] Sutter, *Let Us Now Praise Famous Gullies*, 119. Regarding the severity of consequences relating to negligent soil practices in the century before Great Depression, Sutter comments that such practices "transformed the ecology, hydrology, and geomorphology of many southern watersheds in ways that may last for thousands of years."

[20] Ibid., 111, 125, 129.

[21] Using distinguished Southern historian Howard Odum's studies as foundation, Sutter concludes that, "While erosion was by no means confined to the Southeast, the region clearly had more than its share of severely eroded land by the 1930s." Ibid., 111–112.

[22] Ibid., 87–89.

un-American" and even "Bolshevik" in the words of local North Carolina politician S. H. Hobbs.[23] The wealthy banking and manufacturing class labeled FDR a traitor. Left-wing radicals like Governor Huey Long of Louisiana felt FDR had not gone far enough: they wanted income leveling and government seizure of personal or inherited assets in excess of a million dollars.[24] Further, as World War II approached, many in Congress, including those who had initially supported FDR, became increasingly unreceptive and even hostile to core New Deal initiatives such as conservation and production controls. According to Sutter, "[T]he abused land was still there, but now there were strong impulses to increase production."[25]

Despite these detractors, FDR took bold actions tangibly positioning his policies squarely in the middle of living rooms across America. According to historian Anthony Badger, FDR's New Deal programs "brought the federal government into new areas of North Carolina life … the federal government became for the first time an institution that was directly experienced."[26] One of Roosevelt's boldest initiatives was the Agricultural Adjustment Act (AAA) of 1934. This unprecedented act, as well as several follow-on acts, addressed land use and conservation in two ways. First, the government assumed significant responsibility for planning agricultural production through a domestic allotment system for key crops, enforced by pecuniary penalties against farmers disregarding acreage and planting restrictions, and more important, by government largesse for those who did comply. Not only did the farmer receive payments for not planting, by adhering to rigid production restrictions, he received the benefit of propped up and stabilized prices, and a reasonable assurance of top prices for the acres they placed under the plow.

Second, follow-on adjustments to the AAA regimen economically rewarded farmers who implemented soil conservation and progressive land-use measures. Indeed after 1936, rather than receiving allotment payments, farmers received "soil-building payments."[27] Thus, remuneration was directly connected to conservation, as qualifying for payments required farmers to participate in soil conservation and land-use programs. This economic and environmental program was significant in the

[23] Badger, *Prosperity Road*, 86, 156.
[24] Alan Brinkley, *Voices of Protest: Huey Long, Father Coughlin, and the Great Depression* (New York: Vintage Books, 1983), 55, 71–73, 144–145.
[25] Sutter, *Let Us Now Praise Famous Gullies*, 104.   [26] Badger, *Prosperity Road*, xv.
[27] Wright, *Old South, New South*, 232.

South. With so much at stake, the program worked, enrolling the majority of tobacco farmers by 1941. They adopted these conservation plans to stay enrolled, get the guaranteed price, and receive government payments. As the holdouts adjusted to these new restrictions and regulations, eventually 99.9 percent of tobacco farmers voted for crop controls and soil conservation measures. They consistently reaffirmed this vote for every year but one over the next 70 years.[28] According to Paul K. Conkin, whether the farmers were initially enthusiastic about soil conservation was immaterial. The conservation plans were effective over time, and farmers eventually embraced the logic of mitigating the long-term effects of soil erosion (see Figure 7.3).[29]

Soon, what was an incentivized habit became standard practice. Soil renewing crops such as grasses and legumes appeared with more frequency, and other anti-erosion features began to dot the countryside. Farmers particularly favored taking land out of production for legumes and pastures, planting trees on eroded hillsides, and building ponds to hold runoff water.[30] The year 1936 saw a 23 percent reduction in tobacco acreage as well as the associated benefits of conservation and replenishment of soil.[31] On the heels of some of the worst dust storms in American history, as well as devastating agricultural price drops, these pre–World War II interventionist policies received a hearty reception from American farmers desperate for relief. Badger labeled this an amazing feat in "intervention of a detailed nature by the federal government in the individual economic lives of three hundred thousand tobacco growers" that "had to be achieved in a democratic society without the bureaucratic apparatus of a police state."[32] Further highlighting the significance of the moment, when announcing his soil conservation initiative, President Roosevelt announced, "The history of every nation is eventually written in the way in which it cares for its soil." FDR exclaimed he was glad the nation was finally "emerging from its youthful state of heedless exploitation and is beginning to realize the supreme importance of treating the soil well."[33]

---

[28] Conkin, *A Revolution Down on the Farm*, 68; *United States Senate Special Committee Investigating the National Defense Program*, "Cigarette Rations," 12165 (hereafter *USSSC Report*); and Badger, *Prosperity Road*, 58.

[29] Conkin, *A Revolution Down on the Farm*, 73–74.   [30] Ibid., 74.

[31] Badger, *Prosperity Road*, 124.   [32] Ibid., 235.

[33] Franklin D. Roosevelt: "Statement on Signing the Soil Conservation and Domestic Allotment Act," March 1, 1936, *The American Presidency Project*, ed. Gerhard Peters and John T. Wooley, www.presidency.ucsb.edu/documents/statement-signing-the-soil-conservation-and-domestic-allotment-act (accessed July 26, 2019); Sutter, *Let Us Now*

FIGURE 7.3 Erosion control work by CCC in Newberry, SC, 1942. CCC workers fighting soil erosion in gulley adjacent to planted pines and farm fields. Newberry soil was depleted in the nineteenth century by tobacco and cotton, and in the twentieth century, cotton cultivation continued the erosion process.
Source: Bureau of Agricultural Economics, Department of Agriculture, NARA. National Archive Identifier: 522798. Image in the public domain

Over the course of two centuries, the United States transformed from a loose conglomeration of colonial family farms to a globally networked agro-industrial nation of market-driven producers. This system underwent extreme testing during the Great Depression, yet on the eve of World War II, it reached a new balance. New federal interventions in the agro-economy appeared to benefit the farmer, the consumer, *and* the environment. The tobacco belt's worst fears seemed misplaced; there was such a thing as good government policy regarding cultivation of tobacco, adequate supply to the market, and the conservation of land. The outbreak of World War II, however, brought new doubts to the surface:

Praise Famous Gullies, 92. Further, in an even more defining moment, historian Paul Sutter points out that the government's official 1938 "state of the soil" report boldly challenged the nation to care for its soil "after several centuries of sinful soil mining."

could this "win-win" policy survive the demands of all-out mobilization? More specifically, how would tight control of tobacco allotments and soil fare against the gigantic wave of cigarette-smoking GIs and intense pressures to respond.

THE SKYROCKETING DEMAND FOR CIGARETTES IN WORLD WAR II

Tom Brokaw once labeled the generation of Americans who fought in World War II the "greatest generation." To this, one could add that they were the greatest generation of smokers and nicotine addicts. By 1944, the army's official policy, *War Department Circular 285*, gave soldiers access to 9 to 12 free cigarettes per day as part of their rations, and one additional pack (16 cigarettes) they could purchase. However, field commanders took the cigarettes designated for sale and placed them in the ration accessory packs assembled in theater. So in reality, every soldier was authorized, on average, 16 free cigarettes per day, and as high as 30 if one included additional cigarettes they were authorized to purchase.[34] This is an astonishingly high figure considering the fact that the per capita consumption rate in America in 1940 was five cigarettes per day.[35]

The role of wars and the military in spreading smoking culture has often gone unrecognized. One could argue the widespread cigarette habit took root in American life in a single season of a single year: the summer of 1918. One year after entering the Great War, military officials including Army Chief of Staff General Peyton March became exceedingly aware of the demand for cigarettes among the doughboys in France. In March's memoirs, he recalls:

Tobacco was obtainable by the soldiers only by buying it, and many tired men were deprived of the use of this solace because they had no money, while more fortunate comrades with means of their own were getting all the tobacco ... [therefore] I directed that an order be issued making tobacco a part of the ration for issue to the soldiers.[36]

Largely nonsmokers as they left civilian life, after meeting up with smokers in the army, even more smokers among their British and French

---

[34] *USSSC Report*, 12148, 12111, 12270.   [35] Proctor, *Golden Holocaust*, 57.
[36] The Papers of General Peyton March, Box 8, Folder marked "Speeches and Writings – Drafts, The Nation at War," Library of Congress, *The Nation at War* (Garden City, NY: Doubleday, Doran & Co, 1934), 366.

allies, and then the military's cigarette distribution program, the American doughboys quickly picked up the habit.[37]

This habit, initiated by the war and the military cigarette distribution program, was also encouraged by mechanical, chemical, and production developments. From 1891 to 1910, cigarette producers perfected flu curing, aging, and the machines used to mass produce cigarettes, creating a cheap, smooth, deeply inhalable product enabling the most inexperienced smoker or virgin starter to become a sophisticated, veteran smoker in no time.[38] The process of flu curing and aging turns the leaves a bright golden yellow, and more importantly, alters the alkaline levels, making them more neutral, and more deeply inhalable as compared to cigars. This deep inhaling allows for more nicotine absorption at a faster rate – and subsequent addiction. Robert Proctor calls this aging and curing process the "deadliest invention in the history of modern manufacturing."[39] Once initiated to the rigors of combat and the lifestyle of smoking, World War I combat soldiers became smoking veterans who demanded more and more cigarettes. At one point, when asked what he needed to win the war, General John J. Pershing exclaimed, "You ask me what we need to win this war. I answer tobacco, as much as bullets."[40]

Most historians agree that more than any other single factor, the Great War "legitimized the cigarette" and "moved cigarettes into the mainstream of American culture ... by linking them to an icon of manliness and civic virtue: the American soldier."[41] The decision by the government to give soldiers billions of cigarettes during World War I created an enduring American image: the soldier and the cigarette. Moreover, this image legitimized what had been disreputable behavior and helped make it an accepted and widespread cultural practice, a part of daily life.

During World War II, this connection between soldiers, tobacco, and cigarettes, continued to soar. To a combat soldier, whether fighting in 1918 or 1944, a cigarette delivers certain physiological effects allowing

---

[37] March, *The Nation at War*, 377–378.
[38] Brandt, *The Cigarette Century: The Rise, Fall, and Deadly Persistence of the Product That Defined America* (New York: Basic Books, 2007), 27–31.
[39] Proctor, *Golden Holocaust*, 34–36.
[40] Richard Kluger, *Ashes to Ashes* (New York: Alfred Knopf, 1996), 58; Cassandra Tate, *Cigarette Wars: The Triumph of "Little White Slaver"* (New York: Oxford University Press, 1999), 71.
[41] Jarrett Rudy, *The Freedom to Smoke: Tobacco Consumption and Identity* (Montreal: McGill–Queens University Press, 2005), 110–111, 132; Tate, *Cigarette Wars*, 65–66; Julian Sivulka, *Soap, Sex, and Cigarettes: A Cultural History of American Advertising* (Boston: Wadsworth Cengage Learning, 1998), 166.

him to cope, steady his hands for shooting, and increase his ability to take shock and risk. After World War II, industry scientists proved the pharmacology of nicotine was irresistibly appealing to soldiers. They found that "cigarette smoking was a diversional activity," a general adaptation to stress when flight is not an option, and a "defense mechanism" delivering a "tranquilizing effect" offering a sense of euphoria. In contrast to nonindustry scientists, who connected the cigarette to pulmonary disease, these scientists described the euphoria and release of a smoke as "pulmonary eroticism," a term used to describe the euphoria and release of smoke. Whether it was a calm trigger finger, or this form of tobacco-driven eroticism, in a war placing men in the front lines over an extended period, cigarettes became a vital element of the soldier's kit (see Figure 7.4).[42]

In addition to these pharmacological effects on combat perseverance, some very practical reasons made cigarettes appealing. A soldier's life included intense moments of terror coupled with drawn-out seasons of boredom, and for many soldiers, cigarettes were essential for passing the time. They also helped cover up the strong odors of the battlefield and of bodies that rarely enjoyed baths or showers.[43] Further, smoking gave soldiers a sense of normalcy in an otherwise chaotic environment. While living an animal-like existence, soldiers relished the freedom to smoke. Caught up in the savagery of combat, a smoke provided a solemn moment of reflection and a bit of relief from the jolt of the battlefield. Cigarettes acted as a medium of exchange and greeting between soldiers living among the cold machinery of war. Simply stated, cigarettes enabled soldiers to maintain composure and focus in the midst of difficult circumstances. Reflecting on the chaos of the Normandy invasion, observers recalled a shoreline littered with empty cartons of cigarettes "as far as eye could see." Famous war correspondent Ernie Pyle said he had met 10 soldiers who had smoked their first cigarette on the morning of the D-Day invasion.[44] Cigarettes were combat motivation in a convenient, transportable, tradable, disposable stick. Of course, they were also highly addicting, which increased demand for the product as the war progressed.

---

[42] William L. Dunn Jr., ed., *Smoking Behavior: Motives and Incentives* (New York: John Wiley and Sons, 1973), 1–3, 34, 45, 291; Count Corti, *A History of Smoking* (London: George G. Harrop & Co, 1931), 261.
[43] Jarrett Rudy, *The Freedom to Smoke: Tobacco Consumption and Identity* (Montreal: McGill–Queens University Press, 2005), 132–134, 141.
[44] Kennett, *G.I.: The American Soldier in World War II*, 94.

FIGURE 7.4 Marines at Peleliu smoking cigarette in barren foxhole. "From field to foxhole ... Marine Private First Class Douglas Lightheart (right) cradles a 30-caliber machine gun in his lap, while he and his buddy Private First Class Gerald Churchby take time out for a cigarette, while mopping up the enemy on Peleliu Islands, 7/14/1944."
Source: World War II Photos, NARA. National Archives Identifier: 532538. Image in the public domain

Thus, soldiers not only needed but demanded cigarettes during World War II. From the start of the war, the army requisitioned billions of cigarettes to meet the requirements of 16 million men and women destined to serve.[45] Americans only consumed 2.5 billion cigarettes a year in 1900, and 18 billion on the eve of World War I. However, the number climbed dramatically afterward, hitting 45 billion in 1920 and 134 billion in 1935. Ten years later, the numbers had tripled and risen to astronomical levels: in 1945 alone, Americans smoked 341 billion cigarettes. In 1935, the average American adult smoked 1,564 cigarettes a year. In 1944, the figure was 2,240 per year. By 1945, the annual rate rose to 3,449 cigarettes for every adult in America – more than twice what it was just a decade earlier.[46]

[45] Kennedy, *Freedom from Fear*, 636–637.   [46] Proctor, *Golden Holocaust*, 57.

World War II soldiers, supplied by the army's extensive cigarette distribution program, heavily increased consumption figures. The army supplied soldiers with nearly 350 billion cigarettes through meals and daily rations during the war.[47] In terms of consumption rate, the year 1944 is quite telling: the army's adjusted consumption rate had swollen to a projected 114 billion cigarettes, which represented the planning number it assumed for 1945. The 114 billion cigarettes *for the army alone* is astonishing considering the *entire* US adult population smoked only 134 billion cigarettes just a decade earlier.[48]

Several small vignettes further illustrate the near fanatical relationship between soldier and cigarette during World War II. Historian Lee Kennett describes how upon enlistment, GIs were "offered cigarettes at every turn … some local draft boards presented each departing selectee with a carton."[49] To meet the demand, the army established an entire division in the Quartermaster Corps dedicated to cigarette procurement. During the war, American fighting men smoked nearly one out of every five cigarettes produced in the United States.[50] The highest-ranking American generals had much to say about them as well. General Dwight D. Eisenhower smoked as much six packs of cigarettes a day as he paced back and forth, hands thrust in pockets, awaiting news from the front.[51] In praise of cigarettes, General Douglas MacArthur once instructed a citizens' group how to dispose of the $10,000 it had raised for soldiers. Rather than

[47] The US Senate Special Committee Investigating the National Defense Program, Part 26, "Cigarette Rations" September–December 1944, 12283, 12107, 12270, 12272–12184, and 12289, http://legacy.library.ucsf.edu/tid/fwz24foo/pdf (accessed November 15, 2013). This total number of cigarettes procured for soldiers during World War II can be found by detailed analysis of figures reported by the industry and the army in the Truman Committee Hearings plus some extrapolation based on the testimony. The army/industry reported procurement totals for 1944 (for soldiers overseas and in stateside training) was 114 billion cigarettes. This became their procurement planning number for 1945 as well. Testimony was provided that the overseas procurement number for 1943 was 31 billion. One can assume that the figure for 1942 overseas consumption would have been 20 to 30 billion. Further, the army reported that army consumption rate stateside in 1944 was 22 billion. Based on this figure, I assume that throughout the war the army's average yearly stateside consumption rate was about 20 billion a year. When totaled, the Army had to procure roughly 350 billion cigarettes during World War II and demobilization to meet the soldiers' needs.

[48] Proctor, *Golden Holocaust*, 57; *USSSC Report*, 12107, 12109, 12270, 12272–12284.

[49] Kennett, *G.I.: The American Soldier in World War II*, 94.

[50] Eric Burns, *The Smoke of the Gods: A Social History of Tobacco* (Philadelphia: Temple University Press, 2007), 198.

[51] See Rick Atkinson, *An Army at Dawn: The War in North Africa, 1942–1943* (New York: Henry Holt and Co., LLC, 2002), 60–61.

sending blankets, beverages, or inspirational literature, MacArthur said, "The entire amount should be used to buy American cigarettes."[52] After the war, the army named four massive demobilization camps in Europe for the war's most popular cigarette brands: Camps Lucky Strike, Twenty Grand, Old Gold, and Phillip Morris.[53] The soldiers entered the war with cigarettes, fought with cigarettes, and demobilized with cigarettes.

The demand for cigarettes, both domestically and at the fighting front, grew to such proportions that in 1944, tobacco lobbyist Joseph Kolodny noted that it was impractical even to predict a ceiling for cigarette consumption in America: "The production and consumption of cigarettes has leaped to astronomical heights in recent years, yet the saturation point is not yet in sight. As a matter of fact, no one is capable of forecasting when a point of saturation will be reached. It is rather silly to even contemplate any limit on cigarette consumption."[54] He further claimed given an adequate supply of cigarettes, the demand for them "has virtually no limits." Kolodny also observed civilians and soldiers under wartime conditions could suffer much in terms of rationing of supplies and food, but not cutting their cigarette supply. Indeed, if faced with limits, Americans were likely to "go nuts" without them and "holler [their] head off."[55]

Yet by the fall of 1944, a diminishing cigarette supply is exactly what the nation faced. In an environment of dwindling supply and overwhelming demand, elements of the federal government swung into action to first understand and then rectify the shortages. Some also hoped to use the situation to push back New Deal environmental, soil, and production regulations.

THE TRUMAN COMMITTEE HEARINGS, 1944

The army's massive logistical obligation to support the requirement of nearly two packs of cigarettes a day per soldier created a considerable domestic shortage. Many also feared the war dragging into 1946 or further – a real possibility in 1944 – and the government failing to meet soldiers' smoking demands. This looming problem garnered the attention of a powerful congressional inquiry in the fall of 1944. Led by Senator

[52] Burns, *The Smoke of the Gods*, 198.
[53] W. Paul McKinney et al., "Comparing Smoking Behavior of Veterans and Nonveterans, *Public Health Reports*, 112, no. 3 (1997): 215; The 225th AAA Searchlight Battalion Veterans Association, "The Cigarette Camps: US Army Cigarette Camps in the Le Havre Area," http://skylighters.org/special/cigcamps/cigintro.html (accessed July 26, 2019).
[54] *USSSC Report*, 12283.   [55] *USSSC Report*, 12285.

Harry Truman, government officials concerned with the opportunity for graft and war profiteering formed the Truman Committee in 1941 to exercise oversight over the rapidly expanding war economy. In an effort to resolve the domestic cigarette crisis, as well as plan for soldiers' access to cigarettes, the committee leaned heavily on the US Army to provide testimony regarding cigarette procurement. They also called on leading cigarette industry executives, agricultural experts, land-use specialists, and logisticians.

The forecasted 1945 army consumption rate would require 30 percent of all cigarettes made in America during 1944.[56] To meet both civilian and military requirements in 1945, the cigarette industry had to produce an unprecedented 400 billion cigarettes.[57] Camel alone designated 51.5 percent of its entire cigarette output in 1944 for soldiers. Seeking full explanation of these figures and assumptions, a panelist at one point interrupted the army colonel giving details on cigarette procurement to ask the question on everyone's mind: "Do you just assume that every soldier in the United States Army smokes?" The colonel promptly replied with an emphatic and frank "Yes!" The legislators and army officials on the panel never wavered in their determination to do whatever required to assure soldiers unfettered access to cigarettes. The army was clear on its intentions: "We are committed to buying whatever the demand is in theatre." The committee echoed this dedication: "If the theatre commanders, if the boys, are getting all the cigarettes that they require, then we are off to a good start ... we want to be sure that they are getting the cigarettes first, and in sufficient supply to meet their demands."[58]

With these words, the Truman Committee signaled the nation's intention to respond to the soldier demand for cigarettes. Yet at what cost? Data proving that cigarettes cause heart and lung disease did not emerge until 1952, long after the war was over. Even then, it was a hotly debated issue for the next 50 years. The vast majority of Americans did not give much thought to smoking as a deadly disease. In fact, during this period smoking was linked more to patriotism than disease. Americans were encouraged in their patriotism by American Tobacco, whose packages of Lucky Strikes were *sans* green dye because "Lucky Strike Green Has Gone to War." Was the home front willing to forgo cigarettes to ensure soldiers had adequate supply? Considering the majority of American

[56] *Business Week*, "Cigarette Famine," October 14, 1944, 19.
[57] *USSSC Report*, 12116, 12130, 1228.   [58] *USSSC Report*, 12108, 12112, 12111.

adults were smokers, this required a substantial commitment.[59] In the face of huge demand, some began to question the rationale of tightly restricted cultivation and production. Environmental regulations, and the philosophy undergirding them, became an intense issue of debate.

The New Deal had only recently implemented tobacco cultivation restrictions and soil conservation. Thus, the Truman Committee's enthusiasm to do "whatever was required" to extract cigarettes from the land ran up against commitments to soil conservation and land allotment restrictions. With cigarette production tied directly to tobacco leaf cultivation, the New Deal policies governing tobacco land allotments and leaf production came under debate. For example, as a result of allotment programs, and in the face of a World War II demand curve increasing at a rate of 15 percent per year, the government capped tobacco acreage at a 7 percent annual growth rate to avoid price fluctuations and irrational use of soil.[60] As military planners, industry executives, and politicians attempted to match cigarette supply with increasing demand, these policies blocked anyone tempted to allow the war to preclude prudent resourcing of land.

Anti-New Deal conservative Senator Homer S. Ferguson (R–MI), keenly aware of supply shortages, exploding demand, and the strategic consequences of a cigarette famine, tried to take advantage of the situation. From the earliest days of the New Deal, a small but growing group consistently characterized FDR's programs as government overstretch and shackling of the free market.[61] During Truman Committee hearings, they took aim at the soil conservation and allotment programs viewed as the root cause of the cigarette shortage.[62] Some reasoned that if Americans wanted billions of cigarettes, chief among these soldiers, then the

---

[59] John Burnham, *Bad Habits: Drinking, Smoking, Taking Drugs, Gambling, Sexual Misbehavior, and Swearing in American History* (New York: New York University Press, 1993), 102; Brandt, *Cigarette Century*, 96–98. Burnham's research reveals that by mid-century, 80 percent of American males between 18–64 used tobacco, and the majority of those were cigarette smokers.

[60] *USSSC Report*, 12176, 12283.

[61] In addition to those mentioned in this essay, others notables, either as groups or as individuals, who opposed the New Deal include Governor Huey Long (D–LA), William Lemke (R–ND), John Nance Garner (D–TX and FDR's VP for first two terms), Carter Glass (D–VA), W. R. Hearst (Publisher), and Hugh Johnson (former Administrator of the National Rifle Association). For this topic, see Alan Brinkley's *Voices of Protest* or David Kennedy's *Freedom from Fear*.

[62] For more, see Alan Brinkley, *Liberalism and Its Discontents* (Cambridge, MA: Harvard University Press, 2000).

answer should be to ramp-up acreage and production. It was good for the soldiers, and it was good for the economy. At one point, Ferguson asked, "If we are going to have any prosperity at all" aren't the "boys ... at the front" and "people all over the country" going to have to smoke more? Of course, the cigarette enterprise representative was happy to respond with a hearty "We hope so!"[63] Ferguson was essentially arguing the cigarette shortage was symptomatic of an American economy hamstrung by FDR's overreach. The controls hindering opportunities to exploit skyrocketing demand annoyed him. Among these contentious regulations was tight government control over land use, disguised, in Ferguson's eyes, as soil conservation.

With the New Deal under such scrutiny, war planners contemplated the reaction of American soldiers and factory workers to restricted cigarette access. Focusing his ire on FDR's managed agro-economy as the real culprit, Ferguson sarcastically asked, "Isn't it true that we paid growers *not* to grow tobacco in 1943 ... and we penalized other growers for growing too much tobacco ... which could be used for cigarettes?"[64] The answer was a resounding "yes!" Ferguson argued this was the sickening irony of the entire cigarette shortage episode. The US government paid exorbitantly for lower production and soil conservation from 1941 to 1944, causing the cigarette shortage they were desperately trying to overcome in the middle of a world war. Further, the economic impact of a strong, global American cigarette industry hung in the balance. In Joseph Kolodny's closing statement to the commission, he said,

American leaf tobacco and cigarettes will enjoy a larger and more active demand among foreign nations after the war than at any time in history ... the men in the armed forces – striding audaciously across the global map with their omnipresent cigarette – are doing a super job of selling the rest of the world on ... American tobacco. Lend-lease exports of leaf tobacco likewise contribute toward the build-up of a vastly expanded post-war market ... all this missionary work will go for naught if the production of leaf tobacco is not stepped up sufficiently to allow for a large exportable surplus after the war.[65]

---

[63] *USSSC Report*, 12181.
[64] *USSSC Report*, 12126 and Glenn L. Johnson, "Burley Tobacco Control Programs: Their Over-All Effect on Production and Prices, 1933–1950," *Bulletin 580*, Kentucky Agricultural Experiment Station, The University of Kentucky, February 1952, 195. The penalties for growing tobacco in excess of planned allotments varied, but generally included stiff penalties like revocation of tax certificates and a per pound charge for overproduction and a $5,000 fine for warehousemen misreporting data.
[65] *USSSC Report*, 12285

If America was to position itself as the world's foremost purveyor of cigarettes, was sacrificing or significantly adjusting centrally planned land-use and soil conservation policies a viable policy option? Was it the end of "win-win" deal between farmers, the government, and the land?

THE GOOD NEWS: GOOD POLICY SURVIVES

The nation's industrial production capacity during World War II was nothing less than astonishing. The American labor force produced 300,000 airplanes, 61,000 tanks, 12.5 million rifles, and 41 billion rounds of ammunition during World War II.[66] Add to this nearly 350 billion manufactured cigarettes for military consumption. These products, be they tank treads or cigarettes, required mountains of natural resources. Whether water to produce electricity, ore to make metal, or rubber for tires, war consumes vast amounts of natural resources. Tobacco for cigarette production was no different.

Yet tobacco acreage growth was capped at a very conservative rate during World War II. As much as the New Deal appeared to dig America out of the Depression and save its depleted and scarred landscape, it obstructed substantial increases in tobacco leaf production. The main concern now was the availability of suitable tobacco to meet the surging war requirements. Cigarettes require three-year aged tobacco, and the industry quickly burned through its reserves. For example, cigarettes produced in 1944 required tobacco leaves harvested in 1941. The industry was not willing to sacrifice quality to meet quantity requirements. It rejected the use of unaged tobacco. Thus, this commitment to the aging process forced utilizing reserve stocks of aged tobacco to meet the 1944 increase. However, this short-term fix failed to satisfy the problems of the out years. They had to address production from 1943 to 1944 to meet forecasted demand from 1945 to 1947 by substantially increasing acreage. Despite these efforts, planners forecast shortages for 1945 and 1946.[67]

To right this cigarette shortage, why could the industry not just produce a few billion more? A lobbyist representing cigarette wholesalers suggested a notional 35 percent increase in land allotted for tobacco in 1945 to meet

---

[66] The National World War II Museum, "By the Numbers: Wartime Production," www .nationalww2museum.org/learn/education/for-students/ww2-history/ww2-by-the-numbers/ wartime-production.html (accessed November 14, 2014).

[67] *Business Week*, "Cigarette Famine," October 14, 1944, 19–20; *USSSC Report*, 12142.

future demand forecasts and restore depleted tobacco reserves.[68] New Deal crop control, allotment, and soil conservation programs stood in the way of such drastic increases. With the cap set at a max 7 percent growth per year, a 35 percent increase was certainly out of the question. Though industry executives were gushing over seemingly unlimited demand, declaring it was "silly" even to envision a ceiling, tobacco growers had a stubborn memory of near-zero demand for new leaf a mere decade earlier, as well as centuries of boom and bust in their collective memories.[69] The New Deal was their deal, and they circled the wagons.

Despite badgering from North Carolina Senator Josiah W. Baily and other anti-New Deal politicians, who attributed the late 1930s improvement in the agro-economy to an act of God rather than the federal intervention they so loathed, FDR's agricultural and land-use programs had worked quite well, particularly for tobacco.[70] From 1933 to 1935, tobacco prices had doubled and then remained stable.[71] Removal of surplus and runaway production generated this price stabilization and market confidence. Moreover, this trend continued with the passage of the Soil Conservation and Domestic Allotment Act of 1936, which replaced the 1934 Act and further positioned soil conservation as part of the economic recovery. Planners in the Department of Agriculture were happy with the 1936 Act because they had been anxious to "shift from short-term emphasis on production control to the long-term aim of genuine adjustment" and strategic use of the land. The old 1934 program was weak on these issues; the new program provided "incentives for genuine conservation practices."[72] In the end, these government-mandated control measures were only part of the maturation of an activist federal government and long-term reform measures with far-reaching implications for farming, environmentalism, and agro-capitalism in America.[73]

These agro-enviro-economic policies became a cherished norm among America's tobacco farming communities. Growers grew to support

---

[68] *USSSC Report*, 12121.

[69] *USSSC Report*, 12176, 12283; Johnson, "Burley Tobacco Control Programs, 11, 18.

[70] Badger, *Prosperity Road*, 96.

[71] Bruce J. Schulman, *From Cotton Belt to Sun Belt: Federal Policy, Economic Development, and the Transformation of the South, 1938–1980* (Durham, NC: Duke University Press, 1994), 17.

[72] Badger, *Prosperity Road*, 124.

[73] This last sentence is informed by a close reading of Kennedy, *Freedom from Fear*; Lind, *Land of Promise*; and Alan Brinkley's *End of Reform* and *Liberalism and Its Discontents*. Additionally, for a focused treatment of the evolution of compulsory crop control oriented on a bottom-up, as well as top-down lens, refer to Badger, *Prosperity Road*.

government policy and caps on tobacco production, rejecting the free
market principles of *laissez faire* so much a part of their Jeffersonian
roots. Moreover, they reacted militantly to any drastic increase in land
allotments. They were more than content to pursue life, liberty, and
happiness through steadfast adherence to these government-imposed crop
size and land-use restrictions. With a nice check from the government, the
aggressive land "gobblers" of America's past became the happy soil
conservers of America's future.[74] During Truman hearing testimony, this
sentiment came through loud and clear when the farmer's representative,
Mr. E. Y. Floyd, stated that the overwhelming majority of tobacco
farmers were "practically all in and all very happy about" these policies,
and that they were the "difference between success and failure."[75] Call it
conservation or largesse, these tobacco farmers were happy with their
new deal and even the conservation measures attached to it. America's
iconic agrarian Thomas Jefferson might regard these developments as
anathema; however, they were lifeblood to the modern farmer.[76]

This support for good government policy found its voice in the Truman
Committee. Tobacco growers, drained by the disastrous price fluctuations
plaguing them for decades, repeatedly told the Truman Committee they
were not in the least interested in sacrificing crop support programs for
increased acreage.[77] In a rare example of solidarity, one cigarette industry
executive stated, "I assuredly would not recommend under present circumstances that all controls be eliminated. I know nobody who is willing
to face again the conditions that we had in 1930–1932 in leaf tobacco ...
when farmers were going all but hungry."[78] Another said he considered a

---

[74] Gloria L. Main, *Peoples of a Spacious Land: Families and Cultures in Colonial New
England* (Cambridge, MA: Harvard University Press, 2001). By using the term "gobblers," I hearken back to Gloria Main's description of early colonial land settlement.
Regarding the Puritans' *mentalité* toward land and enterprise, Main comments that
"wherever they went, Puritans made deals, launched enterprises, [and] started
plantations ... [they were] land gobbling engine of growth" fortified by a relentless and
very "American pursuit of private property."

[75] *USSSC Report*, 12165–12166. Mr. E. Y. Floyd was a North Carolina tobacco farmer
who was elevated to the Extension Service from 1925–1933, and then to the AAA from
1933 to 1943. He had extensive working knowledge of the farmers and their concerns.

[76] My judgments and descriptions of Thomas Jefferson's *mentalité* are greatly influenced by
Joseph Ellis's outstanding book *American Sphinx: The Character of Thomas Jefferson*
(New York: Alfred A. Knopf, 1996).

[77] *USSSC Report*, 12144, 12164–12172.

[78] *USSSC Report*, 12144, and Badger, *Prosperity Road*, 22. Badger gives figures showing
that North Carolina flue-cured tobacco growers earned $93.4 million in 1928, and only
$34.9 million in 1932.

situation whereby farmers once again chased a "disaster," and that growers were loath to permit a situation creating the price fluctuations and unpredictability they were accustomed to before allotment. Conversely, some within the cigarette industry did push for "more manpower and more acreage." Yet tobacco growers were not budging. They were satisfied with the allotment program and government oversight of soil use. Even if they might miss the promising opportunities for growth represented by the remarkable expansion in cigarette consumption during World War II, they remained resolute. Tobacco farmers were firmly behind FDR's managed economy and soil programs and came to rely on crop allotments as a substantial portion of their annual income. Subsequently, these benefits became a cornerstone of tobacco state politics.[79]

The war did not drag into 1946 or later, and despite pressures to throw out the soil conservation measures central to the agricultural allotment system, FDR's beloved New Deal agricultural and environmental programs held firm.[80] If measuring good policy is only linked to the degree to which the government, the farmer, and the environment are able to cooperate to the benefit of each and supply the resources for war, it was truly a good news, win-win situation. Yet if, in this evaluation of good policy, the degree to which these policies supported public health are included, the news is less positive.

THE BAD NEWS: POLLUTING THE HUMAN LANDSCAPE

Adhering to sound agro-economic-environmental policies, disciplined domestic cigarette rationing, and aggressive planning by the army, the nation overcame the challenges presented by the World War II cigarette shortage. As a bonus, politicians and war planners simultaneously reaffirmed commitments to the principles of soil conservation and managed agro-production, both relatively new ideas in America. Further, due to the nation's concerted, even zealous efforts, soldiers serving overseas or

---

[79] *USSSC Report*, 12171, 12140, 12164, 12166. For specifics regarding the "farmers' voices" regarding their overwhelming support, see the testimony of farmer and North Carolina AAA representative Mr. E. Y. Floyd on pages 12163 to 12171 of the Truman Committee Transcript.

[80] Conkin, *A Revolution Down on the Farm*, 82. After the 1936 Soil Conservation and Allotment Act, the average tobacco acreage per farm continued to steadily drop and hover around two acres for decades after World War II. This is testament to the success of the AAA legislation.

training stateside saw absolutely no cigarette shortage. In lieu of a cigarette famine, in fact, soldiers experienced a cigarette avalanche.[81]

However, this good news was also the root of some very bad news: the wholesale entrenchment of the cigarette habit as not only a norm, but a celebrated aspect of American society. The numbers are alarming. After issuing 5.5 billion manufactured cigarettes to soldiers during the entirety of World War I, just 26 years later during World War II the government oversaw the production and distribution of nearly 350 billion. This drastic spike in state-sponsored military smoking transferred into society. From 1940 to 1950, American's per capita consumption of cigarettes doubled from 5 to 10 cigarettes per day, representing the largest 10-year spike in the entire twentieth century.[82] By 1950, 80 percent of all American males were avid users of tobacco, with the vast majority using cigarettes as their chosen form of nicotine intake.[83]

Further, before World War I, with only 140 cases worldwide prior to 1900, lung cancer was so rare that medical school students considered examining a cadaver with the disease a rare event. After initiating the cigarette ration in World War I, consumption of cigarettes began a rapid climb. By 1925, there were 2,837 cases of lung cancer reported in America. After World War II, when smoking soared to even greater heights, the number of domestic lung cancer cases increased to 18,313 by 1950.[84]

Despite scientific data in 1952 definitively linking smoking to lung cancer, as well as the 1964 Surgeon General's Warning to smokers, the government continued to issue cigarettes to soldiers as part of their rations in both the Korean and Vietnam wars. By 1985, when those who were 25 in 1945 turned 65, the number of lung cancer cases stood

---

[81] *USSSC Report*, 12110–12111.   [82] Proctor, *Golden Holocaust*, 57.

[83] Burnham, *Bad Habits*, 101; The American Lung Association (ALA) Research and Program Services Epidemiology and Statistics Unit, "Trends in Tobacco Use," July 2011, www.lung.org/assets/documents/research/tobacco-trend-report.pdf (accessed July 26, 2019). Burnham's research uncovers that 80 percent of all American men used tobacco of some form, with two-thirds given to using cigarettes. The ALA reports that "for U.S. males, smoking prevalence peaked in the 1940s and 1950s at approximately 67%. For females, smoking prevalence peaked in the 1960's at approximately 44%." The bottom line from all this data: men issued cigarettes during the war left the war and became part of the "vast majority" tobacco users in America after the war.

[84] Brandt, *Cigarette Century*, 3; Proctor, *Golden Holocaust*, 45, 57. These statistics and linkages to cigarette smoking are the subject of much controversy and litigation. After four decades executing a litigation strategy aimed at plausible deniability, the cigarette industry moved to a shrewd, opposite strategy. Arguing in the late 1990s that it was well known that smoking cigarettes was dangerous to health and that consumers were assuming the risk, they attempted to transfer risk to the smoker, not the industry.

at an alarming 123,146. During this same period, research revealed 52.2 percent of uniformed personnel under age 20 smoked, compared to 21.2 percent of high school seniors.[85] In the army, 63 percent of noncommissioned officers smoked, and 57 percent of junior enlisted soldiers were avid smokers.[86] These were high numbers when compared to the civilian smoking rate of 32 percent.[87]

Thus, the massive groundswell of cigarette-smoking World War II veterans was instrumental in establishing Americans as among the world's leading consumers of cigarettes, with an associated decline in public health.[88] By the 1980s, the cigarette smoking World War II veterans plus the generation of smokers they raised created a well-documented public health epidemic. The consequences of government policies regarding production of tobacco and consumption of cigarettes in relation to military veterans and their dependents is profound. Sanctioned by the government, active duty soldiers, veterans, and their dependents possessed a multitude of opportunities to continue their military smoking habit through generous smoking benefits guaranteed them by their elected representatives. The government provided cigarettes in Veterans Affairs (VA) hospital facilities and offered access to low-cost, subsidized cigarettes in the Post Exchange (PX) and commissary. Despite numerous attempts, the Department of Defense was not able to institute smoking cessation measures until 1986 and was not able to remove smoking subsidies for military smokers until 2001.[89] Old habits die hard.

CONCLUSION

This episode in the environmental history of World War II is only part of the greater story of American history. From its earliest days, America has been a nation comfortable with contradiction. On one hand, World War

---

[85] Walter Pincus, "Pentagon Doctor Seeks to Reduce Cigarette Sales," *The Washington Post*, January 5, 1986, A1, A16; James Savarese & Associates, "Economic Impact: Proposal to Raise Cigarette Prices in Military Commissaries," May 5, 1986, 7, http://legacy.library.ucsf.edu/tid/cff22doo/pdf (accessed January 10, 2015).

[86] Larry Carney and Jim Tice, "Army Broadens Ban on Smoking July 7," *The Army Times*, June, 23, 1986, 10, http://legacy.library.ucsf.edu/tid/dkc36boo (accessed January 15, 2015).

[87] *The Senate Congressional Record*, August 6, 1986, at S10534, http://legacy.library.ucsf.edu/tid/pxw66woo/pdf (accessed February 28, 2013).

[88] Proctor, *Golden Holocaust*, 45, 57.

[89] Elizabeth A. Smith, Virginia S. Blackman, and Ruth E. Malone, "Death at a Discount: How the Tobacco Industry Thwarted Tobacco Control Policies in US Military Commissaries," *Tobacco Control*, 16, no. 1 (2007): 40.

II saw the affirmation of wise government policies regarding the rational extraction of tobacco resources from the land. The war also demonstrated that the United States could provide overwhelming resources in a global war effort without resorting to a command economy or a police state. On the other hand, the war and its aftermath showed how the growing federal bureaucracy encouraged a mounting public health disaster. During the 1980s, Secretary of Defense Caspar Weinberger recognized the irony of his soldiers' long affair with the cigarette. Assessing a nation struggling to pay for military and retiree health care yet addicted to the tax receipts from cigarette sales, Weinberger summed up the entire episode best with his assertion that, "The tobacco issue has presented the government with a paradoxical situation attempting to balance the negative health impacts against the positive economic impacts."[90]

---

[90] Office of the Asst. Secretary of Defense (Health Affairs) and Office of the Assistant Secretary of Defense (Force Management and Personnel), "Department of Defense Report on Smoking and Health in the Military," March 1986, 24, http://legacy.library .ucsf.edu/tid/kic36b00 (accessed January 15, 2015).

PART IV

NEW LANDSCAPES

Cities and Coasts

8

A Watery Grave?

World War II and the Environment on the American Gulf Coast

Christopher M. Rein

Just before midnight on July 30, 1942, German U-boat captain Hans-Günther Kuhlmann peered through the periscope of *U-166* at a 5,000-ton steamship running north in the Gulf of Mexico toward the safety of the mouth of the Mississippi River. The SS *Robert E. Lee*, bearing a name from the last war to touch the Gulf's shores, was on the final leg of a perilous voyage from Port of Spain, Trinidad, and had, along the way, rescued a number of survivors of ships sunk by U-boats.[1] Kuhlmann and his boat were on their first trans-Atlantic patrol, hoping to avoid the substantial antisubmarine forces off the American eastern seaboard in favor of the lightly defended but lucrative petroleum-laden targets in the vast Gulf of Mexico. The U-boat had already sunk three smaller vessels, including a 2,300-ton ship off the coast of Cuba, but the current victim was the crew's largest. It was also their last.

At 11:37 p.m., the *Lee*'s escort, *Patrol Craft (PC)-566*, commanded by Lieutenant Commander Herbert Claudius, reported a torpedo explosion aft on the *Lee*. *PC-566* immediately located the sub using sonar and began dropping depth charges. Not long thereafter, an ominous oil slick blackened the Gulf's surface, and the crew of *PC-566* claimed success. They immediately turned their attention to the lives of the crewmembers and passengers aboard the *Lee* and were able to save all but 25 of the more than 400 souls on board before the ship slipped below the waves.

---

[1] The *Lee* had been chartered by the Aluminum Company of America (Alcoa) to supply its expanding operations along the northern coast of South America. See Matthew Evenden, "Aluminum, Commodity Chains, and the Environmental History of the Second World War," *Environmental History* 16, no. 1 (January 1, 2011): 69–93.

Despite prosecuting what appeared to be a successful attack on the U-boat, the navy reprimanded Claudius for the loss of the *Lee*. Two days later, a US Coast Guard Grumman J4F *Widgeon,* flying from a recently militarized airfield near Houma, Louisiana, also reported sighting and depth-charging a U-boat in the open Gulf nearly 100 miles south of that city, and not far from where the *Lee* had slipped below the waves. After the war, the Coast Guard corroborated the attack with the reported loss of *U-166* near that time and credited the two crew members with a successful attack, awarding both military decorations.[2]

In 2001, a contractor working for Shell and British Petroleum (BP) surveying the Gulf's floor located two shipwrecks immediately adjacent to each other in the area of *U-166*'s sinking of the *Robert E. Lee*. The first was indeed the *Lee*, but the second was *U-166*. Claudius's crew on *PC-566* had indeed done their job, successfully sinking the U-boat, while the partially trained crew of the Coast Guard aircraft had probably attacked a whale, or possibly another U-boat known to be in the area. Sadly, in 2010, while operating less than five miles away, a BP-leased oil rig exploded, resulting in the release of more than five million barrels of crude into the Gulf in the worst oil spill ever in a marine environment. The geographic proximity of the final resting places of the *Lee*, *U-166*, and the *Deepwater Horizon* rig, and the highly toxic dispersant and globs of raw crude oil that now presumably coat all three, symbolically link the area's military and industrial infrastructure established during World War II, the massive expansion of petroleum resources in the region to sustain the US military's global hegemony won during the war, and the significant environmental transformation and degradation of the American Gulf Coast.

From the mouth of the Rio Grande River in Texas to Key West in Florida, the US Gulf Coast stretches for more than 1,600 miles along the western, northern, and eastern edges of the Gulf of Mexico (see Map 8.1). Since the era of European colonization, this coastal region has seen conflict between Spanish, French, English, and later American military forces, as posts along strategic waterways afforded access to and control over a large area of the continent's interior. Excellent natural harbors spawned coastal communities in Tampa, Mobile, Biloxi, New Orleans,

---

[2] For details of the attack, see Brian Clark Howard, "72 Years Later, Snubbed Captain Credited with Downing German U-Boat," *National Geographic*, December 19, 2014, http://news.nationalgeographic.com/news/2014/12/141217-german-u-boat-u-166-gulf-mexico-archaeology-history/ (accessed June 7, 2016); and "Ships Hit by U-Boats: Robert E. Lee," *U-Boat.net*, http://uboat.net/allies/merchants/1981.html (accessed June 7, 2016).

MAP 8.1 Cities and military installations along the American Gulf Coast. Created by the author.

and Galveston, linking them to both the wider world of ocean commerce as well as to the coastal ecosystem in which each resided. Natural factors, especially the malaria and yellow fever that thrived in the damp, mosquito-laden subtropical environment, limited growth throughout the early twentieth century but advances in public health science coupled with massive flood control and drainage programs that reduced mosquito breeding habitats increased survival rates and made coastal cities more survivable and livable.[3] By the dawn of the twentieth century, refrigeration technology pioneered by John Gorrie at Apalachicola on the Florida Gulf Coast (and the associated technology of air conditioning) promised more comfortable living and heralded a population boom in the once-remote coastal region.

In his 2017 Pulitzer Prize–winning work on the Gulf of Mexico, Jack Davis masterfully catalogued the history of human interaction with this most American sea and convincingly argued, "The Gulf's history, as we shall see, is America's history."[4] But his volume, aside from brief treatment of munitions dumping and the impact of warfare on nature, largely omits discussion of military affairs in general, and World War II in

[3] See, for example, Craig Colten, *Unnatural Metropolis: Wresting New Orleans from Nature* (Baton Rouge: Louisiana State University Press, 2006) and Melanie Wiggins, "Combatting Yellow Fever in Galveston," *Southwestern Historical Quarterly*, 119, no. 2 (January 2016): 234–252.
[4] Jack Davis, *The Gulf: The Making of an American Sea* (New York: W. W. Norton, 2017), 7.

particular, as pivot points in the American remaking of the Gulf of Mexico.[5] At the dawn of World War II, America's Gulf Coast was still very much its "third coast," lagging behind the settlement and development already well established on the Atlantic and expanding along the Pacific coasts. Outside of the port cities, which did a booming trade with Central America and, after the opening of the Panama Canal in 1914, across the Pacific, sleepy fishing villages and long stretches of wild, pristine coastline typified the American Gulf Coast. In 1940, only three cities ranked among country's 100 largest: New Orleans (#15), Houston (#21), and Tampa (#84). Outside of these ports, smaller communities shipped timber from the coastal plain's pine belt or packed seafood for markets in larger cities. But World War II substantially transformed the region. It brought armed conflict to the Gulf's shores for the first time since 1865, with Axis submarines attacking Gulf shipping, especially tankers laden with oil and gasoline, the lifeblood of modern militaries fighting in Europe and across the Pacific. Even more important, the military and industrial infrastructure spawned to support World War II combat led to permanent military bases and a massive expansion in the region's petrochemical infrastructure. Federal investment remade coastal communities, delivering much-needed capital, in the form of both contracts and wages, which fueled impressive growth along the coast. This federally funded wartime infrastructure not only reshaped the region throughout the war but also spurred growth during the Cold War that followed and continues to the present day.

In particular, urban centers such as Houston, Tampa, and New Orleans boomed during the war. Smaller cities such as Fort Myers/Naples (77), Sarasota/Bradenton (72), McAllen/Edinburgh (65), and Baton Rouge (70) joined the list of the nation's 100 largest, with Lafayette (108), Mobile (129), Corpus Christi (118), Pensacola (109), Brownsville (127), Beaumont (130), and Tallahassee (139) lingering just outside. Each of these communities experienced tremendous growth during and after the war, either as a direct result of military bases established nearby, or the production of industrial commodities in demand by the military (the US military has been the single largest user of petroleum in the world).[6]

---

[5] Ibid., 98–99, 328–329.
[6] For a full discussion of the Department of Defense's energy use, which, in the 1990s alone exceeded that of two-thirds of the world's countries, see J. R. McNeill and David Painter, "The Global Environmental Footprint of the US Military, 1789–2003," in *War and the Environment: Military Destruction in the Modern Age*, ed. Charles Closmann (College Station: Texas A&M University Press, 2009), 24.

By 2016 the Houston and Tampa metropolitan areas had rocketed up the list to #5 and #18, respectively, while New Orleans slipped to #46, after the devastation and depopulation caused by Hurricane Katrina. Despite its population woes, New Orleans is still the busiest port in the United States.

Much of this new development took place in environmentally sensitive coastal areas where shallow water tables exacerbated the effect of pollution and slow tidal flows kept waste in circulation or facilitated environmental absorption rather than dispersal. While inland cities could safely discharge effluent into fast-moving streams that would carry waste far away, coastal settlements since Jamestown have found that their effluent often returns to them on each incoming tide, as stagnant waters allow pollutants and waste to linger and accumulate. When coupled with the vast diversity and productivity of estuary ecosystems, increased development in coastal areas can damage built and natural environments and the flora and fauna that live there. In addition, the shallow gradients of coastal plains and high susceptibility to flooding can exacerbate storm-related damage and pollution, as the Houston area witnessed during Hurricane Harvey, when power outages led to toxic releases and floods inundated retention ponds, discharging massive amounts of toxins into the local environment.[7]

World War II was not the sole cause of the tremendous growth in the region, but massive federal investment, much of it initiated during the war years, provided a stimulus for further infrastructure development and the significant environmental change of the period referred to as the "Great Acceleration" of the Anthropocene.[8] While many of the problems presented here are not unique to the region, they do "lend themselves to a regional approach."[9] When examined holistically, it is clear that environmental changes initiated during World War II were a significant, if largely unacknowledged, factor in the ecological transformation of one of the country's most important and productive coastal environments.

---

[7] See Joel Tarr, ed., *The Search for the Ultimate Sink: Urban Pollution in Historical Perspective* (Akron, OH: University of Akron Press, 1996).

[8] Robinson Meyer, "The Cataclysmic Break That (Maybe) Occurred in 1950," *The Atlantic*, April 16, 2019, www.theatlantic.com/science/archive/2019/04/great-debate-over-when-anthropocene-started/587194/ (accessed April 17, 2019).

[9] Air-conditioning, in particular, has had a significant role. See Robert S. Thompson, "The Air-Conditioning Capital of the World: Houston and Climate Control," in *Energy Metropolis: An Environmental History of Houston and the Gulf* Coast, ed. Martin Melosi and Joseph Pratt (Pittsburgh, PA: University of Pittsburgh Press, 2007); W. Jeffrey Bolster, "Opportunities in Marine Environmental History," *Environmental History* 11, no. 3 (July 2006): 584.

MILITARY ACTIVITY ON THE AMERICAN GULF COAST FROM
THE SIXTEENTH CENTURY TO WORLD WAR II

During European colonization, continental rivals often clashed on or near the American Gulf Coast. In 1559, Spanish conquistador and explorer Tristan de Luna founded a temporary settlement on bluffs high above Pensacola Bay. The colony suffered fearfully from a hurricane that September, forcing the Spanish to abandon the site, and allowing St. Augustine, settled in 1565 on Florida's Atlantic Coast, to earn the title of the oldest continually occupied European settlement in North America. French explorers established their first colonies at Biloxi on the Mississippi coast in 1699 and on the shores of Mobile Bay in 1702, before finally settling in the flood-prone site of New Orleans on the banks of the Mississippi in 1718 as the capital of their New World empire.

But the British, and later their American progeny, eventually crowded both declining powers out of the Gulf. After American violations of Spanish neutrality, most notably by Andrew Jackson during and immediately after the War of 1812, which also featured an abortive British attempt to reclaim New Orleans, the United States eventually consolidated control over the Gulf and began erecting a string of masonry forts to protect key points, extending from Dry Tortugas in the Keys to the approaches to New Orleans. In 1828, it also established a naval reservation on the barrier island between Pensacola Bay and the Gulf of Mexico, due largely to the extensive stands of native live oak (*Quercus virginiana*), an exceptionally dense wood highly valued for ship construction that gave early American warships such as the *USS Constitution* the nickname, "Old Ironsides." Today, the Naval Live Oaks Reservation is part of the Gulf Islands National Seashore and features one of the last undeveloped stretches of the northern Gulf Coast.[10]

During the American Civil War, the Gulf again became the scene of combat, as federal forces successfully neutralized the outdated masonry forts defending New Orleans, Biloxi, Mobile, and Pensacola and denied these ports to the Confederacy. The coast then became the scene of raiding, especially on Confederate salt works, as that increasingly scarce commodity became critical to southern efforts to preserve meat for soldiers and civilians. Tampa enjoyed a flurry of activity in 1898 as the primary port of embarkation for American forces headed to Cuba

---

[10] National Park Service, "The Live Oak Tree: A Naval Icon," www.nps.gov/guis/learn/historyculture/the-live-oak-story.htm (accessed November 18, 2016).

during the Spanish-American War, including the famed "Rough Riders," and their commander-turned-president, Theodore Roosevelt. In fear of forays from the Spanish Navy, many older masonry forts underwent extensive modification with concrete emplacements and the installation of heavy seacoast guns. But, as the new century dawned and American military enterprises expanded across the globe, and especially into the Pacific, the Gulf languished as a forgotten backwater in the defense establishment.

The development of aviation after 1903 briefly revived the Gulf's fortunes within the military, particularly after World War I. While the army remained focused on inland training areas and the navy built up its vaunted "Great White Fleet" into a two-ocean navy, with principal bases on the Atlantic and Pacific coasts, both army and navy aviation establishments eyed the Gulf South region as an ideal area for aviation training. "In the pioneering days," a report later found, "the need for favorable flying weather and an agreeable climate received paramount consideration."[11] With its long summers, snow- and ice-free winters and the availability of large overwater training areas free of vertical impediments and suitable for emergency landings, the Gulf Coast region rated highly with aviation advocates in both services. During the interwar years, Brooks, Randolph, and Kelly Fields, near San Antonio, hosted most of the army's primary and advanced flight training, and the Army Air Corps relocated its Tactical School from Langley Field in Virginia to Maxwell Field outside Montgomery in the 1920s.[12]

Eyeing a role as an economic defense force during the isolationist and depressed 1930s, the Army Air Forces established air bases near principal ports, eventually including MacDill Field near Tampa, Eglin Field at Fort Walton Beach, Brookley Field at Mobile, and a reactivated Ellington Field outside of Houston. Many of these fields benefitted from designation as Works Progress Administration (WPA) sites and became eligible for additional federal assistance due to their location within 100 miles of the coast.[13] As a result of further wartime expansion, the navy's entire

---

[11] Frederick Shaw ed., *Locating Air Force Base Sites: History's Legacy* (Washington, DC: Air Force History and Museums Program, 2004), 6.

[12] Shaw found the Air Corps "concentrated its attention in Texas, particularly at San Antonio, because of its excellent weather, climate and topography." Ibid., 17. Vincent P. Caire, *Military Aviation in the Gulf South: A Photographic History* (Baton Rouge: Louisiana State University Press, 2016). https://lsupress.org/books/detail/military-aviation-in-the-gulf-south/ (accessed November 11, 2019).

[13] Ibid., 26.

aviation training infrastructure eventually found a home around the Gulf's shores, with major naval air stations at Key West, Pensacola, and Corpus Christi and supporting fields further inland in Beeville and Kingsville Texas and Milton, Florida.

Aviation's foothold in the Gulf made it easy to convert these airfields into active bases for antisubmarine patrols when, in 1940, the U-boat menace threatened and spurred even further expansion of the navy and AAF's training infrastructure. By December 1940, Harding Field, near Baton Rouge, Dale Mabry Field at Tallahassee, Drew Field at Tampa, and the municipal airports at Orlando and New Orleans all hosted operational groups. Tyndall Field, near Panama City, Florida, became a gunnery training school.[14] During the war, new fields joined existing bases in a massive expansion, including flight training fields at Lake Charles, Louisiana; Biloxi, Mississippi; Sarasota, Homestead, and Sebring, Florida; Valdosta, Georgia; and Dothan and the famed Tuskegee school for African American aviators in Alabama, as well as additional training bases at Victoria and on Matagorda Island, and a gunnery range at Harlingen, Texas. The government transferred the sparsely populated scrub pines and swampland behind Eglin, which had been administered by the Forest Service as the Choctawhatchee National Forest, to the Army Air Forces, where it became the air force's largest weapons testing range, after the AAF had previously operated a small range near there for the Air Corps Tactical School at Maxwell. When that school closed for the war, the AAF acquired more than 200,000 acres near Avon Park, Florida, where airmen developed and refined new weapons and techniques at the Army Air Forces School of Applied Tactics at Orlando.

Many of these bases shut their doors after the war, but both the navy and the air force recognized the value of the open ranges over the Gulf of Mexico and developed wartime bases to host training exercises during the Cold War. Homestead and Key West hosted "aggressor" air-to-air training squadrons for the air force and navy, respectively, until Homestead was heavily damaged by Hurricane Andrew in 1992. Similarly, Tyndall played host the annual "William Tell" air-to-air interception

---

[14] As a child in the 1970s, I recall collecting spent lead slugs from the dunes behind the base's white sandy beaches, a phenomenon common on other former training ranges, including Longboat Key near Sarasota. See Bret Hauff, "Former Longboat Bombing Range Not Scheduled for Clean Up until 2047," *YourObserver.com*, January 3, 2018, www.yourobserver.com/article/former-longboat-bombing-range-not-scheduled-for-clean-up-until-2047 (accessed January 10, 2018).

exercise throughout the Cold War on its ranges over the Gulf while Eglin still owns the massive wartime weapons range that covers a significant percentage of Florida's panhandle. Tragically, Tyndall suffered significant damage in the October 2018 landfall of Hurricane Michael, a Category 5 storm that devastated the base and damaged almost 20 advanced F-22 fighters that sheltered against the storm in hangars on the base.[15] Following the navy's and air force's lead, the army also gravitated toward the Gulf Coast for aviation training, and now conducts all its helicopter pilot training at Fort Rucker, located on the site of a World War II–era training base just inland near Dothan, Alabama. All these facilities became economic engines for the surrounding communities, fueling growth in sensitive coastal ecosystems and leading to heavy aviation activity over important wetlands.

Compared to the navy and the air force, the army displayed less of an interest in the Gulf Coast proper during World War II, with the exception of Camp Gordon Johnston, established near Carrabelle, Florida as an amphibious training center in 1941, which used the nearby coastal barrier islands of Dog Island and St. George's Island to train troops for the D-Day landings in 1944. The base closed shortly after the end of the war and is now a retirement village, cementing the linkage between wartime infrastructure and postwar development. But usually the military retained its wartime bases, expanding existing training posts and developing new ones to support the massive wartime demand. These include bases for the active-component of the army on the edge of the coastal plain at Fort Hood, outside of Killeen, Texas; Fort Polk, near Leesville, Louisiana; and Fort Benning, near Columbus, Georgia.

State National Guard establishments followed the active-army's lead in repurposing major wartime training camps into extensive postwar training areas, including Camp Blanding, Florida and Camp Shelby, Mississippi. Both sites make extensive use of coastal longleaf pine ecosystems home to several endangered and threatened species, including the red-cockaded woodpecker and the gopher tortoise. In many places, already protected areas have been designated off limits for training and are managed cooperatively with the Nature Conservancy, facilitating conservation efforts for those species. The army's wartime emphasis on

[15] Kyle Mizokami, "More Than a Dozen F-22s May Have Been Damaged or Destroyed by Hurricane Michael," *Popular Mechanics*, October 15, 2018, www.popularmechanics .com/military/aviation/a23792532/f-22s-damaged-destroyed-hurricane-michael/ (accessed April 17, 2019).

southern bases also had subtle effects on the nation's foodways, as local producers sought additional markets for agricultural goods. In Louisiana, both rice and sweet potato growers actively marketed their products to the growing complex of wartime army training bases in the central part of the state, hoping to introduce national palates to what until then had been regional dishes.[16]

World War II bases also highlighted the poor state of the region's road infrastructure. The inadequate road network revealed during the War Department's massive training exercises in 1940 and 1941, which became known as the Louisiana Maneuvers, ensured the region's share of the attention paid to developing transportation infrastructure during and after the war. During the exercise engineers had to strengthen bridges and regrade roadbeds to support military vehicles.[17] The Federal Highway Act of 1944 mandated improved connections between populations and "defense areas," which now included the Gulf. As a result, the Gulf States especially benefitted from the new interstate highway system, which provided both a central artery, Interstate 10, across the northern Gulf, as well as a number of spurs connecting points inland to the coast, including Houston's Gulf Freeway, authorized in 1945. The port of Beaumont, in particular, rapidly expanded during the war years, became a principal embarkation point for forces from the interior scheduled to ship out for Europe in the event of an emergency there.

With this infrastructure in place, cities were now free, and even encouraged, to expand into surrounding areas, fueling further growth, including in many of the country's new tourist destinations.[18] As Harvey Jackson argues,

In 1941, all along the northern rim of the Gulf Coast, from Pass Christian, Mississippi, to Panama City, Florida, there were a score or more of little villages that survived on fishing and a trickle of tourists from not too far away, vacationers who came down to spend a week or so in the few "mom and pop" motor courts. They'd swim a little, fish a little, eat raw oysters, buy something tacky at a local shop, and some, freed from hometown social restraints, would visit local night clubs, dance and drink and get rowdy. After the war their numbers increased.

---

[16] Jason Theriot, "Cajun Country during World War II," *Louisiana History* 51, no. 2 (Spring 2010): 137, 145.

[17] Christopher Gabel, *The US Army GHQ Maneuvers of 1941* (Washington, DC: Center of Military History, 1991), 58.

[18] Tom Watson McKinney, "Superhighway Deluxe: Houston's Gulf Freeway," in *An Environmental History of Houston and the Gulf Coast*, ed. Martin Melosi and Joseph Pratt (Pittsburgh: University of Pittsburgh Press, 2007), 148–172.

Driving down on military-improved roads, [emphasis added] they came mainly from Alabama, Mississippi, and Georgia, and brought with them the culture of the rising southern white middle class.[19]

Florida's "Emerald Coast" alone hosts major navy and air force bases in Pensacola, Fort Walton Beach, and Panama City and improved access to these areas provided the necessary infrastructure for a postwar tourism boom on the "Redneck Riviera," including Panama City Beach's claim to be the nation's "Spring Break Capital."

SHIPBUILDING AND PETROLEUM PRODUCTS: WARTIME INDUSTRIAL DEVELOPMENT ON THE GULF COAST

While the navy did not base any major warships in the Gulf during the war, wartime demands still had a profound impact on the area. In addition to an increase of smaller vessels, primarily convoy escorts, across the Gulf, the area witnessed a significant influx of industrial shipbuilding as a result of war contracts, much of which has continued to the present. In 1940, the Northeast hosted a majority of the nation's shipbuilding in a concentrated area that stretched from Bath, Maine to Newport News, Virginia, while the Gulf and Pacific coasts hosted only a handful of minor yards. The concentration in the Northeast made economic sense – the region boasted a burgeoning population of skilled laborers experienced in manufacturing and was also in close proximity to the nation's primary steel manufacturing corridor, stretching from Pennsylvania to the Midwest, as well as the sea lanes to Europe. Narrow locks on the Detroit and Niagara Rivers, coupled with foreign control of the St. Lawrence River, hampered development of new shipyards on the Great Lakes, meaning mills in Gary, Cleveland, and Pittsburgh sent steel plates by rail over the spine of the Appalachians to public and private shipyards in Boston, New York, and Philadelphia.

But the development of a southern steel industry centered on Birmingham, Alabama in the early twentieth century, combined with excellent ports and cheap labor along the Gulf Coast, made the region a viable alternative for a maritime construction industry looking to diversify

---

[19] Harvey H. Jackson, III, "The Rise and Decline of the Redneck Riviera: The Northern Rim of the Gulf Coast since World War II," *Southern Cultures* 16, no. 1 (Spring, 2010): 7–30. For a full discussion, see Jackson, *The Rise and Decline of the Redneck Riviera: An Insider's History of the Florida–Alabama Coast* (Athens: University of Georgia Press, 2012).

geographically, especially after the 1914 opening of the Panama Canal. In addition, the threat of saboteurs, either along the coast or from among the large, foreign-born populations of eastern cities also spurred shipbuilding along the Gulf Coast, with its primarily native-born population and remoteness from the seat of the war. While U-boat attacks did occur in the Gulf, they paled in comparison to those along the eastern seaboard, as New Orleans was almost half again as far from Nazi bases in France as New York. Further, the absence of steel manufacturing on the West Coast (though a mill eventually opened in California) and the limitations on the Great Lakes meant that, as one historian explained, "the possibilities of the Gulf for shipbuilding stood out all the brighter. It had a favorable climate and was protected from attack."[20]

A study of the shipbuilding industry completed shortly after the war reported that, as early as 1940, defense officials recommended "serious consideration should be given to locating these plants in the South in order to distribute the burden and to utilize to best advantage the labor available." While labor shortages were already appearing in the Northeast, "In the southern states, on the other hand, there are large numbers of workers who would be available for unskilled work or for training. Other industries are not competing keenly for labor." It appeared that the region's agrarian history, now reaching the end of a long, lucrative period of monoculture cotton production, largely as a result of the devastating boll weevil infestation in the 1920s and 1930s, was becoming an asset for war production.[21] The agricultural decline provided a ready pool of former farmers and fallow fields with declining value or delinquent tax payments facilitated military acquisition for training bases and ranges.

Tight schedules and high demand for production meant that manufacturers and the military could ill-afford labor losses due to illness. As late as 1936, more than 4,000 Americans, mostly in southern states, had *died* from malaria, while thousands more suffered the disease's debilitating effects. By 1946, this number had dropped to 400, and malaria deaths virtually disappeared in subsequent years. Much of this could be attributed to the efforts of the Office of Malaria Control in War Areas (MCWA), renamed in 1946 the Communicable Disease Center (CDC) and, today, the

---

[20] Frederic Lane, *Ships for Victory: A History of Shipbuilding under the US Maritime Commission in World War II* (Baltimore: Johns Hopkins University Press, 1951), 49.

[21] See James Giesen, *Boll Weevil Blues: Cotton, Myth and Power in the American South* (Chicago: University of Chicago Press, 2011).

Center for Disease Control, and Prevention still headquartered on the fringes of the country's historical malaria belt, in Atlanta, Georgia. Officials chose the Atlanta location because it was also the headquarters of the Army's 4th Corps area, responsible for military bases across the Southeast and the direction of the regional malaria-control program.[22] An army doctor, Major Walter Reed, confirmed the mosquito as a vector in yellow fever epidemics and the service remained interested in protecting soldiers' health as a guarantor of combat power. These programs also utilized military aircraft to pioneer aerial dusting, which enabled a much wider dispersal of insecticides that had been possible previously, codifying a practice that had far-reaching consequences.[23]

As it did elsewhere, the massive aerial spraying of DDT and other pesticides during and after the war seriously damaged the Gulf's coastal ecosystems. As the highly persistent DDT built up in the environment and the tissues of smaller fish, it eventually wound its way up the food chain to apex predators, where it accumulated in toxic quantities. By the 1970s, the state of Louisiana had lost all its native brown pelicans (*Pelecanus occidentalis*), an ecological and public-relations disaster for the self-proclaimed "Pelican State." After environmental regulations finally banned DDT in 1972, trapped birds from less-affected areas in Florida had to be reintroduced to rebuild the state's population.[24]

As a result of these efforts to expand production bases and to take advantage of workers now protected from a more dangerous disease environment, shipbuilders augmented existing yards in the Mobile area (Alabama Drydock and Gulf Shipbuilding), New Orleans (Delta Shipbuilding), and Houston (Houston Shipbuilding) with three practically new facilities: Tampa Shipbuilding, Ingalls Shipbuilding in Pascagoula, Mississippi, and Pennsylvania Shipyards in Beaumont, Texas.[25] These three were soon followed by an additional yard building small warships

[22] Albert Cowdrey, *This Land, This South: An Environmental History* (Lexington: University Press of Kentucky, 1983), 170; Centers for Disease Control and Prevention, "Our History – Our Story," www.cdc.gov/about/history/ourstory.htm (accessed June 9, 2016).

[23] David Vail, *Chemical Lands: Pesticides, Aerial Spraying, and Health in North America's Grasslands since 1945* (Tuscaloosa: University of Alabama Press, 2018).

[24] For a full accounting of the army's efforts in the United States, see *Preventative Medicine in World War II*, vol. IV, *Communicable Diseases: Malaria*, ed. John Coates and Ebbe Hoff (Washington, DC: Department of the Army, Office of the Surgeon General, 1963), ch. 3. For a history of DDT use during and after the war, see David Kinkela, *DDT and the American Century: Global Health, Environmental Politics, and the Pesticide That Changed the World* (Chapel Hill: University of North Carolina Press, 2011).

[25] Lane, *Ships for Victory*, 34–35.

FIGURE 8.1 Line-up of women welders, including the women's welding
champion of Ingalls Shipbuilding Corp., Pascagoula, MS, 1943.
Source: Women's Bureau, Department of Labor, National Archives and Records
Administration. National Archives Identifier: 522890. Image in the public domain

operated by Consolidated Steel in Orange, Texas.[26] While most warship
construction remained concentrated on the East and West coasts, Gulf
yards specialized in the vital merchant shipping that enabled the Allies to
win the Battle of the Atlantic and landing craft that supported military
operations in Europe and across the monumental expanses of the Pacific
(see Figure 8.1).

Critical to this effort was the famous Liberty ship, the backbone of
merchant fleets in both World War II theaters. Born of a design that would
permit quick, modular construction with a welded – as opposed to
riveted – frame, the Liberty ship design valued ease of construction over
durability, as evidenced by several of the vessels breaking apart at sea. But

---

[26] For an excellent summary of individual perspectives on the shipyard and how it wrought
larger changes in the town, see Louis Fairchild's, *They Called It the War Effort: Oral
Histories from World War II Orange Texas* (Austin: Texas State Historical Commission,
2012).

TABLE 8.1 *Liberty ships built on the Gulf Coast*

Shipyard	Merchant ships built
Alabama Drydock & Shipbuilding Co. Mobile, AL	20
Delta Shipbuilding Co. New Orleans, LA	188 (32 Tankers) (24 Colliers)
J. A. Jones Construction Company Panama City, FL	102 (8 Tank Transports) (28 Boxed Aircraft Carriers)
Todd-Houston Shipbuilding Corporation Houston Shipbuilding Corporation Bend Island, Houston, TX	208

Source: American Merchant Marine at War, "Liberty Ships Built during World War II Listed by Shipyard," www.usmm.org/libyards.html (accessed June 8, 2016).

the ease of construction permitted dizzying numbers to be built at incredible speed; in a publicity stunt, a West Coast shipyard assembled one of the more than 2,700 ships in just over 100 hours. Gulf Coast shipyards played a significant role in Liberty ship construction, as well as the associated Victory ships and fuel tankers, constructing 518 of the 2,710 total, or 19 percent, primarily at Mobile, New Orleans, and Houston, but more than 100 at a new yard operated by Jones Construction in Panama City, Florida (see Table 8.1). All four cities had direct rail connections with the steel mills in Birmingham, which produced enough plate to supply additional yards along the southeastern Atlantic coast as well.

Another clear example of the direct linkage between the Gulf Coast's environment and the prosecution of the war can be found in the development of the Landing Vehicle, Tracked (LVT), also known as the *Alligator*, which became a mainstay of amphibious operations across the Pacific. Following the record-breaking Labor Day hurricane of 1935, which devastated the Florida Keys, killing hundreds at Civilian Conservation Corps camps located there, the storm tracked up the western coast of Florida before making landfall in the extreme northeast Gulf, near Cedar Key. As a result, most of south Florida's Gulf Coast remained in the storm's right-front quadrant, where the highest winds and storm surge inundated coastal communities around Tampa. The resulting landscape, neither land nor water, frustrated rescuers who found it too wet for vehicles but too dry for boats. An enterprising inventor, Donald Roebling, developed a hulled vehicle with bulldozer-style tracks whose treads doubled as paddles when submerged, enabling the vehicle to float across water and climb through swampy ground. After seeing the vehicle in a feature in *Life* magazine, Marine Corps planners ordered a prototype for testing and eventually

FIGURE 8.2 A side view of the Roebling Alligator tractor as it moves through a swampy area. The tractor is a Donald Roebling creation and is the vanguard for the present Marine LVTP-7 tracked landing vehicle.
Source: American Forces Information Service, US Department of Defense, National Archives and Records Administration. National Archives Identifier: 6348245. Image in the public domain

placed an order filled initially by a factory in Dunedin, Florida, and later supplemented by additional facilities in Lakeland, Florida and in California. LVTs, carrying 20 combat-loaded soldiers or more than two tons of cargo, became essential in the Pacific, as the craft could successfully traverse the shallow coral reefs that fringed many islands before swimming across the lagoons that lay between the reefs and the shore. The military eventually fielded more than 18,000 LVTs in several variants, and an amphibious tractor, or "amtrac," the direct descendant of the LVT, remains a vital part of the Marine inventory today (see Figure 8.2).

While legacy yards in the Northeast and along the West Coast have declined, the Gulf States now boast 12 of the nation's 20 active large shipbuilders and 5 of the 10 parent companies, including World War II–era legacy facilities in Tampa, Mobile, and Pascagoula and new yards along the Louisiana and Texas Coasts.[27] While some of this added capacity can be attributed to the explosive growth of the oil and gas industry after World War II, much of the construction takes place at facilities opened during the war and has benefitted from skilled labor trained during the war, as well as the return of servicemen experienced with industrial activities in maritime environments as a result of the navy and Merchant Marine service during the war.[28]

---

[27] Shipbuilding History, "US Builders of Large Ships," www.shipbuildinghistory.com/shipyards/large.htm (accessed July 29, 2019).
[28] Jason P. Theriot, *American Energy, Imperiled Coast: Oil and Gas Development in Louisiana's Wetlands* (Baton Rouge: Louisiana State University Press, 2014), 41, 51.

No discussion of shipbuilding along the Gulf Coast would be complete without mention of the famed Higgins boats, built by Andrew Higgins at his New Orleans shipyard, which Dwight Eisenhower famously called "the ship that won World War II" because it enabled amphibious assaults across the globe. In the 1930s, Higgins began designing cheap, shallow-draft supply boats for the expanding oil and gas industry, which was then pushing further into Louisiana's coastal wetlands. Higgins's boats, with the addition of a bow ramp for rapid discharge of assaulting soldiers, became the "Landing Craft, Vehicle and Personnel," or LCVP, which could be driven directly onto a beach, facilitating amphibious assaults in Europe and across the Pacific. Higgins eventually built more than 12,000 LCVPs, more than half of the total wartime production, as well as other amphibious craft at his yards in New Orleans and Houma, Louisiana, using wood primarily from southern forests.[29]

But the boat's connection to the rapidly expanding oil and gas industry is perhaps more prophetic for the Louisiana and Texas Gulf coasts. Military hardware, including technologies developed during the war such as the helicopter, which can be used to ferry critical parts and personnel to oil rigs located in remote coastal locations, supported the massive postwar expansion of the nation's oil and gas industry. The "Muskrat Line," the first of many significant natural gas pipelines built after the war that channeled the methane formerly burned off as "flare" at drilling sites into a cheap energy source for customers far inland, benefitted from wartime expertise gained in laying pipelines for aviation and other fuels for the military across the various theaters in the decade prior. As historian Jason Theriot notes, a region that handles fully one-quarter of the nation's oil and natural gas supply also boasts 40 percent of the nation's wetlands and 80 percent of its wetlands' loss. While some of this loss can be attributed to natural subsidence and the flood control levees along the Mississippi River that now funnel its formerly sustaining sediments into the deep waters of the Gulf, the many oil and gas access and pipeline canals cut into Louisiana's coastal marshes have upset a delicate ecosystem, allowing salt water to intrude into brackish and fresh marshes, killing essential vegetation and increasing coastal erosion, enhancing the region's susceptibility to devastating storms, such as Hurricane Katrina.

---

[29] For a full treatment, see Jerry Strahan, *Andrew Jackson Higgins and the Boats that Won World War II* (Baton Rouge: Louisiana State University Press, 1994). Eisenhower's endorsements can be found on page 3.

Inshore, the development of the oil and gas industry and its related products had a profound impact on the Gulf South's built and natural environment. As an example, the loss of Southeast Asian rubber plantations to Japanese military expansion in 1941 and 1942, which restricted Allied access to 90 percent of the world's natural rubber supply, forced war industry planners to search for a substitute.[30] Rubber was essential for the production of truck and aircraft tires and tank treads, the sinews of a modern war effort, as well as thousands of other items, from wiring insulation to radiator hoses. Chemists from both academia and industry united to produce a suitable synthetic rubber substitute, known as Buna-S, using petroleum, which was also in heavy demand to fuel these same machines of war. Domestic manufacturers began production at a number of plants across the country but quickly concentrated the industry along the Gulf Coast, near the site of most of the nation's petroleum production and refining capacity. During the war, six new plants in an arc along the northwestern Gulf Coast produced more than 40 percent of the nation's synthetic rubber (see Table 8.2). By the 1970s, Texas alone manufactured 80 percent of the nation's synthetic rubber, which had largely supplanted natural rubber in domestic consumption.[31] Synthetic rubber production proved a godsend to the US war effort, which had stockpiled less than a year's supply of natural rubber at the beginning of the war, but it had significant long term effects.[32] While synthetic rubber spared fragile tropical ecosystems from intensive agricultural development for the production of natural rubber, it also shifted the environmental burden, in the forms of toxic byproducts, into communities along the American Gulf Coast.

While historians have debated whether wartime industrialization really transformed the southern economy, even skeptics acknowledge that the war ignited the rapid expansion of the petrochemical industry along the Gulf Coast.[33] For example, Baton Rouge, home to one of the most important refineries during the war (and still one of the largest in the world),

---

[30] See Paul Wendt, "The Control of Rubber in World War II," *The Southern Economic Journal*, 13, no. 3 (January 1947): 203–227, and Mark Finlay, *Growing American Rubber: Strategic Plants and the Politics of National Security* (New Brunswick, NJ: Rutgers University Press, 2009).

[31] Will H. Shearon Jr., "Synthetic Rubber Manufacture," *Texas State Historical Association: Handbook of Texas Online*, www.tshaonline.org/handbook/online/articles/dmsgx (accessed June 16, 2017).

[32] For a full accounting, see Vernon Herbert and Attilio Bisio, *Synthetic Rubber: A Project That Had to Succeed* (Westport, CT: Greenwood Press, 1985).

[33] See Robert Lewis, "World War II Manufacturing and the Postwar Southern Economy," *The Journal of Southern History* 73, no. 4 (November 2007): 840.

TABLE 8.2 *Synthetic rubber production, 1940–1945*

Plant	Owner	Production, long tons
Lake Charles, Louisiana	Firestone	118,098
Port Neches, Texas	Firestone	114,769
Port Neches, Texas	BF Goodrich	119,342
Houston, Texas	Goodyear	111,147
Baton Rouge, Louisiana	Copolymer Corp.	90,680
Baytown, Texas	General Tire	78,151
	Total, Gulf Coast	**632,187**
Akron, Ohio	Firestone	95,505
Louisville, Kentucky	BF Goodrich	149,962
Borger, Texas	BF Goodrich	94,892
Akron, Ohio	Goodyear	84,763
Los Angeles, California	Goodyear	66,082
Naugatuck, Connecticut	Uniroyal	70,015
Institute, West Virginia	Uniroyal	247,631
Los Angeles, California	Uniroyal	56,507
Louisville, Kentucky	National Synthetic	72,734
	Total, Rest of US	**938,091**
	Grand Total	**1,570,278**

Note: Thanks to Mr. Dave Gustafson of Bridgestone Americas, Nashville, TN, for his assistance with this research.
Source: Adapted from "Report on the Rubber Program, 1940–1945, Supplement No. 1, 1945," (Washington, DC: Rubber Reserve Company, 1946), 51–56, https://babel.hathitrust.org/cgi/pt?id=mdp.39015051785528;view=1up;seq=3 (accessed June 16, 2017).

which produced 100-octane aviation gas that gave Allied aircraft an edge in combat, as well as an aluminum-producing plant-processing bauxite shipped down the Mississippi from Arkansas, doubled in size during the war years. While the city retained traditional economic bases as the center of state government and home to the state's flagship higher education institution, petrochemicals substantially expanded the local economy, drawing in a new population from the surrounding rural parishes.

Baton Rouge spread from a fairly compact city clustered on the river's high levees into the surrounding coastal plain, which, in most places, sits only a few feet above sea level and is drained by smaller rivers and streams in broad valleys with slight gradients that are highly susceptible to flooding. Many of the new suburbs spilled into neighboring Livingston, Ascension, and West Baton Rouge parishes, largely duplicating "white flight" patterns in other southern cities. Unfortunately, this expansion into marginal areas with poor drainage eventually yielded catastrophic consequences, confirming the old adage that "nature bats last." In August

2016, much of the city suffered a deluge of between 20 and 30 inches of rain from a posttropical storm. The water, at least, was color blind, inundating both predominantly white suburbs as well as older black communities relegated to lower lying areas. As was the case in New Orleans during Hurricane Katrina, only the "old" city, high on the river's natural levees, escaped the worst of the destruction.

Baton Rouge's wartime growth, and also the wartime demand for refined petroleum and other chemicals spawned a corridor of industrial development from Baton Rouge to New Orleans known as "Cancer Alley." The latter name carries the greatest significance, as toxic chemicals released into the air and water have created some of the highest cancer rates in the nation, which disproportionally affect the region's largely black inhabitants. Baton Rouge hosts several National Priority List (Superfund) sites, including the notorious Devil's Swamp Lake and the Petro-Processors of Louisiana sites, both near predominantly African American Scotlandville. Cancer rates from Baton Rouge to New Orleans, along the "Cancer Alley" that hosts more than 150 processing plants, are consistently among the highest in the nation and disproportionally affect the region's poorest inhabitants, who are unable to simply move away, in what scholars have described as "environmental racism."[34]

POSTWAR LEGACIES

The military's increased presence along the Gulf, established during the World War II years, continued well into the Cold War era, with significant impacts for much of the region's flora and fauna. Historians of American military activity across the globe have found that

U.S. military bases generated massive amounts of hazardous wastes as part of their normal operations. The routine maintenance of the vast numbers of ships, aircraft, combat and support vehicles, and weaponry produced such pollutants as used oil and solvents, polychlorinated biphenyls (PCBs), battery and other acids, paint sludge and heavy metals, asbestos, cyanide, and plating residues. Sometimes the size of small cities, US bases also produced large amounts of ordinary garbage, medical wastes, photographic chemicals and sewage. Often these wastes, toxic and nontoxic alike, were disposed of casually.[35]

---

[34] Matt Black and Trymaine Lee, "Cancer Alley: Big Industry, Big Problems," *MSNBC*, August 10, 2015, www.msnbc.com/interactives/geography-of-poverty/se.html (accessed November 1, 2016); James C. Cobb, *The South and America since World War II* (Oxford: University Press, 2012), 217.
[35] McNeil and Painter, "The Global Environmental Footprint of the US Military," 21.

This was especially true at sites along the Gulf. During the Vietnam War, the navy base at Gulfport, near Biloxi, Mississippi became the primary shipping point for toxic defoliants, including Agent Orange. The powerful herbicide frequently leaked from storage containers, usually 55-gallon metal drums, and seeped into the soil and the sensitive coastal ecosystem surrounding the base. The Department of Defense contracted out much of the disposal to private companies, who had less financial incentive to carry the munitions to designated areas far from the coast and often reduced costs by dumping them closer to shore, representing an increased and continuing threat to both the environment and local residents.[36]

In 1945, in another example of less-pernicious effects, the navy moved its Mine Warfare Center from Maryland to a base in Panama City, Florida, which had been established in 1942 to support amphibious training. As development increased along the Atlantic and Pacific coasts, and the navy saw increased opposition to the use of remote training ranges, most notably at the island of Vieques, off the coast of Puerto Rico, the Gulf of Mexico, and its military-friendly population became a more attractive locale. In 2004, the navy announced that it intended to increase activities in the vicinity of the naval base at Panama City, prompting a statement of concern from the Animal Welfare Institute. The organization worried that increased activities, especially the use of sonar offshore, would harm marine mammals, including five endangered species of whales and dolphins. Beach activities had the potential to impact nesting success for threatened sea turtles and many threatened and endangered species of migratory birds transited the Gulf each year. Without an increased presence in the region, initiated during the emergency years of World War II, the Gulf might not have become a space contested between the navy and environmentalists.[37]

Some of these flora and fauna have even been recruited into the military directly. In the 1960s, the navy implemented its Marine Mammal Program, which used dolphins and sea lions to detect mines and other objects in murky waters and mark them for removal or disposal. Though declassified after the end of the Cold War and now headquartered in San Diego, some of the research, including trapping of native bottlenose

---

[36] Edwin Martini, *Proving Grounds: Militarized Landscapes, Weapons Testing, and the Environmental Impact of US Bases* (Seattle: University of Washington Press, 2015).

[37] The Animal Welfare Institute, "Increase in US Navy Activities in the FL Panhandle Likely," https://awionline.org/content/increase-us-navy-activites-fl-panhandle-likely (accessed June 8, 2016).

dolphins (*Tursiops truncatus*) apparently took place at various sites in the northern Gulf. After training, the navy deployed dolphins to both Vietnam and the Persian Gulf and retains a force of approximately 75 marine mammals today.

The war years also spurred globalization and increasingly connected the sleepy, Gulf Coast fishing and shrimping ports to a larger global economy, often with beneficial effects but also contributing to the introduction of highly destructive invasive species. Beginning in 1945, surplus equipment shipped back to the continental United States from the Pacific theater began arriving in Gulf ports, including Houston, New Orleans, Lake Charles, and Galveston, through the Panama Canal. Much of the equipment arrived packed in wooden shipping crates, produced in the theater from locally sourced timber, while warships held stocks of shoring timbers, used to support buckled bulkheads during damage control, which were often procured locally across the Pacific as well. Deep within many of the already sodden and rotting timbers burrowed the Formosan termite (*coptotermes formosanus*).

Originating in the damp jungles of southern China, the termite adapted readily to the humid, subtropical Gulf Coast. Formosan termites gather in much larger colonies than indigenous species and range over a much larger area, making infestations difficult to control and eradication thus far impossible. In New Orleans, the Formosan termite has taken a toll on both historic structures and the city's stately old-growth live oak trees (*quercus virginiana*), costing the city more than $300 million per year in control costs and damages. One author has even speculated that Formosan termite infestations may have contributed to floodwall failure during Hurricane Katrina, as builders often used oiled bagasse (sugar cane residue) as a cushion between floodwall sections, which the termites then consumed, opening gaps and compromising the structural integrity.[38] From its coastal beachhead, the termite has invaded the entire Southeast and now ranges as far north as Tennessee, wreaking havoc on built and natural environments as it spreads and prompting the liberal application of pesticides in vain attempts to control it. Similarly, entomologists trace the arrival of the now-ubiquitous southern fire ant (*Solenopsis invicta)* to prewar and wartime-era shipments from South America through the port of Mobile. The fire ant also adapted readily to the southern environment, proving lethal to cattle and, in rare cases, allergic humans, while

---

[38] Gregg Henderson, "The Termite Menace in New Orleans: Did They Cause the Floodwalls to Tumble?" *American Entomologist* 54, no. 3 (Fall 2008): 156–162.

generating massive applications of pesticides that were often more dangerous than the ants, all in a futile attempt at control.[39]

Much of the surplus military equipment either transported home from the war fronts or produced and then never used during the Cold War that followed eventually overwhelmed military storage facilities, leading to a search for a cost-effective disposal program. The depths of the Gulf of Mexico, a reservoir for effluents from the center of the North American continent as well as the coastal bays and rivers that drain the Southeast, became an attractive option for cost-conscious defense officials beginning as early as 1946.[40] A recent study estimated that millions of pounds of unexploded bombs litter the Gulf's floors, where they pose a threat to fishermen, oil and gas interests, and even beachgoers, as one case in Tampa demonstrated in 2012 when a World War II–era bomb had to be detonated on a local beach. While unexploded ordnance poses a brief, if immediate threat, containers of chemical agents, including mustard and phosgene gas, have been dumped as well, resulting in a more insidious threat as storage containers rust and break down.[41]

Just as the triple wrecks of the *Robert E. Lee*, *U-166*, and the *Deepwater Horizon* symbolize the deep connection between the war and the Gulf's environment, so too do a cluster World War II–era platforms now serving as artificial reefs off the Gulf Coast. Not far off the Texas coast, a total of 12 Liberty ships and 2 tankers, many fabricated in Gulf Coast shipyards, sit as quiet memorials under roughly 100 feet of water. Once cleaned and scrubbed of most toxic materials, the ships became readily available structure for corals and reef-dwelling fish and other aquatic organisms. Since the mid-1970s, these World War II veterans have served to offset some of the significant environmental damage their construction helped create by providing new habitat for Gulf species as well as recreation opportunities for anglers and divers alike. Off the Alabama coast, additional Liberty ships and more than 50 army main battle tanks serve a similar purpose, while in Florida the *USS Oriskany*, an Essex-class aircraft carrier commissioned in October 1945, serves a comparable

---

[39] See Joshua Blu Buhs, *The Fire Ant Wars: Nature, Science and Policy in Twentieth-Century America* (Chicago: University of Chicago Press, 2004).

[40] For a full discussion, see Joel Tarr, *The Search for the Ultimate Sink* (Akron, OH: University of Akron Press, 1996).

[41] For a recent dissertation (and hopefully forthcoming book) covering the global aspects of weapons dumping, see Alex Souchen, "The Peace Dividend: Munitions Disposal and Canada's Second World War, 1943–48" (PhD diss., University of Western Ontario, 2016).

purpose. On May 17, 2006, preset explosives ripped more than 20 holes in *Oriskany*'s sanitized hull, sending it to the bottom 200 feet below the Gulf's surface in less than an hour. In the decade that followed, the ship's passageways and hanger deck have been colonized by coral and reef fish, and the site, known locally as the "Great Carrier Reef," is now one of the top diving sites in the world.

CONCLUSION

While the Liberty shipwrecks and the *Oriskany* demonstrate some positive changes resulting from World War II–era activity along the Gulf Coast, most of the changes have placed additional stress on a sensitive littoral environment. While the conflict brought some combat directly to the Gulf's shores, the most significant long-term effects came from the industrialization and urbanization spurred by the war's industries and support infrastructure. In Louisiana alone, the war years saw an increase of 39 percent in urban populations while rural populations declined by 4 percent.[42] At the same time, oil and gas development, also spurred by wartime activities and defense needs, grew exponentially, sometimes running afoul of other uses of the Gulf, as when the Deepwater Horizon disaster devastated tourism and fisheries alike following the 2011 disaster. While the region seems to be recovering from that disaster, many of the long-term consequences are still being discovered.

World War II played a central role in the transformation of the Gulf Coast from a sleepy backwater to an economic powerhouse, fueling growth, development, and ecological degradation. Altering natural environments to make them more amenable to human habitation took a number of forms, but the most significant involved elimination of disease-carrying vectors that made the Gulf a healthier place to live, and the development of industry and both military and civilian infrastructure that made it possible for new residents to earn a living along and behind the Gulf's sandy shores. Successful prosecution of a global conflict transformed regions with previously untapped natural resources, both on land and at sea, and especially along the interstices of both.

Historically, the Gulf Coast has survived all manner of threats, gracefully absorbing all that man can throw at, and into, it, and occasionally pushing back as it spawns a Category 5 hurricane and hurls it against the

[42] Jerry Purvis Sanson, *Louisiana during World War II: Politics and Society, 1939–1945* (Baton Rouge: Louisiana State University Press, 1999), 239, 285.

receding coastline. But a warming climate suggests storms of greater intensity and heavier rainfall will increase along the Gulf Coast – in 2016, 2017, and 2018, tropical systems devastated Baton Rouge, Houston, and Panama City, respectively. Rather than attempt to fortify against the threat, mankind and the Gulf would both likely benefit from an environmental "Marshall Plan" that rehabilitates the Gulf and rebuilds connections between humans longing for "natural" spaces and one of the few remaining, still untamed coastal environments. Such efforts, already underway all along the Gulf by scientists, policy makers, and industry, hold out hope for the better future that animated many Americans to make such extraordinary efforts during the war years.

9

World War II and the Urban Environment

Redirecting American Politics in Los Angeles and Beyond

Sarah S. Elkind

Like many American cities, Los Angeles was built upon real estate speculation, mind-boggling boosterism, and war. World War II diversified and expanded the city's industrial sector; Cold War defense contracts sustained Southern California's automobile, tire, chemical, and aerospace industries for much of the twentieth century. Oil under residential subdivisions and commercial centers fueled the Pacific fleet. Los Angeles' industries and business organizations consciously used their contributions to military preparedness to cement their political influence, and to protect themselves from regulation and labor activism. These political phenomena are, perhaps, the most significant aspect of the urban environmental history of World War II in the United States because American cities experienced the environmental impact of World War II primarily through industrial production and its legacies, and because regulating industry is such a critical component of American politics.

Of course, World War II had profound physical impacts on American cities. For example, the population of San Francisco's industrial suburbs grew by 50 percent; water use, and therefore sewage, more than doubled.[1]

---

[1] Parts of "World War II in the Urban Environment" were previously published in "Extracting Property Values and Oil: Los Angeles's Petroleum Booms and the Definition of Urban Space," *Jahrbuch für Wirtschaftsgeschichte/Economic History Yearbook* 57, no. 1 (2016), and "The Nature and Business of War: Drilling for Oil in Wartime Los Angeles," in *Cities in Nature: Urban Environments of the American West, Essays in Honor of Hal K. Rothman*, ed. Char Miller (Reno: University of Nevada Press, 2010), 205–24.

"Sewer Disposal Problem," *Oakland Tribune*, February 12, 1945, in "Sewage N-Z" loose-leaf binder, East Bay Municipal Utility District Records Office. For more on wartime

Sewers spewed raw sewage onto tidal flats and inlets leaving "quite uniform evidence of sewage pollution" including "floating or stranded fecal and other sewage particles" all along the shore, forming "a black organic putresible mud that covers much of the area" and could be smelled as much as two miles inland.[2] The decomposition of organic wastes from sewage and from the region's many fruit and vegetable canneries depleted the dissolved oxygen in shoreline waters – one study found large areas with no dissolved oxygen at all. Fish and marine species suffocated, and anaerobic decay released foul-smelling gases, including enough hydrogen sulfide to cause "an inestimable amount of damage to the paint of buildings and marine structures" along the waterfront.[3]

Los Angeles experienced something very similar. As early as 1939, engineers reported serious sewage disposal problems and ocean contamination at the city's sewage treatment plant. The Department of Health closed 10 miles of public beaches to keep people out of the contaminated water. These quarantines stayed into effect until 1947, because the waters of Santa Monica Bay – where the sewage entered the ocean – had "become a common cesspool," and "sands intended for quiet sunbathing [were] smeared with the scum of human filth."[4] The overburdened sewage system allowed "offensive" industrial wastes to flow into the Los Angeles River, and unidentified gases to explode in the city's sewer lines.[5] In both San Francisco and Los Angeles people complained

---

growth in the San Francisco Bay Area, see Marilynn S. Johnson, *The Second Gold Rush: Oakland and the East Bay in World War II* (Berkeley: University of California Press, 1993).

[2] "Sewage A-M," 2, loose-leaf binder, East Bay Municipal Utility District Records Office, Oakland; Charles Gilman Hyde, Farnsworth Gray, and A. M. Rawn, "Report upon the Collection, Treatment and Disposal of Sewage and Industrial Wastes of the East Bay Cities, California," (n.p., 1941), 57, Crown Law Library, Stanford University, Palo Alto; Committee of East Bay Engineers, "Preliminary Report upon Sewage Disposal for the East Bay Cities of Alameda, Albany, Berkeley, El Cerrito, Emeryville, Oakland, Piedmont, San Leandro, Richmond to the East Bay Executive Association," (Oakland: 1938), 7, Bancroft Library, Berkeley; R. C. Kennedy, "Report on Sewage Collection and Disposal for Special District 1," 5, East Bay Municipal Utility District Records Office.

[3] Committee of East Bay Engineers, "Preliminary Report," 8–9.

[4] "Shoreline Development Study for Los Angeles," *The American City* 59 (August 1944): 11; "Court Order to Open Beach Swimming Area," *Los Angeles Times*, February 2, 1946, Fletcher Bowron Collection, Huntington Library, San Marino, California. Hereafter cited as Bowron Collection.

[5] Report to the Los Angeles County Board of Supervisors by the Los Angeles County Smoke and Fumes Commission, March 13, 1944, attachment to A. H. Campion to Board of Supervisors, May 11, 1944, 4. John Anson Ford Collection, Huntington Library. Hereafter cited as J. A. Ford Collection.

vociferously about these problems; their elected officials threw up their hands, lamenting that wartime shortages of labor and material kept them from building new public works. In other words, local officials blamed the federal government for the environmental hardships of the war years; this, too, contributed to the postwar political realignment that is central to the environmental history of World War II in urban America.

Before World War II, many Americans viewed corporations with suspicion. Big business, in particular, was regarded as an unwelcome centralizing and modernizing force in a nation that liked to imagine itself as a decentralized, entrepreneurial, and agricultural society. After the war, and because of the war, this perception changed. The population whose livelihood depended on industry grew. Military production enjoyed a special status during World War II, which protected industries in Los Angeles and elsewhere from public scrutiny and local control even after peace returned. The business community collaborated with government in managing the war economy, and in the process bridged the divide between business and government at the federal level.[6] Wartime austerity and, before that, 10 years of economic depression fueled Americans' embrace of consumer goods and the industries that produced them. Finally, and most significantly, the war gave American industry the opportunity to portray itself as the defender of American democracy. Together, these phenomena helped the business community and opponents of New Deal interventionist politics redefine government power as a threat to American freedom and democracy, and the private sector, including large corporations, as the critical counterweight to government authority. World War II set the stage for the most important political realignment of the twentieth century, a realignment that is particularly visible in Los Angeles' oil and air pollution politics, but that touched every industrial city in mid-century America.

OIL AND PATRIOTISM OVERWHELM REGULATIONS

A surprising amount of Southern California's oil lies scattered under residential lands, public parks, and beaches in Los Angeles. Midway through World War II, federal officials estimated that the nation needed to double or triple petroleum production to meet military, industrial, and consumer needs. And that was in spite of gasoline rationing imposed

---

[6] Alan Brinkley, *The End of Reform: New Deal Liberalism in Recession and War* (New York: Vintage, 1995).

largely to conserve rubber. Oil companies in Southern California responded by doubling applications to drill new oil wells in the Los Angeles region, and by bringing wells into production that yielded poor quality grade crudes that were environmentally costly to refine and burn.[7]

But oil exploitation in Los Angeles had a very destructive history. During the periodic oil booms between the 1880s and 1920s, oil companies had bulldozed entire city blocks, and fires regularly ripped through oil fields, feeding on tightly packed wooden derricks, open oil tanks, and spilled crude.[8] In 1944, an activist recalled this dangerous and devastating past to convince Los Angeles officials to block oil exploration in residential areas: "I ... saw beautiful sections of this city ruined and I hope that such will never come again. Human greed and avarice, unless restrained, would destroy our beautiful beaches, our residential areas, without any compunction."[9] In the 1920s, the devastation – and damage to real estate values – wrought by the oil industry inspired Angelenos to outlaw oil drilling on land zoned for residential or commercial development and on their beaches. They did not countenance oil companies' efforts to reverse these drilling rules in the 1940s, even in the face of the war emergency.

The oil industry was able to overcome a surprising amount of this opposition, largely by linking urban oil exploration to patriotism and the war effort. By the end of the war, new wells sprouted in Los Angeles' central business district, in one of the city's major public parks, and on the grounds of Beverly Hills High School. Oil company personnel used strong-arm tactics, political name-calling, and overly rosy projections of royalty income to collect signatures in favor of new oil drilling in these

---

[7] "California Gets on with Its Drilling," *Petroleum World* 40 (1943): 17. For an example of costly extraction of low-grade, heavy crude, see "California Drilling in Big Gain over '42," *Petroleum World* 40 (1943): 22.

[8] For a description of the impact of oil booms on Huntington Beach, see Jim Combs, "Another Oil Boom Brings Chaos to Huntington Beach," *Fortnight* 18, no. 6 (March 16, 1953): 11–13. As one holdout resident described the scene: "These oil men have taken everything except the food in the icebox.... My back yard is an oil well, a sump hole. My fence is gone and the inside of my house is a mess." But *Fortnight* reported that most Huntington Beach residents were so money-struck that they welcomed even the chaos and filth.

[9] Marshall Stimson to Ed Ainsworth (Times editor), February 9, 1944, Box 1, Marshall Stimson Collection, Huntington Library. Hereafter cited as Stimson Collection. For news coverage of these regulations, see, "Drilling Ordinance Looms: Huntington Beach to Call Special Election Soon to Ascertain Public Sentiment on Question," *Los Angeles Times*, August 6, 1930; "Santa Monica to Reconsider" *Petroleum World* 29 (November 1932): 37.

neighborhoods.[10] The appeals to patriotism were explicit: "If there was any possible shortage of oil for war purposes, I am sure no patriotic citizen would have an instant's objection to such drilling in any portion of the City of Los Angeles."[11] Using the war emergency thus allowed the industrial and business communities to bypass public opinion, and to assert that they knew better the needs of the public than did the public.

Angelenos who supported wartime drilling in their city did so despite considerable experience of the destructive power of oil development. In the first eight years of Los Angeles' oil industry, companies large and small drilled more than a thousand wells in the Los Angeles City Field near downtown.[12] Each subsequent oil discovery yielded a similar stampede, bringing both incredible wealth and a myriad of problems to the city. Natural gas explosions, runaway wells, noise, odor, and sprayed or spilled oil befouled the community. Fires raged out of control among tightly packed, wooden derricks, open oil tanks and spilled crude. To curb the worst excesses of oil development, the Los Angeles City Council prohibited oil drilling near city parks and used zoning to restrict drilling near residential and commercial areas.[13] These repeated experiences with oil drilling in residential and recreational areas solidified Los Angeles

[10] "Other City Drilling Programs Proposed," *Petroleum World* 40 (August 1943): 64. On Seaboard Oil's proposal to drill under Elysian Park, see "Council Okehs Oil Drilling for Duration" *Daily News* October 10, 1943; "Drilling Row End in Sight," *Los Angeles Times*, October 27, 1943; "Drilling Row End in Sight," *Los Angeles Times*, October 27, 1943; "Elysian Drilling Injunction Asked" *Los Angeles Times*, December 18, 1943, all in box 74, Newspaper clippings files, Bowron Collection; Stimson to Ickes, June 19, 1943, Box 1, Stimson Collection.

[11] A. Wardman to Bowron, July 23, 1943 (cc to Stimson), Box 1, Stimson Collection. Proponents of regulation tried on occasion to turn anticommunist rhetoric on its head, but it rarely worked. For example, when a shortage of chlorine extended the quarantine on Los Angeles beaches, one newspapers blamed Cold War anticommunism for distracting city officials from the public's real business: "While the city fathers perfume the city hall with their operations against 'communism,' their inaction on matters of first-rate civic concern to millions of Angelenos has brought about the pollution of the city's beaches." See "Beach Cities Flay LA over Surf Closing," *Los Angeles Herald*, September 3, 1947, J. A. Ford Collection.

[12] William R. Freudenberg and Robert Gramling, *Oil in Troubled Waters: Perceptions, Politics and the Battle over Offshore Drilling* (Albany: State University of New York Press, 1994), 15, 72–73; Daniel Yergin, *The Prize: The Epic Quest for Oil, Money and Power* (New York: Simon & Schuster, 1991), 25, 28–29.

[13] "That Oil Ordinance," *Los Angeles Times*, January 25, 1897. Additional city ordinances, lawsuits or other legal means to curb oil nuisances were recorded in 1901, 1926, 1929. See "Measures to Stop the Oil Nuisance," *Los Angeles Times*, May 3, 1901; "War to Bar Oil Leaks in Sea Starts," *Los Angeles Times*, November 9, 1926; "Oil Pollution Evil Banished," *Los Angeles Times*, March 21, 1929.

residents' and civic leaders' commitment to restricting oil exploration within city limits. Meanwhile, Los Angeles' extensive oil production and refining and its important port facilities made this region extremely important for the American military effort. Over the course of the war, federal officials challenged and eventually overruled local regulations in hopes of increasing oil production for aircraft, tanks, trucks, and ships. Oil companies expanded oil drilling and production across Los Angeles; federal pressure to increase oil production in the city altered the physical environment and transformed the political environment as well.

In the early 1930s, Angelenos disagreed about whether the right to drill for oil on private property trumped the rights of abutters to protect their property from the nuisances and dangers of oil drilling, about how to resolve the competing mineral rights of all property owners in an oil field, and about the relationship between individual property rights and the communal benefit from zoning and industrial regulation. Opponents of the drilling in residential neighborhoods and near public parks also emphasized the importance of real estate values to individual and community prosperity. As the 1930s wore on, however, attention shifted from questions of property and community to the behavior and intentions of the oil companies. The chaotic development of oil deposits in the Venice-Del Mar oil field cemented Angelenos' commitment to regulating drilling in residential areas. In 1929 and 1930, property owners in Venice Beach demanded unrestricted drilling in the Venice-Del Mar oil field, in violation of zoning ordinances that specifically excluded oil production in residential areas. The Los Angeles City Council buckled before the pressure; derricks, tanks, and pump houses quickly displaced homes. Residents who stayed in their homes faced life in a noxious industrial zone. Property values fell. The oil field "played out" after two or three years, in part because rapid production and excessive drilling quickly lowered the gas pressures necessary to push oil out of the ground. The "fiasco at Venice," prompted the Los Angeles City Council President to propose an outright ban on oil drilling in residential Los Angeles in 1931. For the next decade, opponents of oil drilling routinely cited the destruction in Venice to justify stronger enforcement of zoning ordinances and other restrictions on oil drilling throughout Los Angeles.[14]

---

[14] "Venice Rushes to Drill," *Los Angeles Times*, March 31, 1930; "Oil Drilling Move Killed," *Los Angeles Times*, January 29, 1932; "Oil Drilling Scotched," *Los Angeles Times*, January 30, 1932; "Randall Would Restrict Areas for Oil Drilling," *Los Angeles Times*, January 30, 1932; "Oil Drilling Ban Favored," *Los Angeles Times*, February 4,

Public consensus against drilling in residential areas did not survive World War II. The military's trucks, tanks, ships, and planes required unprecedented amounts of oil, and Southern California oil fields were the primary source of fuel for the navy's Pacific Fleet. The oil industry responded briskly to wartime calls for more oil. In just two months in 1942, California producers opened 100 new wells and increased the state's oil flow by 6 percent. One company invested so much money in drilling and exploration that it could not pay its employees.[15] Firms in Los Angeles renewed proposals for wells in protected residential sections of the city. Even though their support for the war would precipitate a reassessment of urban drilling, Angelenos remained skeptical of the oil companies' motives, and quite concerned about their city and their property values.[16] Throughout the war years, Angelenos struggled to decide if drilling was truly necessary for the war effort or if oil companies were taking advantage of the emergency to gain access to oil that local regulations had placed off limits.

The first of the wartime urban drilling proposals came before the Los Angeles City Council a month after Pearl Harbor. In January 1942, J. E. Elliot and Shell Oil proposed a deep well in Gilmore Island, between the La Brea Tar Pits and West Hollywood. Even though Gilmore Island was unincorporated county land, the city of Los Angeles claimed jurisdiction because Shell's project would affect neighborhoods inside the city. Residents of these neighborhoods opposed Shell's proposal, deriding it as "a wildcat oil scheme," and speaking

1932. For invocations of the destruction of Venice, see "Hearing Slated on Oil Drilling," *Los Angeles Times*, January 18, 1932; "That Oil-Drilling Scheme," *Los Angeles Times*, January 19, 1932; and Sarah S. Elkind, "The Nature and Business of War: Drilling for Oil in Wartime Los Angeles," in *Cities and Nature in the American West*, ed. Char Miller (Reno: University of Nevada Press, 2010), 205–214.

[15] "California Petroleum Situation – December 1942," February 8, 1943, in "Statistics: California Situation," Petroleum Administration for the War Records, Box 138, National Archives, Laguna Niguel, California. In December 1942, California's 18,500 wells produced 774,000 barrels of oil per day; "Minutes of the Annual Meeting of Shareholders of Burnoel Petroleum Corporation," July 31, 1942, in Burnoel Petroleum Company Papers, Huntington Library.

[16] For a discussion of oil company practices that excited public opposition, including oil drilling along California's shoreline, see Sarah S. Elkind, *How Local Politics Shaped Federal Policy: Business, Power and the Environment in Twentieth Century Los Angeles* (Chapel Hill: University of North Carolina Press, 2011), 17–51; and Sarah S. Elkind, "Public Oil, Private Oil: The Tidelands Oil Controversy, World War II, and Control of the Environment," in *The Way We Really Were: The Golden State and the Second Great War*, ed. Roger Lotchin (Urbana: University of Illinois Press, 2000), 120–142.

against it at public hearings.[17] Under pressure from the city council, Shell developed a plan to reduce noise, odors, and danger at the site. Los Angeles officials faced enormous pressure to approve the Gilmore Island project. Shell justified the project as necessary for the war. Secretary of the Navy Frank Knox and the federal Office of Production Management urged Los Angeles city officials to approve new oil wells throughout Los Angeles. Los Angeles mayor Fletcher Bowron initially sided with residents; he vetoed drilling permits, arguing that drilling at Gilmore Island threatened the rights of the city and the interests of nearby property owners.[18]

Bowron was outraged that oil companies wanted to use the war emergency to circumvent hard-won regulations, and he was incensed that federal officials sided with the oil companies. He and his allies feared that wartime drilling could to turn the whole city into an oil field, and that the resulting damage to "the city as a whole would far outweigh any possible gain that might arise from drilling in certain limited areas."[19] They saw no reason for further exploration in Los Angeles until the navy had exhausted alternative, established sources of supply. In 1942, Bowron did not have the votes on the city council to block war emergency drilling permits. Heeding war emergency rhetoric, the Los Angeles City Council approved a drilling permit for a residential neighborhood near Los Angeles harbor and overrode Bowron's Gilmore Island veto.[20]

Although Shell found no oil at Gilmore Island, the 1942 drilling permits unleashed a small flood of applications for new exploratory wells, mostly in residential areas where the council had previously – sometimes repeatedly – refused to let oil companies drill. Seaboard Oil Company's

[17] "Proposed Gilmore Strip Oil Drilling Debated," *Los Angeles Times*, June 18, 1942; "Mayor Vetoes Oil Ordinance," *Los Angeles Times*, September 22, 1942.

[18] Howard Kegley, "California Oil News," *Los Angeles Times*, February 21, 1942; "Gilmore Island Oil Drilling Opponents Ask for More Time," *Los Angeles Times*, June 4, 1942; "Proposed Gilmore Strip Oil Drilling Debated," *Los Angeles Times*, June 18, 1942; "Gilmore Island Oil Drilling Plea Supported by Knox," *Los Angeles Times*, May 27, 1942; "O. P. M. Urges Permit to Drill for Oil on Gilmore Island," *Los Angeles Times*, May 28, 1942; "Mayor Vetoes Oil Ordinance," *Los Angeles Times*, September 22, 1942.

[19] Marshall Stimson, "Statement," February 9, 1944, Box 1 "Oil Drilling in the City of Los Angeles" in Stimson Collection; "Oil Drilling Vote Deferred," *Los Angeles Times*, June 27, 1942; "Council Defeats Move to Repeal Drilling Action," *Los Angeles Times*, July 21, 1943.

[20] "Lone Bid Submitted in Park Oil Project," *Los Angeles Times*, March 26, 1943; "Attack on Oil Drilling Move Proves Futile," *Los Angeles Times*, April 17, 1943; "Gilmore Island Oil Drilling Program Speeded," *Los Angeles Times*, October 30, 1942.

proposal for a well below Elysian Park was typical.[21] In 1931, the city council had rejected a different oil company's permit to drill a test well extending under Elysian Park, from a residential area few blocks southeast of what is now the I-5 – Route 2 interchange.[22] Like Shell, Seaboard promised to enclose its derricks and machinery to protect nearby homes from noise and damage. Seaboard justified drilling under Elysian Park to help win the war, thus giving the project the same patriotic sheen that Shell had employed in its Gilmore Island bid.[23] With these assurances, and hoping to profit from oil royalties, two thousand homeowners signed leases with Seaboard. Seaboard then brought the plan before the Los Angeles City Park Commission, which approved the Elysian Park well in late February 1943.[24] However, drilling proposals sparked significant opposition in 1943. In February, opponents of Seaboard Oil held a mass meeting to protest. The outcome of city elections in March reflected the mounting opposition, too. Council candidates reported that constituents held "indignation mass meetings" if candidates seemed to endorse oil drilling in neighborhoods, while oil companies "vowed vengeance" if council members opposed oil wells. Candidates won who promised to ban new oil drilling in residential areas.[25] Mayor Bowron took this opportunity to propose new regulations that would have allowed the city to close new wells in residential areas within six months of the end of the war. These regulations also would have given the Los Angeles Zoning

---

[21] Howard Kegley, "California Oil News," *Los Angeles Times*, November 5, 1942. In the aftermath of the approval of Gilmore Island, oil companies came forward with proposals to drill in the Salt Lake Field, the Sherman field, Fox Hills Country Club, the Westwood Hills Golf Course, on La Cienega at Third Street, near the Chatsworth Reservoir on Woodlake Avenue, west of Los Angeles airport, and at Soto and Valley Blvd. near the site of the Ascot Speedway. See "Oil Drilling Interest Soars," *Los Angeles Times*, December 15, 1942; "Oil Drilling Vote Deferred," *Los Angeles Times*, June 27, 1942.

[22] Ramsey Petroleum sought to drill here in 1931. Seaboard began working on its proposed well in 1937. See Howard Kegley, "Oil News," *Los Angeles Times*, September 4, 1937.

[23] "Ruling on Elysian Park Oil Drilling Deferred," *Los Angeles Times*, August 11, 1943; "Oil Decision Put Off Again," *Los Angeles Times*, August 18, 1943; "Planning Board Backs Elysian Park Oil Test," *Los Angeles Times*, August 25, 1943; "Standard of California's War Program," *Petroleum World* 40 (August 1943): 22; "Oil Shortage Facing State, Says Attorney," *Los Angeles Times*, September 2, 1943.

[24] "Ruling on Elysian Park Oil Drilling Deferred," *Los Angeles Times*, August 11, 1943; "Elysian Park Oil Drilling Offers to Be Sought Today," *Los Angeles Times*, February 25, 1943.

[25] "Bowron and Hampton to Address Meeting," *Los Angeles Times*, March 2, 1943; "Oil Becomes Factor in City Elections," *Los Angeles Times*, March 29, 1943; "Council Asked to Ban Beach Oil Drilling," *Los Angeles Times*, February 26, 1943; "Attack on Oil Drilling Move Proves Futile," *Los Angeles Times*, April 17, 1943.

Administrator power to prohibit any oil operations that "cause[d] grave harm to" or "diminish[ed] seriously the value or detract[ed] from the use" of adjacent property.[26] The City Planning Commission urged Bowron to ban urban drilling outright, but acknowledged that military needs made such a ban unlikely.

The oil industry enjoyed enough support in Washington to override both local regulation and public opposition. Secretary of the Navy Frank Knox, called for more oil "to win the battle of the Pacific," and thus gave the petroleum industry a critical military justification for expanded oil production in Los Angeles. Harold Ickes and the Petroleum Administration for the War (PAW) also rejected Los Angeles' proposed regulations.[27] Ickes had staffed the PAW with oil company executives and put the organization in the hands of a former vice president of Standard Oil of California. Industry influence was compounded by the PAW's dependence upon another group of oil executives, the Petroleum Industry War Council, for policy recommendations.[28] This type of industry-government collaboration was standard practice during World War II and was seen as essential to secure industry cooperation with the federal government's unprecedented intervention in the economy. This integration of oil executives into the federal policy-making apparatus gave them enormous influence over the urban environment during and after the war.

Back in Los Angeles, Mayor Bowron and his allies found the oil industry's influence, as well as military and strategic justifications for oil production, equally impervious. The director of the Los Angeles office

[26] "Oil Drilling Law Backed," *Los Angeles Times*, June 12, 1943; "Council Defers Action on Wilmington Drilling," *Los Angeles Times*, May 6, 1943.

[27] Carrington King, "PAW Gives California the Green Light," *Petroleum World* 40 (April 1943): 18. For the Secretary of the Navy's position, see Martin Van Couvering, "Searching for Oil in the City When Los Angeles Was Young – and Now!" *Petroleum World* 40 (March 1943): 56.

[28] Robert Engler, *The Politics of Oil: A Study of Private Power and Democratic Directions* (New York: McMillan, 1961), 278–279. See also Harold Ickes, *Fightin' Oil* (New York: Alfred A. Knopf, 1943). On industry influence on the federal government during World War II more generally, see Alan Brinkley, *The End of Reform: New Deal Liberalism in Recession and War* (New York: Alfred A. Knopf, 1995); Louis Galambos, *The Public Image of Big Business in America, 1880–1940* (Baltimore: Johns Hopkins University Press, 1975); Clayton Koppes, "Environmental Policy and American Liberalism: The Department of the Interior, 1933–1953," *Environmental Review* 7, no. 1 (1983): 17–41; Gerald D. Nash, *United States Oil Policy, 1890–1964: Business and Government in Twentieth Century America* (Pittsburgh: University of Pittsburgh Press, 1968), and Oliver Zunz, *Making America Corporate, 1870–1920* (Chicago: University of Chicago Press, 1990).

of PAW called for rapid development of "every field and pool in the state, including those within the city of Los Angeles."[29] Nine months later, PAW reduced production from some California oil fields while continuing to push drilling in Los Angeles.[30] Under pressure from Ickes and PAW, Bowron reluctantly supported Seabord's Elysian Park project and other wells without time restrictions. Public opinion, however, remained unchanged. At one public hearing in August 1943, more than four hundred property owners demanded that city officials limit oil operations to the duration.[31] Bowron had repeatedly made this same argument, calling upon oil companies to match the sacrifices that wartime drilling imposed on residential property owners. Oil companies always countered that they could not afford to drill new wells unless they could operate them for seven or more years. For its part, Seaboard Oil protested restrictions designed to make oil drilling untenable. In October, the city council finally approved Seaboard's test well for Elysian Park; Seaboard promised to drill a well so "unobjectionable" that opposition to urban drilling would soon "dissipate."[32]

Throughout 1943, opponents of drilling disputed the navy's need for oil from residential Los Angeles. They complained that oil production threatened property values and questioned the oil industry's motives. If Los Angeles had to permit drilling during the war, they insisted, all oil production in residential neighborhoods must end when the war ended. They called the oil industry "a selfish type of enterprise," accused major oil firms of trying to set up monopolies or corrupt local government and called upon city officials to protect their real estate investments. They warned "that there is a group hiding behind the American flag, working for a selfish interest."[33] Bowron and other opponents of wartime drilling

---

[29] Ickes to Bowron, January 19, 1943, 3, in Box 56, Bowron Collection; "'Every Field and Pool Must Be Drilled,' – PAW," *Petroleum World* 40, no. 8 (August 1943): 21.

[30] "Oilmen Denounce Ickes Output Cut in Gas Crisis," *Los Angeles Times*, November 17, 1943, in Newspaper clippings files, Bowron Collection.

[31] "Oil Drilling Deadlock in City May Be Broken," *Los Angeles Times*, August 6, 1943; "Ruling on Elysian Park Oil Drilling Deferred," *Los Angeles Times*, August 11, 1943.

[32] "Oil Muddle in the City of Los Angeles," *Petroleum World* 40 (August 1943): 21. "A Noiseless Well in the Heart of the City," *Petroleum World* 40 (March 1943): 30–40 and ff.; "Exploration for Oil Planned without Disturbing Sites," *Los Angeles Times*, February 14, 1943; "Final Oil Hearing Set," *Los Angeles Times*, September 25, 1943; "Elysian Park Drilling Voted," *Los Angeles Times*, November 9, 1943.

[33] Bruce Murchison, "Mr. Springer – Speaking for a Group of Neighbors in Elysian Heights," and J. O. Smith, as quoted in "Notes Taken at Public Hearing on the Oil Drilling Ordinance, Thursday Afternoon, July 1, 1943," 3–4.

saw the PAW's and the navy's pressure to drill in Los Angeles as evidence that the oil industry had captured federal oil policy and had turned the war into an excuse to circumvent local regulations.[34]

In the wake of the Seaboard decision, the city council approved still more exploratory wells in residential neighborhoods. Bowron continued opposing urban drilling, and remained convinced that oil companies were "not actuated by purely patriotic motives but by expectation of profit" because they refused to close emergency wells at the end of the war.[35] Strong opposition to oil wells continued in most affected neighborhoods, but commitment to the war effort tempered that opposition. Some who opposed drilling in residential areas in principal could accept oil wells if oil companies also sacrificed. These comments by homeowners were typical: "If the government really needs the oil, I will let them drill in my front yard and turn the proceeds over to the Red Cross, if they will agree to stop when the war is over" and "The Government took my son and can take my oil – but why should I ruin my home to make an oil company richer?"[36] These Angelenos could not countenance "wrapping the flag" around urban drilling for profit, or using the war emergency to weaken city planning.

Although opposition to urban drilling remained strong in those neighborhoods overlaying oil deposits, elsewhere in the city Angelenos saw drilling as a necessary sacrifice to win the war. Appeals to patriotism, wartime emergency, and sacrifice cast local resource policy issues in terms that undermined local industrial regulations and allowed oil companies to drill in areas where oil production was prohibited. But the oil debates in Los Angeles also reveal that World War II altered urban environmental politics in the twentieth century. Wartime institutions, such as the PAW and the Petroleum Industry War Council, gave American businesses a powerful voice in national policy. The presence of oil company executives in these agencies rather abruptly reoriented federal policy from countering

---

[34] Stimson to Ickes, June 19, 1943, Box 1 "Oil Drilling in the City of Los Angeles" in Stimson Collection.

[35] Bowron to the city council, January 31, 1944, 3, box 56, Bowron Collection. See also, "Mayor Signs Oil Measure," *Los Angeles Times*, November 28, 1943.

[36] As quoted in "Larger Reserve of Oil Urged at Council Hearing," June 24, 1943; D. G. Springer (Save Your Homes Association) to Stimson, March 8, 1943, Box 1, Stimson Collection. For more letters on urban drilling, see R. G. Winter, "Why the Delay"; Mrs. A. L. Gribling, "Wells Favored"; Kenneth J. McIntosh, "Why Limit It"; Olga Dickenson, "Produce It Quickly"; and P. J. Yorba, "Permission Favored," all in *Los Angeles Times*, February 14, 1944.

the power of business to collaboration between business and government. In Los Angeles, this policy realignment extended far beyond oil, as city and county officials instituted air pollution control policies that depended upon the cooperation of industrial polluters.

WARTIME INDUSTRY, SMOG, AND BUSINESS INFLUENCE
IN LOCAL POLITICS

In the summer of 1943, as the Los Angeles City Council debated Seaboard Oil's drilling permit, an acrid cloud of "lacrimous fumes" settled over downtown Los Angeles. City officials received letter after letter complaining that the smoke destroyed the community, "depressed ... [the] spirits," and threatened the public health.[37] These complaints focused on a chemical plant owned by Southern California Gas but expanded by the federal Rubber Reserve Corporation to produce butadiene for wartime synthetic rubber production. When Mayor Bowron complained to the Rubber Reserve Corporation that fumes from this plant threatened the "health and welfare of people in this area," he placed local conditions before national needs much as he had during the oil drilling debates.[38] The federal response, that closing the plant was "contrary to the best interests of the war effort," likewise echoed the PAW's insistence upon drilling in residential Los Angeles.[39] Los Angeles' efforts to control air pollution reflect the urban environmental history of World War II in this conflict between federal and local concerns and its contribution to public frustration with federal power, in the importance of war industry in building

[37] H. O. Swartout to Board of Supervisors, September 21, 1943, Box 25, J. A. Ford Collection; Elbert D. Owen to Los Angeles City Council, August 17, 1943, and Emily K. Krug to Mayor Bowron, September 1944, both attached to Fletcher Bowron to J. W. Livingston, August 11, 1943, Los Angeles City Archives, Box A 832, Communication 15399; Jerrie M. Rossen to Los Angeles City Council, September 17, 1944, Los Angeles City Archives, Box A 851, Communication 18283; Bowron to William L. Stewart, October 16, 1943, Bowron Collection; Frederic A. Kane to Los Angeles City Council, September 8, 1944, Los Angeles City Archives, Box A 851, Communication 18283.

[38] Bowron to J. W. Livingston, August 11, 1943, Bowron Collection. The County Grand Jury adopted Bowron's resolution calling for closing of the butadiene plant in September 1943. See "Adopted by the Grand Jury of the County of Los Angeles, this 20th day of September, 1943," Box 1, Bowron Collection.

[39] Bradley Dewey to Los Angeles City Council, October 22, 1943, City Archives, Box A 835, Communication #16028; "U. S. Rebukes City's Suit on Gas Fumes," Los Angeles Daily News, October 26, 1943; "Council Halts Suit to Close Butadiene Plant," Los Angeles Times, October 28, 1943; "Butadiene Gas Suit Dropped," Los Angeles Examiner, October 28, 1943, all in Bowron Collection.

industrial infrastructure, and in the political influence that pollution control gave to the business community.

Los Angeles' decades-long battle to control smog began during World War II but did not succeed until car emissions were controlled by the Clean Air Act of 1970.[40] Before 1950, when car exhaust was proved to be a major cause of smog, uncertainty about the causes and consequences of air pollution divided Los Angeles. Smog pitted residents of heavily polluted but nonindustrial neighborhoods against heavy industry, dividing the business community and confounding public officials. Into this complicated political setting stepped the Los Angeles Area Chamber of Commerce (LAACC). Every step that local officials took to clean the air seemed only to increase both Angelenos' expectations and their anger when smog persisted. The LAACC feared that public anger about smog would prompt demands to halt industrial growth, and thus cripple the city's industrial future. So, the LAACC led air pollution control efforts by participating in public hearings, sending representatives to smog control committees, drafting legislation, sponsoring research, and pressuring their own membership to reduce their factory emissions. The LAACC's influence over air pollution policy in Los Angeles demonstrates the way wartime environmental problems enhanced business influence over American politics at the local as well as the federal level.

The first investigation of Los Angeles' air quality explained that "an air pocket" or temperature inversion trapped "industrial waste, smoke, gases and fumes" including formaldehyde, ammonia, sulfuric acid, and other chemicals, from "foundries, oil refineries, chemical manufacturing plants, fish canneries, smelters, electroplating plants, fertilizer plants, packing plants, soap factories and waste disposal plants" in downtown Los Angeles.[41] Nevertheless, Mayor Bowron and most Angelenos blamed

---

[40] Comprehensive works on air pollution include David Stradling's *Smokestacks and Progressives: Environmentalists, Engineers and Air Quality in America, 1881–1951* (Baltimore: Johns Hopkins University Press, 1999), Scott Hamilton Dewey, *Don't Breath the Air: Air Pollution and U. S. Environmental Politics, 1945–1971* (College Station: Texas A&M University Press, 2000), and Peter Thorsheim, *Inventing Pollution: Coal, Smoke, and Culture in Britain since 1800* (Athens: Ohio University Press, 2006). On Los Angeles' story in particular, see James E. Krier and Edmund Ursin, *Pollution and Policy: A Case Essay on California and Federal Experience with Motor Vehicle Air Pollution, 1940–1975* (Berkeley: University of California Press, 1977).

[41] Charles L. Senn, to George M. Uhl, July 30, 1943, Box 25:3 (1944), J. A. Ford Collection. For newspaper coverage of the original report, see "Cause of Gases Sought by City," *Los Angeles Times*, September 22, 1942.

Southern California Gas's downtown butadiene plant for the fumes that filled the streets in 1943. The Rubber Reserve Corporation defended butadiene as vital to the war effort, and chided Bowron for complaining about a mere inconvenience during the war emergency. Angelenos fired off an "avalanche of public protest" that prompted Los Angeles County Supervisors to convene both a grand jury and a Smoke and Fume Commission to investigate air pollution. The grand jury found that butadiene plant fumes interfered with other essential war work and threatened public health in Los Angeles, Pasadena, Altadena, and other communities.[42] The City of Los Angeles sought an injunction to halt operations at the butadiene plant. The Rubber Reserve Corporation closed the plant to install equipment to reduce fumes.

The butadiene plant reopened in December 1943, but haze and eye irritation – now labeled "smog" – returned in the summer of 1944 and spread from downtown to the suburban communities of the San Gabriel Valley.[43] This persuaded nearly everyone that the problem was larger than the butadiene plant. Speculation about causes dominated smog debates for the rest of the year. City and federal health officials blamed the climate and cars, respectively. The county health department attributed the problem to the combined emissions industry, locomotives, automobiles, and home incinerators.[44] Los Angeles Mayor Fletcher Bowron repeatedly threatened to prosecute industrial polluters. *The Citizen News* suggested it was "time to adopt a policy against any more factories for Los Angeles."[45] Even the *Los Angeles Times* criticized industry: "the

[42] "Relief from Gas Fumes Promised in December," *Los Angeles Times*, September 15, 1943; "Gas Fumes to Be Curbed," *Los Angeles Times*, September 23, 1943, and Bowron to Dr. J. W. Livingston (Rubber Reserve Co., Washington, DC), August 11, 1943, both in Box 1, Bowron Collection. In October 1943, all the Los Angeles newspapers carried full-page advertisements emphasizing importance of butadiene plant to war effort: "War Fumes and War Rubber," *Los Angeles Times, Los Angeles Examiner, Los Angeles Herald-Express, Citizen News*, and *Daily News*, October 18, 1943 from Newspaper clippings files, Bowron Collection.

[43] "City 'Smog' Laid to Dozen Causes," *Los Angeles Times*, September 18, 1944; "Blanket over Downtown Area Lifts," *Los Angeles Times*, September 24, 1944; Louis Seymour Jones, "Man-Made 'Smog,'" *Los Angeles Times*, September 25, 1944.

[44] "Three-Point Plan to Combat Fumes Offered," *Los Angeles Times*, October 7, 1944; "County Officials Agree on Joint Fumes Action," *Los Angeles Times*, September 22, 1944; "D. A. Plans Test Suit in City's Smoke Fumes War," *News*, August 31, 1944, Newspaper clippings files, Bowron Collection.

[45] "Policy," *Citizen News*, September 21, 1943; "Lesson," *Citizen News*, October 27, 1943; "D. A. Plans Test Suit in City's Smoke Fumes War," *Los Angeles Daily News*, August 31, 1944, all in Newspaper clippings files, Bowron Collection.

question is the welfare of millions of residents here versus the selfish interests of a few major industrial concerns."[46]

The LAACC reacted to this rising clamor with a three-year campaign for regional smog control during which they modeled ordinances, organized county-wide smog conferences, and provided the city and county with air pollution research.[47] In most American cities, business organizations resisted smoke control regulations; the LAACC's cautious support for regulation stands out. With the blessing and assistance of the LAACC, the newly formed Los Angeles County Air Pollution Control District (APCD) imposed strict smoke rules on gray iron foundries and oil refineries, some of the dirtiest industries in the region, and started working with other businesses to develop emissions control devices.[48] County officials sought to reduce pollution from tugboats, locomotives, and diesel trucks; private dumps that burned garbage; and citrus farmers who burned tires to protect their trees from frost. Together with the LAACC's aggressive voluntary smoke controls, these measures did reduce industrial pollution in 1940s Los Angeles.

Smog returned every summer, and with it public outcry and accusations that business-government cooperation hindered air pollution control. The Altadena Property Owners League, a neighborhood improvement organization based in the unincorporated foothill community of Altadena, was one of several civic organizations that challenged the legitimacy of the LAACC's increasingly central role in air pollution policy. Altadena and its neighbors suffered mightily from smog but had few polluting industrial plants. The Altadena Property Owners League and the LAACC agreed that Los Angeles needed uniform county-wide smog rules but had little else in common. Where the Altadena Property Owners League hoped such

[46] "The History, Legal and Administrative Aspects of Air Pollution Control in the County of Los Angeles," report submitted to the Board of Supervisors of the County of Los Angeles, May 9, 1954, Bowron Collection, Box 59.

[47] Morris Pendleton in Board of Directors, Steno Reports, October 19, 1944, 1–3, Box 28, California Historical Society Collection of Los Angeles Area Chamber of Commerce Records and Photographs, Special Collections, University of Southern California, Los Angeles, California. Hereafter cited as LAACC Records.

[48] Christine M. Rosen discusses the range of business responses to air pollution, from obstruction to engagement, in "Businessmen against Pollution in Late Nineteenth Century Chicago," *Business History Review* 69, no. 3 (1995): 351–397. Swartout to Board of Supervisors, August 1, 1944, "Subject: The Fumes and Smoke Problem – Progress Report," 2, Ford Collection, Box 25; "Report to the Los Angeles Board of Supervisors by the LA County Smoke and Fumes Commission," March 13, 1944, 3, Ford Collection, Box 25. The Air Pollution Control District was made up of the County Board of Supervisors and an appointed director.

regulations would reduce smoke pollution in absolute terms, the LAACC worried inconsistent regulations would turn Angelenos against industry as a whole or would push plants into being lenient instead of forcing firms to reduce emissions.[49]

The LAACC and the Property Owners League also disagreed over what should be regulated. In 1944, the LAACC created its own smoke and fumes committee, headed by Morris B. Pendleton, to study of air pollution from household incinerators, car exhaust, sewage, and boiler smoke, as well as industrial firms. They found that foothill cities, including Altadena, suffered not just from smoke generated by downtown industries but also from local incinerators. Pendleton warned that public anger about smog would become "a source of harassment to Southern California industry of all sorts" unless LAACC members reduced their smoke, pressured their recalcitrant colleagues to do the same, and supported government action to "take care of the recalcitrant members of industry who will not listen to reason."[50] Pendleton's strategy of research, policy recommendations, and voluntary smoke reductions earned the LAACC a special status in public policy debates.

The competition between the Altadena Property Owners League and the LAACC revealed itself explicitly in the fall of 1944, as the Altadena Property Owners League pressed for a county ordinance limiting the density of industrial smoke.[51] At one hearing, the president of the Altadena Property Owners League warned that "[i]f the authorities don't do something about this, the people will."[52] This threat worried the LAACC. The LAACC board of directors dismissed the Altadena group as part of a "hysterical movement" that was "attempting to get up an argument with us."[53] More importantly, Pendleton and the LAACC sought to move smog policy out of the public arena, preferring to work directly with the

---

[49] Morris Pendleton speech before LAACC Board of Directors, Steno Reports, October 12, 1944, 8, LAACC Records.

[50] LAACC Board of Directors Minutes, September 14, 1944, 3–4; Morris Pendleton speech before LAACC Board of Directors, Steno Reports, October 12, 1944, 8, both in LAACC Records.

[51] "Brief of Meeting Held in Pasadena City Hall, October 19, 1945, at 2 p.m. by the Action Committee on Smog," 2–4; H. F. Holley, "Memo for files," October 22, 1945, both in E. E. East Collection, Southern California Automobile Club archives, Los Angeles, California.

[52] "D. A. Plans Test Suit in City's Smoke Fumes War," *News* August 31, 1944, Newspaper clippings files, Bowron Collection.

[53] LAACC steno reports, September 14, 1944, 11; LAACC Steno Reports, September 22, 1944, 12, both in LAACC Records.

elected officials. Fearing that the Altadena Property Owners League would pressure the county supervisors to pass sweeping, damaging regulations, the LAACC pressed for moderate measures to reduce smoke through improved efficiency and voluntary cooperation.

As was the case with oil drilling, the war contributed to Los Angeles' air pollution woes. The LAACC excused some pollution on the grounds that wartime production controls kept industry from acquiring or making the kinds of equipment that they needed to reduce pollution. Factory owners also seized upon the logic of vital military production to protect themselves from smoke regulations. Standard Oil officials at the El Segundo refinery, for example, argued that "government pressure to increase the production of 100 octane gasoline for war purposes was largely to blame for their inability to operate their plant in a way that would avoid all the nuisances that could be avoided under normal conditions." Executives at General Chemical Company in Manhattan Beach "frankly admitted that new processes put into operation to meet wartime needs had resulted in the emission of noxious oxides of sulfur." Swartout also reported that the American Cyanamid Company in Azusa was "busy on orders from the Chemical Warfare Division of the Army ... of such secret and urgent nature that entrance to the main part of the plant was not permitted."[54]

In October 1944, the County Board of Supervisors finally announced a draft ordinance to reduce smoke from stationary smokestacks, including household trash incinerators, dumps, and orchard heaters. The county based its measure in part on a draft provided by the LAACC. The attention to smokestacks prompted the Western Oil and Gas Association to speak out against the measure.[55] Pendleton, in contrast, urged his colleagues to support the county measure even though it did nothing to control vehicle emissions. According to him, the county supervisors, eager to get county smog control efforts started, consciously drafted a limited ordinance, hoping that it would pass quickly. Pendleton promised that both local and federal officials would consult the LAACC about

[54] H. O. Swartout to Board of Supervisors, "Subject: The Smoke and Fumes Nuisances – Second Progress Report," September 27, 1944, 2–3, J. A. Ford Collection.

[55] LAACC Steno, October 12, 1944, 8, LAACC Records; "The History, Legal and Administrative Aspects of Air Pollution Control in the County of Los Angeles," report submitted to the Board of Supervisors of the County of Los Angeles, May 9, 1954, Bowron Collection. See also Dewey, *Don't Breathe the Air*, 43–45. See also Krier and Ursin, *Pollution and Policy*, 46–51.

improving regional smoke control rules.[56] With that reassurance, the
LAACC supported the county ordinance.

In November 1944, the Los Angeles County Board of Supervisors
called for a county-wide air pollution conference. Discussion over who
should organize this event revealed the depth of the LAACC's influence.
The supervisors assumed that their own smoke control committee would
plan the conference. Los Angeles mayor Fletcher Bowron, however,
argued that the LAACC's smoke committee should take the lead. In a
letter to Pendleton, Bowron described the supervisors' air pollution committee as "merely some citizens that have no more authority and far less
representation than your own committee."[57] LAACC involvement also
promised to send a message about the industrial community's "willingness to seek a solution" to air pollution. A little over a year into the air
pollution control debates, the LAACC had secured for itself a dominant
role in local policy making.

The county ordinance drafted in 1944 yielded limited results. It created
a county smoke control agency with the authority to regulate polluters in
unincorporated communities, but no authority over incorporated municipalities. Several of the most heavily industrialized cities refused to either
adopt the county's model ordinance or attend regional smoke control
conferences.[58] The disappointing results of county regulations made the
new county smoke agency look soft on industrial pollution, which
angered Angelenos, like those in the Altadena Property Owners' League.
The head of county smoke control efforts, H. O. Swartout, believed he
could develop air pollution regulations "with benefit to the community
and with profit to many smoke producers." He warned that aggressive
regulations would damage the region's economy. Publicly, he explained
that wartime conditions hindered aggressive smoke abatement.[59]

---

[56] Morris Pendleton speech before LAACC Board of Directors, Steno Reports, October 19,
1944, 2–3, LAACC Records.

[57] Bowron to Morris B. Pendleton, November 2, 1944, Bowron Collection.

[58] "The Shame of Smog," *Los Angeles Times*, September 26, 1946, Newspaper clippings
files, Bowron Collection; "Brief of Meeting Held in Pasadena City Hall, October 19,
1945, at 2 p.m. by the Action Committee on Smog," 2–4, E. E. East Collection, Southern
California Automobile Club archives.

[59] H. O. Swartout to Board of Supervisors, "Recommendation: That Your Honorable
Board Give Consideration to the Advisability of Passing a 'Smoke and Fumes' Ordinance
Embodying Substantially the Following Provisions," June 18, 1945, 3, J. A. Ford Collec-
tion. See also H. O. Swartout to Board of Supervisors, "Subject: The Smoke and Fumes
Nuisances – Second Progress Report," August 1, 1944, 3, J. A. Ford Collection.

Swartout's cautious approach earned him the LAACC's support even as it highlighted the environmental costs of war industries. For its part, the LAACC consistently praised the city and county for their cautious and "reasonable" approach to air pollution regulation during these early years. In the face of near universal public criticism from individuals, the Western Oil and Gas Association and other business groups, the LAACC's consistent support for city and county pollution control efforts reinforced their political influence locally, even as public frustration with ineffective regulation surged.

CONCLUSION

The end of the war in 1945 solved neither air pollution nor oil drilling for Los Angeles. Oil companies continued to seek oil in residential areas after World War II. Although they could no longer cite the war emergency, they did warn that the region's economic future depended upon finding ever more oil resources.[60] Residential drilling continued, particularly in those parts of the city where property values were low or residents lacked political influence. Technological innovations reduced the noise, danger, and mess of oil development, and in the process normalized what had, in the early 1930s, seemed an infringement upon residential property. The main consideration in oil policy was no longer whether oil drilling represented an exercise or an infringement on property rights, but how to ensure enough oil to fuel the postwar and then the Cold War economy. The urgency behind postwar oil debates reflected two stark facts: in 1944, California's oil consumption outpaced local production, and then, in 1952, the United States outgrew domestic oil supplies.[61]

By August 1946, only four cities had adopted the county smoke ordinance: Glendale, South Pasadena, Beverly Hills, and Bell. Meanwhile, Vernon and Torrance, two of the most industrial cities, demonstrated that they had no intention of regulating factory emissions. Lack of local progress drove proponents of smog controls, including the Foothill Cities

---

[60] Continental Oil Co. executive, as quoted in "Oil Well Showdown," *Daily World*, June 21, 1946, Newspaper clippings files, Bowron Collection.

[61] G. Egloff, "Petroleum and National Defense," *Science* 92, no. 2397 (December 6, 1940): 520; "Tideland Oil," *Business Week*, February 12, 1944, 32–33; "Summary of Remarks of Harold L. Ickes before the Petroleum Industry War Council, January 12, 1944 on Some of the Problems of a National Oil Policy," in National Oil Policy Committee File, Records of the Petroleum Administration for the War, Box 70, Division 5, National Archives, Laguna Niguel, California.

Smog Abatement Committee, the League of California Cities, and the Automobile Club of Southern California, to push for state action and the creation of a semiautonomous Air Pollution Control Board in 1947.[62] The LAACC did not always succeed in shaping Los Angeles air pollution policy, but did succeed in defining themselves as indispensable allies of embattled air pollution control officials. The fact that the LAACC made concerted and sincere efforts to reduce air pollution first voluntarily helped, too.

The oil industry secured influence by collaborating with federal, not local, officials. Like the Rubber Reserve Corporation and other polluting industries, oil companies linked otherwise unpopular activities to the war effort, sacrifice, and patriotism. They thus quelled opposition, undermined industrial regulations, and gained access to areas that Los Angeles had placed off limits to oil development. Moreover, wartime policy changes and institutions also allowed American businesses to redefine national policy goals. During and after the war, a new emphasis on economic growth overshadowed prewar policies designed to mitigate corporate influences. Given the explosive growth of industry, industrial jobs and population in Los Angeles during World War II, elected officials' attention to industrial prosperity after the war was understandable. However, the urban history of World War II also reveals the ways declarations of national emergency altered American politics, undermining legal protections that communities established to limit powerful interests, protect minorities and civil rights, and shape their environments.

[62] Beach Vasey to Earl Warren, "Assembly Bill 1," June 10, 1947; Harold Kennedy to Earl Warren, June 9, 1947, 3 in Governors Ch. Bill File, Ch. 632 (AB 1), 1947, California State Archives.

PART V

NEW FRONTIERS

Microbes, Molecules, and Atoms

10

Battling Insects and Infection

American Chemical and Pharmaceutical Expansion during World War II

Martha N. Gardner

World War II marked a dramatic success for military medicine. Among the 16 million American soldiers who served during the war, approximately 405,000 died – a horrifying number, but one that could have been much higher.[1] Injured soldiers' chances of surviving surpassed that of any previous war – and were twice that of World War I.[2] Numerous factors explain this success – from the availability of whole blood to streamlined transportation – but new chemical and biological treatments stand out as life savers. Previously, soldiers had died from wound infections; insect-borne diseases, such as typhus and malaria; and sexually transmitted diseases, such as syphilis and gonorrhea. Now new, effective treatments greatly reduced morbidity and mortality rates.[3] However, this heralded success had environmental and public health implications for military and civilian life, both during the war and in the years that followed.

[1] Nese F. DeBruyne and Anne Leland, American War and Military Operations Casualties: Lists and Statistics. *Congressional Research Service* (January 2, 2015), 2 and Bernard D. Rostker, *Providing for the Casualties of War: The American Experience through World War II* (Santa Monica, CA: Rand Corporation, 2013), 267.

[2] Rostker, 247 and "Quick Care Saves American Troops," *New York Times*, July 2, 1944, 5.

[3] Graham A. Cosmas and Albert E. Cowdrey, *United States Army in World War II: The Medical Department: Medical Service in the European Theater of Operations* (Washington, DC: Center for Military History, US Army, 1992), 234; and Mary Ellen Condon-Rall and Albert E. Cowdrey, *United States Army in World War II. The Medical Department: Medical Service in the War against Japan* (Washington, DC: Center for Military History, US Army, 1998), 205, 349, 387.

World War II, as business historian Alfred Chandler has noted, created "an extraordinary surge of growth" for US industry that gave leading chemical and pharmaceutical companies "a cornucopia of new products."[4] Government organized and funded chemical research and production that drove this surge. Industry was, he asserted, "transformed by wartime programs."[5] No new products did more to transform American medicine than penicillin and DDT. As one public health leader proclaimed in 1946, "DDT stands – with penicillin – as one of the two greatest contributions to public health science which have been made in the last decade."[6]

These wartime advances reshaped American chemical and pharmaceutical industries. While many of the scientific innovations predated the war, companies' massive expansion of industry grew from the war. The federal government poured millions of dollars into the well-established chemical industry and the emerging pharmaceutical industry. "It took a world war of catastrophic dimensions," Senator Claude Pepper observed in 1945, "to jar enough money out of the national pocket to enable medical research men to conduct their work on an adequate scale."[7]

The pharmaceutical and chemical expansion spurred by World War II had wide-ranging environmental costs not at first fully understood. This chapter examines how the development, production, and use of the insecticide DDT, the germicide hexachlorophene, and the antibiotic penicillin affected the environment. In 1962, Rachel Carson characterized the production of synthetic chemicals during and after World War II as a "chemical barrage ... hurled against the fabric of life."[8] However, the urgency of wartime meant that immediate measures to save soldiers prevailed over more carefully weighed solutions that might have considered the long-term effects of this "barrage" more fully.

---

[4] Alfred D. Chandler, "The Competitive Performance of US Industrial Enterprises since the Second World War," *Business History Review* 68, no. 1 (Spring 1994): 5–6.

[5] John Kenly Smith Jr., "World War II and the Transformation of the American Chemical Industry," in *Science, Technology and the Military*, ed. E. Mendelsohn, Merritt Roe Smith, and P. Weingart (Dordrecht: Springer Science and Business Media, 1988), 307.

[6] Charles Winslow, "Taking Stock of DDT," *American Journal of Public Health* 46, no. 6 (June 1946): 658.

[7] Claude Pepper, "Isn't Health Important to the Nation?," *New York Times*, May 20, 1945.

[8] Rachel Carson, *Silent Spring* (Boston: Houghton Mifflin Harcourt, 2002), 297; Sandra Steingraber, *Living Downstream: A Scientist's Personal Investigation of Cancer and the Environment* (New York: Vintage Books, 1998), esp. ch. 5, 87–117; and Edmund Russell, *War and Nature: Fighting Humans and Insects with Chemicals from World War I to Silent Spring* (New York: Cambridge University Press, 2001).

DDT: THE "ATOMIC BOMB OF THE INSECT WORLD"

During World War I, typhus, carried by lice, had killed hundreds of thousands of soldiers in Europe. American military leaders planning for World War II knew this precedent well.[9] DDT remedied this problem. A synthetic pesticide developed in the late 1930s that blocked disease and nuisance caused by insects, DDT killed insect carriers of typhus and malaria,[10] as well as bedbugs and flies. Its containment of a typhus outbreak in Naples during the winter of 1943–44 illustrated its potency.[11] Similarly, DDT played hero in the Pacific theater. In 1945, US Department of Agriculture (USDA) entomologist Frederick C. Bishopp recalled how DDT spraying in the Pacific theater of the war met an "urgent need" to eliminate flies that carried dysentery.[12] By early 1945, US General James Simmons declared DDT "[w]ar's greatest contribution to the future health of the world."[13]

Although DDT was not new, the war prompted its rediscovery and mass production. It was originally synthesized in 1874. In 1939, Paul Müller, a chemist at the Swiss company Geigy A. G., found and tested the compound when looking for a chemical to stop the infestation of the Colorado potato beetle. In 1940, Geigy started to market DDT internationally, and a sample arrived at the laboratory of Edward Knipling, an entomologist at the USDA Bureau of Entomology in Orlando, Florida, who was the primary designer of the military's insect strategy. Knipling and his colleagues quickly found DDT to be very promising – far more effective than pyrethrum, the botanical pesticide that had been used until

---

[9] Edmund Russell, *War and Nature*, 27. There is a rich literature on epidemic disease and mortality rates in previous war. See for example J. R. McNeill, *Mosquito Empires* (New York: Cambridge University Press, 2010).

[10] For malaria, see Frank Snowden, *The Conquest of Malaria: Italy, 1900–1962* (New Haven, CT: Yale University Press, 2006).

[11] Waldemar Kaempffert, "DDT, The Army's Insect Powder, Strikes a Blow against Typhus and for Pest Control," *New York Times*, June 4, 1944; Snowden, *The Conquest of Malaria*, 198–212; and Margaret Humphreys, "Kicking a Dying Dog: DDT and the Demise of Malaria in the American South, 1942–1950," *Isis* 87, no. 1 (March 1996): 12.

[12] Frederick C. Bishopp, "The Medical and Public Health Importance of the Insecticide DDT," *Bulletin of the New York Academy of Medicine* 21, no. 11 (November 1945): 576.

[13] Terence Kehoe and Charles Jacobson, "Environmental Decision Making and DDT Production at Montrose Chemical Corporation of California," *Enterprise and Society* 4, no. 4 (December 2003): 646. See also Judith Bennett, *Natives and Exotics: World War II and Environment in the Southern Pacific* (Honolulu: University of Hawaii Press, 2003), ch. 3.

then.[14] As Director of the Agricultural Research Service of the USDA Sandy Miller Hays later explained, "The modern age of agricultural chemicals had begun ... to the detriment of many years of research on other alternatives."[15]

Previous American approaches to eliminating insect-borne disease had focused on the draining of wetlands and swamps to eliminate insect breeding grounds, which clearly would not help combat the insects already swarming the soldier in wartime.[16] In contrast, DDT killed disease-carrying insects immediately. Insect elimination – "vector control" – rather than methods that prevented their propagation gained dominance during and after the war.[17] DDT also had staying power – "persistence" and "residual effect" – as well as no discernible toxicity for humans. The chemical remained potent for months after its original application; insects still died on contact with walls and floors sprayed with a DDT solution months earlier. This quality saved the military from having to apply the substance repeatedly.[18] It was also this quality that created environmental problems.

The war spurred a remarkable boost in output. The United States produced under 200,000 pounds in 1943, but 13 million pounds in the first half of 1945 alone. The number of companies producing the chemical also expanded, as the military demand outpaced the capability of the Geigy factory in Cincinnati. By 1945, DuPont and Hercules Chemical Company, as well as numerous smaller companies, all produced DDT, though Geigy still dominated, producing 50 percent of the total.[19]

---

[14] David Kinkela, *DDT and the American Century: Global Health, Environmental Politics and the Pesticide That Changed the World* (Chapel Hill: University of North Carolina Press, 2011), 15–18.

[15] Sandy Miller Hays, "20th-Century Insect Control," *Agricultural Research* 40, no. 7 (July 1992): 4.

[16] For the army's medical corps work at the Panama Canal early in the century, see Joseph A. LePrince and A. J. Orenstein, *Mosquito Control in Panama: The Eradication of Malaria and Yellow Fever in Cuba and Panama* (New York: The Knickerbocker Press, 1916).

[17] Leo Slater and Margaret Humphreys, "Parasites and Progress: Ethical Decision-Making and the Santee-Cooper Malaria Study, 1944–1949," *Perspectives in Biology and Medicine* 51, no. 1 (Winter 2008): 107–108; Randall M. Packard, *The Making of a Tropical Disease: A Short History of Malaria* (Baltimore: Johns Hopkins University Press, 2007); Elizabeth W. Etheridge, *Sentinel for Health: A History of the Centers for Disease Control* (Berkeley: University of California Press, 1992), 10–11.

[18] Bishopp, "The Medical and Public Health Importance of the Insecticide DDT," 575.

[19] Russell, *War and Nature*, 147–148.

While the success of DDT on the frontlines of Europe and the Pacific received the most attention, military areas in the United States also turned to DDT during the war for insect control. The creation in 1942 of Malaria Control in War Areas (MCWA), a new branch of the US Public Health Service, illustrates the ongoing concern within the United States.[20] The organization's founding mission was to control malaria in a thousand military areas across the southeastern United States. While ditch digging for drainage was the primary method used in 1942, by 1944 DDT, the wartime "miracle insecticide," had eclipsed other methods. Residual DDT spraying on the walls of dwellings and workplaces every six months became standard.[21]

As wartime demand expanded DDT production exponentially, concerns about environmental damage from factories did not receive much attention. Calls for federal regulations to prevent industries from polluting water had emerged in the 1930s but disappeared in the World War II fervor. Regulations did not emerge again until the 1960s. Instead, water laws were passed at the state level, and were typically not very strong.[22] The American public generally did not discover environmental protection until the 1960s. "Some environmental problems," law professor Jonathan H. Adler explains, "were regarded as the inevitable, if not wholly desirable, consequence of industrial progress and economic growth."[23]

Wartime success prompted continued use afterward, and the MCWA, which was renamed the Center for Disease Control and Prevention (CDC) in 1946, aimed to apply DDT to eradicate malaria from the country once and for all. By this time, the disease was uncommon in the United States, but the fear of a disease reserve existing among mosquitoes and of GIs bringing the disease home fueled concern.[24] CDC workers sprayed more

---

[20] See for example US Public Health Service and Tennessee Valley Authority, *Malaria Control on Impounded Water* (Honolulu: University Press of the Pacific, 2005).

[21] John Parascandola, "From MCWA to CDC – Origins of the Centers for Disease Control and Prevention," *Public Health Reports* 111, no. 6 (November–December 1996): 549–550.

[22] William L. Andreen, "The Evolution of Water Pollution Control in the United States – State, Local, and Federal Efforts, 1789–1972: Part II," *Stanford Environmental Law Journal* 22, no. 215–294 (2003): 215.

[23] Jonathan H. Adler, "When Is Two a Crowd? The Impact of Federal Action on State Environmental Regulation," *Harvard Environmental Law Revue* 31, no. 67 (2007): 73. See also Gerald Markowitz and David Rosner, "Building a Toxic Environment: Historical Controversies over the Past and Future of Public Health," in *History and Health Policy in the United States*, ed. Rosemary Stevens, Charles E. Rosenberg, and Lawton R. Burns (New Brunswick, NJ: Rutgers University Press, 2006), 130–150.

[24] Slater and Humphreys, *Parasites and Progress*, 108.

than 500,000 homes and privies with DDT every three months in late 1945, and 5 million homes between 1947 and 1950, although public health officials found no clear evidence of its necessity or effectiveness. With no reported cases after that time, the CDC discontinued spraying.[25]

Along with the CDC, huge local government, agricultural, and consumer markets formed for DDT as well. Even though an official from USDA cautioned in 1945 that "there is a great deal that is yet to be learned about how to safely use DDT," production of DDT mushroomed from 10 million pounds in 1944 to a peak of more than 182 million pounds in 1962–63.[26] The War Production Board did not impose any limits on the DDT producers' ability to sell, though they warned of the lack of complete knowledge and recommended caution.[27] In agriculture, DDT took over as the "go-to" pesticide, used on everything from Washington apples to New York potatoes to Kansas cattle (to kill off the flies that bothered them).[28] Farmers and ranchers found that its use dramatically improved outputs.

Consumer and local government use expanded rapidly as well, and wartime optimism about DDT helped to speed its acceptance. Journalists predicted as early as 1944 that "gardening will be much simpler" in the United States with DDT.[29] The American public saw DDT as a miracle pesticide. Companies heavily promoted it, using the wartime success to buoy sales. Advertisements for garden and home pesticides appeared across the country. And cities also were quick to turn to DDT to control mosquito and fly season, with at least 600 cities across the country using fog machines to spread DDT. The American public dreamed of a "pest-free world" that seemed within their grasp, as they marveled at DDT's power.[30] According to public health leader Charles Winslow, DDT had achieved the status of "the atomic bomb of the insect world," a glowing phrase used to show how completely it could wipe out annoying and disease-carrying insects.[31]

[25] Humphreys, "Kicking a Dying Dog," 14.
[26] John Perkins, "Reshaping Technology in Wartime: The Effect of Military Goals on Entomological Research and Insect-Control Practices," *Technology and Culture* 19, no. 2 (April 1978): 182. For the Department of Agriculture quotation, see "Public to Receive DDT Insecticide," *New York Times*, July 27, 1945.
[27] Russell, *War and Nature*, 162–164.
[28] Perkins, *Reshaping Technology in Wartime*, 181; "DDT Increased Potato Crop," *New York Times*, December 5, 1945.
[29] Dorothy H. Jenkins, "Around the Garden," *New York Times*, June 11, 1944.
[30] Russell, *War and Nature*, 165–175.
[31] Charles Winslow, "Taking Stock of DDT," 657.

However, even during the war not everyone appreciated this broad-spectrum obliteration of insects. Not all insects were pests, and some naturalists and entomologists worried about the harm to ecosystems. From DDT's initial use, journalists and scientists cautioned that such an "insect war" might "backfire."[32] While positing that judicious use of DDT could be effective, naturalist Edwin Way Teale in 1945 warned "If the insects, the good, bad, and indifferent insects, were wiped out in a wide area, the effects would be felt for generations to come."[33] In agriculture, DDT killed not only the pests that ate crops, but also insects like bees and beetles that helped farmers. DDT's affordability and effectiveness typically outweighed farmers' concerns about these adverse effects, but many did note them.[34]

Naturalists also raised concerns about the effects on wildlife, but findings were inconclusive. While some observed harm to birds and especially fish soon after the war, other studies found DDT to be safe.[35] But few did long-term research. One warning came from the head of the US Fish and Wildlife Service, who in 1945 advised that our "incomplete knowledge of its actions on many living things, both harmful and beneficial," created a need for great caution.[36] But wartime optimism and DDT's ability to wipe out pests eclipsed such concern.

DDT's wartime beginnings also affected how Americans explored its potential risks. As Food and Drug Commissioner Paul Dunbar explained in 1949, soldiers' exposure to DDT was short-lived, and it was a cost-effective way to fight malaria and typhus. In contrast to brief wartime exposure, postwar Americans made the chemical an ongoing part of their lives.[37] The wartime imperative that had facilitated the development and use of DDT also shaped the risks on which scientists concentrated when examining its potential harms. The focus of attention was on toxicity for humans and animals after initial exposure, rather than on more long-term or widespread effects. The swift adoption of DDT in a wide variety of settings made it very difficult to study its effects exhaustively.[38]

---

[32] Jane Safford, "Insect War May Backfire," *The Science News-Letter* 46, no. 6 (August 5, 1944): 90.

[33] Quoted in James Erwin Schmitt, "From the Frontlines to *Silent Spring*: DDT and America's War on Insects, 1941–1962," *Concept* 39 (2016): 19.

[34] David Kinkela, *DDT and the American Century*, 31, 72–73.

[35] Thomas R. Dunlap, "Science as a Guide in Regulating Technology: The Case of DDT in the United States," *Social Studies of Science* 8, no. 3 (1978): 271–272.

[36] Quoted in Cristobal S. Berry-Caban, "DDT and *Silent Spring*: Fifty Years After," *Journal of Military and Veterans' Health* 19, no. 4 (October 2011): 21.

[37] Quotation in Russell, *War and Nature*, 57.

[38] Dunlap, "Science as a Guide in Regulating Technology," 273.

Even so, by the 1960s, Americans generally recognized that DDT and other synthetic chemicals were fundamentally altering the American landscape. Indiscriminate killing of insects meant that pheasants and other wildlife lost a vital source of food.[39] And Americans had come to believe that DDT exposure was damaging to wildlife and humans alike, even when "used as directed." The publication of Rachel Carson's *Silent Spring,* in 1962, caused a dramatic shift in public awareness. A year later, President Kennedy's Scientific Advisory Committee issued a report on American use of pesticides, asserting that *even when proper precautions were taken,* they caused widespread "collateral damage," including the devastation of fish and birds.[40]

Finally, the benefits of DDT and similar pesticides, like toxaphene and dieldrin, ran into problems because of insect resistance. Cases of resistant strains of flies and other insects began to appear as early as 1946, and scientists warned farmers to use the pesticide judiciously.[41] Numerous media reports documented flies and mosquitoes becoming impervious to DDT spray.[42] The language used continued to employ war imagery, with mosquitoes developing armor after a "nine-year war," thus the farmer required new "weapons." Others called again for the older methods of insect control, such as swamp drainage, but were mostly ignored.

DDT's ban from domestic use in 1972 marked a significant change in the public attitude toward the chemical, and toward persistent synthetic chemicals more broadly. However, American companies were not yet banned from producing it for international markets. And recent biological studies have shown that DDT still persists in river fish tissue even though its use was prohibited in the United States more than 40 years ago.[43] Also, consumers, farmers and municipalities continued to turn to synthetic pesticides for relief from insects.

---

[39] Larkin Powell, "Hitler's Effect on Wildlife in Nebraska: World War II and the Farmed Landscape," *Great Plains Quarterly* 35, no. 1 (Winter 2015): 23.

[40] Naomi Oreskes, "Science and Public Policy: What's Proof Got to Do with It?," *Environmental Science & Policy* 7, no. 5 (2004): 373.

[41] Christian W. Simon, "Insecticide Resistance versus Antimicrobial Resistance: Biological Issues in Historical Perspective," *Gesnerus* 60 (2003): 238.

[42] "Flies Resist DDT," *New York Times,* October 31, 1948; "Mosquitos Developing an Armor against DDT after Nine-Year War," *New York Times,* March 14, 1952.

[43] Karen A. Blocksom, David M. Waters, Terri M. Jicha, James M. Lazorchak, and Theodore R. Angradi, "Persistent Organic Pollutants in Fish Tissue in the Mid-Continental Great Rivers of the United States," *Science of the Total Environment* 408, no. 5 (2010): 1180–1189; E. Pulford, B. A. Polidoro, and M. Nation, "Understanding the

HEXACHLOROPHENE, WORLD WAR II, AND THE "GERMICIDAL GOLD RUSH"

DDT was the most iconic chemical emerging from World War II, but there was an onslaught of others as well, including synthetic chemicals designed to control disease bacteria that threatened fighters and civilians alike. Hexachlorophene, a germicide, emerged before World War II and grew exponentially during and after the war, at the beginning of what scientists, environmentalists, and historians have labeled our "chemically altered environment."[44]

As was typical of American chemical companies, hexachlorophene's producer, Givaudan-Delawanna, embraced the trend toward synthetics. Previously, Givaudan had specialized in essential oils, but in the mid-1930s the company decided to expand its offerings. "The future," a Givaudan publication proclaimed in 1935, "belongs to synthetics." In 1938, the company opened a bacteriology lab, hoping to venture into the pharmaceutical market. A year later hexachlorophene was among a series of chemicals synthesized by Givaudan chemist William S. Gump.[45]

Hexachlorophene's producer was typical of industry in its patriotic support of the war effort. With the title "Givaudan Goes to War" blaring across the cover of the March 1943 *Givaudanian*, the company devoted its entire issue to the war. "Research," the publication proclaimed, "is a weapon of war," and Givaudan research laboratories had achieved "results of significant importance to the war effort." By 1943 this manufacturer of more than four hundred chemicals was providing 25 percent of its production directly to the war effort, an additional 50 percent more was indirectly connected, and the company predicted that these percentages would grow higher.[46]

One chemical contribution heralded by the company came in the form of an odorless white powder they labeled "G-11," later naming it hexachlorophene. When added to soaps and other hygiene products, it killed germs. The *Givaudanian* claimed, "Such a germicidal soap should be regarded as an outstanding contribution ... to the protection of the health

Relationships between Water Quality, Recreational Fishing Practices, and Human Health in Phoenix, Arizona," *Journal of Environmental Management* 199 (2017): 242–250.

[44] Benjamin Ross and Steven Amter, *The Polluters: The Making of Our Chemically Altered Environment* (New York: Oxford University Press, 2010).

[45] "Givaudan Has Fully Equipped Bacteriology Labs," *Givaudanian* XVI (February 1939): 7–8.

[46] "Givaudan Goes to War," *Givaudanian* (March 1943), 1–7.

of the soldiers and civilians." G-11 could "diminish the spread of disease" and be "a great boon to the soldier fighting in the foxholes, who must battle against both human and bacterial enemies, whether he be in New Guinea, Tunisia, or at fronts still to be opened."[47]

Whether hexachlorophene ultimately provided this protection to soldiers during the war is unclear: neither the company nor the military mention its use in public documents. However, its sister chemical, "G-4," developed in the same "G" series at Givaudan, was a fungicide that soldiers used to prevent athlete's foot, and military suppliers added it to textiles, including clothing and tents, to prevent mildew.[48] The production push created by war assisted in the synthesis and development of hexachlorophene, spawning a chemical that would have a plethora of postwar medical and consumer uses.

Along with boasting of its wartime potential, Givaudan-Delawanna began to market the chemical in the United States during the war. In 1941, when hexachlorophene was first patented, company representatives began promoting the product in medical schools and hospitals, pursuing the industry's trend toward integrating research, production, and marketing.[49] As its inventor Gump explained in an article devoted to hexachlorophene in the spring of 1945, this chemical was both "bacteriostatic" and "bactericidal" against staphylococcus.[50] This highly prevalent type of bacteria created irritating skin conditions as well as deadly infections, so hexachlorophene's utility seemed clear.[51] Hexachlorophene also had a cumulative effect, decreasing significantly the number of resident and transient flora on the skin. It spread widely and became ubiquitous. As surgeon Philip Price explained in 1952,

---

[47] Ibid., 7.

[48] "A Non-Irritating Compound for Mildewproofing Textiles," *The Givaudanian – Industrial Aromatics Division* (March–April 1943): 1; "Combined Fungicides for Mildewproofing," *The Givaudanian – Industrial Aromatics Division* (September–October 1945): 1–2.

[49] Correspondence between Gump and Carl W. Walter, Carl W. Walter Papers, Countway Library, Harvard Medical School; "Surgeon's Soap: Hands Made Sterile in Three Minutes with New Compound," *New York Times*, November 7, 1948.

[50] William Gump, "The Development of a Germicidal Soap," *The Givaudanian* (March–April 1945): 5.

[51] Hexaclorophene is effective against gram-positive bacteria but not against gram-negative bacteria like Streptoccocus. Walsh McDermott, "The Problem of Staphylococcal Infection," *British Medical Journal* (October 13, 1956): 837–840; Henry R. Shinefield and Naomi L. Ruff, "Staphylococcal Infections: A Historical Perspective," *Infectious Disease Clinics of North America* 23, no. 1 (2009): 1–15.

"Four years ago the product had scarcely been heard of; today only the exceptional hospital is without it."[52]

pHisoHex became the primary hexachlorophene product in hospitals, though many others also populated the advertising pages of hospital industry magazines. Created by the Winthrop Chemical Company in the early 1950s, the "pHisoHex" brand name combined the name of their skin detergent called "pHisoderm" with an abbreviated version of hexachlorophene. Soon known for its distinctive green bottle, the product became a familiar sight in medical settings, used not only to disinfect for surgery but also as a cleanser for hospital personnel and patients.

When hospitals confronted alarming epidemics of deadly, resistant staph infections in the late 1950s, notably in infant nurseries, pHisoHex sales boomed. Individual anecdotes, Winthrop promotional materials, and hospital research all refer to the use of pHisoHex to prevent the spread of infection.[53] Many ads directly referred to nursery infections, claiming that pHisoHex provided a "tenacious film" that provided "a constant barrier against Staph and other bacteria." Another ad trumpeted that hospitals were "IN TOTAL HOSPITAL WAR AGAINST STAPH." The framework of resistant infection as the enemy with hexachlorophene as the savior became the norm.[54]

Givaudan-Delawanna moved to extend the market beyond hospitals as well. Hexachlorophene was often labeled a "wonder drug" in ads; an October 1945 article in *Popular Science Monthly* had predicted this wartime product could "transform our daily lives" at home.[55] Inventor

---

[52] P. B. Price, "Fallacy of a Current Surgical Fad – The Three-Minute Preoperative Scrub with Hexachlorophene Soap," *Annals of Surgery* 134, no. 3 (September 1951): 476. See also H. Cleland, "Hexachlorophene (G11) in the Surgical Scrub: A Brushless Surgical Wash," *Canadian Medical Association Journal* 66, no. 5 (May 1952): 462–464; C. V. Seastone, "Observations on the Use of G-ll in the Surgical Scrub," *Surgery, Gynecology & Obstetrics* 84 (1947): 355–360; A. J. Canzonetti and M. M. Dalley, "Bacteriologic Survey of Scrub Technics with Special Emphasis on Phisoderm with 3 Per Cent Hexachlorophene," *Annals of Surgery* 135, no. 2 (February 1952): 228–233.

[53] C. D. Farquharson, S. F. Penny, H. E. Edwards, and Elizabeth Barr, "Staphylococcal Skin Infections in the Nursery," *Canadian Medical Association Journal* 67, no. 3 (1952): 247; Harold J. Simon, Sumner J. Yaffe, and Louis Gluck, "Effective Control of Staphylococci in a Nursery," *New England Journal of Medicine* 265, no. 24 (1961): 1171–1176; and Louis Gluck and Harrison F. Wood, "Effect of an Antiseptic Skin-Care Regimen in Reducing Staphylococcal Colonization in Newborn Infants," *New England Journal of Medicine* 265, no. 24 (1961): 1177–1181.

[54] See *American Journal of Nursing* 60, no. 11 (November 1960): 1568.

[55] "Soap Washes Hands Clean as a Surgeon's," *Popular Science Monthly*, October 1945, 82–83.

William Gump also touted his chemical, asking, "Why should not every person be using this germ-killing soap every time he washes his hands, for bathing, for shaving, for laundering, and on other occasions? . . . There is every reason why, in the interests of general health, in the reduction of contagion and epidemics, a germicidal, non-toxic, and non-irritating chemical should become an ingredient of a large part of the soap made in this country."[56] Notably, unlike numerous other chemicals used in soaps, hexachlorophene did not irritate skin, a quality important to both the medical and consumer markets.

Hexachlorophene did catch on quickly, for two important reasons. First, as a Dial soap slogan soon claimed, it could "stop odor before it starts" by killing the bacteria that grew on sweat. A new product in 1948, Dial soap had become the leading soap brand in the country by 1953.[57] Deodorants, soaps, lotions, makeup, feminine hygiene sprays, air conditioner filters – more than 400 consumer products in all – eventually included hexachlorophene for this deodorizing effect. Second, hexachlorophene killed bacteria responsible for acne and other skin conditions. Its effectiveness had advertisements in newspapers and magazines touting it, and the green bottles of pHisoHex became a staple in the bathrooms of American teenagers. As early as 1950, the trade journal *Chemical Industries* noted the "Germicidal Gold Rush" sweeping the country, with hexachlorophene sales steadily growing until the early 1970s.[58]

The wholesale use of hexachlorophene, the "total war" according to pHisoHex advertisements, wiped out both civilian and soldier bacteria indiscriminately, just as DDT had wiped out both "good" and "bad" insects. In fact, benign strains of staphylococcus and other bacteria can serve important health purposes, as recent research about the role of the microbiome in maintaining health attests. The seamless elegance of hexachlorophene products wiping out any bad odor, blemish, or germ held great appeal, but dissenting voices at the time suggested other approaches to combating germs might be safer and preserve the "good" germs that improved health and protected people. Work by physician Henry Shinefield and his colleagues to artificially colonize hospital patients with a benign strain of staph to prevent the more deadly strain from infecting

---

[56] Gump, "The Development of a Germicidal Soap," 7.

[57] Fairfax M. Cone, *With All Its Faults: A Candid Account of Forty Years in Advertising* (Boston: Little, Brown & Company, 1969), 204.

[58] "What's New: Germicidal Gold Rush," *Chemical Industries* (April 1950): 504; "Sweet Smell of Success," *Chemical Week* (January 4, 1969): 13, 16.

patients showed impressive results during a wave of deadly antibiotic-resistant hospital infections in the late 1950s and early 1960s.[59] However, such work – wiping a germ out by infecting someone with another germ – did not receive the same kind of positive attention.

However, by the late 1960s, scientists determined that products with hexachlorophene posed a danger to those exposed. Research at the Environmental Protection Agency (prompted by a proposal to have hexachlorophene used as a pesticide) in late 1969 showed that exposure to hexachlorophene severely damaged rat brains. By 1972, an article in the *FDA Papers* laid out how even when used correctly, hexachlorophene could build up in the bloodstream and attack the nervous system, causing brain damage and weakness. Because hexachlorophene was patented in the early 1940s, during wartime fervor, it had escaped more rigorous testing that was required by the 1960s. Most people just assumed that its safety was established.[60] The popularity of the chemical, speculated one physician in 1966, had bred "carelessness."[61]

Moreover, because so many different products had hexachlorophene in them, risk analysis would have needed to assess cumulative exposure to be accurate, not each individual product separately. It was one thing if your soap contained hexachlorophene, but if your soap, lotion, toothpaste, and deodorant all contained it, your level of exposure increased greatly. Food and Drug Administration (FDA) Commissioner Charles Edwards declared that the public had been "needlessly and massively exposed" to a chemical with clear indication of potential damage.[62]

The death of 39 infants in France from hexachlorophene overexposure in 1972 put the nail in the coffin for consumer use of hexachlorophene in consumer goods. Although these deaths occurred when a baby powder manufacturer accidentally added double the normal level of hexachlorophene, the toxicity at this higher level alarmed consumers and regulators alike.[63] In 1972, the FDA banned hexachlorophene from consumer

---

[59] Henry R. Shinefield, John C. Ribble, Marvin Boris, and Heinz F. Eichenwald, "Preliminary Observations on Artificial Colonization of Newborns," *American Journal of Diseases of Children* 105, no. 6 (1963): 646–654; Rene Dubos, "Staphylococci and Infection Immunity," *American Journal of Diseases of Children* 105, no. 6 (1963): 643–645.

[60] Wayne L. Pines, "The Hexachlorophene Story," *FDA Papers* (April 1927): 11–16.

[61] A. B. Coleman, Letter to the Editor, *Pediatrics* 37, no. 6 (June 1966): 1031.

[62] Richard D. Lyons, RD. "F.D.A. Curbs Use of Germicide Tied to Infant Deaths," *New York Times*, September 23, 1972.

[63] Ibid., 65.

products, except when used in extremely low concentrations as a preservative in cosmetics. The problem added to the growing alarm about chemicals. "Once again," *New York Times* health columnist Jane Brody wrote, "a synthetic drug long thought to be beneficial to man is suspect."[64]

Hexachlorophene's production process also posed a serious environmental threat. Hexachlorophene is a chlorinated phenol, and the process of production can create dioxin (TCDD) as a byproduct, as in the production of Agent Orange.[65] Two major chemical accidents at chemical plants synthesizing hexachlorophene in the 1970s made it notorious. In both Seveso, Italy and Times Beach, Missouri, dioxin contamination resulted in large-scale evacuations and environmental damage.[66] There was also evidence of TCDD in the sediments and river water near Givaudan-Delawanna's main plant in New Jersey.[67]

Hexachlorophene's effect on the human skin environment – as well as on land and water – is another area of concern. The residual effect that strengthens its ability to keep nursery infants and surgeons' hands sterile also diminishes the diversity of the skin microbiome, an effect that many now see as harmful. But the marketing of hexachlorophene and its successors reflected and abetted the prevalent American belief in the desirability of wiping out as many germs as possible. Hexachlorophene still serves as a disinfectant in hospitals, although new products have largely replaced it. The problem of synthetic chemicals like it and DDT is that they have created a "chemical body burden," which scholars are continuing to study and assess.[68]

---

[64] Jane E. Brody, "Hexachlorophene: What Price Deodorant?," *New York Times*, December 12, 1971.

[65] For a recent description of Agent Orange in the United States, see Susan L. Smith, *Toxic Exposures: Mustard Gas and the Health Consequences of World War II in the United States* (New Brunswick, NJ: Rutgers University Press, 2017).

[66] Hites, Ronald A. "Dioxins: An Overview and History," *Environmental Science & Technology* 45, no. 1 (September 2010): 16–20.

[67] Robert Hazen, Bruce E. Ruppel, Keith Lockwood, Robert Mueller, Edward Stevenson, and J. J. Post, *A Study of Dioxin (2, 3, 7, 8 Tetrachlorodibenzo-p-dioxin) Contamination in Select Finfish, Crustaceans and Sediments of New Jersey Waterways* (Trenton, NJ: New Jersey Department of Environmental Protection, Office of Science and Research, 1985), 1, 10, 32. See also Renate D. Kimbrough, "The Epidemiology and Toxicology of TCDD," *Bulletin of Environmental Contamination and Toxicology* 33, no. 1 (1984): 636–647.

[68] Joseph W. Thornton, Michael McCally, and Jane Houlihan. "Biomonitoring of Industrial Pollutants: Health and Policy Implications of the Chemical Body Burden," *Public Health Reports* 117, no. 4 (July–August 2002): 315–323.

PENICILLIN: "GOOD MICROBES FIGHT BAD ONES"

Penicillin also brought out the complexities of a "total" war against bugs and germs. As with DDT's development, the wartime threat of disease facilitated the development of penicillin. Here too, World War I was a recent memory for military planners; wound infections had killed thousands of Doughboys on the front lines.[69] Venereal disease had also crippled troop readiness.[70] Additionally, the American pharmaceutical industry had come of age during the interwar years, with a significant "burst of research activity," and new collaboration between industry and university researchers.[71] As historian John Lesch explains, the industry's newfound success had created "an unprecedented flow of new medicines onto the market and into medical practice."[72] At the time, medical authorities and journalists heralded the changes wrought by these medicines as a "therapeutic revolution."[73]

Sulfa drugs became the first important treatment for infection, and remained so during World War II, acting as a "harbinger of a new medical day," as one prominent science journalist termed it in the early 1940s.[74] Researchers at the German chemical giant IG Farben had developed this chemical treatment for infectious disease in the early 1930s, using what Lesch has called a "systematic approach to innovation." They synthesized Prontosil, the first sulfa drug, from a red dye, discovering that it could wipe out streptococcal infections in animal hosts.[75] The treatment,

[69] Bernard D. Rostker, *Providing for the Casualties of War: The American Experience through World War II* (Santa Monica, CA: Rand Corporation, 2013), 190.

[70] Allan M. Brandt, *No Magic Bullet: A Social History of Venereal Disease* (New York: Oxford University Press, 1987), 170–171; John Parascandola, "John Mahoney and the Introduction of Penicillin to Treat Syphilis," *Pharmacy in History* 43, no. 1 (2001): 3–13.

[71] John Parascandola, "Industrial Research Comes of Age: The American Pharmaceutical Industry, 1920–1940," *Pharmacy in History* 27, no. 1 (1985): 12–21.

[72] Jeremy A. Greene, Flurin Condrau, and Elizabeth Siegel Watkins, "Introduction: Medicine Made Modern by Medicines," in *Therapeutic Revolutions: Pharmaceuticals and Social Change in the Twentieth-Century*, ed. Jeremy A. Greene, Flurin Condrau, and Elizabeth Siegel Watkins (Chicago: University of Chicago Press, 2016), 9–10.

[73] For a thoughtful consideration of the historical idea of "therapeutic revolution," including sulfa drugs, see Scott Podolsky and Anne Kveim Lie, "Futures and Their Uses: Antibiotics and Therapeutic Revolutions," *Therapeutic Revolutions: Pharmaceuticals and Social Change in the Twentieth-Century*, ed. Jeremy A. Greene, Flurin Condrau, and Elizabeth Siegel Watkins (Chicago: University of Chicago Press, 2016), 11–42.

[74] The quotation is from Greene et al., Therapeutic Revolutions, 9.

[75] John E. Lesch, *The First Miracle Drugs: How Sulfa Drugs Transformed Medicine* (New York: Oxford University Press, 2007), 51–67. Head of the pharmaceutical division Heinrich Horlein brought chemists Fritz Meitzch and Joseph Klarer together with

however, was imperfect, and resistance appeared often and quickly.[76] Even as sulfa drugs continued to be used, penicillin became the most celebrated and efficacious treatment during the war.[77]

Sulfa drugs were chemicals synthesized in a chemistry lab, as with DDT and hexachlorophene. In contrast, penicillin was a fungus. As with other antibiotics, it was part of the natural world. As one medical journalist pointed out in 1944, penicillin was different from the bacteria-killing sulfa drugs that preceded it because it was "the result of a naturally occurring antagonism between microorganisms."[78] Although researchers initially hoped that penicillin could be synthesized chemically, attempts were unsuccessful until after the war.[79] Requiring different methods of research and development, antibiotics also carried distinct environmental consequences.[80]

Like DDT, penicillin was not a wartime find. Alexander Fleming originally discovered it in 1928, but only in the early 1940s did Oxford researchers Howard Florey and Ernest Chain fully examine its potential.[81] Finding penicillin promising, Florey traveled to the United States in 1941 to drum up financial support, and the United States provided vital production innovations and funding. Several government agencies shared the responsibility with pharmaceutical corporations and research foundations for developing and producing penicillin. The Office of Scientific Research and Development's (OSRD) subdivision the Committee on Medical Research (CMR), the Department of Agriculture, and the War Production Board (WPB) all had important roles in moving penicillin research and production forward. Fifteen companies and 13 universities

---

pathologist Gerhard Domagk, in a collaboration that produced Prontosil, the trade name for sulfanilamide.

[76] Vered Schechner, Elizabeth Temkin, Stephan Harbarth, Yehuda Carmeli, and Mitchell J. Schwaber, "Epidemiological Interpretation of Studies Examining the Effect of Antibiotic Usage on Resistance," *Clinical Microbiology Reviews* 26, no. 2 (April 2013): 289–307.

[77] Cosmas and Cowdrey, *United States Army in World War II*, 542; Condon-Rall and Cowdrey, *United States Army in World War II*, 254, 294; John Parascandola, "John Mahoney and the Introduction of Penicillin to Treat Syphilis," *Pharmacy in History* 43, no. 1 (2001): 3–13; and John E. Lesch, *The First Miracle Drugs*, 207–221.

[78] Jane Stafford, "Penicillin," *The American Scholar* 13, no. 4 (Autumn 1944): 469.

[79] John P. Swann, "The Search for Synthetic Penicillin during World War II," *The British Journal for the History of Science* 16, no. 2 (July 1983): 189.

[80] E. Chain and H. W. Florey et al., "Penicillin as a Chemotherapeutic Agent," *The Lancet* (August 24, 1940): 226.

[81] Robert Bud, *Penicillin: Triumph and Tragedy* (New York: Oxford University Press, 2007).

and research foundations came together with government to mass produce penicillin, building 21 penicillin plants during the war.[82]

Penicillin's effect on soldiers' mortality was unprecedented, fundamentally transforming the injury experience for soldiers. Surgeons found they could close injuries earlier and conduct more risky surgery without the same fear of infection.[83] One military historian estimated that from D-Day in June of 1944 until the end of the war, "U.S. military deaths from infection approximated zero." Gangrene, the familiar and dreaded companion of injured soldiers, no longer grew in wounds; this made amputations resulting from infection unnecessary.[84] Thousands were saved, though exact estimates are difficult because of what historian Robert Bud has termed the difficulty of drawing a line between "careful observation and ecstatic response" to this unprecedented medical treatment.[85]

Wartime demand created production expansion, though mass production of this unstable mold was no easy task. Central to the development of the process was the work of the USDA's National Regional Research Laboratory (NRRL). Researchers there developed a new fermentation process that increased the yield of penicillin more than 10 times.[86] The penicillin collaborators shifted production from a "crude" "low-yielding" process using bed pans and glass bottles to more efficient production of commercial-grade penicillin in 10,000-gallon tanks.[87] By 1943, mass production had begun, with Pfizer, Merck, and Squibb functioning as the central producers.[88] But, as with DDT, ecological concerns took a backseat to the wartime desire for immediate cures.

---

[82] Peter Neushul, "Science, Government, and the Mass Production of Penicillin," *Journal of the History of Medicine and Allied Sciences* 48, no. 4 (1993): 394.

[83] Clinton K. Murray, Mary K. Hinkle, and Heather C. Yun, "History of Infections Associated with Combat-Related Injuries," *Journal of Trauma and Acute Care Surgery* 64, no. 3 (2008): S224–S225.

[84] Vincent J. Cirillo, "Two Faces of Death: Fatalities from Disease and Combat in America's Principal Wars, 1775 to Present," *Perspectives in Biology and Medicine* 51, no. 1 (2008): 121–133.

[85] Bud, *Penicillin*, 59.

[86] "Further Note on Penicillin Production," *British Medical Journal* 2, no. 4365 (September 2, 1944): 314.

[87] Roswell Quinn, "Rethinking Antibiotic Research and Development: World War II and the Penicillin Collaborative," *American Journal of Public Health* 103, no. 3 (2013): 427. See also Arthur Daemmrich, "Synthesis by Microbes or Chemists? Pharmaceutical Research in the Antibiotic Era," *History and Technology* 25, no. 3 (September 2009): 237–256 and David C. Mowery and Nathan Rosenberg, *Paths of Innovation: Technological Change in Twentieth-Century America* (New York: Cambridge University Press, 1999), 96.

[88] Peter Neushul, "Science, Government, and the Mass Production of Penicillin," *Journal of the History of Medicine and Allied Sciences* 48, no. 4 (October 1993): 371–395.

Penicillin came back from the war with a huge consumer market and companies equipped to fill their demand.[89] Countless anecdotes of penicillin saving soldiers on the brink of death appeared in the popular – as well as the medical – press.[90] One 1944 advertisement in *Life Magazine* showed a medic treating a wounded soldier on the front, declaring "thanks to penicillin, he will come home." The advertisement had an image of a petri dish of the penicillin mold in one corner. Penicillin, it asserted, "may well be ... the greatest news event of World War II."[91] Penicillin's storied potency against dread killers, like pneumonia and scarlet fever, became well known.

Wartime optimism and the belief in the power of medicine made the defeat of all infectious disease seem possible. Extending far beyond penicillin, the search for new antibiotics took center stage, with penicillin the hero and disease the enemy.[92] A 1947 *New York Times* article titled "Good Microbes Fight Bad Ones" chronicled how "all over the world, medical men are searching for ... another penicillin."[93] Antibiotics pioneer Selman Waksman in 1948 voiced his optimistic hope that "before long all human and animal diseases, and possibly also plant diseases, will be combated if not completely eliminated."[94] The future for antibiotics, according to Waksman and many others was "bright indeed."

By March 1945, American factories produced enough penicillin to release it to the general public, not just to soldiers on the war front, setting the stage for the postwar years, when antibiotics became pervasive in civilian life.[95] Combined production in the United States and Great Britain ballooned from 21 billion units in 1943 to 6.8 trillion in 1945.[96] Seventy years after World War II, production reached millions of metric

---

[89] Cosmas and Cawdrey, *United States Army in World War II*, 619.

[90] See Boris Sokoloff, *The Story of Penicillin* (New York: Ziff-Davis, 1945); Boris Sokoloff, *The Miracle Drugs* (New York: Ziff-Davis, 1949); and Bud, *Penicillin*.

[91] Advertisement for Schenley Laboratories, *Life Magazine*, August 14, 1944, displayed at *ExplorePAHistory.com*, http://explorepahistory.com/displayimage.php?imgId=1-2-FA8 (accessed July 30, 2019).

[92] Hannah Landecker, "Antibiotic Resistance and the Biology of History," *Body & Society* 22, no. 4 (2016): 28.

[93] Francis Rawdon Smith, ""Good Microbes Fight Bad Ones," *New York Times*, August 10, 1947.

[94] Quoted in "Victory of Biotics over Disease Seen," *New York Times*, June 17, 1948.

[95] Quinn, "Rethinking Antibiotic Resistance and Development," 429.

[96] M. M. Manring, Alan Hawk, Jason H. Calhoun, and Romney C. Andersen, "Treatment of War Wounds: A Historical Review," *Clinical Orthopaedics and Related Research* 467, no. 8 (August 2009): 2184.

tons a year.[97] As with DDT's observed effectiveness making public health leaders no longer use traditional practices of draining swamps, so too did penicillin make medical personnel deemphasize traditional infection control practices like handwashing. Confidence in the antibiotic miracle meant that Americans threw caution to the wind, with misuse and overuse of penicillin rampant.[98]

However, there were also more cautious voices in the postwar period, calling for a nuanced view of antibiotics and infection. Most notably, Rene Dubos, a microbiologist and successful microbe hunter, focused attention on the ecological complexity of interactions between microbes and humans. He argued that the interaction between disease and treatment was no zero-sum game.[99] In his prescient book of essays *Mirage of Health* (1959), Dubos compared antibiotic use to an American cowboy. In a typical Western story, the cowboy would swoop into town and wipe out all the villains. But what happens after that neat story ends? Dubos posited that more villains were on the horizon and that more was needed to stop them than a cowboy hero. "The belief that disease can be conquered through the use of drugs," he emphasized, "fails to take into account the difficulties arising from the ecological complexity of human problems."[100] Antibiotics had not, in fact, conquered disease, but instead offered "relative protection ... at the cost of a huge ransom."[101]

Dubos also warned that resistance to antibiotics developed almost as quickly as penicillin production did. The problem of resistance had been well known long before penicillin, but Americans' confidence in their ability to find more and more successful treatments kept physicians, the pharmaceutical industry, and the American public from focusing on the consequences. Americans held onto the belief that if drugs and chemicals could be "used as directed," risks would be insignificant without any proof.

By the 1960s, some infectious disease doctors began to warn that antibiotics had disrupted the ecological balance between microbes and fomented ever stronger pathogens. As medical historian Scott Podolsky

---

[97] Landecker, "Antibiotic Resistance and the Biology of History," 24.

[98] Stuart B. Levy, *The Antibiotic Paradox: How Miracle Drugs Are Destroying the Miracle* (New York: Springer, 2002).

[99] Carol L. Moberg, *Rene Dubos, Friend of the Good Earth: Microbiologist, Medical Scientist, Environmentalist* (Washington, DC: American Society for Microbiology, 2005).

[100] Rene Dubos, *Mirage of Health: Utopias, Progress and Biological Change* (New York: Anchor Books, 1959), 138.

[101] Ibid.

has shown, leading infectious disease scientists, including Joshua and Esther Lederberg and Maxwell Finland, warned of "superbugs" emerging to combat the antibiotic "superdrugs."[102] One 1962 *New York Times* commentary on the topic warned that "germ-killers extraordinary ... conquerors of disease have come up against raw, resistant strains. And the battle is not yet decided."[103] Today, intractable resistant infections like MRSA and C-Dif pose a concrete and serious public health threat in the United States and worldwide, making this warning a reality.[104]

Production of penicillin also created unprecedented waste for which no easy means of disposal existed. The problem was recognized at the time. As the war ended, one industrial chemist noted, "temporary expedients in dealing with these problems were no longer justified."[105] One account, from an Industrial Waste Symposium in 1947, detailed the magnitude of the problem with specific reference to penicillin, explaining that "tons of raw materials are fermented to produce a few pounds of finished product."[106] Whereas plant managers had once disposed of waste in previously established sewer systems and in local streams, without industrial scientists identifying adverse effects, now the much greater volume created a need for sewage systems within factories as well. Additionally, waste from penicillin production inhibited the usual disposal and breakdown processes, "sealing up" trickler beds and retarding waste breakdown.

More recent research has shown that this waste has fostered antibiotic resistance. While typical studies of antibiotics in the environment have often focused on disposal of drugs and on residual antibiotics in human waste, environmental researchers have uncovered the significant level of antibiotics left in the industrial waste from antibiotic production.[107]

---

[102] Scott H. Podolsky, *The Antibiotic Era: Reform, Resistance, and the Pursuit of a Rational Therapeutics* (Baltimore: Johns Hopkins University Press, 2015), 154–158.

[103] Lawrence Galton, "When Wonder Drug Meets Wonder Bug," *New York Times*, April 8, 1962, 78.

[104] Centers for Disease Control and Prevention, *Antibiotic Resistance Threats in the United States, 2013*, www.cdc.gov/drugresistance/pdf/ar-threats-2013-508.pdf (accessed July 30, 2019); World Health Organization, *The Evolving Threat of Antimicrobial Resistance: Options for Action* (World Health Organization, 2012), https://apps.who.int/iris/handle/10665/44812 (accessed July 30, 2019).

[105] E. L. Knoedler and S. H. Babcock Jr., "Industrial Wastes ... Pharmaceutical and Biological Plants," *Industrial and Engineering Chemistry* (May 1947): 582.

[106] Ibid.

[107] Jerker Fick, Hanna Söderström, Richard H. Lindberg, Chau Phan, Mats Tysklind, and D. G. Joakim Larsson, "Contamination of Surface, Ground, and Drinking Water from Pharmaceutical Production," *Environmental Toxicology and Chemistry* 28, no. 12 (2009): 2522–2527.

Producers also repurposed the waste, creating unanticipated environmental effects. The corn steep liquor used as penicillin's fermentation medium became feed for domestic animals. Farmers soon found that this new feed unexpectedly triggered "dramatically faster growth, less disease, and earlier marketability" of their animals. The medical innovation of antibiotics therefore spurred increased meat consumption among Americans and prompted farmers to house their animals indoors.[108] Some pharmaceutical companies also highlighted how fermentation byproducts from penicillin production could accelerate growth of agricultural produce. Pfizer created a "demonstration farm" in the 1970s to illustrate how penicillin byproducts greatly improved soil and promoted growth.[109]

Recent research has also begun to reveal the potential long-term consequences of antibiotic exposures on the human race. Microbiologists have recently focused on how diseases have evolved since the beginning of the antibiotic era, focusing on how the great increase in autoimmune diseases and allergies could be connected to how antibiotics have altered the microbial communities in and on humans.[110] The problem of weight gain in the United States, some warn, might also have connections to antibiotics. The environment in and around us has clearly been altered by the widespread production and use of antibiotics.

THE COMPLEX LEGACY OF THE WARTIME THERAPEUTIC REVOLUTION

A world without antibiotics, antibacterial cleansers, and synthetic insecticides is hard to imagine. Each is a success story of the twentieth century, saving lives and improving life. Their emergence in World War II shaped their incorporation into American life fundamentally. The imperative to save soldiers from disease and infection was the testing ground of penicillin, hexachlorophene, and penicillin – and they came through with flying colors. But this success during these few years did not illustrate their long-term safety, though it did make them appealing to relieved and patriotic Americans emerging from the war.

---

[108] Landecker, "Antibiotic Resistance and the Biology of History," 26–27.

[109] Timothy K. Reynolds and Michael E. Johnson, "The Pfizer Demonstration Farm," in *Bulletin No. 26: Recycling Mycelium – A Fermentation Byproduct Becomes an Organic Resource*, ed. William A. Niering et al. (New London, CT: Connecticut Arboretum, 1981): 17–22.

[110] Martin J. Blaser, "Who Are We? Indigenous Microbes and the Ecology of Human Diseases," EMBO Reports 7, no. 10 (October 2006): 956–960.

The very effectiveness of all three substances was in itself an indication of environmental disruption. As the PSAC concluded after its careful examination of DDT, "Precisely because pesticide chemicals are designed to kill or metabolically upset some living target organism, they are potentially dangerous to other living organisms."[111] Not only disease-carrying insects, but other insects, animals, and potentially even humans were therefore at risk. So too with hexachlorophene and penicillin, which wipe out germs indiscriminately. Some scientists expressed caution at the time, but the risks were not immediately discernible, or else they were seen as insignificant in the face of saved lives and productive agriculture.

The assessment of risks at the time was also shaped by the war – and was not what it would later become. Industrial pollution without significant regulation was one area of significant environmental cost that continued to persist even after restriction and regulation. *Silent Spring* helped to transform public awareness in 1962, and the regulatory setting of the industry began to change. DDT was banned in the United States in 1972. So too was hexachlorophene for consumers because of the dangers of neurotoxicity. Antibiotic resistance in humans has made clear the harms that have come with the use and misuse of antibiotics.

Additionally, the more complex shifts in our environments, both human and land, are important to gauge as well. The war years, with their critical contributions to the industrial development of these chemical and pharmaceutical solutions and the attitudes surrounding them, had enduring consequences. Two Institute of Medicine (IOM) reports attest to growing awareness and concern about some of these consequences. In the early 1990s, on the heels of the HIV/AIDS epidemic's emergence, the IOM conducted an extensive study of "emerging microbial threats," warning that even though "drugs, vaccines and pesticides" were "important weapons" in the "battle against infectious disease," their use had created complacency and overconfidence as well as producing newly virulent and resistant enemies.[112] The need for more care and study in the deployment of these weapons was clear.

---

[111] As quoted in Naomi Oreskes and Erik M. Conway, *Merchants of Doubt* (New York: Bloomsbury Press, 2010), 221.

[112] Stanley C. Oaks Jr. Robert E. Shope, and Joshua Lederberg, eds., *Emerging Infections: Microbial Threats to Health in the United States* (Washington, DC: National Academies Press, 1992). Alfred M. Prince and Lindsley F. Kimball, "Emerging Infections: Microbial Threats to Health in the United States," *Journal of the American Medical Association* 270, no. 3 (1993): 384.

More recently, a 2014 IOM report had a different focus: that of "microbial ecology." Leading off with a quotation from Joshua Lederberg, a prominent microbiologist and policy maker, the report highlighted the importance of moving beyond war metaphors of conquering enemies. Lederberg had urged in 2000 that "a more ecologically informed metaphor, which includes the germs'-eye view of infection, might be more fruitful."[113] The report went on to highlight that resident microbes in the trillions occupy each human body and fundamentally shape human health. Rather than trying to simply "wipe out" insects and microbes indiscriminately, current public health leaders focus on the need to explore the effects of chemicals and drugs in a more nuanced manner.

Our bodies and the ground around us document the enduring presence and adverse effects of penicillin, DDT, and hexachlorophene – medical weapons of war and peace. DDT's continuing presence in the environment still restricts breeding of bald eagles and other wildlife, while antibiotic resistance is a growing global health threat.[114] Lack of effective regulation of industrial pollutants compounded this damage. And the mindset of immediate medical fixes, deemed necessary during the war, has hidden the broader ecological consequences.

---

[113] Alison Mack, Leigh Anne Olsen, and Eileen R. Choffnes, eds., *Microbial Ecology in States of Health and Disease: Workshop Summary* (Washington, DC: National Academies Press, 2014).

[114] Jelle P. Hilbers et al., "Using Field Data to Quantify Chemical Impacts on Wildlife Population Viability," *Ecological Applications* 28, no. 3 (2018): 771–785.

11

Shattered Worlds

Place, Environment, and Militarized Landscapes at the Dawn of Atomic America

Ryan H. Edgington

On a cool morning in the isolated southern New Mexico desert, scientists and military personnel gathered for what they knew would be one of the twentieth century's most historic moments. Three ... Two ... One ... A thunder roared across the desert. It was July 16, 1945, at 5:29:45 am Mountain Standard Time. The assembled onlookers watched the first successful atomic device explode at the Trinity site 50 miles northwest of Alamogordo, New Mexico. No one knew for certain what would happen. Everyone shielded themselves with protective eyewear and were told to turn away from the blast. Manhattan Project scientist Enrico Fermi took bets as to whether the fission-type plutonium implosion weapon would annihilate New Mexico or the entire world.[1] When the test came to an end, a 6-foot-deep crater with a 250-foot radius was left behind. At the equivalent of 20 kilotons of TNT, it was the largest explosion in human history. The blast destroyed vegetation two thousand feet from ground zero.[2]

The explosion struck some as both awe inspiring and frightening. Austrian-born physicist Otto R. Frisch, an émigré, forced from Europe by fascism, who helped to build the device, described the scene: "Suddenly and without any sound, the hills were bathed in brilliant light, as if somebody had turned the sun on with a switch." He added, "After some

---

[1] Richard Rhodes, *The Making of the Atomic Bomb* (New York: Simon & Schuster, 1986), 664.

[2] The best treatment on the Trinity test remains Ferenc Morton Szasz, *The Day the Sun Rose Twice: The Story of the Trinity Site Nuclear Explosion, July 16, 1945* (Albuquerque: University of New Mexico Press, 1984), 79, 136.

seconds I could keep my eye on the thing and it now looked like a pretty perfect red ball as big as the sun, and connected to the ground by a short grey stem."[3] As he watched the fireball reach the heavens, J. Robert Oppenheimer, head scientist of the project, quoted the Indian epic poem *Bhagavad Gita*: "I am become Death, Shatterer of Worlds."[4] Oppenheimer understood that the Manhattan Project, the secret program created in 1942 to beat the Germans to the first nuclear weapon, would transform the world technologically, militarily, and environmentally.

To understand how nuclear power shaped America during the war, we must look toward the triad that exists between cultures, economies, and the environment. These are the "understories" of early Atomic America. As the geographer Jake Kosek explains, "nature has been the primary target through which bodies and populations – both human and nonhuman – have been governed, and it has been the primary site through which institutions of governance have been formed and operated."[5] World War II altered how nature was valued by the government, which in turn transformed environments across the country. Nonhuman nature, as an actor in history, alters cultures and their economies through the dynamics of environmental change. Economies shape how cultures are formed and change with time. Completing the circle, human cultures alter nature based upon human economic needs and cultural desires.[6]

Many different places were influenced by and played a role in what I call Atomic America. Emerging during World War II, Atomic America consisted of an interlinked nuclear landscape: a web of nuclear testing sites, scientific laboratories, and nuclear material production facilities spanning the United States. Twenty critical sites emerged during the war to help the Manhattan Project succeed. Each one of the locales played a role in what scholars call "Big Science." Before World War II, scientific research often happened on an individual or team level, with little, if

---

[3] Quoted in Robert Chadwell Williams and Philip L. Cantelon, *The American Atom: A Documentary History of Nuclear Policies from the Discovery of Fission to the Present, 1939–1984* (Philadelphia: University of Pennsylvania Press, 1984), 46.

[4] There are several translations for the poem. I use the most common one I have seen attributed to Oppenheimer. For an account of that moment, see Szasz, *The Day the Sun Rose Twice*, 88–91.

[5] Jake Kosek, *Understories: The Political Lives of Forests in Northern New Mexico* (Durham, NC: Duke University Press, 2006), 25.

[6] On the interrelationship between nature, culture, economy see Arthur McEvoy, "Towards an Interactive Theory of Nature and Culture," in *The Ends of the Earth: Perspectives on Modern Environmental History*, ed. Donald Worster (Cambridge: Cambridge University Press, 2011), 211–229.

any, federal funding, and often in small laboratories affiliated with a university.[7] As Jeff A. Hughes explains, scientific experimentation during these years was a "table-top" endeavor.[8] With the onset of the war and the Manhattan Project, however, science scaled up to include large teams of researchers. Part of that process included more federal investment in scientific exploration, as the cost of research increased.[9] The Manhattan Project epitomized this shift from individual to industrial scientific research.

Nuclear technologies did not merely explode in far off places. They reshaped scores of local landscapes across the United States, where people had long lived and worked. Big Science had local implications – and it is these local stories that will be the focus of this chapter. At Trinity site, few working within the Manhattan Project thought about the local "worlds" shattered by the bomb. Once the range of cattle ranchers, by 1945 Trinity site became part of White Sands Missile Range, the largest military installation in the United States. Cordoned off from public use, visitors would not have access to the site until the 1960s, nor would anyone totally understand the environmental impact of what had transpired there. For decades, the site loomed large in the American public's imagination. But, of course, the place took on special meanings for locals. The environmental consequences for those who lived in the area were weighty. Cattle were contaminated. Birds died. Local families suspected their health maladies were caused by the unpredictable, invisible forces unleashed that day.

All militarized landscapes, whether the shipyards of Oakland or a munitions plant in Wisconsin, have complicated local histories. Agrarian landscapes became massive weapons plants. Coastal fisheries became naval stations. Those conversions changed the people who lived there permanently. Militarized landscapes did not exist in a vacuum. Instead, they occurred as a web of interconnected places linked by the past, present, and future. Such linkages shaped the nuclear landscapes created during World War II.

---

[7] Lawrence Badash, *Scientists and the Development of Nuclear Weapons: From Fission to the Limited Test Ban Treaty* (Amherst, NY: Humanity Books, 1995), 4–5. As Badash notes, the advent of Big Science was more of a process than a moment. It began to emerge as early as the nineteenth century, but took on new meaning during the war.

[8] Jeff A. Hughes, *The Manhattan Project: Big Science and the Atom Bomb* (New York: Columbia University Press, 2002), 7; see also Vincent C. Jones, *Manhattan: The Army and the Atomic Bomb* (Washington, DC: Center of Military History, 1985).

[9] Badash, *Scientists and the Development of Nuclear Weapons*, 4–6.

While nuclear landscapes existed across the United States, some of the most important existed in the American Southwest, and in New Mexico in particular. In this chapter, which is divided into three sections, I document three important nuclear landscapes created during World War II. They reflect the broader process of militarization during the Manhattan Project. They also show that while there were global implications for the making of an Atomic Bomb, those implications were immediately felt at the local level.

This chapter's first section lays out the national scope of Manhattan Project installations, and then examines Los Alamos, where city planning played a vital role in transforming a mountainous landscape into a vibrant military and scientific city. The next section examines the Navajo Nation (the Diné) in the Four Corners region of the American West and what happened when uranium – essential to building nuclear weapons during the war – was found on their land. Last section examines how the Trinity explosion remade ranchlands into testing grounds and eventually a massive missile range. The explosion contaminated humans, plants, and animals. It ultimately became a site of conflict as scientists, the military, and everyday Americans wrestled over the meaning of atomic power as both a good and bad technology. Los Alamos, Navajo Country, and the Trinity site were foundational sites in Atomic America. Each location evolved as part of an environmental process where nature, culture, and economy intertwined. This chapter recovers these stories.

THE CITY ON THE HILL: LOS ALAMOS AND THE MANHATTAN PROJECT

In the present-day Santa Fe National Forest, deep in the Sangre de Cristo Mountains, lies a little-known campground called Cowles. It is easy to miss Perro Caliente ("Hot Dog" in Spanish), a small ranch not far from the campsite. It was a place that physicist J. Robert Oppenheimer knew well. Diagnosed with tuberculosis as a child, Oppenheimer followed many "lungers" to New Mexico.[10] While there, a family friend introduced him to Perro Caliente. In 1925, he described the place to a friend: "We have done only a few expeditions. Pecos Baldy and over towards the Truchas; Lake Peak and the divide, which was superb; and a feeble attempt to penetrate the caves at Pancuela." Perro Caliente was a site of

---

[10] Jon Hunner, *J. Robert Oppenheimer, the Cold War, and the Atomic West* (Norman: University of Oklahoma Press, 2012), 42–43.

exploration. Oppenheimer and his brother Frank loved northern New Mexico. It became a second home to them.[11]

Partly because of his experiences at Perro Caliente, in 1942 Oppenheimer, in negotiation with the US military, chose New Mexico as the central site for the Manhattan Project. He selected Los Alamos, or the secret Site Y (as it came to be known), not far from Perro Caliente. A former boys' school on the Pajarito Plateau just below the Jemez Mountains, it was isolated (for security reasons) yet accessible and possessed a moderate climate. It was an environment that Hispanics and Native Americans had utilized for food and timber for centuries. Los Alamos became the nexus of the Manhattan Project and the site where the scientific theory underlying the bomb was researched. World War II transformed the Pajarito from a merely local place to a site of national security tied to the rest of Atomic America.

Los Alamos's growth reflects how planned towns became part of World War II–era Atomic America, changing the environments where they existed from farmlands and ranchlands to sites of national security and scientific endeavors. The Manhattan Project connected scores of sites across the United States. The project was massive in scope, reflecting the emergence of Big Science. Oak Ridge, Tennessee, first called Clinton Engineer Works, was the project's headquarters as designated by the Army Corps of Engineers, which obtained the land for the project. Surrounded by several ridges and just southwest of the Clinch River, at the 70-square-mile Oak Ridge facility, engineers and scientists separated U-235, or fissile uranium, from U-238, or steady uranium.[12] U-235 was used in the bomb, nicknamed "Little Boy," dropped on Hiroshima, Japan.[13] Scientists considered the weapon used on Hiroshima so failsafe that they did not bother testing it. At Hanford Engineer Works on the Columbia River near Richland, Washington, engineers and scientists worked to create plutonium from U-238.[14] Plutonium would become the

---

[11] Quoted in Alice Kimball Smith and Charles Weiner, eds., *Robert Oppenheimer: Letters and Recollections* (Cambridge, MA: Harvard University Press, 1980), 40.

[12] On the acreage of Oak Ridge, see Alan Axelrod, *Encyclopedia of World War II: Volume I* (New York: Facts On File, 2007), 538.

[13] On Oak Ridge see Charles O. Jackson, *City behind a Fence: Oak Ridge, Tennessee: 1942–1946* (Nashville: University of Tennessee Press, 1981).

[14] The best source on Hanford remains *Michelle S. Gerber, On the Home Front* (Lincoln: University of Nebraska Press, 1992); See also Kate Brown, *Plutopia: Nuclear Families, Atomic Cities, and the Great Soviet and American Plutonium Disasters* (New York: Oxford University Press, 2013), ch. 1. Brown examines the process of choosing Hanford as a site for the plutonium production facility as a part of the Manhattan Project.

core of the bomb tested at the Trinity site and the bomb, dubbed "Fat Man," dropped on Nagasaki, Japan.

In addition to Los Alamos, Oak Ridge, and Hanford, ordnance plants across the United States and Canada also played important roles in the Manhattan Project. Plants in Morgantown, West Virginia, Sylacauga, Alabama, and Trail Point, British Columbia, produced heavy water necessary to "moderate" the ideal isotope of uranium necessary for the bombs.[15] A plant in Wabash, Indiana produced RDX (cyclotrimethylene-trinitramine), the explosive compound used in the Los Alamos program to study explosives prior to the Trinity test. The plant also experimented with heavy water.[16] Chalk River Laboratories in Ontario also produced heavy water.[17] At Dayton, Ohio, the Dayton Project was tasked with helping build the "triggers" to explode both bombs.[18]

There were several other laboratories in addition to Los Alamos. At the end of 1942, the University of Chicago Metallurgical Laboratory, led by physicist Enrico Fermi, completed the first sustained nuclear chain reaction, a critical step in making a bomb.[19] The Radiation Laboratory (RAD Lab), led by physicist Ernest Lawrence in Berkeley, California, and affiliated with the University of California, played a vital role in the separation of uranium.[20] At Rochester University in New York, scientists studied the health consequences of radiation, which was crucial for both the success of the test and in understanding the impact of the weapons on human populations. But the long-term effects of radiation for both humans and the environment would not be completely known until well after the Trinity test.[21]

Other programs also contributed to the Manhattan Project (see Map 11.1). Project Ames at Iowa State University studied uranium and

[15] On Alabama Ordnance Works see Allen Cronenberg, *Forth to the Mighty Conflict: Alabama and World War II* (Birmingham: University of Alabama Press, 2003), 51–52; Research on Morgantown's role in the war is scant see: Anthony Cave Brown and Charles B. MacDonald, *The Secret History of the Atomic Bomb* (New York: Dell Publishing, 1977) 143–145. For a very brief analysis on Cominco see Chris Waltham, "An Early History of Heavy Water," *arXiv physics* (June 2002), 5–9, https://arxiv.org/abs/physics/0206076 (accessed July 12, 2016).

[16] Lillian Hoddeson, *Critical Assembly: A Technical History of Los Alamos during the Oppenheimer Years, 1943–1945* (New York: Cambridge University Press, 1993), 164–166.

[17] Brian Buckley, *Canada's Early Nuclear Policy: Fate, Chance, and Character* (Montreal: McGill-Queen's Press, 2000), 31–34.

[18] Hoddeson, *Critical Assembly*, ch. 7.   [19] Szasz, *The Day the Sun Rose Twice*, 13–16.

[20] Benjamin P. Greene, *Eisenhower, Science Advice, and the Nuclear Test-Ban Debate, 1945–1963* (Stanford, CA: Stanford University Press, 2007), 81–82.

[21] Szasz, *The Day the Sun Rose Twice*, 119–123.

MAP 11.1 World War II–era Manhattan Project sites. Created by the author.

plutonium production and had a direct relationship with the initial work in Chicago. Mallinckrodt Chemical Facility in St. Louis, Missouri, produced uranium. Project Camel in Inyokern, California (later China Lake) and affiliated with the California Institute of Technology, conducted research into detonators, specifically for the implosion device tested at Trinity. Project Alberta in Wendover, Utah, worked on delivery systems for the weapons used on Japan.[22] Finally, two critical companies controlled the uranium mining industry in the American West: Vanadium Corporation of America based in Monticello, Utah, and US Vanadium Corporation, based in Uravan, Colorado.[23]

Although a national network, all the atomic places created during the war – from Oak Ridge to Hanford – shaped the futures of the communities

[22] On the role of Project Ames in the atomic bomb project see Hoddeson, *Critical Assembly*, 26, 207–213; There are only scant resources on Mallinckrodt, see US Nuclear Regulatory Commission, "Mallinckrodt Chemical Inc.," *United States Energy Commission*, www.nrc.gov/info-finder/decommissioning/complex/mallinckrodt-chemical-inc-facility.html (accessed September 21, 2016); on Project Camel see "Nuclear Notebook," *Bulletin of the Atomic Scientists* 49, no. 7 (September 1993): 56; on Project Alberta see James P. Delgado, *Nuclear Dawn: The Atomic Bomb, from the Manhattan Project to the Cold War* (New York: Bloomsbury Publishing, 2011), ch. 4.

[23] On Yellowcake Towns see Raye C. Ringholz, *Uranium Frenzy: Saga of the Nuclear West* (Logan: Utah State University Press, 2002); Michael A. Amundson, *Yellowcake Towns: Uranium Mining Communities in the American West* (Boulder: University Press of Colorado, 2002).

of which they became a part. No place shows this better than Los Alamos, an area humans have called home for thousands of years. Long before the 1940s, indigenous peoples, Spanish and America settlers, federal agencies, and the timber industry all competed for the Pajarito Plateau – and each group transformed the environment of the region in the process. Prior to the arrival of Euroamericans, diverse Puebloan people, including the pueblos of San Ildefonso (Po-Woh-Geh-Owingeh) and Santa Clara (Kha'po), relied on the mountains for seasonal sustenance. Recurrent burning, both man-made and natural, benefited livestock owners who fed their cattle with the rich grasses that the process of burning supported. By the late 1700s, Spanish settlers, called *pobladores*, had settled in the Española and Pojoaque Valleys. A growing number of cattle and sheep grazed on land grants deeded by the Spanish Crown to settlers, displacing Native communities from traditional sites of sustenance.[24]

Cattle and sheep ranching undermined the delicate ecosystem of the Pajarito. Rainfall totaled 10 to 14 inches a year. On the Pajarito, bunch-grasses sat in thin soil, which made them vulnerable to overgrazing. Introduced in the eighteenth and nineteenth centuries, cattle taxed the land and depleted grasses. As historian Hal Rothman notes, "Like many other parts of the Southwest, the Pajarito Plateau was an ecological trap. Its thick grama grasses, abundant ponderosa pine trees, and numerous bears, wild turkeys, and other game at higher elevations promised much to the nineteenth-century eye."[25] The reality is that the ecosystem was more vulnerable than early settlers realized.

By the end of the Mexican-American War in 1848, Americans arrived with a new vision for the region. Even though mandated by the Treaty of Guadalupe-Hidalgo, the United States often ignored Spanish land grants by suggesting that property lines were not drawn properly. Well before World War II, federal agencies, including the United States Forest Service, created in 1905, the National Park Service, created in 1916, and eventually the War Department, took control of the region's natural resources. In 1916, Bandelier National Monument was established to protect Puebloan ruins there.[26] In 1932 it was transferred from the Forest Service to the National Park Service.

When World War II began, Los Alamos became a military and scientific boomtown cut mostly from Forest Service lands, transforming local

---

[24] Hal Rothman, *On Rims and Ridges: The Los Alamos Area Since 1880* (Lincoln: University of Nebraska Press, 1992), ch. 1 in general, 15–16.
[25] Rothman, *On Rims and Ridges*, 17, 28.   [26] Ibid., chs. 6–7.

land use practices. City planning became critical to the success of the project. Like many military sites, despite planning efforts it was a ramshackle place. This trend embodied the hasty development of Los Alamos and other military sites to meet the immediate needs of the war effort. Like other Manhattan Project military installations, Los Alamos was intended to embody efficiency and fortitude during the war. At first, Oppenheimer believed perhaps as few as 60 scientists and personnel would be needed to complete the project. But by 1943 the number had ballooned to somewhere between six and seven thousand. In response, the Army Corps of Engineers laid out Los Alamos in a way that created a sense of community for military personnel, scientists, and the workers in town. Town amenities interwove with various forms of housing. As one resident noted, housing came in the form of "barracks, garages, and crackerboxes."[27] Yet, Oppenheimer encouraged planning that included "naturally" curving streets, open space, and views of the surrounding environments.[28]

To get to Los Alamos from the railroad in Lamy, New Mexico, military personnel and scientists headed north from a no-name secret office at 109 East Palace Avenue in Santa Fe before climbing by car over a rugged road to the isolated "Hill." The road was makeshift, with dangerous switchbacks. What the researchers at Los Alamos found was a far cry from the residences they found at the most prestigious colleges and universities of North America and Europe, where they had worked.[29] Today it stands out in New Mexico for its lack of Pueblo Revival and Spanish colonial architecture. It looks more like a Levittown, the first suburbs built after World War II, than New Mexico's nearby capitol city, Santa Fe.[30]

---

[27] Phyllis Fisher quoted in Carl Abbott, "Building the Atomic Cities: Richland, Los Alamos, and the American Planning Language," in *The Atomic West*, ed. Bruce Hevly and John M. Findlay (Seattle: University of Washington Press, 1998), 93–94.

[28] Carl Abbott, "Building the Atomic Cities: Richland, Los Alamos, and the American Planning Language," in *The Atomic West*, ed. Bruce Hevly and John M. Findlay (Seattle: University of Washington Press, 1998), 97; Mark Fiege, *The Republic of Nature: An Environmental History of the United States* (Seattle: University of Washington Press, 2012), ch. 7.

[29] On the "invention" of Los Alamos, see Jon Hunner, *Inventing Los Alamos: The Growth of an Atomic City* (Norman: University of Oklahoma Press, 2004), chs. 1–2.

[30] Levittowns were some of the first postwar American suburbs, which were planned using wartime housing as a model. See David Kushner, *Levittown: Two Families, One Tycoon, and the Fight for Civil Rights in America's Legendary Suburb* (New York: Walker & Co., 2009).

The massive growth of Los Alamos in the first few years of the war led to conflict, as military personnel and scientists sought to create community in a place with various classes of local people.[31] Furthermore, despite its remote location and high-level of importance, managers at Los Alamos often clashed with other federal agencies. The National Park Service wrestled with the presence of the secret site. One site in particular, the Otowi area of Bandelier National Park, became a point of contention. The Army Corps of Engineers had planned to build a road through Otowi without National Park Service consent. As Rothman notes, "the situation became a standoff," with neither side budging. The Park Service remained steadfast, as did Site Y personnel. While near the end of the war the two sides attempted to work together, the "conflict illustrated that the balance of power had changed on the Pajarito Plateau." A site of contest between local residents and federal agencies even before the war became a place of conflict both inside and outside the fences of Los Alamos.[32]

The laboratory at Los Alamos, which remains active today, was not seen as an economic boon by everyone.[33] Rothman writes:

Working at the lab was a double-edged sword. The jobs paid better than anything else in the region, but the work done by locals was largely menial. Maintenance jobs abounded, as did openings for groundskeepers, laborers, helpers and other similar positions. This category was informally reserved for Anglo, Hispano, and Indian residents of the area, leading to a situation where people of importance in local communities worked at demeaning and inconsequential jobs at Los Alamos.[34]

For many, the environmental reorganization of the area recalled a colonial past.

For local residents, Los Alamos embodied a history of environmental dispossession at the hands of the federal government and the industrialization of the local forests, a process that had already begun much earlier. Scientists at the Manhattan Project had few, if any, ties to the area. For locals, the site became a reminder of state and federal land grabs that prevented them from using forest resources in their everyday lives.[35]

---

[31] Historian Hal Rothman also leaned on the idea of a "sense of place" in the region, albeit one increasingly contested after the United States had arrived. See Rothman, *On Rims and Ridges*, 226.

[32] Ibid., 226–230.   [33] Kosek, *Understories*, 229.

[34] Rothman, *On Rims and Ridges*, 239.

[35] A good example of this is William deBuys, *Enchantment and Exploitation: The Life and Hard Times of a New Mexico Mountain Range* (Albuquerque: University of New Mexico Press, 1985); see also Kosek, *Understories*, Introduction.

In contrast, for those who would count themselves as staunch Cold Warriors seeking to upend the Soviet Union's stranglehold on Eastern Europe and East Asia after the war, the environmental impact of Los Alamos on the local communities and the surrounding region was a necessary sacrifice.

ŁEETSO: URANIUM, THE NAVAJO NATION, AND THE COLD WAR LEGACY

In 1990, Juanita Jackson found a bump on her neck. Her daughter, Lorissa, took her to Northern Navajo Medical Center in Shiprock, New Mexico, which was operated by the Indian Health Service. The bump had spread to her lymph nodes. The doctors found that the cancer had begun in her breast and lungs. She moved in with her son, Pete, near the city of Farmington, New Mexico, to be closer to necessary medical facilities. As time passed, it became clear to her family that her health was declining. She could not sleep. She hallucinated. She was breathing deeply. Then, surrounded by her loved ones, she died on July 24, 1992. She was to turn 59 the next day.[36]

While Jackson's story may not appear to have much to do with World War II, it reveals the enduring ways in which environmental changes during the war touched local communities in Atomic America. Jackson, like hundreds of members of the Diné (Navajo) community, succumbed to sickness from uranium mining on Navajo lands, which began in 1942. As the Navajo Nation became a site of material extraction for the Manhattan Project, war, nature, and bodies collided.

Without the Navajo Nation's uranium, the bombs created at Los Alamos and dropped on Japan at the end of the war would not have been possible. With 92 protons in its nucleus, Uranium is nature's heaviest element. When fashioned into a weapon, it is also extremely explosive. As one scholar explains it, "The subatomic innards of U-235 spray outward like the shards of a grenade; these fragments burst the skins of neighboring uranium nuclei, and the effect blossoms exponentially, shattering a trillion trillion atoms within the space of one grain of sand."[37]

---

[36] This story is derived from the seminal study of uranium mining on the Navajo Nation: Judy Pasternak, *Yellow Dirt: An American Story of a Poisoned Land and a People Betrayed* (New York: Free Press, 2010), 163–165.

[37] Tom Zoellner, *Uranium: War, Energy, and the Rock That Shaped the World* (New York: Penguin, 2009), ix–x.

In other words, scientists saw uranium as an extremely radioactive natural element, and perfect for a bomb. Diné homelands happened to be rich in uranium, a substance that came from *łeetso*, the Diné word for "yellow rock."

The Navajo Nation resides in the Four Corners region, where Utah, Arizona, Colorado, and New Mexico meet. Most Navajo live in Arizona. But small towns dot the landscape including Shiprock and Sheep Springs, New Mexico; Shonto and Tuba City, Arizona; and Oljato, Utah. The countryside is known for its deep desert canyons, the high spires of Monument Valley, and small rivers such as the Canyon de Chelly and the San Juan. In the heart of Navajo Country is Dinétah, the ancestral homelands of the Navajo, which lies in present-day New Mexico south of the San Juan River and north of Chacra Mesa.[38] Dinétah sits roughly 250 miles northwest of the Trinity site and 260 miles west of Los Alamos.

Łeetso became extremely valuable during World War II. Early in the war, most US uranium came from the Belgian Congo in Central Africa (now the Democratic Republic of the Congo). But Manhattan Project commander Brigadier General Leslie Groves, who worried about the loss of the precious substance to Nazi submarine attacks, sought a domestic source. Knowledge of its existence in Navajo Country had deep roots. During World War I, John Wetherill, a local trader, was asked by the military to search out an ore called carnotite, which was rich in radium. His knowledge of the Navajo and their lands made him a good contact to find it. Carnotite was used, in part, by French scientists Marie and Pierre Curie in their studies of radium, which would help in planning for an eventual nuclear weapon.[39]

For thousands of years, since the origin of Diné (as told in the Diné Bahane' creation story), the Navajo had colonized the areas surrounding Dinétah.[40] The extraction of uranium from their lands was one event in a long history of exploitation of the Diné people. They had been removed from their lands during the 1864 long walk to the Bosque Redondo in present-day eastern New Mexico. The long walk resulted from new American colonial desires to settle the region without interference from Indian raiding. The government and military saw Navajo raiding as a scourge on

[38] For more on Dinétah and Navajo Country see Marsha Weisiger, *Dreaming of Sheep in Navajo Country* (Seattle: University of Washington Press, 2009).

[39] Pasternak, *Yellow Dirt*, chs. 2–4; On the Curies see Rhodes, *The Making of the Atomic Bomb*, ch. 2.

[40] For more on the Navajo creation story see Paul G. Zolbrod, *Diné Bahane: The Navajo Creation Story* (Albuquerque: University of New Mexico Press, 1987).

early US colonial endeavors in the Southwest. The long walk decimated the Navajo people. Fundamentally, the introduction of disease, metallurgy, and livestock changed traditional ways of living for the Navajo. In 1868, they returned to their homelands from the Bosque Redondo.[41]

Sheep herds had been an important part of life for the Navajo. Introduced by the Spanish in the 1600s and 1700s, sheep became a critical aspect of Navajo culture. Blessingway, a critical cultural ceremony, illustrated the importance of sheep: in the fifth world, Diyin Dine'é (spirits) made sheep and sent them to the Navajo for survival.[42] By the beginning of the Great Depression, Navajos grazed somewhere near 1.3 million sheep and goats on their lands. But as drought ravaged the region and grasses shriveled during the 1930s, the Bureau of Indian Affairs, under Commissioner John Collier, sought to cull those populations through abject slaughter of herds in the name of "livestock reduction." Many were simply burned. In the process, the Diné suffered the loss of a vital social, spiritual, and economic resource.[43] The destruction of sheep devastated the spiritual and cultural ways of the Navajo during the decade prior to the war. It also echoed earlier exploitation by incoming Euroamericans. As herds were cut significantly to ward off soil erosion, the Diné found themselves in economic despair. Rarely did the federal government consult with tribal leaders about the cultural and spiritual importance of sheep to the Nation.[44]

Enter vanadium, an element in carnotite that became critical to the war effort. During World War II, vanadium was used to strengthen armor plate, which was useful in military vehicles.[45] As early as 1942, the army's vanadium procurers had entered contracts with two companies, Vanadium Corporation of America (VCA) and US Vanadium.[46] But more significantly, carnotite rock, it turned out, includes not just vanadium, but also uranium. Uranium was initially seen as an annoyance in the extraction of vanadium. But it soon took on new value for the Manhattan

---

[41] Pasternak, *Yellow Dirt*, 3.

[42] Weisiger, *Dreaming of Sheep in Navajo* Country, 18, 64, 74–75.

[43] See ibid.; Pasternak, *Yellow Dirt*, 21.

[44] For more on Dinétah and Navajo Country see Marsha Weisiger, *Dreaming of Sheep in Navajo Country* (Seattle: University of Washington Press, 2009).

[45] Pasternak, *Yellow Dirt*, 28–29.

[46] Ibid., ch. 4; The entire Four Corners region was rich in Uranium. For more see: Michael A. Amundson, *Yellowcake Towns: Uranium Mining Communities in the American West* (Boulder: University Press of Colorado, 2002); Raye C. Ringholz, *Uranium Frenzy: Saga of the Nuclear West* (Logan: Utah State University Press, 2002).

Project. Army procurers of vanadium started buying what they called "B," or uranium sludge. For every six pounds of vanadium mined, the government received one pound of uranium.[47]

Four men discovered *leetso* in the 1940s. The first was Luke Yazzie, who lived in Cane Valley east of Monument Valley on the Navajo Nation. Yazzie was Diné and found out about the value of the rock from Harry Goulding, an Anglo one-time sheepherder and trade post owner. Yazzie had seen the yellow rock as a child. At the behest of Goulding, he brought what he could find to the trader, who presented it to Denny Viles, Vice President and Field Manager of VCA.[48] Confirming its value, the VCA and the Navajo Nation signed contracts after the War Department raised concerns about procuring supplies from Africa. Mining began first at a site called Monument Valley No. 1 in 1942, and a short time later at Monument Valley No. 2 in 1943. At the second mine, uranium was so plentiful that the VCA saw it as a great boon to their business. The economic boost to the Navajo Nation for the lease of the second mine was $3,000 from the company, four times what the VCA paid to lease the first one.[49]

Yet there remained a dimension of exploitation. As Judy Pasternak explains, the leases on uranium mines in Navajo Country were legal. However, Navajo council delegates "wanted to be helpful to the United States, and they were glad to accept royalties for the tribal coffers, but they felt strongly that *their people should also be cashing in on the boom.*"[50] Like other Americans toward the end of the war, the Diné sought the amenities that came with growing consumer affluence – kitchen stoves, trucks, televisions – and the American dream: a decent home. With the loss of sheep, mining uranium became a practical form of employment. Yet, at least during the late war years, economic returns from uranium mining remained slim. During 1944, in a single section of Monument Valley, more than 54,000 dollars was made by mining companies on uranium mining. VCA cashed in as the Cold War heated up. Yet Viles paid a mere $739.83 for rights to Monument Valley No. 1.[51] The total amount of uranium used in the Manhattan Project mined from Navajo lands during the war was 12.5 percent of the total uranium mined for the project, or 2.7 million pounds. Yet, in the act of opening Navajo

---

[47] Pasternak, *Yellow Dirt*, 44.   [48] Ibid., 36–37.
[49] Traci Brynne Voyles, *Wastelanding: Legacies of Uranium Mining in Navajo Country* (Minneapolis: University of Minnesota Press, 2015), 92; Pasternak, *Yellow Dirt*, ch. 4.
[50] Pasternak, *Yellow Dirt*, 60. Emphasis added.   [51] Ibid., 44.

lands to uranium mining during the war, VCA made it clear just how rich the area was in the element. Monument Valley No. 1 alone produced ten thousand tons of ore.[52] When the war ended, mining did not stop. It expanded to meet the needs of the growing US nuclear arsenal.

The impact on Navajo health shows the legacy of uranium mining and the exploitation of the Diné. During the war, there were no discussions about the health impact of mining uranium within the Navajo Nation, although knowledge of the impact of radiation on health stretched back to the research of the Curies.[53] By the 1950s and 1960s, uranium was needed to beat the Soviet Union in the nuclear arms race. On Navajo lands, new roads were built. Modern mining technologies came to the Navajo Nation. So too did the health problems from mining, which swept through the mostly Navajo workforce. It was not just Juanita Jackson who suffered. Oral histories speak of health problems that followed uranium mining, a direct result of the project to build nuclear weapons. As one resident, George Tutt Sr., recently explained:

Direct injuries, there were none. Just machinery used to haul the ore out, they called it a "scoop creep." We would haul one ton of ore with it. It operated with a diesel engine. One of these crushed me. It crushed me against a rock, but that's what happened. I don't remember when it was. That was the only injury I sustained, but I was not injured that bad.[54]

But he went on to suggest that he later experienced "some respiratory problems. It was obvious, because I was short of breath when I walked up hills. I would get sweaty and short of breath. The health examinations traced the problem back to mining, and it has affected me."[55] Jackson and Tutt were just two individuals caught up in the uranium fever.

The element's health and environmental impact had developed among the Navajo as uranium mining expanded during World War II. Despite warnings from the Indian Health Service, the US Public Health Service, and the Atomic Energy Commission, mining went forward to support the creation of nuclear weapons and energy in the Cold War years. Sheep died as mining tailings leached into the soil due to runoff, and uranium-laced

---

[52] Ibid., 51. [53] Rhodes, *The Making of the Atomic Bomb*, ch. 2.
[54] Timothy Benally, "I Have Revisited the Places I Used to Work: Oral History of Former Miner George Tutt," in *The Navajo People and Uranium Mining*, ed. Doug Brugge, Timothy Benally, and Esther Yazzie-Lewis (Albuquerque: University of New Mexico Press, 2006), 11–24.
[55] Ibid., 16.

rock was used in the bedding under the foundation of houses, schools, and places of worship. Tailings piled up and people got sick as the aftereffects of mining led uranium to seep into the soil and water near mining sites.[56]

Brynne Voyles has called the process of using Navajo lands for uranium mining *wastelanding*. Calling a place a wasteland, she says, "renders an environment and the bodies that inhabit it pollutable."[57] The federal government, private mining companies, and Diné leadership did just this by expanding mining in the Navajo Nation without proper health studies. This means that the process of industrialization in the Navajo Nation includes having the power to dictate the value of desert landscapes otherwise seen as worthless. In other words, if the government can define the value of a desert place, it can also own it and the people that live there. In sum, VCA and other corporations transformed Navajo Country into an industrial landscape as part of Atomic America during World War II with long-term consequences for the Diné.

THE WALK OF THE DEAD: THE TRINITY TEST SITE AND REGIONAL CONTAMINATION

When Robert Oppenheimer spoke of a "shatterer of worlds" at the Trinity site, he probably was not thinking about the history of the local desert landscape. Instead, he envisioned the potential future destruction of the planet in atomic war. Yet, the first nuclear explosion, the culmination of the work done at all the Manhattan Project sites, also dramatically reformed the local landscape. Scientists, military personnel, and civilians from across the United States had played a role in making the Trinity test and reconfiguring the area into a militarized landscape.[58]

Many Americans may see the area of the first nuclear explosion, as Susan J. Tweit writes, as a "barren, wild, and worthless" desert.[59] Indeed, the Army Corps of Engineers selected the site for the test in part because

---

[56] To learn more about the long-term effects of uranium mining see Pasternak, *Yellow Dirt*; Brynne Voyles, *Wastelanding*. On the specific use of uranium in buildings see Pasternak, *Yellow Dirt*, ch. 9.

[57] Brynne Voyles, *Wastelanding*, 9.

[58] Unless otherwise noted, this section is based upon Szasz, *The Day the Sun Rose Twice*; Edgington, *Range Wars*, chs. 1–2.

[59] For more on this perception of the region see Susan J. Tweit, *Barren, Wild, and Worthless: Living in the Chihuahuan Desert* (Tucson: University of Arizona Press, 2003). Historian C. L. Sonnichsen went so far as to see the area as a foreboding place explicitly because of how barren it seemed. See Sonnichsen, *Tularosa: The Last of the Frontier West* (Albuquerque: University of New Mexico Press, 1980), esp. ch. 1.

of its isolation and lack of population. But, for thousands of years, indigenous communities had lived in the region, including the ancient Jornada Mogollon Indian tribe. By the early 1700s, the Comanches and Apaches competed for control of the area through raiding on horseback, making permanent settlement by the Spanish and, after the Mexican Revolution in 1821, citizens of Mexico, impossible. Searing summer heatwaves and brutal winters added to the difficulty of settlement. The area was so dangerous that the Spanish called parts of the trail that passed through the area from Mexico City to colonies in northern New Mexico "the walk of the dead."[60]

The end of the Mexican-American War in 1848 brought a massive change in the way that Euromericans interacted with the environment and community of the desert Southwest. Following the defeat of Mexico in 1848, and despite arid desert conditions (getting only 11 inches of precipitation per year), cattlemen with hundreds of thousands of livestock poured into southern New Mexico from points east. They overgrazed the desert grasslands from the 1870s well into the 1930s, while persistent drought and a lack of water sources further undermined economic and environmental conditions for the livestock economy.[61] Environmental carelessness prompted the State of New Mexico and the federal government, under the auspices of the Grazing Service (later the Bureau of Land Management), to step in to regulate grazing districts. By 1940, almost all southern New Mexico rangelands had fallen under government control. Private property owners were forced into leases with the government for the duration of the war.

Thus, in addition to its historical isolation, the federal control of the area gave Oppenheimer and Groves ample reason to select the site.[62] But that history does not completely explain the Manhattan Project's interest in the location. Federal control was critical, but so were several other factors. The proposed site had to be flat and without significant population; be close to Los Alamos; and have a generally good climate; and, in particular, little rainfall. Finally, the location needed lookout points and the ability for scientists to move around to take radiation readings. Scientists and military personnel made a nuclear laboratory in the desert.[63]

On that July 1945 morning, the region – and the world – was forever changed by the Trinity test. When the device exploded, scientists fanned

[60] Edgington, *Range Wars*, ch. 1.   [61] Ibid.

[62] This rationale is explained in Szasz, *The Day the Sun Rose Twice*, 29–31.

[63] Edgington, *Range Wars*, 59.

FIGURE 11.1 Crater left by Trinity Test, 1945.
Source: Photo courtesy of National Nuclear Security Administration/Nevada Field Office,
www.nnss.gov/pages/resources/library/Media.html (accessed July 31, 2019)

out into the desert to measure fallout readings. All participants were
required to follow the "Trinity Exposure Record," which monitored
radioactive exposure with a maximum exposure of 0.1 roentgens per
day (a measurement of exposure to gamma rays and x-rays).[64] At
Ground Zero, the tower that held the device was completely obliterated
and replaced by a massive crater and a strange substance dubbed "Trinitite," a green glass-like material created as sand fused together at the
moment of detonation (see Figure 11.1). Radiation readings depended on
the positioning of monitors. Despite preparations for making sure that
winds did not affect the test, the plume broke into three parts, moving
north, west, and northeast. Thus, readings were as low as 2.0 roentgens
in some places to as high as 20 roentgens elsewhere. A small gorge
northeast of the site had such high readings it was dubbed "Hot
Canyon." At one measurement site, army personnel "buried steaks they

[64] Szasz, *The Day the Sun Rose Twice*, 117–118.

were cooking on an open fire because they thought they were too much contaminated ... and pulled out."[65]

The test altered the entire desert environment in unexpected ways. Manhattan Project ornithologists, herpetologists, entomologists, biologists, soil scientists, heath physicists, and botanists measured the effects.[66] They talked to the ranchers who still lived around the site. One claimed that fallout had turned half his beard white. Although evidence was not conclusive, birds and rodents also experienced the impact of fallout from the test. By 1948, 407 animals were collected for examination. Of the birds examined, 33.3 percent exhibited effects from radiation exposure. Effects included unusual changes to the digestive tract and deformation of their feet.[67]

Many locals talked of "atomic calves" that they claimed had experienced loss of hair and blistering on their backs. According to one report from Los Alamos, as many as 350 cattle experienced some form of radiation exposure. Symptoms included discoloration and scabs, but the cattle seemed to live normal lives. In 1949, the Atomic Energy Commission, which had been created in 1946, said that the 73 cattle studied seemed normal in every way. However, those "severely exposed" showed skin cancer on their backs at the end of their lives.[68]

The blast damaged soils and plant life as far as five thousand feet from ground zero. Moreover, the dynamics of the desert environment complicated the problem. Blowing dirt and flash floods transported radiation to other places and into the ground. Cattle feces were used to measure the degree to which grasses were affected by radiation. A study done in 1947 explained that, near Hot Canyon, waste samples "were definitely radioactive."[69] High winds moved dust from the area around the crater, creating problems in measuring radiation. As a UCLA scientist assigned to measure fallout explained, all one needed to do was to experience the "five heavy dust storms (so far)" to understand the problem of collecting data from the blast.[70]

But it was not just the area around Trinity that felt the effect of winds. Within 15 minutes of the blast the cloud moved in different directions.

---

[65] Quoted in Barton Hacker, *The Dragon's Tail: Radiation Safety in the Manhattan Project* (Berkeley: University of California Press, 1987), 103.

[66] This group was known as the UCLA Group. See Szasz, *The Day the Sun Rose Twice*, 136.

[67] These numbers can be found in Edgington, *Range Wars*, 67.

[68] Szasz, *The Day the Sun Rose Twice*, 132–135.   [69] Edgington, *Range Wars*, 68.

[70] Quoted in ibid., 69. See also Szasz, *The Day the Sun Rose Twice*. See ch. 6 for more details on the local effects of the blast.

The north cloud made it as far as Las Vegas, New Mexico 260 miles north of Trinity site. The northeast section rose to between 45,000 and 55,000 feet and moved from New Mexico across the Midwest, through New York, and into New England.[71]

It is hard to know the full implications of radiation across New Mexico and the United States due to the test. As historian Ferenc Szasz argues, "This was America's first acquaintance with radioactive fallout."[72] It was a nascent science and an uncertain technology that scientists needed more time to understand. Nonetheless, in February 2017, a study commissioned by an organization called the Tularosa Basin Downwinders Consortium showed that local residents near Trinity site suffered significant incidences of diseases from breast cancer to kidney disease, which they attributed to the Trinity test. Recently, the Centers for Disease Control and Prevention explained that no one around the area was warned not to ingest food or water contaminated from the blast.[73]

At Trinity, local stories swirled in the postwar years as to the health impact of the test, but few tangible facts emerged to back them up. Ranchers, however, remembered all too well what had happened to their land: missiles replaced livestock. The McDonald family, for example, owned the house where scientists constructed the device for the Trinity test. After the war, the newly created White Sands Missile Range consumed the Trinity site. Former cattle lands became the domain of the Department of Defense, under the auspices of the US Army. By the end of the 1970s, more than 60,000 missiles had been tested there.[74] Ranchers lost access to their land. The roots of that process began during the war and protests from locals continue to the present day. For example, in the 1980s, Dave McDonald, who snuck back to his family's ranch, set up signs that read "No Trespassing" and "Road Closed to the US Army." He initially refused to leave despite warnings, but eventually agreed after negotiations with New Mexico's congressional delegation. Ranchers would never again return to their properties.[75]

The fears of exposure to radiation also lingered. The Tularosa Basin Downwinders Consortium sought to amend the Radiation Exposure Compensation Act of 1990 (RECA) to receive compensation and

---

[71] Szasz, *The Day the Sun Rose Twice*, 115.   [72] Ibid., 116.

[73] Dennis Carroll, "New Health Survey at Nuclear Test Site Details Decades of Illnesses, Deaths," *Santa Fe New Mexican*, February 11, 2017, www.santafenewmexican.com/news/local_news/new-health-survey-at-nuclear-test-site-details-decades-of/article_4cfc0b66-67ae-5a5d-a542-6977b5164e7d.html (accessed February 15, 2017).

[74] See Edgington, *Range Wars*, Introduction.   [75] Ibid., chs. 1 and 5.

healthcare benefits. They cited that residents of Arizona, Utah, and
Nevada had received such benefits, but nobody near Trinity site had.
They noted that health-related compensation would result in better economic outcomes, which included a decline in the stress related to family
finances and the long-term effect of family financial health. For the
government to take those issues into consideration would result in a
greater ability to gain health insurance and healthcare within the
community.[76]

LEGACIES

Although different places with different local histories, these three parts of
the Southwest – Los Alamos, the Navajo Nation, and Trinity site – shared
a common history of environmental transformation as part of Atomic
America. Indeed, the relationship between Los Alamos, the Navajo
Nation, and Trinity site reflects upon how the Manhattan Project tied
multiple places together, even though the environmental impact may have
been different for each site.

In the years after the war, Los Alamos's population exploded. By 1957,
the town had ballooned to more than 12,000 residents and was a thriving
community committed to the exploration of nuclear energy, but mainly
nuclear weapons.[77] As the Cold War wore on, the Los Alamos National
Laboratory also generated regional fears about the environmental and
health impact of nuclear research. In particular, nuclear research led to
nuclear waste. Locals would experience this aspect of nuclear research
strongly. In 2000, the Cerro Grande wildfire raged across the Pajarito
Plateau, forcing 25,000 people to evacuate the area. "One of the most
striking cultural aspects of the Cerro Grande fire," anthropologist Joseph
Masco explains, "was how many New Mexicans experienced the blaze as
nothing less than a nuclear apocalypse."[78]

As of 2006, the scientists and administrative personnel at Los Alamos
lived in the fourth wealthiest zip code in the United States. Yet the

[76] Tularosa Basin Downwinders Consortium. "Unknowing, Unwilling, and Uncompensated: The Effects of the Trinity Test on New Mexicans and the Potential Benefits of
Radiation Exposure Compensation Act (RECA) Amendments" (February 2017), 51–53,
www.trinitydownwinders.com/health-impact-assessment (accessed September 20, 2017).
See the report generally for health impacts of the Trinity site in the area.
[77] Hunner, *Inventing Los Alamos*, especially the introduction and chapters 3 and 4.
[78] Joseph Masco, *The Nuclear Borderlands: The Manhattan Project in Post-Cold War New
Mexico* (Princeton, NJ: Princeton University Press, 2013) 39, 289–290.

surrounding pueblos and towns, which are more than 70 percent Native and Hispanic, count among some of the poorest places in the country.[79] As Darryl Lorenzo Wellington explains:

Representatives of Las Mujeres Hablan (The Women Speak), a coalition of New Mexican women seeking global disarmament, would add to the list by underscoring that the Manhattan Project acquired New Mexico lands by wielding an act of eminent domain against tribal peoples and Hispanic villagers. That process had deep ties to the project to build the bomb during World War II. It is also a reminder of the profound role the federal government has played in the region. With nuclear weapons came another round of environmental dispossession for local populations.[80]

A local advocate, Ike DeVargas was frank about living under the cloud of Los Alamos. He disliked the Forest Service and the surge of environmental activism since the 1970s in the area. But more than anything else, he holds particular disdain for the city on the hill. As DeVargas says, "There is nothing surprising about Los Alamos. There is a long history of white folks screwing brown folks."[81] The economic disparities between Los Alamos and Española have resonated through local communities.

For the Navajo, there were expected limitations on mining during World War II. Between 1942 and 1943, they explicitly insisted that the VCA pledge to avoid waste and keep the land in as fine a condition as it had been prior to uranium mining. In other words, the land should be conserved per Navajo spiritual and cultural values.[82] What followed instead was environmental decay and health problems across Diné lands. Houses were built atop uranium tailings, livestock became sick, and incidences of cancer exploded in the Navajo Nation.[83] In 1993, the *New York Times* published an article called "A Valley of Death for the Navajo Uranium Miners." In that article, Clifford Frank Sr., a former miner dying of lung cancer, explained that he was living in a dilapidated trailer with his wife on a mere $324 in federal benefits. While the federal government had apologized for the health risks associated with uranium mining, many members of the Navajo Nation remained in poverty and without health benefits.[84]

[79] Kosek, *Understories*, 19, 230.
[80] Darryl Lorenzo Wellington, "In the Shadow of the Manhattan Project." *New Politics* (Winter 2014), 45.
[81] Kosek, *Understories*, 240.   [82] Pasternak, *Yellow Dirt*, 49.   [83] Ibid., pts. 3 and 4.
[84] Keith Schneider, "A Valley of Death for the Navajo Uranium Miners," *New York Times*, May 3, 1993, www.nytimes.com/1993/05/03/us/a-valley-of-death-for-the-navajo-uranium-miners.html (accessed March 13, 2018).

In the years after the use of nuclear weapons on Japan, which ended the war, a lofty patriotism emerged that lauded the Trinity test as an unmitigated good.[85] In New Mexico, within weeks of the bombing of Hiroshima and Nagasaki, news appeared about the Trinity test. Local economic boosters began calling for a monument and a museum at Trinity site. Some mentioned bringing the Enola Gay, the plane that had dropped the bomb on Hiroshima, to the site. Even the National Park Service, which administered nearby White Sands National Monument, sought to connect pristine sand dunes to the site using a series of trails.[86]

In the end, none of these schemes was implemented. Instead, an obelisk was placed at the site, located on present-day White Sands Missile Range. On the fiftieth anniversary of the test in 1995, people came from all over the world to reflect on the test's global importance. However, they came to remember events in *other places*, primarily the devastation of Hiroshima and Nagasaki. Japanese citizens, World War II veterans, protesters (including one who threw fake blood on the obelisk), and the media all made their way to Trinity site. Few knew or thought about the local environmental history of the place where the test happened, despite a sign at Ground Zero that suggested visitors not chew gum or apply makeup and warnings that pregnant women not visit the site altogether.[87] In 2017, the Tularosa Basin Downwinders Consortium challenged the idea that the Trinity test has no adverse health impacts. Their report further stated, "No epidemiological studies of resultant health effects have ever been performed on Trinity test downwinders or New Mexico downwinders." The consortium encouraged further studies of cancer incidents around the site and greater oversight from the federal government.[88]

As Kosek notes, there are "understories" to environments.[89] Nuclear landscapes during World War II had their own "understories." Nuclear weapons did not merely explode. Instead, their meanings were shaped by complex local histories. They also created environmental legacies molded

---

[85] There were also detractors that looked at the bomb as something not only bad but also counter to humanity's moral obligation to one another. One need look no further than the very scientists who built the bomb. They became some of the greatest detractors of further nuclear weapons development in the years after the war. For more on this see Paul Boyer, *By the Bomb's Early Light: American Thought and Culture at the Dawn of the Atomic Age* (Chapel Hill: University of North Carolina Press, 1985).

[86] See Edgington, *Range Wars*, ch. 2.   [87] Ibid.

[88] Tularosa Basin Downwinders Consortium, "Unknowing, Unwilling, and Uncompensated," 75–78.

[89] See Kosek, *Understories*.

from the process of militarizing landscapes critical to the war effort. Narrowing the history of early Atomic America to merely one of environmental decay denies those complex processes. Myriad peoples played a role in the construction of Atomic America during World War II and they understood it in diverse ways. As importantly, the environmental impact also depended on the sites selected for laboratories and testing.

Environmental history is an interaction between cultures, economies, and environments.[90] National security at a time of war was paramount for the War Department and the scientists, military personnel, and civilians engaged in building the bombs dropped on Japan at the end of the war. The environment became a part of the early push for Big Science, as universities and new laboratories became involved in wartime weapons development. This meant transforming many rural places into military sites. In the years to come, Los Alamos would continue to design the weapons that required uranium from Navajo Country and the Trinity site remained a powerful reminder of the outcome of the rush to build the bomb.

[90] McEvoy, "Towards an Interactive Theory of Nature and Culture," 211–229.

PART VI

CONSERVATION

I 2

Total War and the Total Environment

World War II and the Shift from Conservation to Environmentalism

Thomas Robertson

As the essays in this volume make clear, World War II was a total war similar to World War I but much longer, more widespread, more mobile, and more resource intensive. Its effects reached into every corner of American life, aiming to mobilize every atom and molecule from Florida to Alaska. Most conspicuously, the United States created miraculous new productive capacity to supply its massive military forces the vast supplies they needed – everything from wheat, soybeans, and cigarettes to airplanes and alloys. Vast amounts of oil, electricity, and coal and a range of new wartime technologies and chemicals fueled this productive explosion. A new geography emerged during the war – speed-based and urban, focused on northern industrial, coastal, and Sunbelt areas – as well as a new material culture of plastics and alloys. A new economic-environmental system took hold in the country based on faith that the new Keynesian growth economy could, in the future, provide not only the "guns" that US national security appeared to require but also the "butter" – the food, homes, cars, and refrigerators – that seemed central to a new, affluent standard of living.

As these changes unfolded, new ideas about conserving and protecting nature also emerged, a shift from a "conservation" focus on efficient use of resources to a broader "environmental" focus.

In the 1920s and 1930s, conservation meant something very different in the United States than it did after the environmental movement of the late 1960s and 1970s. Two examples show this. First, during the interwar decades, the Ford Motor Company's massive industrial plants near Detroit were repeatedly celebrated as paragons of conservation planning because of their large-scale efforts to recycle materials, repurpose byproducts, and cut waste in resource use. At the time, above all else, conservationists prized resource efficiency and planning. But they generally said little about – they barely even noticed – what would later become key "environmental" concerns: the vast quantities of dirty, toxic substances Ford's factories spewed into the air and dumped into nearby rivers.[1]

Another example comes from the massive New Deal dams of the 1930s, such as the Colorado River's Boulder Dam and the Colombia River's Bonneville Dam. Conservationists lauded these dams as models of efficient resource planning, as they prevented the "waste" of water flowing to the ocean unused for irrigation and power generation. "Conservation is thrift and the avoidance of waste," wrote Paul Sears, one of conservation's most visible theorists, in 1941. "It is management with an eye on the future as well as the present. It is responsible conduct, based upon a desire for permanent and stable prosperity."[2] But in later decades, many environmentalists would see dams as scars upon the landscape, destroyers of habitat, and defilers of wild rivers. Prewar conservation celebrated long-term sustainability but conceived of the threats posed to nature – and the very understanding of what nature was – narrowly. Nature was a storehouse of disparate resources, and the chief enemy was waste.[3]

In contrast, environmentalists of the 1960s and 1970s, although more heterogeneous than remembered, stressed resource efficiency but also several other concerns: an ecologically based idea that nature was interconnected, complex, and vulnerable, even fragile; a profound unease with modern technology and human interference in nature; a deep, even apocalyptic worry about human survivability; a greater sense that material consumption was pushing up against nature's limits, now viewed

---

[1] Christopher W. Wells, *Car Country: An Environmental History* (Seattle: University of Washington Press, 2012), 204.

[2] Paul Sears, *The Foundations of Conservation Education* (Washington, DC: National Wildlife Federation, 1941), 38.

[3] For many years, historians have been complicating the narrative of a simple shift from prewar "conservation" to postwar "environmentalism." Several different strands of early-twentieth-century conservation existed, each one complex and contingent in its own right. Some overlapped. In addition, some early-twentieth-century reformers showed elements of postwar environmentalism, including reformers who decried the unhygienic conditions of urban areas as well as "preservationists" such as John Muir who pushed for the protection of wild places. See, for instance, Robert Gottlieb, *Forcing the Spring: The Transformation of the American Environmental Movement* (Washington, DC and London: Island Press, 2005); Char Miller, *Gifford Pinchot and the Making of Modern Environmentalism* (Washington, DC: Island Press, 2013).

globally; and a concern about protecting the natural amenities that brought a high quality of life. These ideas showed themselves in the major concerns of the 1960s and 1970s: pesticides and pollution, atomic weapons and energy, population growth and unsustainable resource use, and open space and wilderness protection.[4]

This chapter argues that mid-twentieth-century national security imperatives created problems and knowledges that spurred the shift from early-twentieth-century "conservation" to 1960s "environmental" thinking. Even as it reinforced the conservationist call for efficient natural resource development, total war during the 1940s, which set patterns that would expand during the Cold War, sowed the seeds for new environmentalist ways of thinking. As this book makes clear, total war depended upon nature: natural resources were mobilized from a wider catchment area than ever before but also manipulated more intensively than ever before to create new, more powerful tools of production and new, more powerful weapons of destruction. Deploying these powerful new technologies as well as the organizational power of the federal government, the American war machine mobilized rivers, forests, farms, subsoil metals, and even the magic of molecules and the power of subatomic particles. As nature was pulled increasingly into the furnace of total war, the war forced a rethinking of what conservation meant. In a 1944 article called "Conservation and War," the biologist Walter Taylor called for "a drastic shifting of emphasis."[5]

---

[4] The classic study of environmentalism is Samuel P. Hays, *Beauty, Health, and Permanence: Environmental Politics in the United States, 1955–1985* (New York: Cambridge University Press, 1987). Recent works include Adam Rome, *The Bulldozer in the Countryside: Suburban Sprawl and the Rise of American Environmentalism* (New York: Cambridge University Press, 2001); Adam Rome, "'Give Earth a Chance': The Environmental Movement and the Sixties," *Journal of American History* 90, no. 2 (2003): 525; Michael Egan, *Barry Commoner and the Science of Survival: The Remaking of American Environmentalism* (Cambridge, MA: MIT Press, 2007); Thomas Robertson, *Malthusian Moment: Global Population Growth and the Birth of American Environmentalism* (New Brunswick, NJ: Rutgers University Press, 2012); James Morton Turner, *The Promise of Wilderness: American Environmental Politics since 1964* (Seattle: University of Washington Press, 2012); David Stradling, *The Environmental Moment, 1968–1972* (Seattle: University of Washington Press, 2012); Adam Rome, *The Genius of Earth Day: How a 1970 Teach-In Unexpectedly Made the First Green Generation* (New York: Farrar, Straus and Giroux, 2014); Thomas Jundt, "Dueling Visions for the Postwar World: The UN and UNESCO 1949 Conferences on Resources and Nature, and the Origins of Environmentalism," *Journal of American History* 101, no. 1 (2014): 44–70.

[5] Walter P. Taylor, "Conservation and War," *Nature* 37 (January 1944): 41.

Most of what little historians have written about conservation during the war years has focused mostly on atomic power.[6] "The age of ecology opened," historian Donald Worster has written, "on the New Mexican Desert, near the town of Alamagordo, on July 16, 1945, with a dazzling fireball of light and a swelling mushroom cloud of radioactive gases."[7] Except for atomic power, most courses on twentieth-century environmental history skip over the war years. Worster is right to emphasize nuclear weapons as a driver of postwar environmental views. However, long before the summer of 1945, total war and all that it entailed – the mobilization of all available resources to maximize destructive power – had profoundly remade American landscapes, patterns of life, and ideas. Observing these changes, many of which are placed under the microscope in this volume, those who cared about nature responded in varied ways, and some began to pioneer the thinking that ultimately blossomed into the environmental movement of the 1960s and 1970s. Concerns about atomic weapons and energy only reinforced new environmental concerns; they did not create them.

This chapter follows the shifts in thinking about nature during the 1940s by examining the complicated reactions to the war by three groups of conservationists. For the first group, the war reaffirmed the traditional conservation goals of planning and efficiency. Harold Ickes – the Secretary of the Interior who had run the nation's conservation programs during Roosevelt's New Deal the decade previously and who found himself in early 1942 having to rustle up supplies for a military of more than 10 million men – decried a decades-long national binge of waste now followed by a "painful hangover" of potentially lethal shortages. Gifford Pinchot, the dean of early-twentieth-century conservation, echoing ideas he had pushed since serving as US Forest Service chief during the Theodore Roosevelt administration, responded to World War II by calling for the "planned and orderly use" of resources, only now on a global scale. His ideas eventually found support from Presidents Roosevelt and Truman.

But a second group of conservationists, buoyed by miraculous wartime economic transformations, developed a more "positive" growth-based conservation during the war that would prove more influential than

---

[6] For an example of how historians of conservation and environment overlook the role of World War II besides atomic power, see Jundt, "Dueling Visions for the Postwar World," 55.

[7] Donald Worster, *Nature's Economy: A History of Ecological Ideas* (New York: Cambridge University Press, 1994), 342.

traditional conservation, at least in the immediate postwar years. David Lilienthal, the director of the Tennessee Valley Authority (TVA), expressed an almost unlimited faith in science, technology, and wartime "machines of wizardry." Julius Krug, who would follow Ickes in the late 1940 as head of the Interior Department, spoke of a "new era" in conservation, one that emphasized technology and production. This group reimagined conservation as planned development using modern technology.

As Lilienthal and Krug's production-based conservation was taking shape during the war, a third strand of thinking moved in more pessimistic directions, pioneering a shift in subsequent decades away from traditional conservation toward more "environmental" forms of nature protection. Not long after seeing army friends die in combat in northern Italy, David Brower, the man who would transform the Sierra Club and environmental politics during the 1950s and 1960s, experienced a life-transforming epiphany while exploring the "dead" wildernesses of the Alps. In the early 1940s, Aldo Leopold, one of the intellectual leaders of the postwar shift in biological science, began to point out that adhering to ecological limits – a new conceptual framework – might help prevent "mobs and wars, unrests and revolutions." Rachel Carson, a wartime researcher for the US Fish and Wildlife Service (FWS), wrote with worry in 1944 about the "startling developments" of the war and, less than a year later, warned about a new wartime chemical then widely being celebrated for its miraculous powers: DDT.

During the war, the concerns of Brower, Leopold, and Carson – about the loss of true wilderness, about resource exhaustion and degradation, and about pollution – emerged as problems on a scale no one had seen previously. This chapter examines their reactions – as well as those of many others – during the war and argues for the importance of the 1940s and total war as a key driver of new thinking about nature and environmental protection.

"SINEWS FOR CONFLICT": CONSERVATION PLANNING AND WAR

As secretary of the interior since Franklin Roosevelt's inauguration in 1933, Harold Ickes had helped update and institutionalize conservation in the 1930s. As part of Roosevelt's New Deal activist response to the Great Depression – an economic crisis that many conservationists also understood as a crisis of relations with nature – the conservation mission of promoting resource efficiency through planning took on particular importance and gained strong governmental backing and much wider application, particularly under Ickes. Conservationists envisioned the TVA and other New Deal projects, for instance, as conservation projects using new governmental planning powers to heal the wounds of soil erosion and prevent the "waste" of water flowing unused to the sea. In the Depression, the mission of conservation increasingly became the efficient mobilization of resources to combat poverty. The title of a 1940 inventory of US natural resources summed up this approach: "Toward Full Use of Resources."[8]

But as the clouds of war gathered over Europe at the end of the 1930s, the work of conservation planning became yoked with national security concerns. The US government intensified resource mobilization, first to supply overseas allies and eventually for America's own war effort. The Lend Lease Act (1941) enabled the United States to provide materials to the United Kingdom and the USSR. After Pearl Harbor in December 1941, resource mobilization became a national mission. To supply a fighting force eclipsing 10 million, the United States needed mountains of raw materials: iron and steel, cotton, wood, electricity, oil, and food of all types. To coordinate this effort, the government drew from New Deal planning tools and New Deal infrastructure projects such as the TVA and Columbia River dams. It also drew from a host of new federal offices and task forces; the effort would not be left to the free market. Planning took on new scale and import: this was conservation planning on steroids.

Nowhere was this new wartime urgency and scale more obvious than in the Department of Interior (DOI), the "landlord" of many federal lands and waters and for decades the chief institutional home of American conservation. For many within the DOI, the war's acute need for resources confirmed the importance of conservation's central mission for the previous half century: careful and efficient resource planning. Indeed, the war showed how "deluded" the United States had been in previous decades about resource management, according to Secretary Ickes in 1942. The country had been on a wasteful spree of overuse of

---

[8] Gardiner Means et al., *Our National Resources: Facts and Problems, toward Full Use of Resources* (Washington, DC: National Resources Planning Board, 1940). For 1930s conservation, see Henry L. Henderson and David B. Woolner, *FDR and the Environment* (New York: Palgrave Macmillan, 2005); Paul Sutter, *Driven Wild: How the Fight against Automobiles Launched the Modern Wilderness Movement* (Seattle: University of Washington Press, 2002); Neil M. Maher, *Nature's New Deal: The Civilian Conservation Corps and the Roots of the American Environmental Movement* (New York: Oxford University Press, 2010); Robertson, *Malthusian Moment*, ch. 1.

water and forest and other resources, Ickes said, and now faced a "painful hangover." Pearl Harbor had profoundly shocked him:

We woke up to find out that we did not have enough steel to do the job; we did not have enough aluminum; we were short of power; we lacked magnesium; our sources of manganese were too far away to do us much good; our supply of timber and lumber did not hold out; our fisheries and other food resources could not be operated on the old basis nor supply enough to meet demand; our coal supply became endangered and the chaos of war tied our petroleum service up into knots.[9]

In response, the DOI organized "drastic action" to "utilize that which was within our reach." The department coordinated a national resource mobilization program to procure "the sinews for conflict – the metals, oil, power, fuel, helium, food, land, water, and timber available for war production." This campaign included an all-out drive to gather resources from around the nation, featuring "increased and hastened production in the mines and in the mills; in the factories and yards where metals are processed and fabricated into planes, tanks, and ships; in the forests, on irrigation projects producing food and in the metallurgical laboratories." It also pushed for the "discovery and exploration of new deposits of strategic and critical minerals."[10] This drastic action to create the sinews for conflict – all built around the conservationist idea of planned resource use – exacted a heavy toll from the nation's ecosystems.

The search for materials took place not only in American forests, farms, and mines (as described in Chapters 4 and 6) but also overseas, as natural resource mobilization turned increasingly global. Many "strategic materials" came from foreign lands. Ickes described "searching the earth for the minerals that were needed in ever-increasing quantities."[11] The 1942 rubber crisis illustrated the problem. When the Japanese seized control of British Malaysia in 1942, supplies of rubber dwindled. "Unless corrective measures are taken immediately," a US commission warned, the United States would face "both a military and a civilian collapse."[12] Similarly, in addition to rubber, a steady supply of new and often rare

[9] Department of Interior, *Annual Report, 1942* (Washington DC: Government Printing Office, 1942), iii.
[10] Ibid., iv.
[11] Department of Interior, *Annual Report, 1945* (Washington DC: Government Printing Office, 1945), v.
[12] Bernard M. Baruch, *Report of the Rubber Survey Committee* (Washington, DC: Government Printing Office, 1942), 5.

materials, such as uranium, was needed to feed the electronics, aviation, and atomic industries. Eventually, US planners compiled a list of 60 strategic resources, of which 30 came entirely from overseas, and took measures to guarantee their supply. Even after the war had ended, the United States continued to stockpile these 60 resources.[13]

As part of this effort to find and secure mineral supplies, geologists from the DOI's Office of Geologic Survey scoured the globe, armed with maps newly compiled by the Office of Geologic Survey.[14] The reach was global, but Latin America was a particular focus because of ample supplies of rubber, aluminum, oil, copper, and other crucial materials. To guarantee expanded supplies, the United States helped build roads and ports, and launched public health programs to enhance worker productivity. After the war, these programs formed the foundation of Point IV international development programs, Harry Truman's innovative economic development programs in the "third world."[15]

By the last year of the war, Ickes had grown distressed by the toll the war exacted from nature. While the DOI was searching for minerals and resources with "meticulous diligence," he noted, the nation was wasting them with "wanton prodigality" in disorganized efforts to fight the war. "The drain on our national natural assets," he stressed, "had been staggering." Indeed, in his view, the costs to nature threatened to turn the war effort into a "Pyrrhic" victory.[16]

Near the war's end, Ickes encouraged first President Roosevelt and later President Truman to organize a global conference on resource conservation, an idea most associated with Gifford Pinchot, a chief architect of early-twentieth-century conservation. As war was breaking out in the late 1930s, Pinchot called for something similar to what he had been championing for decades: the rational, efficient, and fair use of natural resources – now on a global scale – to prevent waste and to increase production. As it had earlier in the century, conservation planning could

---

[13] See John Davis Morgan Jr., *The Domestic Mining Industry of the United States in World War II* (Washington, DC: Government Printing Office, 1949) and Alfred E. Eckes, *The United States and the Global Struggle for Minerals* (Austin: University of Texas Press, 1979), 121–146.

[14] Department of Interior, *Annual Report, 1945*.

[15] Department of Interior, *Annual Report, 1941* (Washington DC: Government Printing Office, 1941), 227. In addition, the United States also helped with soil conservation and even national park programs. Hugh Bennett and soil conservationists provided American advice about soil erosion in 15 Central and South American countries.

[16] Department of Interior, *Annual Report, 1945*, v.

lend order, he believed, to an unruly system where the powerful monopolized resources.

Competition for natural resources, Pinchot believed, had ignited the war. "Since human history began," he wrote President Roosevelt, "the commonest cause of war has been the demand for land." This was because "no Nation is self-sufficient in all the natural resources its safety and prosperity require."[17] Other conservationists made similar arguments during the war, perhaps no one more forcefully than cartoonist Jay "Ding" Darling:

Japan couldn't feed her bulging population on the resources within the borders of her domain. Italy was half starving, by our standards, and had to reach for new resources beyond her legal boundaries. Germany demanded new territory in order that her expanding race could be fed. International burglary was only the instrument by which they sought to satisfy their needs for natural resources. We call it a war of dictatorship against democracy and ignore the fundamental pressure of hunger and depletion of human sustenance. More and more people cannot live on less and less any more than more and more cattle can live on a farm that grows smaller each year.[18]

To avoid more war, Darling, Pinchot, and Ickes believed, the United States had to create a system in which nations could easily and fairly procure the resources they needed (see Figure 12.1).

The core problem, Pinchot believed, was not a shortage of resources but waste and poor planning. "Needless waste or destruction of necessary resources anywhere," Pinchot wrote in 1940, "threatens ... the welfare and security of peoples everywhere."[19] Thus progressive rational planning of resources – "the planned and orderly use" of resources – could reduce global tensions. Pinchot urged Roosevelt to "guide all Nations toward the intelligent use of the earth."[20] This was traditional early-twentieth-century conservation applied worldwide.

Strikingly, as part of his conservation vision, Pinchot also advocated the fair distribution of resources, another core part of conservation. The postwar order must "assur[e] to each nation access to the raw materials it needs."[21] "Fair access" must be the standard. An international conference

---

[17] Gifford Pinchot to FDR, May 1945, Clark Clifford Papers, Presidential Speech File, Box 38, Point IV-Miscellaneous Folder, Harry S. Truman Library (hereafter HSTL).

[18] Darling quoted in Walter P. Taylor, "Conservation and War," *Nature* 37 (January 1944), 42.

[19] Gifford Pinchot, "Conservation as a Foundation of Permanent Peace," *Nature* 146 (August 10, 1940): 184.

[20] Gifford Pinchot to FDR, May 1945.

[21] Gifford Pinchot, "Conservation as a Foundation of Permanent Peace," 184.

FIGURE 12.1 "Ding" Darling, "Speaking of Labor Day" (1939).
Source: Reproduced courtesy of the "Ding" Darling Wildlife Society

could create "a set of principles for securing fair access to necessary raw materials by all Nations."[22] "The Conservation problem," Pinchot added in 1945, "is concerned not only with the natural resources of the earth.... Rightly understood, it includes also the relation of these resources and of their abundance or scarcity to the distribution of peoples over the earth, to the strength or weakness of Nations, to their leaning towards war or toward peace, and to the misery or prosperity, the constant dread or confident security, of their inhabitants."[23]

Ickes pushed for Pinchot's conservation vision. In May 1945, he strongly recommended Pinchot's conference to Truman, noting that President Roosevelt had "expressed himself as favorable to the idea." Ickes highlighted how the war had damaged resources: "The war has taken a heavy toll of the forests, the oil, the coal, and the iron and other metals, and has added to the already heavy depletion of soil resources." Moreover, he stressed, the upcoming years would see a heavy burden on nature because rebuilding war-torn areas would require "great quantities of raw

[22] Gifford Pinchot, "World Conference on the Conservation of Natural Resources," March 28, 1945, Clark Clifford Papers, Presidential Speech File, Box 38, Point IV-Miscellaneous Folder, HSTL, 3.
[23] Gifford Pinchot to FDR, May 1945.

materials, especially of timber, iron, and other building materials." Ickes therefore recommended that the United States undertake "an all-out attack, *far more comprehensive* than anything visualized in the past, against the unnecessary depletion of the world's resources and for their conservation and development."[24]

Truman endorsed some – but, crucially, not all – of Pinchot's vision. In early June 1945, Truman wrote that he was "deeply interested in this subject."[25] A year later, in September 1946, he publicly called for an international conservation conference. "Warfare," he wrote to the US representative at the United Nations, "has taken a heavy toll of many natural resources; the rebuilding of the nations and the industrialization of underdeveloped areas will require an additional large depletion of them."[26] In calling for the conference, Truman echoed conservation's traditional emphasis on waste and the greater good, only this time in a global context. "Waste, destruction and uneconomic use of resources anywhere," he warned, "damage mankind's common estate." Natural resource competition had fueled war: "The real or exaggerated fear of resource shortages and declining standards of living has in the past involved nations in warfare." The need for this kind of conference, he announced, was "never greater."

But Truman said little about Pinchot's vision of equal access to resources, a position that grew harder to support as the Cold War with the Soviet Union, an ally during the war, intensified in the late 1940s.[27] And indeed, despite nominal support for traditional conservation concerns, Truman also helped create a high-consumption, progrowth capitalist economy, both at home and globally, that struck some critics as unsustainable. This progrowth economic system had emerged during the war and even worked its way into traditional realms of conservationist thinking, such as forestry and water. It formed the basis of the second strand of conservation described in this article and came in part from the triumph of consumption-based Keynesian economics, which moved from pump priming to a

---

[24] Harold L. Ickes to Harry Truman, May 31, 1945, Oscar Chapman Papers, Box 60, International Resource Conference Folder, HSTL. Emphasis added.

[25] Harry Truman to Harold L. Ickes, June 6, 1945, Oscar Chapman Papers, Box 60, International Resource Conference Folder, HSTL.

[26] Harry Truman to John G. Winant, US Representative to the United Nations Economic and Social Council, September 4, 1946, Official File 85DD, HSTL. Also see John S. Winant to Dr. Stamper, UN Economic and Social Council, September 13, 1946, Official File 85DD, HSTL.

[27] Harry Truman to John G. Winant.

permanent growth-based economy during the 1940s. It also reflected a shift within many conservation circles to a technology-driven growth agenda. Understanding this second strand of thinking requires understanding the technology-based resource development approach embraced by conservationists such as David Lilienthal and Julius Krug.

PLANNING FOR PRODUCTION: CONSERVATION BECOMES DEVELOPMENT

As Pinchot and Ickes were lobbying for more efficient planning of resources according to traditional conservation goals, other conservationists were headed in a new and different direction, much more focused on technology-driven planned economic development. Early-twentieth-century conservation had never been about locking up resources. It focused on preventing the *misuse* of natural resources, not preventing the *use* of resources. "The planned and orderly development and conservation of our natural resources," Pinchot had written in 1910, "is the first duty of the United States."[28] But planning had involved a delicate balancing between conservation and development. As the twentieth century unfolded, however, and especially during and after World War II, the balance tilted far more toward production, so much so that, for the proponents of this second strand of conservation in the late 1940s and 1950s, conservation began to denote development. Indeed, this new strand of conservationism informed some of the nation's biggest advocates of and planners for economic development. In part this shift included a new emphasis on increased production, especially for war products needed by the military. In part it grew from increasingly powerful forms of technology and increasingly efficient forms of state management. In the process, conservation lost many of its early concerns with democratic fairness and environmental sustainability in favor of technology-driven growth. It was this more active and single-minded concern with encouraging economic development, not just discouraging poor development, that increasingly dominated wartime and postwar programs.[29]

---

[28] Gifford Pinchot, *The Fight for Conservation* (New York: Doubleday, Page & Co., 1910), 20.

[29] Robertson, *Malthusian Moment*. Also see Clayton Koppes, "Environmental Policy and American Liberalism: The Department of the Interior, 1933–1953," *Environmental Review* 7, no. 1 (1983): 17–53; Sarah T. Phillips, *This Land, This Nation: Conservation, Rural America, and the New Deal* (New York: Cambridge University Press, 2007).

This shift toward greater production can be seen in the wartime management of the country's forestry sector, the birthplace of traditional conservation planning in the early twentieth century under Gifford Pinchot. On the one hand, World War II helped to institutionalize Pinchot-style conservation practices, as seen in the vast expansion of industrial tree farms aimed at planned efficient production. The war, pointed out William Greeley, the former head of the Forest Service, "has brought to fruition long-range federal policies in the management of public timber, to encourage sustained-yield forestry operations by private owners.... The temporary forest economy of a pioneer country is gradually being replaced by a permanent forest economy."[30] But, on the other hand, the widespread adoption of scientific forestry went hand in hand with another crucially important development: new technologies that spurred a vast expansion of production. In the Pacific Northwest, for instance, 102 obsolete mills had been replaced during the war by 139 new ones. Equipped with modern technology, the new mills jacked up capacity by an astonishing 350 million board feet. "Without the stimulus of the war and government support," historian Richard Tucker has argued, "neither the Forest Service nor industry could have achieved this expansion of production."[31]

A similar revolution in production and technology remade wartime agriculture. Whereas a decade earlier agricultural conservation meant soil conservation measures, such as contour plowing, during World War II the focus turned to applying fertilizers, and even chemical fertilizers, in the name of restoring and maintaining soil productivity. As Kendra Smith-Howard notes in her article in this volume (Chapter 5), fertilizer use shot up during the war: use of nitrates, phosphate, and potash was 95 percent higher in 1945 than between 1935–1939.[32] "Fertilizers," a 1946 government report explained, "are of greater importance to

---

[30] W. B. Greeley, "Lumber Looks Out of the Foxholes," *Journal of Forestry* 43, no. 9 (September 1945): 799. See also Gerald D. Nash, *World War II and the West: Reshaping the Economy* (Lincoln: University of Nebraska Press, 1990), chs. 3–4; Richard A. Rajala, *Clearcutting the Pacific Rain Forest: Production, Science, and Regulation* (Vancouver: University of British Columbia Press, 1998).

[31] Richard P. Tucker, "The World Wars and the Globalization of Timber Cutting," in *Natural Enemy, Natural Ally: Toward an Environmental History of Warfare*, ed. Edmund Russell and Richard P. Tucker (Corvallis: Oregon State University Press, 2004), 128.

[32] Smith-Howard cites US Congress, House Committee on Appropriations, Hearings on Agriculture Department Appropriation Bill, 1947 (Washington, DC: Government Printing Office, 1946), 248.

agriculture now than ever before." This was because the war had "created increased demands on this country for food, feed, and other crops and at the same time took part of the best manpower off the farm."[33] At the core of this updated conservation was a faith in technology that saw adding chemicals to the soil as restorative, not destructive. Fertilizers, a TVA official explained shortly after the war, could create "a more stable and balanced relationship between modern man and the earth – a relationship in which science and technology will play an increasing role."[34] Though in subsequent decades most environmentalists would see the reliance on chemicals as ecologically damaging, at this juncture in conservation's history, it was conservationists who pushed the use of chemical fertilizers.

At the Department of Interior, Ickes began to notice a shift away from sustainable practices toward what he called a "conservation-and-development program."[35] By the end of the war, as Clayton Koppes has argued, DOI documents revealed two important value shifts: first, economic expansion had replaced the prewar focus on economic fairness and, second, material abundance and increased production had replaced other values such as community cohesion and aesthetic appeal.[36] Family farms were seen as uneconomical compared to big producers, and in public waters social fairness gave way to a drive for high fishing yields. Increasingly, those who held more traditional conservation views combining resource development with goals like fairness or sustainability either shifted their views or left the agency. Ickes resigned in February 1946.

Perhaps nowhere was this emphasis on planning for production more visible than in the DOI's Bureau of Reclamation. In the early twentieth century, the bureau, like the US Forest Service, had been a fountain of conservationist thinking. But during the war, its mission increasingly focused on ramping up electricity production. According to Reclamation Commissioner Harold Bashore in 1942, the bureau oversaw a "spectacular expansion" in electricity-generating facilities and, in the process, became the world's largest power producer. Within a short time after

---

[33] A. L. Mehring, Hilda M. Wallace, and Mildred Drain, *Consumption and Trends in the Use of Fertilizer in the Year Ended June 30, 1944* (Washington, DC: US Department of Agriculture, 1946), 2.

[34] James Rorty, "Soil ... people, and fertilizer technology," published by the Tennessee Valley Authority (Washington, DC: Government Printing Office, 1949), 2.

[35] Department of Interior, *Annual Report, 1945*, xi.

[36] Clayton R. Koppes, "Environmental Policy and American Liberalism: The Department of the Interior, 1933–1953," *Environmental Review* 7, no. 1 (April 1983): 25.

Pearl Harbor, power generation at bureau dams had quadrupled to 14 billion kilowatt-hours a year, mostly for war industries.[37] The new mindset was epitomized by David Lilienthal, chairman of the TVA. Lilienthal clearly thought of the TVA as a conservation project, as it had in fact been intended in 1933. "Resource development," he wrote in 1944, "must be governed by the unity of nature herself."[38] But increasingly he emphasized unbridled faith in the potential of technology: "I believe in the great potentialities for well-being of the machine and technology and science."[39] His writings from 1944 show the mix of technological optimism and bureaucratic faith that defined his brand of conservation:

There is almost nothing, however fantastic, that (given competent organization) a team of engineers, scientists, and administrators cannot do today. Impossible things can be done, are being done in this mid-20th century. Today it is builders and technicians that we turn to: men armed not with the ax, rifle, and bowie knife, but with the Diesel engine, the bulldozer, the giant electric shovel, the retort – and most of all, with an emerging kind of skill, a modern knack of organization and execution. When these men have imagination and faith, they can move mountains; out of their skills they can create new jobs, relieve human drudgery, give new life and fruitfulness to worn-out lands, put yokes upon the streams, and transmute the minerals of the earth and the plants of the field into machines of wizardry to spin out the stuff of a way of life new to this world.[40]

Another influential proponent of this new kind of conservation, which stressed the power of technology to spur greater production, was Julius Krug, secretary of the interior under President Truman from 1946 to 1949. Krug had worked for the TVA during the late 1930s and during the war led efforts to expand dam production as the director of the power branch at the War Production Board (WPB) and later as its overall director. Testifying before Congress in January 1948, Secretary Krug reinforced Truman's call for economic growth on a global scale: "An all out production drive here and in the rest of the world is needed at this time."[41]

In 1949, at the UN conference on conservation in Lake Success, New York, the global conference that grew out of Pinchot's lobbying efforts

---

[37] Harold Bashore, "Report from Harold Bashore, Commissioner of the Bureau of Reclamation" in Department of Interior, *Annual Report, 1941*, 10.

[38] David Lilienthal, *TVA: Democracy on the March* (New York: Harper & Brothers, 1944), 6.

[39] Ibid., xii.   [40] Ibid., 3.

[41] Statement by the President on Receiving Secretary Krug's Report "National Resources and Foreign Aid," October 18, 1947 in *Public Papers of the Presidents of the United States: Harry S. Truman*, vol. 3 (Washington, DC: Government Printing Office, 1966), 474.

during the war, Krug signaled his new thinking by calling for a "new era" in conservation. Until then, he pointed out, conservation had been "largely negative." Earlier conservationists such as Theodore Roosevelt had "dramatized the waste and damage which have resulted from exploitation." But early conservationists did not put forward "constructive ideas as to how we should find the wherewithal to satisfy our ever-increasing needs for the fuels, energy, materials and foods which are the basis of a sound standard of living." Shortly thereafter, Krug wrote Secretary of State Dean Acheson, "Ways must be found for basic development of land and water resources, power and transportation upon which comprehensive and balanced economic progress of an area depend." "Wealth," he emphasized, "is created only by increasing production."[42] For conservationists like Lilienthal and Krug, the Depression-era sense of limits had passed. In its place, a protechnology, growth-based vision of conservation planning very different from traditional Pinchot-style conservation emerged.[43]

TOTAL WAR AND THE EXPANSION OF ENVIRONMENTAL KNOWLEDGE

Meanwhile, a shift in governmental approach toward nature was underway that would have far-reaching consequences. As the war lengthened and broadened, the state involved itself with far more activities involving nature than just the guaranteeing of resource supplies, as important and far-reaching as that was. Because of the imperatives of total war on a global scale, the US government vastly increased the extent to which it studied, planned, and engineered landscapes at home and abroad. It organized a concerted drive – pursued with mushrooming research budgets – to expand and improve knowledge about nature, particularly

---

[42] *Proceedings of the United Nations Scientific Conference on the Conservation and Utilization of Resources*, vol. 1 (Lake Success, NY: United Nations Department of Economic Affairs, 1950), 7; Krug to Acheson, November 30, 1949, UN Scientific Conference Folder, Box 76, Julius Krug Papers, Library of Congress; *Proceedings of the United Nations Scientific Conference on the Conservation and Utilization of Resources*, vol. 1, 6. For an insightful analysis of this conference, see Jundt, "Dueling Visions for the Postwar World." My argument in this chapter largely aligns with Jundt's views, although he seems to suggest that capitalistic motives drove conservation before and after the war, while I point out that conservation was transformed by the war.

[43] Gerald Nash has argued that for many Americans the war refuted Depression-era pessimism. Limits had not been reached. Gerald Nash, "Comment," *Environmental Review* 7, no. 1 (April 1983): 42–47.

the earth sciences such as geography, geology, biology, and meteorology, not just regarding domestic landscapes but also far off ecosystems. Fighting a global, multifront war from the South Pacific to the Arctic and from the Western Pacific to Central Europe required new information, new planning tools, new logistics and transportation methods, and new engineering solutions. These efforts not only spawned a growing body of knowledge but also armies of trained experts. The consequences added up. The new knowledge and new institutions formed an intellectual foundation not just for more exploitation and manipulation of nature but also, eventually, for better understanding the harmful consequences of doing so.

In other words, World War II vastly expanded the "environmental-management state." As Paul Sutter and Adam Rome and others have defined it, the environmental-management state refers to government's role as manager of nature, where "nature" includes not just resources but also everything from weather to waste, and "managing" entailed not just use but also knowledge gathering and protection.[44] Environmental-management entailed far more than explicit programs to protect nature. "Environmental management," Sutter points out, "expands attention beyond conservation, preservation, and environmental regulation to include a broader array of statist activities in areas such as agriculture, science and engineering, public health, internal improvement, warfare and national defense, and international relations."[45] Indeed, the environmental-management state has generally grown alongside US expansion, including overseas expansion. "Environmental management," Sutter observes, "has been central to American expansion from early federal land policy to the management of extra-continental imperial holdings to Cold War–era development efforts around the world."[46]

World War II significantly expanded the American environmental-management state, with important consequences for nature and conservation. The war pushed the US government to expand its coordination and planning of nature in quantity, geographic reach, and intensity. The

---

[44] The environmental-management state is similar to what political historian Bruce Shulman has called the "resource management state" but broader. Paul S. Sutter, "The World with Us: The State of American Environmental History," *Journal of American History* 100, no. 1 (June 1, 2013): 100. For earlier European antecedents, see Richard Grove, *Green Imperialism: Colonial Expansion, Tropical Island Edens, and the Origins of Environmentalism, 1600–1860* (Cambridge: Cambridge University Press, 1995); Peder Anker, *Imperial Ecology: Environmental Order in the British Empire, 1895–1945* (Cambridge, MA: Harvard University Press, 2009).

[45] Sutter, The World with Us," 100.   [46] Ibid.

government became far more involved with far more aspects of nature in far more ecosystems across the country and the planet than ever before. World War II elevated environmental planning to a top priority, well beyond what Theodore Roosevelt, Gifford Pinchot, or even the New Deal had done. If the Depression had pushed the US government to experiment with new regional approaches to resource planning such the TVA, World War II called for extending and institutionalizing such planning on a national and even global scale. As World War II slipped into the Cold War and war mobilization became a permanent feature of American society, the institutions and practices of the environmental-management state also became permanent. The National Security State overlapped in significant ways with the environmental-management state.[47]

The expansion of the environment management state should not at all be confused with becoming an "environmentalist" state with the primary goal of protecting nature, which it decidedly did not become. But, that said, the expansion of the environmental-management state did help create government structures and knowledges that, in some surprising ways, laid a foundation for the environmental movement of the 1960s and 1970s.

For instance, the governmental effort to generate and collect more environmental knowledge during the war profoundly expanded knowledge about places within the United States – for instance, knowledge about Alaska and the Arctic. "We have had meager experience in military operations in the Frigid Zone," wrote US Army Air Corps Chief H. H. (Hap) Arnold in 1940, after an Alaskan tour. To construct and maintain bases effectively, he stressed, American military officials needed to "know considerably more than we did" about the region. Arnold called for distilling the insights of explorer Vilhjalmur Stefansson's 15-volume report on Arctic aviation for ordinary soldiers.[48] Once war broke out, the army called on well-known northern explorers to research cold weather fighting and gear. Additional research grew out of Fort Knox and the army's new Climatic

---

[47] See, for instance, Thomas Robertson, "'This Is the American Earth': American Empire, the Cold War, and American Environmentalism," *Diplomatic History* 32, no. 4 (2008): 561–584; Simone Turchetti and Peder Roberts, *The Surveillance Imperative: Geosciences during the Cold War and Beyond* (New York: Palgrave Macmillan, 2014). Turchetti and Roberts write, "the transformation that took place during the Cold War involved putting the *entire earth* under surveillance, altering the scope, the nature, and above all the extent of scientific interrogation of the planet and its environs" (p. 1).

[48] Major General H. H. Arnold, "Our Air Frontier in Alaska," *National Geographic*, October 1940, 488; and Arnold, *Global Mission* (New York: Harper, 1949), 211–212, as cited in Matthew Farish, "The Lab and the Land: Overcoming the Arctic in Cold War Alaska," *Isis* 104, no. 1 (2013): 9.

Research Laboratory in Lawrence, Massachusetts. The Department of Interior's Office of Geologic Survey also got into the act, conducting extensive mapping programs in Alaska. In addition, the newly formed Arctic Institute of North America, established by a group of explorers and scientists, pushed for in-depth research on arctic areas, and won substantial funding from the military.[49] The war encouraged a similar expansion of research in tropical, coastal, and desert areas.

During the war years, the United States also began to study and map much of the world, with greater coverage and greater detail. It invested heavily in aerial reconnaissance and photography. Map-making missions spread out across the world. Geologists with the Military Geology Unit, part of the Military Intelligence Division, traveled to combat zones in Europe and the South Pacific to prepare operational intelligence and provide scientific advice.[50] Bureau of Mine engineers mapped resources in Latin America as well as, in 1945, newly liberated areas.[51] DOI engineers visited possible dam sites in China's Yangtze River gorge and in India and the Middle East.[52] It was during these years that the DOI grew surprisingly focused on the nation's "exterior" (prompting Megan Black's wonderfully titled article "Interior's Exterior").[53] Other departments, such as the Department of Commerce and the US Department of Agriculture, not to mention the various military services, also vastly expanded their overseas programs.

An important part of this overseas research examined public health. Winning the war meant not only getting enough supplies to soldiers in far-flung battlefields but also keeping them healthy. Doing so in arctic and tropical environments posed unusual challenges. Early in the war in the South Pacific, more US soldiers were incapacitated at the hands of mosquitoes than at the hands of the Japanese. As a result, a "public health war" emerged deploying new tools such as DDT. Fighting a global, total war meant thinking not just about supplying an army overseas but also keeping it whole and healthy, and this led to many new technologies, new programs, and ultimately new forms of expertise.[54]

---

[49] Farish, "The Lab and the Land," 10.
[50] Department of Interior, *Annual Report, 1941*, 111.
[51] Department of Interior, *Annual Report, 1945*, 97.   [52] Ibid., 37.
[53] Megan Black, "Interior's Exterior: The State, Mining Companies, and Resource Ideologies in the Point Four Program," *Diplomatic History* 40, no. 1 (2016): 81–110.
[54] For DDT, see Martha Gardner's essay in this volume (Chapter 10) and David Kinkela, *DDT and the American Century: Global Health, Environmental Politics, and the Pesticide That Changed the World* (Chapel Hill: University of North Carolina Press, 2011).

As the DDT example suggests, the wartime government vastly expanded its exploration and mapping of a whole new range of landscapes: the landscape of cells, molecules, and subatomic particles. During the war, government-funded scientists explored these new realms of human knowledge much the same way US government–funded geologists, botanists, and soldiers explored the US West during the nineteenth century. While some of these fields were well established by the time of the war, others such as subatomic physics were relatively new. Either way, studying these new landscape layers got a huge boost from wartime research and development.

In sum, during the 1940s, governmental capacity and wartime imperatives to manage nature coevolved: the control of nature expanded the scale and intensity of government, and, conversely, government expanded the scale and intensity with which people controlled nature.[55] A surprising amount of what government did in these years involved environmental management and much of what happened with nature often involved governmental action. Such activities would only expand during the Cold War.

As the environmental-management state grew during the 1940s, a third strand of new thinking emerged about how to protect nature: "proto environmentalist" thinking. These new ideas came from people who worked directly for the environmental-management state, or were former soldiers, or were otherwise responding to wartime changes in significant ways.[56] Within this third strand of thinking, three separate but overlapping concerns emerged.

"KILLING WILDERNESS": WAR AND ANTIMODERNISM BEFORE HIROSHIMA

The first concern was antimodernism, a profound unease with urban, technology-based civilization. Historians have long recognized the role that antimodernism has played in the American environmental thinking of the 1950s and 1960s. However, they have rarely noted how important

---

[55] Here I am adapting Edmund Russell's formulation: "War and nature coevolved.... The control of nature expanded the scale of war, and war expanded the scale on which people controlled nature." Edmund Russell, *War and Nature: Fighting Humans and Insects with Chemicals from World War I to Silent Spring* (New York: Cambridge University Press, 2001), 2.

[56] Similarly, the expansion of the British Empire created conditions in which early conservation views developed. Grove, *Green Imperialism.*

World War II was to sowing its seeds. The war fueled a view of man as inherently destructive that profoundly shaped views toward nature after the war. Antimodernism had existed in pockets of American society since the nineteenth century, especially in elite circles. But after World War II it spread widely among the American middle class. The war's promotion of antimodern thinking can be seen in the lives and thoughts of several influential individuals: famed naturalist Aldo Leopold; Fairfield Osborn, the director of the New York Zoological Society and author of *Our Plundered Planet* (1948); Walt Disney, the creator of *Bambi* (1942); writer and naturalist Joseph Wood Krutch; and the already mentioned Sierra Club executive director David Brower.

Few people influenced postwar American thinking about nature more than Aldo Leopold. Leopold is credited with infusing conservation with the principles of ecology, which had gained a foothold in academia in the 1930s. We rarely realize, however, how much his thinking was shaped by the war. As a forest service officer in the 1910s, Leopold had first seen how profoundly far off war could touch American landscapes, and in the late 1930s, as war clouds gathered over Europe, he articulated an anti-modern view that increasingly defined humans as destructive and nature as innocent. A dark tone crept into his writings. His path-breaking 1939 essay "A Biotic View of Land," for instance, written when war was unfolding in Europe, displayed deep unease with the violence of humans toward the earth. Indeed, for Leopold, nothing defined human relations with nature more than violence. "Man's invention of tools," he wrote, "has enabled him to make changes of unprecedented violence." Accordingly, modern life raised two fundamental questions for nature. First, can the land adjust? And second, "Can violence be reduced?" The central work of conservation, he concluded, was to reduce violence. Conservation, he wrote, should lead us "toward a nonviolent land use" (see Figure 12.2)[57]

Director of the Bronx Zoo Fairfield Osborn also began during the war to associate humans with violence and nature with peacefulness. Whereas prewar museums, zoos, and films had often juxtaposed the violence of nature – nature "red in tooth and claw" – with the basic benevolence of human beings, during the war Osborn began to depict human beings as essentially brutal and nature as essentially peaceful. During "an hour of recreation, snatched from these troubled days," he noted at the opening

[57] Leopold, "Biotic View," 728–729.

FIGURE 12.2 "Ding" Darling, "The Ascent of Man–Final Stage" (1941).
Source: Reproduced courtesy of the "Ding" Darling Wildlife Society

ceremony of a new zoo exhibit in 1941, visitors would be "refreshed" for a while from "the spectacle of Man's cruel and needless destruction of himself." "We should have no patience," he explained, "with those unthinking persons who rant that Man, in his present cruelties, is reverting to primitive nature – to the so-called law of the jungle. No greater falsehood could be spoken. Nature knows no such horrors."[58]

Osborn often reiterated such views. "Nature knows nothing comparable to war's destruction," he wrote in 1942. "Her ways are more balanced. They provide no injustices so sudden or so bitter. Combat among other living things is, with rare exceptions, neither so general

[58] Osborn, "The New York Zoological Park," *Science* 93 (May 16, 1941): 467. Gregg Mitman makes a similar point in reference to Osborn, in Gregg Mitman, *Reel Nature: America's Romance with Wildlife on Films* (Cambridge, MA: Harvard University Press, 1999), 86. Also see Gregg Mitman, *The State of Nature: Ecology, Community, and American Social Thought* (Chicago: University of Chicago University Press, 1992), 146–201.

nor so ruthless as that in which man engages."[59] Later in the war, Osborn even attacked political cartoons depicting Japanese soldiers as gorillas – not for dehumanizing the Japanese, but for *humanizing* the gorillas. Gorillas, he felt, were being unfairly tarred with the violence of humans.[60] (As with gorillas, the flipping of views about human society during the war also led to a reappraisal of Neanderthals, another group once seen as inherently violent.)[61]

Indeed, during the war, Osborn began to reframe conservation in terms of violence and peacefulness, just as Leopold had. "Conservation," he wrote in 1944, "may be thought of as a symbol – *a symbol of kindliness* which, denied for the moment as between man and man, can be extended to other living things, mute and without anger."[62] In the widely read *Our Plundered Planet* (1948), Osborn devoted a full chapter to describing man's evolution as a violent predator and destroyer. "The uncomfortable truth," he summarized, "is that man during innumerable past ages has been a predator – a hunter, a meat eater and a killer."[63]

One of the most influential people to share this view was Walt Disney, the filmmaker who left a tremendous imprint on the postwar generation. Disney developed *Bambi* (1942), one of the most culturally important films of subsequent decades, from 1937 to 1942 as war was breaking out in Europe.[64] As Matt Cartmill has shown, the war deeply influenced Disney's depiction of nature and technology in the film. Although the 1920s book contained many examples of one animal killing another, in the late 1930s, as Europe careened toward war, one by one Disney eliminated all predators from the film's forest. In the final version, only one predator remained: Man. Whenever "Man" stepped into the forest, he and his tools – guns, dogs, and fire – did little except wreak

---

[59] Osborn, "The Lesson Not Yet Learned," *Bulletin of the NYZS* 45, no. 5 (September–October 1942): 137.

[60] Osborn, "The Cartoonists' Gorilla," *Animal Kingdom: Bulletin of the NYZS* 46, no. 3 (May–June 1943), 49.

[61] As Elizabeth Kolbert explains, "World War II – not to mention World War I – had shown the sort of brutishness the most modern of modern humans were capable of, and Neanderthals were due for a reappraisal." Elizabeth Kolbert, *The Sixth Extinction: An Unnatural History* (New York: Harry Holt & Co., 2014), 243.

[62] Osborn, "Conservation and War," *Bulletin of the NYZS* 47, no. 3 (May–June 1944): 49. The turn-of-the-century conservationist John Muir also thought of humans as inherently destructive.

[63] Fairfield Osborn, *Our Plundered Planet* (Boston: Little, Brown & Co., 1948), 146.

[64] Disney was not a soldier, but volunteered as an ambulance driver in World War I. See Steven Watts, *The Magic Kingdom: Walt Disney and the American Way of Life* (Boston: Houghton Mifflin, 1997).

environmental terror.[65] Like Osborn, Disney showed that many Americans had begun to display strong antimodernist feelings well before nuclear attack on Japan in August 1945.[66]

This shift mattered. It signaled the ascendance of a central characteristic of postwar environmentalism, the idea of man as a destroyer. Perhaps no one summed up the idea better than Joseph Wood Krutch, a nature writer and philosopher widely read in the 1950s and 1960s. In a 1954 essay, "Conservation Is Not Enough," Krutch called for new ways to protect nature by emphasizing how violence defined human relations with nature: "It is not only the members of his own kind that man seems to want to push off the earth. When he moves in, nearly everything else that lives suffers from his intrusion - sometimes because he wants the space it occupies and the food it eats, but often simply because when he sees a creature not of his kind or a man not of his race, his first impulse is 'Kill it.'"[67]

Few articulated this vehement antimodernism more influentially than David Brower, a World War II veteran and the person most responsible for widening the Sierra Club's political base in the 1950s and 1960s. As a soldier in the 10th Mountain Division, a unit composed of a large number of skiers and outdoorsmen, Brower saw combat in Italy in 1945. His division suffered horrible violence. Although in combat for only 130 days, roughly 1,000 of the Division's 14,000 troops were killed, including some of Brower's Sierra Club friends. Another four thousand were injured. Stationed in Italy's northern mountains for three months after the war's end, Brower had time to explore, and came away deeply disillusioned. He described his feelings in a *Sierra Club Bulletin* article titled, perhaps not coincidentally, "How to Kill a Wilderness": "In such parts of the mountains of Italy, Austria, Switzerland, and Jugoslavia as I have been able to observe are the shattered remains of what must have been beautiful wildernesses. These wild places had their one-time inaccessibility to defend them – their precipices, mountain torrents, their glaciers and

[65] Matt Cartmill, *A View to a Death in the Morning: Hunting and Nature through History* (Cambridge, MA: Harvard University Press, 1993), 161–188.
[66] Also see Ralph Lutts, "The Trouble with *Bambi*: Walt Disney's Bambi and the American Vision of Nature," *Forest and Conservation History* 36 (October 1992): 160–172; and Thomas Robertson, "The Wonderful World of Walt Disney: Nature and Nation in *Bambi* and the 'True Life' Adventures" (MA thesis, University of Wisconsin, Madison, 1999).
[67] Joseph Wood Krutch, "Conservation Is Not Enough," *The American Scholar* 23, no. 3 (1954): 295.

forests. But they lost their immunity; they felt the ravages of a conqueror. And now they're dead."[68] With these words, one biographer noted, "David Brower's fifty-five-year run as point man and conscience of the conservation movement had begun."[69] In 1947 Brower participated in one of his first actions to protect wilderness areas, an effort to stop development of the 11,000-foot San Gorgonio Mountain near Palm Springs, California.

Twenty years later, as the 1960s environmental movement gained steam, Brower again stressed humanity's brutal essence. "Man can undo himself with no other force than his own brutality," he wrote in 1968, not coincidentally a moment when Americans were troubled by another brutal overseas war. "It is a new brutality," he said, then seconded a fellow activist's call for humans to become "a gentler race."[70]

PRODUCTION IS DESTRUCTION: GLOBAL RESOURCE EXHAUSTION AND HUMAN SURVIVAL

A second strand of this new more environmentalist thinking about conservation was concern about overconsumption, resource limits, and environmental degradation. For many Americans, including conservationists like David Lilienthal, the war years kindled an optimistic sense of possibility. With the right planning and technology, Americans could create a new era of growth and abundance. For others, however, the war confirmed and extended the more pessimistic sense of limits that the Depression had fostered. For these conservationists, the war showed that global limits had been reached, and that the resulting poverty and resource competition had fueled conflict and violence. Worse, more war lay ahead. Indeed, humanity's very survival stood at risk. These "limits to growth" conservationists echoed and amplified the closing frontier logic that informed turn-of-the-century conservation and 1930s New Deal conservation, but they applied this logic on a global scale and with new near apocalyptic pessimism.

---

[68] Tom Turner, *David Brower: The Man and the Environmental Movement* (Oakland: University of California Press, 2015), 48. Also see David Brower, *For Earth's Sake: The Life and Times of David Brower* (Salt Lake City, UT: Peregrine Smith Books, 1990), 125–127.
[69] Turner, *David Brower*, 48.
[70] David Brower, "Foreword," in *The Population Bomb*, ed. Paul Ehrlich (New York: Sierra Club-Ballantine Books, 1968), xiii.

Driving this analysis was a novel way of understanding resources. The new logic stressed not just the quantity of resources but also their quality, and not just production but also consumption. Resources were not just running out but additionally being degraded, especially by overconsumption and powerful technologies. Degradation and limits combined to create a sense of crisis. This was the birth of apocalyptic environmentalism.

One of the first to make such an argument was Aldo Leopold, who during the war saw many current and former students and two sons join the service. In a 1941 lecture to his University of Wisconsin students called "Ecology and Politics," Leopold explained the outbreak of war through the lens of ecology, population growth, and unsustainable consumption. "One of the most emphatic lessons of ecology," he began, "is that animal populations are usually self-limiting." "Overpopulated" Europe had approached these limits: "Perhaps the present world-revolution is the sign that we have exceeded that limit, or that we have approached it too rapidly." Leopold offered a similar ecological explanation of the war in a 1943 essay: "Do human populations have behavior patterns of which we are unaware, but which we help to execute? Are mobs and wars, unrests and revolutions, cut of such cloth?"[71]

These points informed Leopold's famous 1944 essay "Thinking Like a Mountain," one of the most influential environmental essays of the post-war decades. Written to explain how his thinking had evolved from his early experience implementing the traditional conservation goal of efficient production in Gifford Pinchot's forest service, the essay mixes in the war's tone and its environmental messages. Essentially, the essay is a rewritten version of his seminal 1939 essay "A Biotic View," which warns of population growth, overconsumption, natural limits, and ecological degradation, told through a story of his early days in the US West. To show how a conservation program to extirpate wolf and increase the number of deer had backfired, Leopold paints a vivid picture of a deer irruption, overconsumption, ecological degradation, and population crash, culminating in a landscape littered with "the starved bones of the hoped-for deer herd, dead of its own too-much." Instead of focusing on one or two

---

[71] Leopold, "Ecology and Politics," undated, I, LP, 10-6, 16. Reprinted in *The River of the Mother of God and Other Essays by Aldo Leopold*, ed. Susan Flader and J. Baird Callicott (Madison: University of Wisconsin Press, 1991), 281–286; Leopold, "Wildlife in American Culture," *Journal of Wildlife Management* 7, no. 1 (January 1943): 5–6. See Robertson, *Malthusian Moment*, ch. 2.

desirable species, Leopold stressed, land managers must learn to think more "like a mountain" – to manage for the long-term perspective ecological health of the land and the entire ecosystem.[72] The essay contains only one explicit reference to World War II, a quick mention of the dangers of "peace in our time" in the final paragraph, but the war context was clear. More important were the essay's larger themes: that human interventions in nature inevitably backfire, and that a population unmindful of its resource base can die of "its own too much." "Thinking Like a Mountain" was published in the late 1940s, at a moment when the recent global conflagration was on everyone's mind, and gained its greatest popularity in the 1960s and 1970s, at a moment of another American war, and another moment of profound worry about overpopulation.

By the time he wrote "Thinking Like a Mountain," Leopold had also begun to worry about the global spread of destructive American economic practices. "The impending industrialization of the world, now foreseen by everyone," he wrote in *Audubon* in 1944, "means that many conservation problems heretofore local will shortly become global." He worried for nature: "No one has yet asked whether the industrial communities which we intend to plant in the new and naked lands are more valuable, or less valuable, than the indigenous fauna and flora which they, to a large extent, displace and disrupt."[73]

The war also spurred Fairfield Osborn to believe that humanity threatened its very survival by destroying its resource base. A former businessman well aware of global resource flows, Osborn realized during the war that society was destroying the material foundation it stood upon. In 1944, he started warning of humanity's "destruction of the living resources of nature." The damage to resources was "infinitely greater" than generally believed, and that humanity's "own existence" was at risk. This was well before the atomic explosions at Hiroshima and Nagasaki. He started writing *Our Plundered Planet* at this time.[74] He started calling for a new broader conservation. In earlier decades, he said, conservation groups

[72] Aldo Leopold, *A Sand County Almanac, and Sketches Here and There* (New York: Oxford University Press, 1992), 132.

[73] Leopold, Postwar Prospects, *Audubon Magazine* 46, no. 1 (January–February 1944), 27.

[74] Fairfield Osborn, *The Pacific World: Its Vast Distances, Its Lands and the Life upon Them, and Its Peoples* (New York: W. W. Norton, 1944), xv. Also see Fairfield Osborn, "Genesis of a Book," *Animal Kingdom* XLVII, no. 2 (1944): 27–32. Quotations from Osborn, *Forty-Ninth Annual Report of the NYZS* (for 1944) (New York, 1945), 4. For the origins of *Our Plundered Planet*, see Frank Rasky, "Vogt and Osborn: Our Fighting Conservationists," *Tomorrow* 9, no. 10 (June 1950): 5–9.

had aimed "solely at the protection of wildlife itself." But recent events had shown that conservation organizations had to take "a broader aspect, with purposes more far-reaching than those previously envisioned."[75]

Leopold and Osborn were not the only people who began to rethink their assumptions about resources during the war. Another was Garrett Hardin, prominent environmentalist in the late 1960s and 1970s and author of one of environmental movement's most influential (if flawed) essays, "The Tragedy of the Commons" (1969), which warned of unbridled resource use in a world of firm ecological limits. Two decades earlier, during World War II, Hardin began the kind of thinking that would lead him to such analysis. While working on a US government project to develop algae as a food source, Hardin began to study the balance of food and people around the world and grew convinced that the solution to the world's food problem lay not in increasing food production through technological breakthroughs but in decreasing demand through population control.[76]

William Vogt, author of the widely read *Road to Survival* (1948) also came to similar conclusions about environmental degradation, resource overuse, and limits during the war. Studying the crash of animal populations in Latin America at the very moment war was exploding in Europe, Vogt realized that animal ecology offered life-and-death lessons for human society. In 1939, Vogt took a job in Peru studying the bird populations on the Guano islands, the coastal islands famous for the bird excrement that made powerful fertilizer. His job was to examine ways to increase the birds' manure production, or as he liked to put it, to "augment the increment of the excrement." Not long after arriving, Vogt witnessed one of the most traumatic aspects of the Guano island ecosystem: a "famine" that killed millions of birds. Encouraged by wildlife ecology to see the flocks as part of a much larger cycling of nutrients, he determined that the die-offs stemmed from a change in the Humboldt Current that had depleted local plankton and anchovy populations. As a result, the bird population had outstripped its resource base.[77] He was

---

[75] Osborn, *Fiftieth Annual Report of the NYZS* (for 1945) (New York, 1946): 4. See Robertson, *Malthusian Moment*, ch. 2.

[76] Garrett Hardin, "Tragedy of the Commons," *Science* 162 (December 1968): 1243–1248; Garrett Hardin, "Carrying Capacity as an Ethical Concept," *Soundings: An Interdisciplinary Journal* 59, no. 1 (Spring 1976): 120–137; Garrett Hardin, "Lifeboat Ethics: The Case against Helping the Poor," *Psychology Today* (September 1974): 800–812.

[77] William Vogt, "Best Remembered," Manuscript, 1962, Folder 2, Box 4, William Vogt Papers (Denver Public Library, Denver, CO).

quick to see lessons for human societies. In 1940, he proposed writing a book on the ecological laws that govern "the living together of plants and animals on the earth" because, "in a day when nations war for 'lebensraum,' such understanding is more than ever important."[78]

Vogt's Latin American expertise soon pulled him into American diplomatic circles. In 1942, he became an advisor for the US War Department, and shortly thereafter, for Nelson Rockefeller's Office of Inter-American Affairs. In 1943, he became the chief of the conservation section of the Pan-American Union, the forerunner of the Organization of American States. In this position, where he worked for a half decade, Vogt studied population and resource dynamics among both animals and humans in Latin America and sounded the alarm about resource depletion and degradation in the region. Latin America, he pointed out in a 1946 newspaper article, was "far from being the rich storehouse of untapped resources that is generally supposed."[79]

Vogt worked strong messages about degradation and limits into *Road to Survival* (1948), perhaps the most influential book about protecting nature before Rachel Carson's *Silent Spring* (1962). In this and other writings, Vogt turned the logic of total war on its head: "We think in compartments," he lamented, and miss the "dynamic, ever-changing relationships between the actions of man and his total environment."[80] He stressed that American landscapes and global ecosystems had reached their limits, and that production was really destruction. "We extract oil, and iron ore, and fine timber, and canvasbacks, and call it *production*."[81] Along with Fairfield Osborn, in the late 1940s and 1950s Vogt led the group of limits-to-growth protoenvironmental conservationists who sharply differed with the progrowth, protechnology strand of conservation that emerged during the war and was spread by Julius Krug, David Lilienthal, and other government officials.

---

[78] "Fellowship Application, Guggenheim Foundation, 1940," Box 5, FF19, VP.

[79] Vogt published several reports from this research: "The Natural Resources of Mexico – Their Past, Present, and Future"; "The Population of Costa Rica and Its Natural Resources"; "The Population of El Salvador and Its Natural Resources"; "The Population of Venezuela and Its Natural Resources," Pan American Union, 1946. Quotation from *New York World-Telegram*, January 18, 1946. For this stage of Vogt's career, see Maureen McCormick, "Of Birds, Guano, and Man," Ph.D. Dissertation, University of Oklahoma, 2005, ch. 3.

[80] William Vogt, *Road to Survival* (New York: W. Sloane Associates, 1948), 142–143. Also see page 86. See Robertson, *Malthusian Moment*, ch. 2.

[81] Vogt, *Road to Survival*, 146.

THE "MENACE OF POLLUTION": THE WARTIME EMERGENCE
OF TOXIC LANDSCAPES

Deep concerns about chemicals and pollution – signature concerns of 1960s environmental activism – also emerged during World War II. As early as 1942, in an article called "No Time to Forget Conservation," US FWS director Ira Gabrielson warned about the toll of wartime factories on America's waterways. "A constantly increasing number of industrial plants are being built," he noted, "which will further pollute these waters."[82] As Sarah Elkind describes in Chapter 10 of this volume, smog emerged as a significant problem in Los Angeles during the war. By 1945, Gabrielson was calling attention to the "menace of pollution." "Pollution," he wrote, "is now one of the most serious and complex of conservation problems." Industry, especially war munitions factories, had not only grown far larger but also spread into previously unaffected areas. Worse, he wrote, "To an already long list of industrial wastes known to be harmful to aquatic life have been added new kinds and additional quantities of harmful wastes from explosives plants, rayon mills, and synthetics manufacture." New types of contaminants were threatening rivers and streams and the animals that depended upon them, including humans.[83]

During the war, the synthetic chemical DDT also emerged as a problem. DDT (as Martha Gardner describes in Chapter 11) had been rediscovered in the late 1930s and during the war became a "miracle" chemical. It found wide use in public health spraying campaigns in military theaters, particularly in the South Pacific, where early in the war malaria and dengue fever were harming more Americans than the Japanese. The FWS, which conducted many of the early tests on DDT, began to notice the chemical's downsides. DDT was, in Gabrielson's words, "an unselective poison." It killed not just its target – disease-carrying mosquitoes and fleas – but also vast numbers of birds, reptiles, and amphibians.[84]

An important figure here is Barry Commoner, the biologist who in the 1960s and early 1970s *Time* magazine would call the Paul Revere of

---

[82] Ira Gabrielson, "No Time to Forget Conservation," *Audubon* 44, no. 2 (March 1942): 75.

[83] Department of Interior, *Annual Report, 1945*, 188. For more on Gabrielson, see Gabrielson, "No Time to Forget Conservation"; Herbert Corey, "Piscatorial Solomon," *Nations Business* 31, November 1943, 36–47; Louis J. Halle "Gabrielson," *Audubon* 48, no. 3 (May 1946): 140–146.

[84] Department of Interior, *Annual Report, 1945*, 184.

ecology because he alerted the American public to so many environmental problems, particularly those stemming from new chemicals and other flawed technology. Commoner first came to understand the ecological problems of new technologies during World War II. Working for the navy in 1942, Commoner, who studied biology before the war, helped design methods for the aerial spraying of DDT for use on Pacific theater beaches prior to American invasions. But not all went as planned. In spraying trials on the New Jersey shore, Commoner discovered that the toxic chemical killed mosquitoes but also thousands of fish. It was a lesson in unintended consequences that stuck with him.[85]

Rachel Carson also came of age as an environmental writer and activist during the war. From her perch as a writer and editor at Ira Gabrielson's FWS, she studied government research on new technologies. Through this work, she came to realize how powerful and possibly dangerous many of the wartime technologies were. "We are all aware that startling developments have come, or are on the way," she wrote in 1944.[86] One of these new technologies was DDT, which she read about in research presented to the FWS. In August 1945, Carson wrote the first of several FWS notices warning of the destructive power of DDT. DDT use in food facilities, she warned fishery managers, "might have serious consequences." A couple of weeks later, the FWS issued a broader warning, noting that, in the rush to protect troops, DDT's "effects on other organisms had to be overlooked." But research showed that even small amounts of DDT could kill birds and fish on a wide scale. Birds and other animals, Carson noted, were "the cheapest, safest, and one of the best means of controlling insect pests." Replacing them with broad use of DDT "could conceivably do more damage than good." Nine months later, Carson wrote a more detailed warning.[87] Two decades later, Carson would write *Silent Spring* (1962), an expose of the ecological dangers of DDT that, more so than any single book, helped ignite the 1960s environmental movement.

Just after the war, Commoner continued his training as an environmental activist, learning a lesson about the public accountability of science that would drive his later environmental activism surrounding

---

[85] Anne Becher, *American Environmental Leaders: From Colonial Times to the Present*, vol. 1 (Santa Barbara, CA: ABC-Clio, 2000); and Egan, *Barry Commoner and the Science of Survival*, 21–22.

[86] Linda J. Lear, *Rachel Carson: Witness for Nature* (New York: H. Holt, 1997), 113–120, quotation from 116.

[87] William Souder, *On a Farther Shore: The Life and Legacy of Rachel Carson, Author of Silent Spring* (New York: Broadway Books, 2013), 113–114.

dangerous new technologies. Commoner worked for the US Senate sub-committee charged with an extraordinarily delicate task: deciding the best way for a democracy in a time of great military uncertainty to oversee atomic weapons. During World War II, scientists, top military officials, and only a handful of civilian officials had administered the nation's atomic program. The program was so secret that Vice President Harry Truman learned of it only after he had become president. The American public learned of it only with the attacks on Hiroshima in August 1945.

Not long thereafter, the May-Johnson Bill proposed maintaining military control of the nation's atomic program. Critics like Commoner felt that, in a democracy, civilians had to control such new, terrifying weapons. Polling scientists, Commoner found they stood overwhelmingly against the idea of military control. His work helped kill the bill and bring about civilian control instead.[88] During the 1950s and 1960s, Commoner pioneered similar efforts to make modern science and technology more accountable to the general public. Commoner's St. Louis Committee for Nuclear Information supplied ordinary citizens with knowledge about the dangers of nuclear fallout and later about household technologies such as detergents. In doing so, he was, in a sense, pursuing the lessons of public accountability he learned in the waning days of World War II. His influential 1971 environmentalist classic, *The Closing Circle*, also laid the blame for most America's environmental problems on technologies created in or just after World War II.[89]

With all these pioneers of new types of environmental thinking – Leopold, Osborn, Brower, Hardin, Vogt, Gabrielson, Commoner, and Carson – it should be noted that they all either worked for or were closely linked to the expanding environmental-management state, either as soldiers or relatives of soldiers, or as government researchers.

CONCLUSIONS: TOTAL WAR AND THE ENVIRONMENT

During World War II, national security imperatives fundamentally altered American relations with nature. Some of the changes had been in the works for decades – such as the transition toward oil and chemicals – but

---

[88] For more, see Anne Becher, *American Environmental Leaders*. Also see Brian Balogh, *Chain Reaction: Expert Debate and Public Participation in American Commercial Nuclear Power, 1945–1975* (Cambridge: Cambridge University Press, 1991).
[89] Barry Commoner, *The Closing Circle: Nature, Man, and Technology* (New York: Knopf, 1971), ch. 8.

the war accelerated the spread of the changes into every corner of nature and society around the country, and intensified them. Other changes sprang from more recent developments. As other historians have noted, the Cold War would further expand and intensify the "great acceleration" of these years. This book argues that that these changes started in World War II, with massive industrial expansion, the industrialization of agriculture and food production, new more powerful technologies, expansion of the oil and electric energy infrastructure, a shift in geography toward urban areas, new "guns and butter" growth-based economic thinking, and new manipulations on the molecular and atomic levels. The expanding control and manipulation of nature went hand in hand with the expanding scale and intensity of modern warfare.[90]

Wartime changes pushed critics such as Aldo Leopold, Fairfield Osborn, William Vogt, Rachel Carson, Barry Commoner, and other leaders of what would become the environmental movement to embrace ideas different from those of Gifford Pinchot and early-twentieth-century conservationists. Like Pinchot, the war turned this group of "protoenvironmentalists" into global thinkers: increasingly, they worried about how new urban, industrial standards of living could fuel international resource competition and even warfare. But, influenced by ideas of ecological theory stressing interconnection and dismayed by the destruction of the war, they developed ideas that differed from traditional conservation. They tended to think more holistically, show more pessimism, and worry about a new set of problems, not just resource shortages but environmental degradation and pollution as well. Compared to most earlier conservationists, they worried much more about human technologies and the increasingly urban spaces where humans lived, not just from where resources came.

The war was crucial for their thinking. Whether because of government service for a quickly expanding "environmental-management state" or for other reasons, they followed the war closer than most, and it transformed their thinking, even before the atomic explosions in August 1945. Their novel ideas developed separately from the advent of nuclear weapons, although atomic power powerfully reinforced many of their key insights. In later years, the new approaches to conservation that this group devised during and immediately after the war would blossom into the central strands of the environmental movement of the 1960s. Many of

[90] Russell, *War and Nature*, 2.

their ideas were evident immediately after the war in their publications and in arenas such as the UNESCO conference at Lake Success in 1949, a kind of protoenvironmental counterconference to the UN conference on natural resources happening concurrently.[91]

Their ideas sharply contrasted with the direction that conservationists such as David Lilienthal and Julius Krug moved during the war. Lilienthal and Krug too had become much more global in their thinking about resource shortages and the movement of materials around the planet. But instead of reinforcing a sense of limits inherited from the Depression, the war showed them the vast potential of planned resource development. Instead of seeing limits to growth, they saw new frontiers of opportunity. This group and the protoenvironmentalists developed radically different understandings of the war. One saw limits fall away and technology as the key to turning untapped resources into new opportunities. The other group saw the technologies unleashed by the war as dangerous tools whose power to transform nature in fundamental ways was unprecedented, poorly understood, and potentially catastrophic.

The war set these different strands of modern conservation on a collision course that would play out in subsequent decades. At first, during the 1950s and 1960s the resource developers like Krug and Lilienthal would gain the upper hand in governmental policy and approach. Their thinking informed the government-led development of big dams and other technologically driven projects aimed at resource development, including a broad new effort to spread the American way of life around the world through "international development." But their missteps would fuel a strong countermovement during the 1960s – a movement of skeptics who questioned the chemical-based agricultural system that developed during the war and spread widely afterward, who wondered whether aggressive resource development and a growth-based economy in the United States and around the world would push the planet beyond its breaking point, who decried the toxic "menaces of pollution" that Ira Gabrielson and Rachel Carson first called attention to during the war, and who saw the downsides to the accelerated pace of life that had driven American life since the war.[92]

---

[91] Thomas Jundt, "Dueling Visions for the Postwar World."

[92] See Thomas Robertson, *Malthusian Moment: Global Population Growth and the Birth of American Environmentalism* (New Brunswick, NJ: Rutgers University Press, 2012).

Index